THE MAKING OF BASINGSTOKE

From Prehistory to the Present Day

Eric Stokes MA, DFC and bar

Edited by Bob and Barbara Applin

BASINGSTOKE ARCHAEOLOGICAL
& HISTORICAL
SOCIETY

Main text © Eric Stokes 2003

This edition © Basingstoke Archaeological & Historical Society 2008

Published by the Basingstoke Archaeological & Historical Society

First published 2008

All rights reserved; no part of this publication may be reproduced, stored in a retrieval system, transmitted in any form, or by any means, electronic, mechanical, photocopying, recording or otherwise, without the prior written permission of the Basingstoke Archaeological & Historical Society

ISBN 978-0-9508095-3-3

2012 2011 2010 2009 2008
10 9 8 7 6 5 4 3 2 1

Printed by Q3 Digital/Litho, Loughborough, Leicestershire

Cover and photos on pages 9 & 29 by BAHS members Ginny Pringle & Dave Allen
Back cover, Borough boundary marker, photo by Debbie Reavell

CONTENTS

	Page
FOREWORD by the Editors	5
TRIBUTES: Tim Herrington	7
Derek Wren	8

Part 1 SETTING THE SCENE

Chapter 1 The Site of Basingstoke — 11
Basingstoke in its geographical context.

Chapter 2 'Because of where it is' — 16
The development of the town because of its nodal position on the communication routes of southern England

Chapter 3 Population — 22
The population growth from Domesday to 1978.

Part 2 THE MAKING

Chapter 4 Early Settlement: Stone Age to Saxon — 31
The archaeological evidence.

Chapter 5 The Medieval Town — 36
The evolution of the town into a self-governing community.

Chapter 6 Markets and Fairs — 47
How the trade of the town was managed and controlled.

Chapter 7 Enclosure 1786 -1788 — 56
The Basingstoke Enclosure Act and its effect on land holdings.

Chapter 8 Coach, Barge and Train — 59
Transport from c1740 to c1900. The importance of the town as a major junction of road and rail routes. Includes an essay by Andrew Duckworth on the coach trade.

Chapter 9 Government by Vestry — 75
Local government as practised in Basingstoke before the 1835 Municipal Reform Act.

Chapter 10 Paving, Lighting and Drains — 87
The work of the Paving Commissioners and the establishment of the Gas Works.

Chapter 11 The Corporation of Basingstoke — 91
Established by the 1622 charter of James I and reformed by the 1835 Municipal Reform Act. How the town was managed - pressure to keep the rates down delayed essential infrastructure improvements.

Chapter 12	**Water and Sewerage**	98
	An expanded discussion of the delays to the improvement in water supply and sewage disposal which led to the 1905 typhoid epidemic.	
Chapter 13	**The Small Market Town**	108
	The 19th century evolution of a largely agricultural town into a small manufacturing one.	
Chapter 14	**Natural Growth**	122
	The continued growth of the town due to its natural and transport advantages.	
Chapter 15	**The Motor-car Age**	134
	The town's nodal position in the developing transport system.	
Chapter 16	**Planned Growth**	140
	The LCC/GLC overspill scheme.	
Chapter 17	**Religion**	152
	The major religious groupings of the town and their development. Contributions by Mary Oliver on the Anglicans and by Derek Wren on the architecture of St Mary's, Eastrop.	
Chapter 18	**Education**	163
	The educational provision (and sometimes the lack of it) in the town from the Petty School, through the National and British schools, to the present day.	
Chapter 19	**Culture and Entertainment**	179
	The provision of amateur and professional entertainment and enlightenment from the 1870s onwards.	
Chapter 20	**Basingstoke Today**	186
	'Today' in this chapter is basically the early 1990s. *Updates by Debbie Reavell, (Chairman of the Basingstoke Heritage Society); Derek Wren; Malcolm Parker, (author of a recent book on Basingstoke) and the editors have been included to bring this chapter up to the present day.*	
APPENDIX 1	Location of places mentioned in the text that have changed names or no longer exist.	195
APPENDIX 2	Basingstoke Public Houses closed/demolished since 1965.	197
APPENDIX 3	Equivalent contemporary values of the Pound – October 2007.	199
BIBLIOGRAPHY AND FURTHER READING		200
INDEX		213

FOREWORD

E.G. Stokes (Eric) was a geographer who taught at Queen Mary's School, Basingstoke, from 1951 until the establishment of Queen Mary's College, where he became Head of Geography and a Senior Tutor until his retirement in 1984.

He took a very keen interest in many aspects of Basingstoke and for many years was Chairman of the local branch of the Workers' Educational Association (WEA). He was responsible for organising, and took part in, many courses on the history and development of the town, some of which resulted in publications such as *Basingstoke – A Social Study* (WEA Southern District), *The Social Implications of a Town Development Scheme* (WEA Study Group, 1962) and *Basingstoke – Expanding Town* (WEA, 1980). Eric had long planned to publish an up-to-date history of Basingstoke to supplement the 19th-century definitive history of the town, *A History of the Ancient Town and Manor of Basingstoke,* by Baigent and Millard, and Anne Hawker's more recent *Story of Basingstoke*. Unfortunately, he became ill and was unable to bring his plan to fruition before his death in 2003.

This text is the latest draft that he produced and it is obvious from notes he left that further revisions were planned. It has been published 'as is' by the Basingstoke Archaeological & Historical Society to make it available in the public domain to provide a resource for those studying Basingstoke's history.

The work was untitled and BAHS, with the agreement of Eric's widow and copyright holder, Mrs Margot Stokes, has called it *The Making of Basingstoke* because it explores different aspects of the development of the town, particularly from the middle of the 19th century onwards. The text, except for the initial scene-setting chapters, deals almost exclusively with what is now referred to as the Basingstoke Urban Area. As a history, there are areas that have not been covered or only briefly mentioned, particularly the 1939-1945 war years and the ever-changing pattern of trading. It is uncertain whether Eric intended to include chapters on such topics. Also the contribution to the wider management of the town, by the owners or tenants of the landed estates that surrounded it, particularly in the 18th and 19th centuries, is only very briefly considered. The book is organised by themes, discussed chronologically within the chapters.

BAHS, with the agreement of Mrs Stokes, has edited the document for publication. There has been some minor rearrangement of the order in which events are discussed and Eric's chapter footnotes and references have been included in the body of the text to aid clarity, but otherwise the text is as it was written. There is some repetition of information from an earlier chapter when the Enclosure of 1788 is discussed but it has relevance in both places. Similarly the problems with the town's water supply and drainage are discussed in the context of the management of the town and more fully in a separate chapter. It was felt that this repetition too is justified. There are some sections that, had he lived, Eric would have further revised to take account of changes that have happened since he drafted this text. The editors have, therefore, added either brief comments within square brackets *[ ]* in the text or short up-dates at the end of some chapters to provide additional information. Some of the up-dates have been provided by those whom we have asked to review particular chapters; where appropriate these comments and updates are identified by the initials of the writer: Ed – the editors; MO – Mary Oliver; DS – Derek Spruce; DW – Derek Wren. An extract from Andrew Duckworth's essay on the coaching trade has been included in Chapter 8. Derek Wren, Malcolm Parker and Debbie Reavell have contributed to the update of Chapter 20. We are grateful to all these contributors.

There was no separate bibliography, so the editors have created one listing all the documents referred to in the text and expanded it to include as many of the publications on Basingstoke, produced over the past 40 years or so, as they can find; this is to help in achieving the aim of providing a resource for those studying the history of Basingstoke. The majority of the books in this bibliography are available in the reference section of Basingstoke Library.

Two appendices have been added with the same aim: the first, locating the position of places and roads mentioned in the text that have changed function or no longer exist; and the second, the public houses closed and/or demolished since 1965. A third appendix lists the comparative values of the Pound at various dates. As explained in this appendix, care should be exercised in how this data is used.

From his research in preparation for this work Eric had collected and published privately a collection of quotes about and illustrations of Basingstoke as *The Things They Say About Basingstoke* (now out of print but available in the Basingstoke Library). The majority of the illustrations that he was proposing to use in this current work are the same as those used in *The Things*. It was decided, therefore, not to use all the illustrations he had collected, although copies will be available in the Resources Room at the Willis Museum; however, maps, diagrams and photographs have been included to provide detail where appropriate. Where possible we have used photographs that have not been published before.

A CD and a printed copy of this work have been given to the Hampshire Record Office, Basingstoke Library, the Willis Museum, the Hampshire County Museums and Archive Service and Queen Mary's College, Basingstoke.

Where reference is made to contemporary buildings the names and/or occupiers are those as of May 2008.

Acknowledgements

Sid Penney kindly supplied photos of some of the buildings that were demolished in the 1960s and Roy Reynolds provided a photograph of his grandfather with his charabanc party; Mary Oliver provided photos from her collection of Town Hall prints; Wendy Bowen and Gill Arnott of the Hampshire County Museums and Archives Service greatly assisted, both Eric and the Editors, with advice and photographs from the Museums Service's collection; Alastair Penfold of HCMAS gave permission for the use of an extract from the 1759 Isaac Taylor map of Hampshire; Sue Tapliss, curator of the Willis Museum, kindly gave advice and provided a copy of their 1860s watercolour of the Town Hall. Sarah Lewin of the Hampshire Record Office gave permission for the use of the 1762 Duke of Bolton's maps and other documents in their Basingstoke collection. Tom Sunley, of the Environment Department of Hampshire County Council provided information from their Archaeological database. The staff of the Hampshire Record Office and the Basingstoke Library willingly answered our queries and located documents. We greatly appreciate the help of all these people.

The extracts from the post 1960 Ordnance Survey maps are reproduced under the terms of Licence 100048022. The census data used in various updates are taken from the Basingstoke & Deane Borough Council's web-site and are reproduced under the terms of Click-Use Licence 2008000214.

The Editors wish to thank Malcolm Parker and Sutton Publishing Ltd for permission to quote from their *Images of England – Basingstoke*.

The Editors also thank John Hollands for helpful comments during his unenviable task of producing the Index and for his help in the Willis Museum Resources Room, also to BAHS members Kate Mattock and Paulline Williams for proof reading; the Editors are extremely grateful to all three.

TRIBUTES

E G (Eric) Stokes MA, DFC and Bar 1919 – 2003

© M Stokes

From Tim Herrington (*Newsletter 165 of the Basingstoke Archaeological & Historical Society, November 2003*)

I count myself lucky to have had Eric as a friend and mentor, eventually helping him to further the cause of the WEA in Basingstoke. Organising classes, educational visits and study groups with him in the WEA committee was a delight – such happy days. My interest in geology and history developed fast under his influence; I recall many magical field trips which focused our attention on the land and history around us. Derek Wren and Eric, with us (not least of all John Arlott) collaborated to produce the 'audio-visual' epic slide show

Basingstoke – The Story of Our Town, now translated to video format. His passing ends a long chapter of devotion to spreading the joys of learning to all who would listen; I salute you, Eric, rest in peace.

From Derek Wren (*Newsletter of the Friends of the Willis Museum*, Winter 2006)

Throughout the time I knew Eric in Basingstoke, he was Chairman of the Workers' Education Association. I met him at a public meeting some time in 1962 and the next week I was a member of a WEA study group considering how Basingstoke could best handle the social problems that would arise from town expansion. From there I moved on to be part of a local history study group. None of the projects that I undertook in those years would have been possible without the support and encouragement Eric gave me.

An earlier study, which Eric had set up with Dr Dunning as tutor, had considered the economic problems of town expansion. This case study appeared as a book *Economic Planning and Town Expansion* but the most popular book which Eric Stokes produced was *The Things They Say About Basingstoke*.

From the 1970s onwards Eric was collecting material and making notes for a definitive history of our town. He continued working on this long after he had retired. The book had been virtually finished by the time he died in 2003 but was not ready for publishing.

The publication, by the Basingstoke Archaeological & Historical Society (BAHS), of this last draft of Eric's work is made as a tribute to the memory of one of the unsung chroniclers of Basingstoke whose efforts, over the years, have not received the recognition that they deserved.

PART 1

SETTING THE SCENE

© Ginny Pringle

*An April 2008 aerial view of Basingstoke from the west.
The Loddon river valley runs east from the bottom right, just south of the railway.
Winklebury hill fort is clearly visible (centre left) with the line of the Silchester to Winchester
Roman road in the foreground.*

Extract from the 2005 Ordnance Survey 1:50,000 map showing the extent of modern Basingstoke

Reproduced by permission of Ordnance Survey on behalf of HMSO © Crown copyright 2008. All rights reserved. Ordnance Survey Licence number 100048022.

1 THE SITE OF BASINGSTOKE

By studying towns as particular elements of the countryside, the geographer can explain above all the physical site and the positional setting of towns and in doing so he is able to supply useful clues not only to their origin and distribution but also as to their function and their changing fortunes.

The Geography Behind History Gordon East, 1938

A prominent feature of the natural landscape of our area is a line of chalk hills, rising in places to between 600 feet and 700 feet above sea level. This westward extension of the North Downs into Hampshire is broken by a large lowland gap, which forms the watershed between the River Test, draining west and south to the Solent, and the River Loddon, which flows east and north to join the Thames near Wargrave. It is within this gap that the Saxon *stoc*, or outlying daughter settlement of the manor of Basing, grew to become *Basingstoches* in Norman times and the Basingstoke of today.

From the vantage point provided by Kempshott Hill or Farleigh Hill, a view to the north shows the line of downs which forms the northern limit of our area. Prominent to the north-west, on the downs above Kingsclere, is Cottington's Hill (754 ft) with its television mast; equally obvious to the north is the North Hampshire Hospital, while away to the east is the tall building of the Automobile Association. Spread out before us is a more or less continuously built-up area, which runs from Chineham and Basing in the east to Oakley in the west. This has been given the name 'the modern urban Basingstoke town area', an indication that 'Basingstoke' is no longer adequate to describe the large concentration of population now found here. Roughly central to our view is a number of tall buildings within a short distance of the railway station.

A move in towards that central area enables us to obtain a clearer idea of the 'physique' of the town. The removal of so many landmarks during the considerable clearance and re-development that have taken place does not make this easy. Less apparent than it once was, is the second element in the site of the town - namely the river. It is useful here to quote the words of Mr C Clark in his talk entitled *The Architectural Development of Basingstoke*, given to the Rotary Club of the town, on 25th January 1930. As part of his general description of the town, he had this to say about its site, 'The town is built on the slopes of the Loddon Valley near to the source of that small river. The physical features of the town itself are this low-lying river valley and its sloping chalk banks, up which the town has advanced on to the level ground beyond.' The low lying ground is at about 260 feet above sea-level; the Market Place is at slightly over 300 feet, while the railway station lies just below the 300 foot contour.

Visits to different parts of the town readily bring out this height difference. The view north down Victoria Street clearly shows St Michael's Church on the valley floor, with the Holy Ghost ruins on the northern side of the valley. Equally convincing is a view southward over the town from the appropriately named South View. The multi-storey car park provides another useful viewpoint, enabling us to look along the valley. It has to be said, however, that the eastern prospect has been much reduced by the construction of a tall (some might say too tall) office block. We should remind ourselves that the central area re-development largely owes its form, that of a 'platform' spanning the River Loddon, to the height difference mentioned above.

At the present time *[early 1990s]*, the Loddon rises at West Ham. Brook Street is an appropriate indication of its course. We have been reminded by the occurrence of flooding in recent years that its original source lay further to the west, in the rather flat valley lying immediately to the west of Buckskin Lane. Mr Clark said of the valley, 'Originally it must have been an impassable marsh. Even now,' (he was speaking of 1930) 'with the exception of that part which has been drained to carry buildings, it remains a series of lagoons fringed with reeds and haunted by moorhen.'

Place-names point to the prevalence of wetter conditions than those which prevail today. There is obviously a great deal of significance in the name 'Noah's Island' for that part of the valley where the *Victory Inn* used to stand, near the junction of Brook Street and Essex Road (the Victory Roundabout). We are now no longer able to judge the appropriateness or otherwise of Frog Lane as an alternative name for Brook Street. The Ordnance Survey marked the area which is now Eastrop Park as 'liable to floods'; part of the lower road to Worting *[not the current Worting Road.]* cannot have been called Water Lane without good reason.

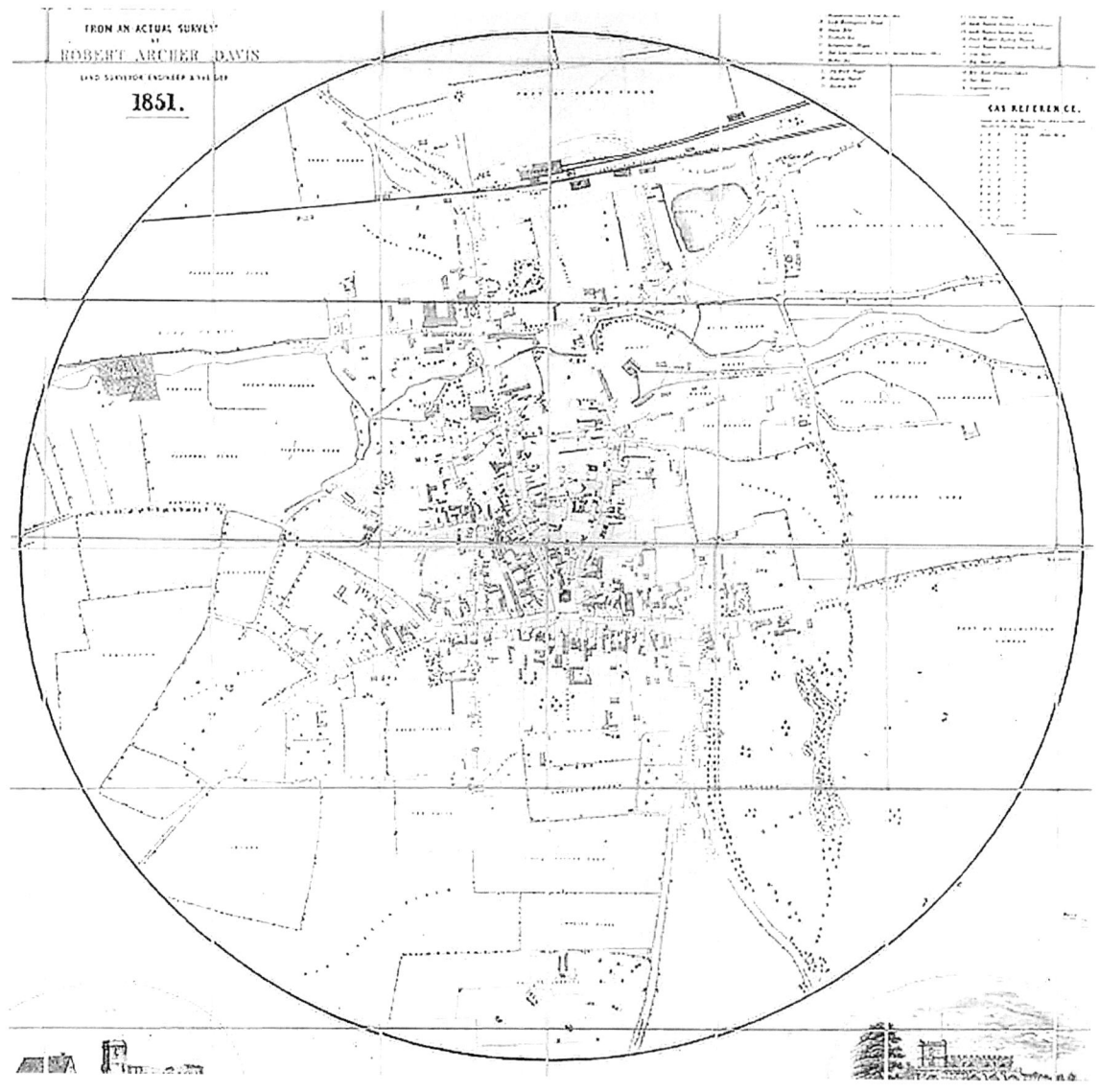

© HCMAS

The 1851 'Archer Davis' Map of Basingstoke

A copy is displayed in the Resources Room at the Willis Museum

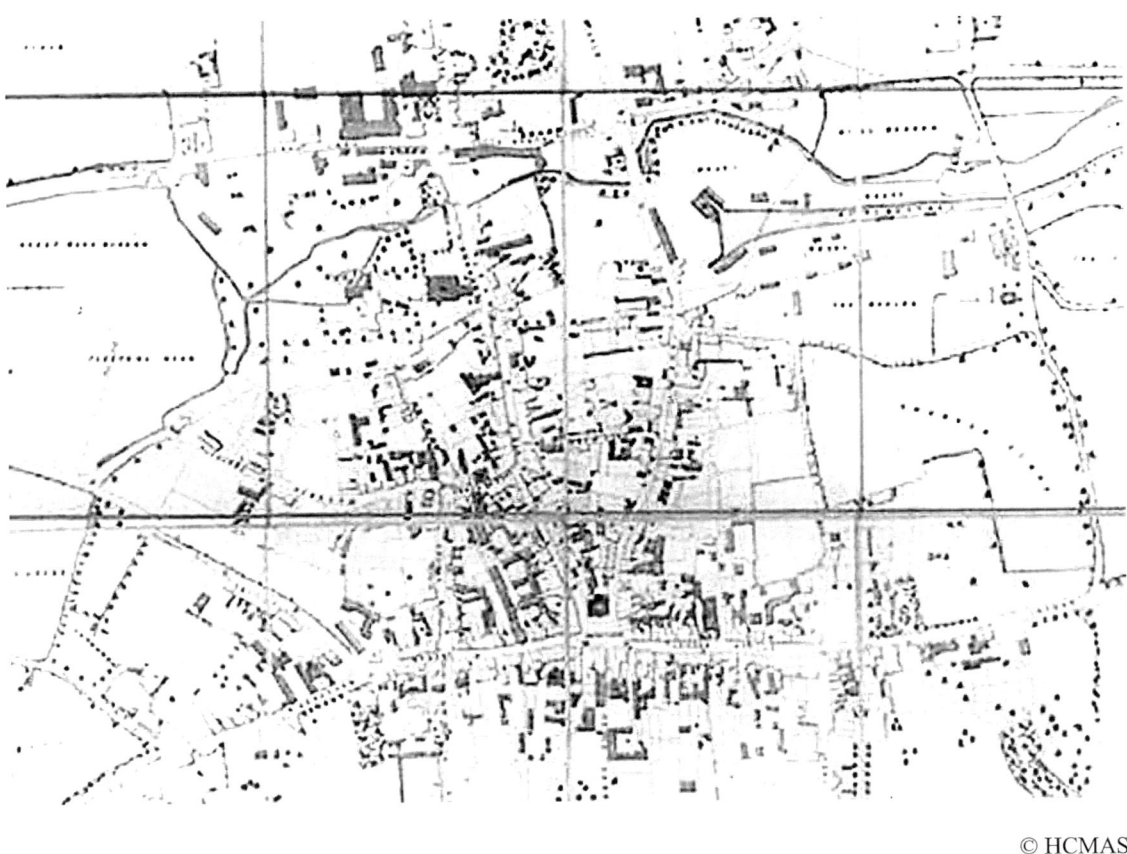

© HCMAS

From the 1851 map. Detail of the central area

Brook Street appears on the 1851 map of the town as Northbrook Street. *[Anne Hawker states that the name means 'North of the Brook' Street.]* There seems never to have been a south brook by that name, but a small tributary did flow in from the south, from its source in Budd's Meadow, via Flaxpool (Flaxfield Road). It followed a course a little to the east of Penrith Road and then along part of Mortimer Lane, to join the Loddon in the south-west corner of what was the Rectory garden (now Glebe Gardens, Church Street). The lie of the land and the evidence of patches of valley gravel point to the probability that the source of the stream lay further to the south along the line of Cranbourne Lane, at a time when the water-table was higher than it is today. Associated with this area is the place-name Foulflood. Foulflood Lane existed until a few years ago; it is now known as Hardy Lane and, indeed, in the early 1950s has flooded at springtime. It is perhaps significant that the terms 'bourne' and 'flood' occur in the same area. Towards the end of the nineteenth century the area was proposed as a possible site for a well to provide a new source of water for the town. *[See page 100.]*

One feature associated with the river that is no longer in existence was the Coppyd Bridge mentioned in old records, which used to span the Loddon at the bottom of Wote Street. The existence of the bridge would appear to provide further evidence that the river used to be larger, even in comparatively recent times. Dr Ballard's *Report upon the Sanitary Condition of Basingstoke [See pages 90 and 96]* in 1871 says of the river, 'At its widest part, as it crosses Wote Street, it is about 12 feet wide, and shallow, with a muddy bottom.' At the bottom of Church Street there appears to have been a causey (causeway), a raised footway, which enabled people to cross the river itself and also the surrounding damp and muddy ground, which could on occasion be flooded.

Today, the river has been brought under control. Rising to the west of the town, at West Ham, it flows as far as Glebe Gardens, from where it is led in a culvert under the Town Centre, to re-appear in Eastrop Park. Here water features, besides regulating the flow, provide amenity in the form of paddling pools and boating ponds. As it nears Basing, it is joined by another tributary, flowing in from Black Dam (Newram Springs). In the early part of the nineteenth century we find the river causing problems to travellers through Basing. In 1826 (30th August) the Vestry resolved 'That a bridge be erected over the River Loddon leading to the Reading turnpike road.' The alternative was to keep the water low enough 'to admit of any carriage or vehicle to pass without alarm or inconvenience to any of His Majesty's liege subjects.'

Although we must not exaggerate the influence of physical factors, there is no doubt that the river and its valley have played an important part in the evolution of the town and its neighbourhood. It is suggested that the smaller size of the Loddon at Basingstoke permitted an easier crossing there than lower down at Basing, and was thus a contributory cause of the growth of the town at the expense of its formerly more important neighbour.

Photo: © R Applin

The Loddon at Glebe Gardens – October 2007

EDITORIAL UPDATE

Now (2008), although the river channel exists in Glebe Gardens it is, more often than not, dry.

Glebe Gardens were originally the grounds of the parsonage to St Michael's Church. There were gardens, lawns, meadows and extensive fish ponds fed by the River Loddon and its tributary which joined it in the garden. The existing Georgian rectory was built to replace the parsonage in 1773. It has been known as Chute House since it was acquired by the Basingstoke & Deane Borough Council in the early 1970s and is named after the Rev. Anthony Chute, vicar of St Michael's from 1938 to 1956.

Photo of print © R Applin

The Old Rectory, Basingstoke

Thomas Warton, (1728-1790), poet, was born at the parsonage on 9 January 1728. He was the younger son of Thomas Warton (1688-1745), vicar of Basingstoke. Warton was educated at home by his father until 16 March 1744 when he entered Trinity College, Oxford, where he eventually became Professor of Poetry as his father had been. Warton was made Poet Laureate in 1785. He wrote a sonnet 'To the River Loddon' which he had loved in his early years. He is commemorated locally by Warton Road at South View carrying his name.

To the River Loddon

Ah! What a weary race my feet have run,
Since first I trod thy banks with alders crowned,
And thought my way was all through fairy ground,
Beneath thy azure sky and golden sun:
Where first my Muse to lisp her notes begun!
While pensive Memory traces back the round
Which fills the varied interval between:
Much pleasure, more of sorrow marks the scene.
Sweet native stream! those skies and sun so pure
No more return to cheer my evening road;
Yet still one joy remains, that not obscure,
Nor useless, all my vacant days have flowed,
From youth's gay dawn to manhood's prime mature;
Nor with the Muse's laurel unbestowed.

Thomas Warton 1777

2   'BECAUSE OF WHERE IT IS'

Basingstoke derives its chief importance from its railway junction and its fine set of seven radiating roads, several of which bifurcate a little out of the town.

Hampshire and the Isle of Wight S E Winbolt, 1949

A settlement is established when a group of people select and occupy a site, favoured by physical features which meet the group's requirements at a particular time. It does not remain in isolation but establishes a relationship with other settlements. Its positional setting (where it is in relation to other places) helps to determine whether it grows, remains static or declines. At an early stage, when almost all movement is over short distances and made on foot, the relationship is a close one with places in its immediate neighbourhood. Later, enlargement of the hinterland comes when, with improved means of transport, links are established with more distant places. A study of the way these links evolved can contribute usefully to our account. Francis Celoria, in *Teach Yourself Local History* (page 70) puts it more strongly: 'No place can be thoroughly studied unless you examine all means of getting to it and away from it!'

Ancient trackways

In *The Old Way from Basingstoke to Salisbury Plain,* H H Coghlan shows two ancient trackways crossing in the neighbourhood of the town, at a point where Pack Lane diverges from the A30 (SU617504). One of these descends from the high ground on the south, via Ellisfield (SU632457), Farleigh Wallop (SU623468) and Hatch Hill (SU619489). It crosses the valley to reach the site of the Iron Age hill fort at Winklebury (SU613529), situated on high ground to the north. It does so via the track known as the Greenway. *[The only extant part is that from Worting Road to Winklebury.]* It then follows a direction slightly north of west, linking up similarly-located hill forts on Ladle Hill (SU479568) at 765ft, Beacon Hill (SU458572) at 859ft and culminating at Walbury Hill (SU374616) at 974ft. The trackway is usually known as the Inkpen or North Hants Ridgeway. *[The current Ordnance Survey Explorer map 144 names the trackway, from North Oakley westwards, as part of the long distance Wayfarer's Walk – a modern name. The route from Winklebury to North Oakley where it joins the Wayfarer's Walk exists partly as trackway and partly as minor roads around Ibworth.]*

The other trackway, which we know as the Harrow Way, reached our area from the east, continuing the line of the North Downs as the Pilgrims' Way. Passing through the village of Well (SU762466), its course is via Four Lanes End (SU727484), Five Lanes End (SU696502) and Polecat Corner (SU671502). Professor C F Hawkes, in *Proceedings of the Hampshire Field Club, 1925,* suggested that the route via Ellisfield and Farleigh Wallop was the original line of the Harrow Way, later superseded by the lower, more direct, summer way via Polecat Corner. Skippett's Lane, Pack Lane and Fiveways (SU602504) mark its course as it continues westward, passing near Oakley and Overton, carefully avoiding the source of the River Test.

Although these two trackways made some contribution to the early peopling of the area, their point of meeting did not become the nucleus around which a permanent settlement might develop.

Roman roads

The same is true of two Roman roads as they passed through the local area. The alignment of one runs to the west of the town and forms, for part of its course, the western boundary of the former borough. This established the link between *Venta Belgarum* (Winchester) and *Calleva Atrebatum* (Silchester). The other road to *Calleva Atrebatum* from *Noviomagnus Regnensium* (Chichester) crossed the River Loddon at Lower Mill, Old Basing, where the causeway taking the road across the river could have provided a foundation for the mill. The convergence of these two roads on this particular part of Hampshire, where others joined them from London, Bath, Gloucester and Salisbury, gave Silchester a nodality which considerably increased its importance, not only locally but to the Roman road network as a whole. There was as yet no town of Basingstoke. (But see Chapter 4)

Anglo-Saxon, Medieval and later

When the Romans began to withdraw their forces to the Continent in order to deploy them in resisting barbarian attacks there, their road system was no longer required to the same extent and gradually deteriorated through lack of use and maintenance. Nevertheless, for several centuries following the departure of the Romans, people continued to use them, or portions of them, if only for very local journeys. Use also continued to be made of the prehistoric trackways; Pack Lane and Chapmansford Farm are names associated with the ancient Harrow Way (Anglo-Saxon *har waeg* meaning 'old road'. It is also known as the *herepath* meaning 'army road'.)

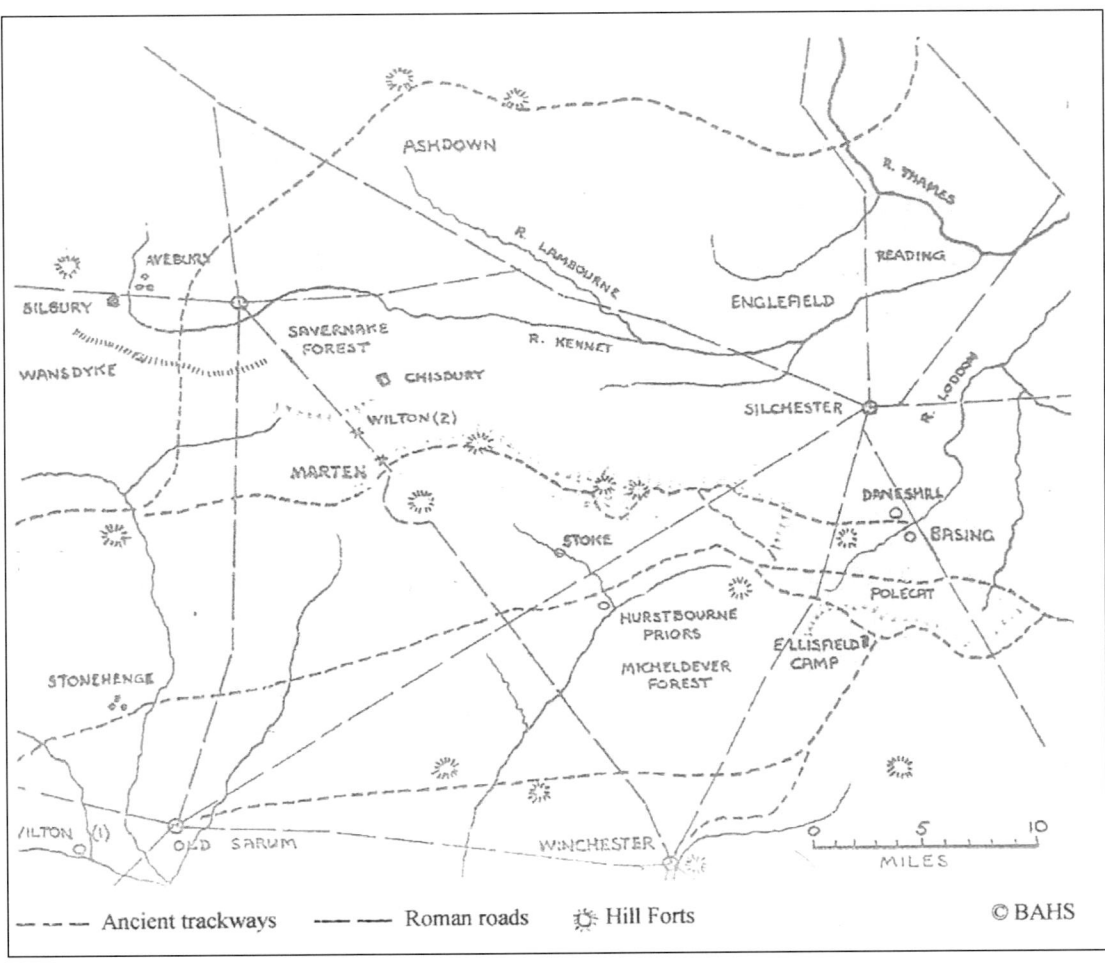

Map showing the ancient routes through north Hampshire

Modern place-names have been used for reference

This map was originally prepared by Frank Mayo for a BAHS Newsletter article on the Anglo-Saxons

Photos: © R Applin

Medieval and later cart ruts on Kempshott Hill

[The photographs on the previous page, taken during the 1985 pre-development excavations at Hatch Warren (Brighton Hill South), show cart ruts running up Kempshott Hill parallel to the present A30 (the hedge line in front of the houses in the lower picture) with the Flowers estate in the background, i.e. looking roughly north. The ruts were at least 40cm deep. The two sets of parallel lines in the foreground in the lower photograph are unexcavated ruts, with the excavated set beyond. There was evidence of at least six sets of ruts towards the hedge-line. This indicates that, as one track became unusable, travellers just moved across the hill to create another. Probably there are more sets under the houses of the Flowers estate.]

We have, at this remove, no means of knowing what and how many journeys of various kinds were undertaken, but it is reasonable to suppose that a large number were made along local lanes such as those now known as Buckskin Lane, Cranbourne Lane and Hackwood Lane, worn by the feet of villagers making their regular visits to the weekly markets. There would have been more 'thoroughfare' on the occasion of the annual fairs held 'about and near' the Chapel of the Holy Ghost at Whitsun and 'within the place called Basingstoke Down near the town of Basingstoke' *[At Kempshott, roughly in the area now bounded by Kempshott Lane, Pack Lane and the A30.]* at Easter and in September. This is when merchants dealing in commodities not produced in the town would be in attendance. Most would have come from a distance and may well have transported their wares by pack-horse. Some would have used wagons to carry bulkier goods; the heavier weight of these would have caused the deep ruts, of which other users had good reason to complain. What is surprising is that, despite all the difficulties, and even dangers, of travel, there was so much movement, sometimes over considerable distances.

The gradual onset of more stable political conditions was accompanied by an increase in the volume of internal trade. Even so, no serious attempts were made to provide roads capable of meeting the needs of the time, until the middle of the eighteenth century, when numerous Turnpike Acts were passed. The roads that resulted were piecemeal solutions to the problem, with local rather than national considerations in mind.

Turnpike Trusts

Daniel Defoe, in his *Tours Through England and Wales* observed the problem caused to traffic by 'the badness of the roads'. He also set out the benefits that could be expected from road improvements. The chosen agency for improvement was the Turnpike Trust. By this means, money raised from the tolls charged for the use of a section of road could be spent on maintaining it in a satisfactory state of repair.

The Trusts serving the Basingstoke area were: the Reading and Basingstoke (1718); the Basingstoke, Odiham and Alton (1736); the Hartford Bridge and Basingstoke (1737); the Andover and Basingstoke (1754); the Stockbridge and Basingstoke (1755); the Basingstoke and Popham (1755); the Basingstoke and Preston Candover (1795) and the Basingstoke and Alton (1795). Tollgates were located at the top of Chapel Hill, at the junction of Hackwood Road and Southern Road, and at Worting. The toll-house at Chineham (Basingstoke to Reading) still exists *[with the addition of a modern replica]*.

A petition which appeared in the *Journal of the House of Commons* in 1737 shows that a local Trust had difficulty in meeting its obligations. The petition was for an Act to repair and maintain the road from Hartford Bridge Hill to Basingstoke and Odiham. It was in the name of 'several gentlemen, freeholders and other persons, living in or near and frequently travelling through the roads from Hartford Bridge, through Basingstoke and Sutton [Sutton

Scotney] to the Borough of Stockbridge, and from Hartford Bridge to Odiham in the County of Southampton.' Witnesses called in support of the petition said, 'That the road ... is in a very Ruinous condition and in some places dangerous to passengers; and that notwithstanding the Statute work hath been duly performed, and several sums of money laid out in amending the same road, the same cannot be effectively repaired without the aid of Parliament.' In 1747, Lord Powlett reported to Parliament that tolls had not produced enough revenue to keep the road in repair. The Trust had eighteen shillings in hand; it owed £1,200, which it had borrowed by the terms of the 1737 Act. A further Act permitted the borrowing of more money to finance the necessary work.

The effect of turnpiking was to increase mobility, making it possible to reach more places more quickly, with greater convenience and assurance of safe, if not always punctual, arrival. Places well situated to provide the facilities that were needed enjoyed greater prosperity through increased commercial activity. This certainly appears to have been the case with Basingstoke, situated where 'the great western road' divided into two in Winton Square. Defoe, writing of the importance of Basing House during the Civil War, said, ' 'Tis incredible what booty the garrison of this place picked up, lying, as they did, just on the great western road, where they intercepted the carriers, plundered the wagons and suffered nothing to pass, to the great interruption of the trade of the City of London.'

One route led down Sarum Hill to Salisbury and beyond (London-Basingstoke-Whitchurch-Andover-Mere-Wincanton-Ilchester-Honiton-Exeter). The other went off in the direction of Winchester (London-Basingstoke-Winchester-Southampton). *Pigot's Hampshire Directory of Wagon and Coach Services* (1824) says of the town, 'It is distant from the metropolis 45 miles. The trade and commerce is much increased by its contiguity thereto and from its being the principal thoroughfare to all parts of the West of England.'

The town was also a crossing-point for coaches running from Southampton to Reading and from Oxford to Portsmouth (Oxford - Newbury - Basingstoke - Alton - Chawton - East Tisted - Petersfield - Portsmouth). This regular coming and going of coaches and wagons made it a place of great 'busyness'.

The coming of the canal and railways

Chapter 8 will deal with the Basingstoke Canal (completed in 1792) and the line of railway from London to Southampton (completed in 1840), together with the subsequent development of the links to other places. Because the railway could provide a shorter transit time between places and also more conveniently carry goods in bulk, it inevitably produced a decline in coach and wagon traffic, particularly over longer distances. *[For example, in 1823 there were 17 coaches daily in each direction from Basingstoke and London. In 1839 (immediately post railway) there was just one. DS]*

However, horse-drawn vehicles did not immediately cease to be of use: they continued to provide the essential link between the town's railway stations and its rural hinterland. This interdependence of town and country, and the network of services provided by local village carriers which grew up to foster it, is a further illustration of the way in which the town's economic activities (and therefore its prosperity) were influenced by its positional setting. The description of the town in a letter to the *Hants & Berks Gazette* in 1887 as 'a miniature metropolis for North Hants' is surely an apt one.

A30

The motor vehicle has been responsible for causing so much change to the local environment that it requires separate treatment (in Chapter 15). For our present purpose, it is enough to remind ourselves that the early years of the 20th century saw the advent of petrol-driven motor vehicles. This entirely new form of transport was the means whereby the road began to regain some of the importance which it had lost to the railway in the previous century. The new vehicles, travelling from London to Basingstoke and beyond, made use of 'the great western road'. With the evolution of the national network of trunk roads, this became the A30, linking London with Land's End. Traffic using it, heading west and south, had to pass through the centre of the town (the Market Place), causing problems of congestion which could be solved only by the construction of a by-pass. The alignment chosen for the new road was 'a quiet country lane' to the south of the town, which had originally been part of the ancient trackway, the Harrow Way. The new stretch of road was fully open to traffic early in 1933. It was eventually to prove inadequate to handle with safety the volume of traffic wishing to use it, a fact that was particularly evident at busy week-ends in the summer months, when long queues of vehicles were a common sight.

M3

Making allowances for an anticipated increase in the volume of traffic between London and the south and west, the Ministry of Transport announced in July 1952 that a new motorway would be built to connect London with Southampton. Its proposed alignment was one parallel to the A30 as far as Popham and then the A33 to Southampton. The ten miles between Black Dam and Popham were opened in May 1971. The main interchange between the motorway and the town's Ringway is at Black Dam, on the London side of the town; another is located at Dummer, three miles south-west of the town.

'A very attractively located town'

When J H Dunning, in a talk in 1963 to the Basingstoke and North Hants Productivity Committee, described the town in this way, he was referring not to its setting in the local landscape but to its potential attractiveness to industry and commerce. Thirty years earlier, the Basingstoke Development Committee had described the town as having 'many special features as a provincial industrial town on account of its geographical position.' In 1944 the Greater London Plan very briefly indicated the importance of communications with other places: 'This is a railway junction and is on the Exeter Road.'

Once it had been agreed to expand the town through a policy of overspill, the responsible authorities had to 'sell' the town as a suitable place in which to live and work. They did so, of course, by stressing the particular advantages it had acquired. Those that were directly attributable to its position in relation to other places may be summarised as:

(a) Good communications by road to London and Southampton by M3 and A33, including Heathrow and Southampton (Eastleigh) airports.
(b) Access to M4 via the improved A33 (the Reading Road).
(c) Access to A34 (for the Midlands).
(d) Good rail services between London and Southampton, and to Oxford, the Midlands and the north (via Reading).
(e) Nearness to attractive countryside - the North Wessex Downs (Area of Outstanding Natural Beauty); convenient access to the New Forest and the Coast.

3 POPULATION

It is by now fairly common knowledge that Basingstoke has been proposed as a reception town under the Greater London Plan for the decentralisation of industry and population from London, and its population will consequently increase to 40,000 or so within the foreseeable future.

Hants & Berks Gazette 16th May, 1947

The way in which a town's population has grown in the past and the reasons for that growth are important matters for study by the local historian. Growth can be 'natural', taking place over a long period, or 'planned' and concentrated in a short span of time. Basingstoke, as we shall see, shows what happens when there is a combination of the two.

A study of growth requires a numerical basis. Unfortunately, it is only since 1801, the year of the first national census, that we have had access to reliable figures of population size. To convey the situation before that date we have to depend on estimates. Taking the figures for Domesday (1086) and using the method proposed by W G Hoskins in *Local History in England,* we find that the 20 villeins, 8 smallholders, 12 freedmen and 6 slaves convert into an estimate of 206 inhabitants. The comparable figure for Basing is 312. These were the two most populous of the fifteen village settlements within the Hundred of Basingstoke, which had a total population of 1,539.

Later estimates are given in the *Victoria County History – Hampshire,* Vol 2, pages 370 and 374. For 1548 a figure of 'not much over 600' is given; the number for 1564 is stated to be 'under 1000'. These figures suggest that it is rather an exaggeration to use the words of the 1622 James I charter *villa populosa* to describe the Basingstoke of the 17th century. 'Large village' is surely a more suitable description.

[There are several 17th-century collections of data that allow an estimate of population to be made. The Diocesan Population Returns for 1563 and 1603, (Dyer & Palliser, 2005), records Basingstoke as having 1000 communicants and zero Recusants and Nonconformists and The Compton Census of 1676, (Whiteman & Clapinson, 1986), records 1580 communicants, one Papist and ten Nonconformists. The Hampshire Hearth Tax Assessment, 1665, (Hughes & White, 1991), records 208 households paying the tax and 139 exempt from tax. Applying the conventional multipliers to these figures gives the populations as:

Date	Recorded number	Multiplier	Population
1603	1000	1.5	1500
1665	347 households	5.0	1735
1676	1591	1.5	2386

These figures should be treated as broad estimates only, particularly as the 1603 recorded number looks very much like a rounded figure. There is no way of telling how many people were left out of these church censuses for whatever reason. The Hearth Tax Assessment returns were collected more rigorously so that the number of households is probably fairly accurate; however, the multiplier is a matter of debate. We are grateful to Dr Jean Morrin of The University of Winchester for bringing these sources to our attention.]

1801-1921

Table 1 shows that the population, which was 2,589 in 1801, had reached 4,263 by 1851 and 9,793 by 1901, the latter including 283 from the incorporation of Eastrop parish into the borough. The local paper, reporting on the 1901 census, regarded the 'steady increase as a satisfactory feature' and added, 'There is every reason to hope that the coming years will witness a continuance of this growth.' It can be seen that, by the turn of the century, numbers were increasing at nearly twice the national average.

It is not possible to give a convincing stage-by-stage explanation of this rapid growth. It is suggested that the enlargement of the town's hinterland through increased railway facilities and the extension of its service functions were important contributors to prosperity and growth. *[Also Wallis and Haslam (later Wallis and Steevens) established The North Hants Ironworks in the town in 1856. This was the first of the larger scale 'industrial' operations that were to be a feature of the town until the 1970s. There were businesses such as Caston's Ironworks already established - acquired by the Wallis family in the 1840s, but these were on a smaller scale. (Whitehead 1983, page 9). Caston was made bankrupt in 1848.]*

TABLE 1

POPULATION GROWTH - BASINGSTOKE BOROUGH AND ENGLAND & WALES 1801 – 1931

YEAR	BASINGSTOKE	DECENNIAL % Increase	ENGLAND & WALES 000s	DECENNIAL % Increase
1801	2,589			
1811	2,656	2.6	10,000	
1821	3,165	19.2	12,000	20.0
1831	3,581	13.1	13,897	15.8
1841	4,066	13.5	15,914	14.5
1851	4,263	4.8	17,928	12.7
1861	4,654	9.2	20,006	11.9
1871	5,574	19.8	22,712	13.2
1881	6,681	19.9	25,974	14.4
1891	7,960	19.1	29,003	11.7
1901	9,793	23.0	32,528	12.2
1911	11,540	17.8	36,070	10.9
1921	12,723	10.3	37,887	5.0
1931	13,865	9.0	39,952	5.5

Source: *Census of Population*

In 1878 there was some reorganisation within the town's clothing industry; this included the opening of a new factory on Station Hill by Gerrish, Ames and Simpkins. The expansion of employment may well have resulted in a slight influx of people into the town. This certainly happened after 1898. In that year Thornycroft gave a significant stimulus to employment by establishing a vehicle-building works here. Within four years the firm was reported as employing 200 workers. About fifteen years later the firm drew the attention of the Borough Council to the difficulty it was having in employing married men. The stated reason was that the provision of housing was failing to keep pace with the growth in population.

1921-1961

From 1921, when it numbered 12,723, the population grew to reach 25,980 in 1961. Three phases of growth can be distinguished in this period. The first of these was from 1921 to 1946; during this time, the average rate of increase was about 0.9% per annum.

Extract from the 6" Ordnance Survey map of Basingstoke © Crown copyright 1912

Extract from the 6" Ordnance Survey map of Basingstoke © Crown copyright 1938
*[Note that the 1938 map shows Queen Mary's School in Vyne Road.
This was not opened until 1940.]*

Although there was some slight movement into the town, due in part to two new firms: Kelvin Hughes in 1937 (aircraft instruments) and Eli Lilly in 1939 (pharmaceuticals), most of the growth was accounted for by natural increase.

Between 1946 and 1952 the population grew by 1,370, of which 712 was natural increase and 658 net immigration. This gave an annual average rate of about 1.5%. Towards the end of this phase there was some increase in employment opportunity; the arrival, in 1949, of Lansing Bagnall, a firm making materials-handling equipment, was the main cause of this.

The third phase of growth may be said to have begun with the building of the Oakridge estate to the north of the town, specifically to accommodate employees of the Atomic Weapons Research Establishment at Aldermaston. Construction began in 1952 and went on until 1954, by which time just over 400 houses had been completed. Assuming a household size of 3.1 persons, we can assume that this contributed an increase of something over 1,200 over the two-year period.

At about the same time the Government relaxed the restrictions on the building of houses for sale, mostly for those on the Clarke estate, north-west of the town, and the Harrow Way estate to the south. Gradually the proportion of local authority houses declined, while there was a considerable increase in the number built for sale. For 1951-1954 it averaged 54 per year; over the period 1955-58 the average was 223; completions reached a peak of 444 in 1959.

The increased availability of houses for sale, combined with greater employment opportunities, attracted a considerable inflow of people, eg 810 in 1952-53 and 952 in 1953-54.

Following the completion of the Oakridge estate, there was a temporary reduction of movement into the town, as is shown by the low values of 73 in 1954-55 and 162 in 1955-56.

During the latter part of this period, i.e. from 1957 to 1961, there was a resumption of expansion. Some of this was accounted for by families moving to the town under the limited overspill agreement of October 1959 for 3,500 houses over ten years to accommodate 12,000. However, the greater part of the inward movement was private, by people coming from the Greater London Area, south-east England and the neighbouring parts of Hampshire, Surrey and Berkshire (see *The Social Implications of a Town Development Scheme*, Basingstoke WEA Study Group on Town Development, 1962). Net immigration averaged 940 per year for the period 1957-61, with a maximum of 1,150 in 1960-61. The rate of growth was 5.2% per year. This was nine times the average for England and Wales - a demonstration that even unforced expansion can be quite rapid.

1961-1978

A population which grows naturally over a long period of time achieves, through slow adaptation to changing political, economic and social forces, a certain degree of balance. That state of balance is upset when a large number of people are 'exported' to entirely new surroundings in a relatively short time. Those in authority are mainly concerned to provide housing for a rapid build-up of numbers, but, as Mr Brooke Partridge, Chairman of the Greater London Council (GLC) Town Development Committee commented in December 1971, there is more to overspill than the mere provision of houses. Employment has to be attracted to the town; resources have to be made available for the various services required by different sections of the community - those of school age, the working population, and the elderly. The success of an overspill scheme, such as the one which began in 1961, is to be judged by the way in which it co-ordinates population movement, housing, employment and the provision of essential services. Predicting the size and structure of an expanding population is a difficult enough exercise; regulating a planned expansion is even more so. Those responsible for this in Basingstoke accomplished the task reasonably well, despite the inevitable variation from year to year in the rate of intake and of natural increase.

Before the October 1959 agreement had made any significant contribution to the peopling of the town, it was replaced by the agreement of 31st October 1961, a tripartite one under the Town Development Act of 1952, between London County Council, Hampshire County Council and Basingstoke Borough Council. This agreement specified not a number of people to be transferred but a number of dwellings to be built. The intention was to provide 11,500 dwellings over a fifteen-year period. Depending on what value is used for average household size, 3.1 or 3.5 persons, this would represent between 36,000 and 40,000 people. Although the agreement was to run for fifteen years instead of ten, the larger numbers involved would mean that the annual intake of people would also be larger than in the case of the earlier agreement. During the period of operation of the scheme, the annual increase fluctuated widely, ranging from a minimum of 980 in 1961-62 to a maximum of 4,590 in 1970-71. The annual rate of natural increase was consistently high, averaging 16.7/1,000 over the peak period of 1963 to 1971, with a maximum of 18.7/1,000 in1965. The birth rate was 26.2/1,000 and the death rate 7.5/1,000. Estimates of what the future population might be varied according to the assumptions made. Projections were calculated, the most detailed of these being those made by J H Dunning, who based his work on the experience of the new towns, *(Dunning, 1963, page 50)*. The values arrived at for the 1976 population ranged from 67,000 to 80,000. In the event, the population achieved by 1976 fell well short of the high value, coinciding instead with the minimum forecast figure of 67,000.

For some time before the overspill agreement was due to end, the GLC had been considering what principles should guide its future policy. It had become concerned about the way in which dispersal of employment and people from the capital was harming its economic and social health. Its views, which had in fact been discussed with local authorities participating in town development, were set out in a consultative document, *Planned Growth Outside London*, which appeared in 1975. Reference to this was made in a report of 30th June 1976, which contained confirmation of the following recommendation, 'that the Council do resolve in principle not to enter into further new agreements in connection with expanding town schemes and, where and when possible, to negotiate amendment or mutually agreed termination of existing agreements with a view to achieving reduction in the present rate and level of activity.'

The Borough Council, too, had been considering what its policy should be. Members took note of the fact that the requirement for overspill housing had declined, because the worsening of the economic climate had discouraged firms from moving to the town. A reduction in the number of overspill houses could release land for use in building houses for sale. This met the views of those councillors who had always thought the Council should try to achieve a better balance between overspill and private housing.

On 1st April 1974, the Borough Council was replaced by a newly-constituted authority - the Basingstoke District Council, formed by the amalgamation of two mainly rural areas, Basingstoke Rural District Council and the Kingsclere and Whitchurch Rural District Council with the Basingstoke Borough Council. This meant that for the first time a rural point of view could directly influence decisions about the future of the town.

Taking advantage of the opportunity offered by the GLC's impending change of policy, the Council decided in July 1976 that the time had come 'to slow down the forced expansion of Basingstoke by building council houses specifically for Londoners and to concentrate instead on a more natural growth of the town and district by encouraging private development.' The main result of this new policy was the extension of the existing central built-up area of the

Borough, towards the east by the development of the Chineham area and towards the west to include the whole of the Brighton Hill area. This enlarged, more or less continuously built-up, area is described officially as 'the modern urban Basingstoke town area'. This larger Basingstoke had a population of 75,300 at the 1981 census.

A much larger unit incorporated the name Basingstoke in 1978 - the Borough of Basingstoke and Deane (Deane being the smallest village in it). This has an area of 245 square miles and had a mid-1974 population of 115,900 (estimated). The main centres of population, apart from the Chineham - Basing - Basingstoke Borough - Brighton Hill concentration, are Oakley, Overton, Whitchurch, Kingsclere and Tadley. Each of these has undergone some expansion in accordance with local plans and each continues to do so. Tadley formed part of the 'package' agreement which substituted (for the abandoned Hook scheme, discussed in Chapter 16) the expansion of Basingstoke, Andover and Tadley. With a population of about 4,500, Tadley was scheduled to receive an intake of 10,000 overspill population; a further increase of 2,500 was expected to come from private migration and natural increase.

Limited expansion was proposed for Oakley, separated from Basingstoke by a relatively narrow stretch of open country. It has experienced a high rate of growth, from 347 in 1951, reaching 3,766 in 1971 and 5,635 in 1981. It has become 'virtually a dormitory, urban-fringe, middle-class village, which functions as a residential area for Basingstoke and London commuters.' *(Livingstone M, 1975.)*

TABLE 2

Age Distribution of Population in Basingstoke

AGE	1951	%	1961	%	1971	%
0-4	1,474	8.7	2,516	9.7	6,280	11.9
5-14	2,216	13.1	4,029	15.5	10,245	19.5
15-24	2,066	12.2	3,043	11.7	7,405	14.1
25-34	2,483	14.6	3,995	15.4	8,755	16.7
35-44	2,537	14.9	3,667	14.2	6,545	12.4
45-54	2,364	13.9	3,235	12.4	5,260	10.0
55-64	1,880	11.1	2,757	10.6	4,000	7.6
64+	1,958	11.5	2,728	10.5	4,090	7.8
Total	16,978	100	25,980	100	52,580	100

TABLE 3

Age Distribution of Population in England and Wales (thousands)

AGE	1951	%	1961	%	1971	%
0-4	3,718	8.5	3,596	7.8	3,905	8.0
5-14	5,974	13.6	6,987	15.2	7,671	15.7
15-24	5,631	12.9	6,079	13.2	7,045	14.5
25-34	6,359	14.5	5,839	12.6	6,062	12.4
35-44	6,688	15.3	6,279	13.6	5,721	11.7
45-54	5,997	13.7	6,450	14.0	6,032	12.4
55-64	4,566	10.4	5,386	11.7	5,817	11.9
65+	4,825	11.1	5,497	11.9	6,495	13.3
Total	43,758	100	46,113	100	48,748	99.9

Source for both tables: *Census of Population*

The considerable increase in the number of people was only too obvious, as one went about the town. Equally noticeable was the 'younging' of the population, a feature which the town shares with other expanding towns such as Aylesbury and Thetford and also new towns like Crawley and Harlow. Tables 1 and 2 above, based on the census figures for 1951, 1961 and 1971, show the changing age structure of the population and enable a comparison to be made with the figures for England and Wales.

EDITORIAL UPDATE

With the passage of time and 3 censuses, the conclusions that can be drawn from the statistics above are not necessarily valid for the current population. The most recent figures may be obtained from the census records in the reference section of the Basingstoke Library. The Basingstoke and Deane Borough Council's website has an extensive analysis of the 2001 census at **www.basingstoke.gov.uk/Community/facts/wards.** *It gives the population of the Borough from the 2001 Census as (rounded figures) 152,000 with 90,000 living in the 'Town urban area'. For the purposes of this text we have defined this as the wards of Brighton Hill N & S, Brookvale, Buckskin, Chineham, Eastrop, Grove, Hatch Warren & Beggarwood, Kempshott, Norden, Popley E & W, Rooksdown, South Ham and Winklebury. Data for the Lytchpit area which should be included in the 'Town urban area' is not available separately (it is included in the data for Basing ward of which it is part), but an estimated number has been included in the 90,000 quoted above. The latest estimate of the Borough population is 162,000, (2008/2009 Guide to Council Tax, B&DBC) with most of the increase taking place in the 'Town urban area'. Note that the Local Government ward boundaries changed in 2008. This does not affect the figures quoted above but may make future comparisons difficult.*

The census data quoted in this update has been accessed and reproduced under the terms of Click-Use Licence C2008000214.

The Hants County Council's website has two addresses that have census information:
www.hants.gov.uk/census/basingstoke
www.hants.gov.uk/factsandfigures/basingstoke

The physical expansion of the town has continued (see Chapter 16).

PART 2

THE MAKING

© Ginny Pringle

An April 2008 aerial view of central Basingstoke from the southwest.

TOWN OF BASINGSTOKE.

BYE LAWS.

I.
Every person who within the said town shall use any dog or dogs for the purpose of drawing, or propelling, or helping to draw, or propel any cart, truck, barrow, or other carriage, or shall employ any dog as a beast of burden, shall forfeit and pay a sum not exceeding forty shillings for the first offence, and not exceeding five pounds for the second and every subsequent offence.

II.
Every person who shall wilfully and wantonly disturb any inhabitant, by pulling or ringing any door or gate bell, or knocking at any door without lawful excuse; or deface with chalk or by any other means any house or building, or shutter, door, gate, or fence, belonging thereto, within the said town, shall, for every such offence, forfeit and pay a sum not exceeding forty shillings.

III.
Every person who shall, in any thoroughfare or public place, within the said town, use any threatening, abusive, or insulting words, or behaviour, with intent to provoke a breach of the peace, or whereby a breach of the peace may be occasioned, shall, for every such offence, forfeit and pay a sum not exceeding forty shillings.

IV.
Every person who shall, within the said town, sell, or distribute, or offer for sale, or distribution, or exhibit to public view, any profane, indecent, or obscene book, paper, print, drawing, painting, or representation, or sing any profane, indecent, or obscene song, or ballad, or write, or draw, any indecent, or obscene word, figure, or representation, or use any profane, indecent, or obscene language, to the annoyance of the inhabitants or passengers, shall, for every such offence, forfeit and pay a sum not exceeding forty shillings.

V.
Every person who shall indecently expose his person, within sight of any other person passing along, or being in any thoroughfare within the said town, shall forfeit and pay a sum not exceeding forty shillings for every such offence.

VI.
Every person who shall make or use any slide upon ice or snow, or drive or trundle any hoop, or fight any dog or other beast, or throw any stone or stones in any street or thoroughfare, within the said town, to the annoyance or danger of any inhabitant or inhabitants, or passenger or passengers, shall, for every such offence, forfeit and pay a sum not exceeding forty shillings.

J. C. SHEBBEARE,
TOWN CLERK.

R. Cottle, Printer, Basingstoke,

© HRO 82M62

Town Bye Laws 1840

4   EARLY SETTLEMENT *Stone Age to Saxon*

In comparison with many other Hampshire towns and villages it is surprisingly lacking in evidences of the past. Yet if the face of things be changed, Basingstoke has some older corners than its suburbs of yesterday would suggest and its archives and histories prove an antiquity indisputable.

Highways and Byways in Hampshire D H Moutray Read, 1908

This antiquity has also been demonstrated from archaeological discoveries made within the area by Mr George Willis (after whom the Willis Museum is named), Mr John Ellaway and their friends on excursions out into the surrounding countryside. *(Proc HFC, 9, 1927 & 12, 1934)* These have been added to by more systematic excavation of sites revealed when land was being cleared for housing and other development.

It is to be expected that an area so favourable to ease of movement would provide evidence of early settlement. The Loddon-Test watershed does this. The discovery of Palaeolithic implements of flint and some of 'stones foreign to the district' near the junction of the two ancient trackways mentioned in Chapter 2 shows movement through or occupation of the area. *The White House* (SU620503) and *The Stag and Hounds* (SU618503) indicate more precisely the location of these finds. *(Roe, D 1968)*

Penrith Road

Nearer to the centre of the town, there is strong evidence of occupation in the form of a 'cooking site' revealed when foundations were being dug for a new road - Penrith Road (SU633518), in 1912. The identification was made by Mr George Willis. His note about the find describes 'a large area of burnt flints in a matrix of earth, 40 feet in diameter, 6 inches deep, lying on a sloping chalk surface under 3 or 4 feet of apparently undisturbed soil.' It is surely of some significance that the site was near a small stream, a tributary of the Loddon. The age of the find is uncertain. *[The location of the note referred to above has not been found in the published literature; however, a taped talk by Mr Willis has these details. A transcript of the tape is in the Resources Room of the Willis Museum. See also Ellaway, 1937.]*

Buckskin

The Buckskin estate in the south-western part of the town incorporates Buckskin Farm. Here there is evidence of occupation from Neolithic through to Iron Age times. The Neolithic is represented by flint implements found on the surface and in tree-throw hollows under the bell-barrow mentioned below. Implements of stone of unconfirmed provenance have also been found. The 1958 Ordnance Survey map (1:25,000 - Sheet SU65) shows round barrows of the Bronze Age, a group of three at SU608511 and a further two at SU604511.

Excavation of a low mound in the Buckskin area, in 1967 *(Allen M J et al, 1995)* revealed the remains of a bell barrow. The mound of loam and flint appears to have been covered with lumps of chalk quarried from its associated ditch, making it a landmark visible from some distance away. It is suggested that the position of one large hole indicates the existence of a 'totem pole'. It is thought possible that the site was one important for the performance of religious ritual.

[Less than a mile to the west there is further evidence of ancient occupation with White Barrow near Mother's Copse and a tumulus in Cow Down Copse between Pack Lane and the B3400 south of Newfound. In 2007, pre-development excavation at Worting between Old Kempshott Lane and the railway revealed evidence of Bronze and Iron Age occupation.]

Daneshill

Although much has been lost beneath the new building that has taken place, many of the features of the archaeology of the Basingstoke area owe their discovery to the work of the bulldozer and mechanical excavator. One such discovery occurred at Daneshill, where seven Bronze Age burial urns were found at SU657539, when contractors were at work preparing a site for new commercial development. There was also evidence of five cremations not enclosed in urns. *(Millett M & Schadla-Hall T, 1992)*

Winklebury

During the period we know as the Iron Age there were times when rivalries developed between neighbouring peoples, making places of refuge necessary. These took the form of hill forts, usually located on the higher parts of an area. Winklebury was such a hill fort. It is unfortunate that the requirements of a large housing development caused most of the evidence of its former defences to disappear. Part of its former site is occupied by Fort Hill School. *(Robertson-Mackay R, 1977, and Smith K, 1977)*

Contractors at work near the site made the interesting discovery at SU618525, of a coffin containing the skeleton of a middle-aged man. Two coins of the Empress Faustina enable the burial to be dated to about 150-170 AD. We may judge from the careful working of the stone, brought at undoubtedly considerable cost from a limestone quarry at Bradford-on-Avon, that the skeleton is probably that of someone important in the local community, perhaps a local landowner. The coffin and skeleton are now displayed in the Basingstoke Willis Museum, together with a life-size figure, suitably apparelled and speaking!

Viables

Viables revealed itself as a small Iron Age settlement on a site displaying no apparent natural advantage (SU632503). From boundary ditches, crop markings and pits it was clearly identifiable as a small farm. It is important for its unique double burial dating from the end of the Iron Age, two female skeletons interpreted as showing a dominant/subservient relationship, the younger appearing to be the more important of the two. *(Millett M & Russell D, 1982 & 1984)*

Ructstall's Hill

This settlement was excavated in advance of the construction of the Rucstalls estate *[the site name in the archaeological report retains the spelling Ructstall's in use at the time of excavation]*. The site, at SU651515, on a spur between two streams tributary to the River Loddon, was occupied with interruptions from Neolithic through to Roman times. *(Oliver M & Applin B, 1978)*

Enclosing ditches, post-holes and pits indicated a small Iron Age farmstead worked by a family group. In addition to pottery sherds and animal bones, clay loom weights and a quern-stone were found.

Fragments of daub, with wattle impressions, give an indication of the type of building, while two small crucibles containing slag show that metal-working had been carried out. Occupation during the Roman period is convincingly shown by glass beads, a bronze brooch, iron nails, spindle whorls and storage jars, as well as five coins of the third and fourth centuries AD. No satisfactory explanation has been given for the presence of a well-made pair of iron dividers in a good state of preservation on what was a typical Romano-British farmstead.

Newtown (May Street and Lower Brook Street)

At no great distance from the Winklebury hill fort, a Romano-British site came to light in 1880. *The Victoria County History* records the find in the following words, 'On the west side of Basingstoke, in the suburb of Newtown, on the north side of the River Loddon. Here roof tiles, nails, paving, ridge tiles and flue-bricks were found, with Samian and other pottery, fragments of glass and part of an iron tool.' S E Winbolt described the site as that of a villa, but this may have been too generous an interpretation. *[The finds were deposited in Reading Museum. See entry in Hampshire Treasures, 1979.]*

Oakridge

If Winklebury is interesting for its coffin, Oakridge is so on account of its well, revealed when site preparation for new housing was taking place. Excavation of the site *(Oliver M, 1993)* indicated occupation by a farming community in both Iron Age and Roman times. Distant from any stream, the settlement was dependent on the well, which was dug 87½ feet into the chalk. At the bottom of the well were the remains of a wooden bucket, a piece of iron chain and what appeared to have been part of the winch for drawing up the water. The evidence points to the occupation of the site at the end of the first century AD, but it would appear that the well went out of use in about 200 AD. It was after this date that the filling-up of the well occurred.

A large number of skeletons of farm animals, (46 cattle, 66 sheep, 32 pigs) came from different levels in the well. The remains of a number of wild animals were also present. The excavation of the well also yielded parts of 27 human skeletons. The nearby Oakridge Centre has a public house called *The Nine Saxons*. *[Demolished 2005]* It should more appropriately have been called *The Twenty-Seven Romano-Britons*.

An iron spearhead, dated to late fifth/early sixth century AD, was found in Stratfield Road, when the site for the original Oakridge estate was in preparation.

West Ham

In the 1950s in an article in the town guide for Basingstoke, Mr Willis wrote, 'The Saxon left little tangible evidence of his tenure of the district.' Finds have been rare but not entirely lacking from within the town. At the turn of the century, when work was in progress in constructing a railway siding at the works of Messrs Thornycroft, in Worting Road, excavation revealed spearheads, a knife and a ladle. There were also gaming pieces made of bone. A more important discovery was of a bronze hanging-bowl, with an escutcheon showing the form of a bird. These objects were interpreted as having accompanied the burial of someone of wealth and importance, possibly a local chieftain *(Smith, R A, 1907/08; quoted in Hinton, D A, 1986)*. They are kept at the British Museum. *[During road works for the Leisure Park, two graves were discovered opposite Davy's Garage. There were no grave goods to date the burials. The graves were very near the valley bottom and close to the course of the Loddon, which may have had ritual significance. Unfortunately the excavators have not published their work.]*

Cowdery's Down

Located to the east of the town, at SU657532, this site was the scene of excavations during the period 1978-1981. *(Millett M & James S, 1983)* Evidence was forthcoming of its use from Bronze Age times onward to the period of the Civil War. Saxon occupation of the site took place in three stages between the late 6th and late 7th / early 8th centuries, with evidence of a high status settlement. The interpretation of the site was favoured by the good state of preservation of the evidence for the different structures, revealed as 'ghost' timber slots in the chalk sub-soil. Initially there were three, eventually ten, of these, described as 'halls'. They differed in type, one of them, larger than the others, being described as a 'feasting-hall'. The site appears not to have been in continuous occupation, but one such as might be visited from time to time by a Saxon landowner on his journeyings from one property to another. In any case, a skeleton staff would have been in permanent residence. Not far away is the site of the dell at Lychpit Farm, the supposed site of the burial of those slain in the battle between Saxons and Danes which took place near Basing in 871 AD. *[This was, in fact, an old chalk pit; now filled in.]* The name Lychpit comes from the Anglo-Saxon *lic*, meaning a corpse. The word lychgate and place-name Lichfield have the same derivation.

It was from Cowdery's Down that Cromwell's guns bombarded Basing House in the summer of 1644, but little evidence of this turned up in the excavations.

Basing

We cannot say why a group of Saxons, the Basingas, chose to establish themselves in the valley of the River Loddon, there to form the nucleus of the village of Basing. Were they, these followers of Basa, perhaps influenced by the existence of an ancient earthwork situated where the ruins of Basing House are found today? Did they find it easier to cross the river by following the road left to them by their predecessors, the Romans?

It was Hugh de Port who by 1086 had caused the settlement to grow to become the most important place in this part of Hampshire, by making it the *caput* or centre of administration of the large number of manors held by him in the county.

In course of time, a *stoc* or small outlying settlement came into existence upstream of Basing. This, known as *Basingstoc* to the Saxons, became *Basingstoches* to the Normans and eventually the town of Basingstoke.

The names of other places in our area reveal their Saxon origin. Oakley originated as *Acleah* (the field with oaks), Cliddesden is formed from *clud* (rock or stone) and *denu* (valley), Sherborne is derived from *sci* (bright, clear) and *brunna* (spring or stream), while Dummer was originally *dun* (hill) and *maer* (pool, pond).

So far as Basingstoke itself is concerned, we can remind ourselves that within its boundaries, the names Kempshott, Winklebury and Worting are all of Saxon origin. This is also the case with the three 'hams' - north, south and west.

EDITORIAL UPDATE

Hampshire Treasures, 1979, *records other early archaeological finds: Neolithic/Early Bronze Age east of the Reading Road bridge in 1883 and Belgic cremation burials and a hut circle in 1882. Unfortunately when the demolition and redevelopment of the town centre took place there was no opportunity for archaeological investigation due to the nature of the building operations taking place; the whole area was very extensively piled.*

Further development of greenfield sites around the town has led to more discoveries: Bronze Age at Beggarwood and Old Kempshott Lane (Worting); Iron Age/Romano-British at Brighton Hill South (Coe D & Newman R, 1993), Park Prewett, Merton Farm (Popley), Beggarwood Lane, Old Kempshott Lane (Worting) and Viables (Vaughn T, 1999 and Hounsell D & Murray J, 2001); Anglo-Saxon at Riverdene (Hall-Torrance M & Weaver S, 2003), and Medieval at Brighton Hill South (Hatch Warren) (Fasham P J & Coe D, 1995).

This last excavation also produced a series of side-by-side cart-ruts in the chalk, the forerunner of the present A30, illustrated by the photographs in Chapter 2.

Many of these excavations are reported in Hampshire Studies (the Proceedings of the Hampshire Field Club) *and other archaeological journals, and all are recorded in the Historic Environment Record in the County Archaeologist's office, Winchester. Finds are held by the Hampshire County Museums & Archives Service.*

Eric Stokes would have been delighted by current archaeological thinking which supports his view of the importance of the geographical position of the Basingstoke area in its development, population growth and land use. This area lies on the boundary between two geological formations: chalk downland conducive to agriculture and the Reading Beds and heavier clays suitable for pastoralism and hunting. It is felt by David Hopkins, the present County Archaeologist for Hampshire, that this position was a significant factor in the concentration of archaeological sites in this area from prehistoric to medieval times.

5 THE MEDIEVAL TOWN

The place of greatest importance in the north of Hampshire during the Middle Ages was Basingstoke. At the time of the Great Survey its inhabitants already possessed some important privileges, among which was its market. It was the meeting place for the hundred... It became in time the governing centre for six hundreds, and lords of neighbouring manors had to make suit at its courts.

A History of Hampshire - T W Shore, 1892.

The King holds Basingstoke in lordship. It has always been a royal manor. It never gave tax nor has the hide been apportioned there. Land for 20 ploughs. In lordship 3 ploughs; 20 villagers and 8 smallholders with 12 ploughs. 6 slaves; 3 mills at 30s; 12 freedmen with 4 ploughs. A market at 30s; meadow, 20 acres; in Winchester 4 men of the suburb(s) paid 13s less 1d. Geoffrey the Chamberlain holds the land of one of these but neither the Sheriff nor the Hundred have ever seen the King's seal for it. Woodland for 20 pigs.

Domesday Book, Hampshire, Julian Munby (Ed), 1982.

Charters

When, in 1972, the Maud Commission, appointed to review local government in England and Wales, proposed that Basingstoke should 'go in with Berkshire', the borough council opposed the suggestion, saying of the town that it had centuries of connection with local government in Hampshire. This connection began in Anglo-Saxon times when Hamtunshire was one of the constituent shires of the Kingdom of Wessex. Like other shires, it was divided into hundreds, which were further subdivided into tythings. In course of time, under the Normans, Basingstoke became the *caput* or centre of administration of six hundreds out of the forty-three into which Hampshire was divided (by 1334 it had been reduced to 37).

The map of *The Ancient Jurisdiction of the Manor of Basingstoke* reproduced from Baigent and Millard's *History of Basingstoke* shows the disposition of these six hundreds - Bermondspit, Chuteley, Holdshott, Odington and Overton, together with the in-hundred of Basingstoke.

As Shore says in his *History of Hampshire*, 'Originally a royal manor administered by the King's bailiff, it acquired in the course of time municipal institutions and became practically a self-governing community possessed of more than ordinary authority over the surrounding hundreds.'

It is not always clear which unit - town, hundred or manor - is being referred to in extant records and so it is difficult to trace the steps by which 'the [ap]proved men of Basingstoke' came to assume full responsibility for managing their own affairs. We can, however, gain some idea from the Pipe Rolls, in which were recorded the various sums collected in rents, fines and taxes, and from the Court Rolls, which gave details of the judgements made against those individuals who failed to conform.

The year 1212 was an important one for the town, for in that year King John granted to the men of Basingstoke the 'firm of the Manor. Fee farm rent - £51.6s.8d.' Fee farm [firm] rent was the annual fixed sum of money which tenants were required to pay the lord of the manor. This meant that they were themselves to be directly responsible for making payment to the King's exchequer. The sheriff, who had hitherto been an intermediary between town and Crown, no longer had any part to play in seeing to the collection of the various dues. As a result he had less opportunity to interfere in, and exercise influence over, the affairs of the town. There was, however slowly it developed, a corresponding increase in the authority of the leading men of the town to speak and to act on behalf of the townspeople generally.

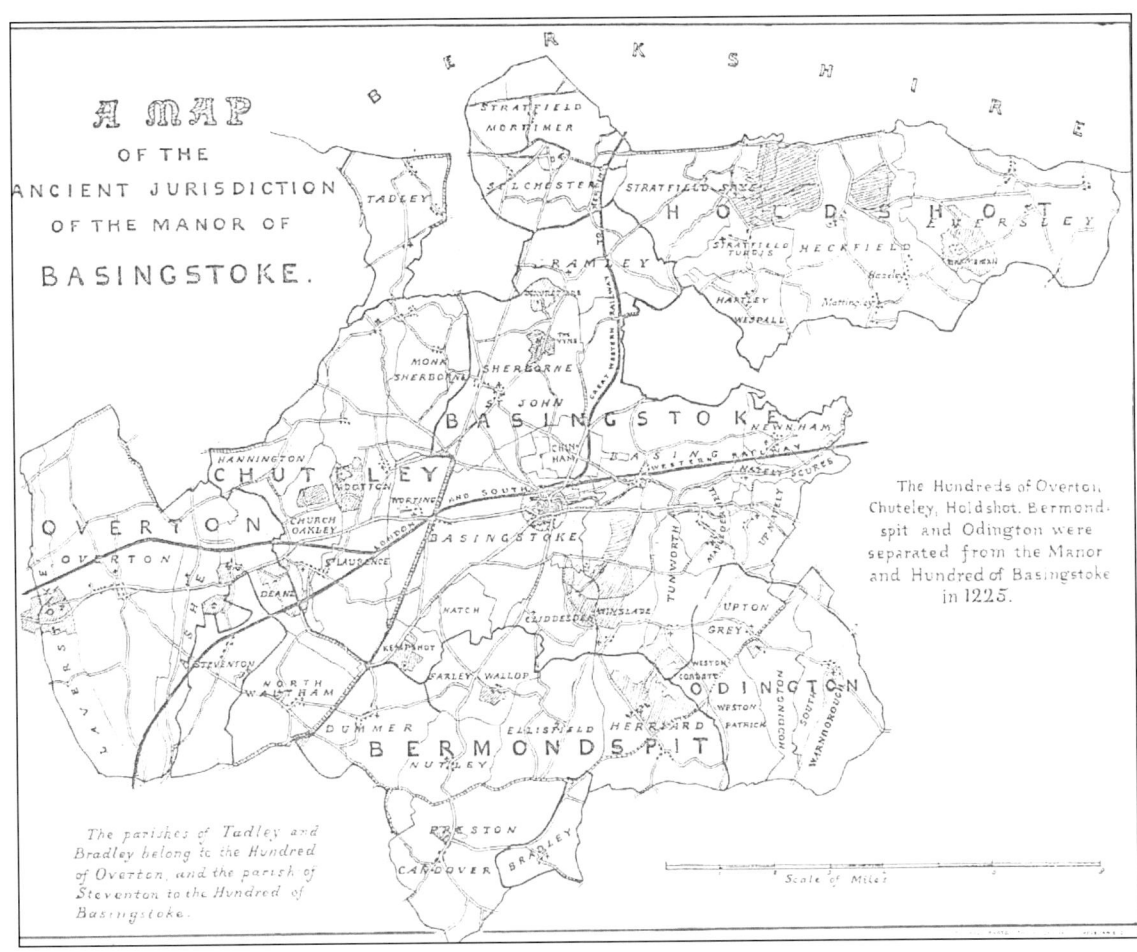

The Ancient Jurisdiction of the Manor of Basingstoke reproduced from Baigent and Millard's *History of Basingstoke*

The annual sum payable by the six hundreds was £104.12s.0d. Unfortunately the manor found it difficult to make the payment regularly. The result of this increasing indebtedness was the separation, in 1227, of the hundred of Basingstoke from the other hundreds. The king retained these in his own hands, but allowed the men of Basingstoke to hold the firm of the Manor at the reduced annual rent (the fee farm rent) of £80. The town still failed to meet its obligations. The situation became clearer in 1256, when Henry III granted to the men of Basingstoke and their heirs the perpetual tenure of the Manor and hundred of Basingstoke.

The charter dated '20 May in the 40th year of our reign' did so in the following terms:

> 'Wherefore we desire, and have firmly resolved for ourselves and our heirs, that the aforesaid men in Basingstoke and their heirs shall in perpetuity have and hold well and peaceably, freely, quietly and wholly from us and our heirs the aforesaid Manor of Basingstoke with all the aforesaid things and with all other liberties and customs appertaining to the farm of the said manor. Rendering thence to our Exchequer every year £80 of Sterling money, namely £40 at the Feast of St Michael and £40 at the Feast of Easter.'

In practice this set the town on the way to becoming a self-governing community.

The sum payable to the royal exchequer was later reduced to £51.6s.8d. In 1547, by an involved series of transfers, it became payable to the Paulet family and the Corporation accounts for 1832-33 show the item, 'To the Right honourable Lord Bolton, Fee farm rent £51.6s.8d.' This was still being paid to Lord Bolton in the 1880s.

More than a hundred years were to elapse before the town acquired full authority to act as a corporate body. It was granted this right in 1392, when the good people of Basingstoke, taking advantage of the assembly of the Parliament at Winchester, petitioned for some relief after serious damage by fire, which resulted in Richard II, with the consent of his Council and Parliament, issuing the following:

> 'Be it known unto all that, taking into consideration the serious injury and utter loss which the good men of our town of Basingstoke have sustained by the ravages of the sudden and unforeseen fire which lately happened in the said town, and from which they will necessarily suffer for a long time to come; and wishing to extend a helping hand in the relief of our aforesaid town and of the aforesaid men, who, by this fortune as well as by other calamities, are greatly impoverished and oppressed; we grant, of our own especial grace, for ourselves and our heirs to the aforesaid town, that they, their heirs and successors, shall be for ever a community in themselves, and for all time shall possess a Common Seal, as aforesaid.
>
> Winchester, 12 February (Richard II, 16)'

Courts and officials

Two men, known as bailiffs, were elected annually to administer the affairs of the town and hundred. They were assisted by two sub-bailiffs, also known as constables, and four affeerors; these latter were responsible for setting the amount of the fine payable, taking into account any special circumstances of the case. There is also mention of the office of provost (John in 1174, William in 1205). It has been suggested that this points to the existence of some form of organization not yet known as a corporation but having a chief citizen or Mayor. The machinery of government consisted of regular meetings of two courts. The records of these bodies show that they were concerned to ensure that the various customs and usages were adhered to by everyone in the interests of the whole community.

The first of these was 'The Court of the hundred of the proved men of the town of Basingstoke and of their manor.' This met on every third Saturday throughout the year. The second was 'The Court Leet or View of Frank-pledge.' This was held twice yearly, in April and November, likewise meeting on a Saturday. The Court Leet continued to meet long after its functions had been assumed by other agencies. In 1880, for example, it met on 16th October in the Town Hall. 'Those present elected manorial officials for the ensuing year. They then adjourned to the Barge Inn to partake of a first rate dinner.' The report continues, 'toasts were given and enthusiastically received, interspersed with some excellent songs. The evening was devoted to social enjoyment.'

Very little documentary evidence of statutory regulation of the town's affairs has come down to us. The document entitled *The Regulations and Constitution of the Manor of Basingstoke* dating from 1389 is the exception. It was a statement of the different usages that had evolved over time in a community whose main concern was the land, its ownership and the way it was used. There appears to have been no corresponding statute giving details of the way in which all other aspects of the life of the town were to be controlled. However, an examination of the court rolls, in Baigent & Millard's *History of Basingstoke*, leaves us in no doubt that a close watch was kept on such matters as 'the preservation of the peace, the punishment of all minute offences against the public good, and all trivial misdemeanors, common nuisances, enquiries as to waifs and strays, the accuracy of weights and measures, the regulation of public trade and all irregularities in the public commons, encroachments, defective fences and highways' (page 234).

The term 'waifs and strays' requires an explanation. Whereas today we normally use the term to refer to unwanted, neglected children, it was formerly used to describe any property which was apparently ownerless. If unclaimed within a fixed period after due notice given, it became the property of the lord of the manor.

Much of the work of the Hundred Court was concerned with cases of debt, (in the course of time almost completely so). The court roll of 1386 shows the sort of case that came before the courts:

> 'Nicholas Bothe is at mercy, because he has not carried out his prosecution against John Bounde on a plea of debt. Fined 6d.
>
> William Gregory, junior, is at mercy for unjustly detaining 3s. due to Nicholas Feldgat on a plea of debt. Fined 6d.
>
> The tything man of Basingstoke, with his assessors present that Edith Gylote justly raised the hue and cry against John Scotmond, therefore the said John is at mercy. Fined 6d.' It was an offence to raise the hue and cry without good reason.

The View of Frank-pledge was the long-established system by which the members of each tything were held to be responsible for the good behaviour of each other. Twice yearly, all the freeholders of the hundred of Basingstoke and all other persons, (not including those under 12 and those over 60, peers, ecclesiastics and women), were obliged to attend the Court Leet, the alternative name of Frank-pledge. Here the chief man of the tything would make 'presentment' to the assembled company. That is, he would report on the 'state of the tything', drawing attention to anything that was amiss. His presentment could be concerned with a wide range of offences against the common good and could include, for example, matters which today would come under the heading of the environment or of consumer protection. A few examples will serve to illustrate the type of case dealt with.

> 1390 - 12 November. 'John Wortynge has two bushels, namely, a greater and a smaller one, and buys by one and sells by the other. John Reynald in like manner has two bushels and so sells his corn to the excess of 6d.' They were each fined 12d., and were to be expelled from the market.
>
> 1399 - 19 April. There were a number of cases of overcharging. No major trade seems to have been free of breaking the law in this way. It was presented that a number of tailors 'took wages in excess of the statute'. The maximum fine was 6d., the least 3d. It was also presented 'that Richard Smyth, Thomas Smyth and William Smyth are smiths and charge excessively, therefore they are at mercy.' Fined respectively 6d., 3d. and 2d. 'Breaking the assize of ale' was a fairly common offence; it is recorded that a number of tapsters were fined for the same offence. *[See page 48.]*

A case of encroachment was reported to the court on 12 November 1407. 'Richard Fynleghe has ploughed up and appropriated to himself a common way called le Greenway, containing four feet in breadth, leading from the highway towards Wyltenyssebury [Winklebury], to the common detriment. Fined 6d. and ordered to amend it against the next court under penalty.'

Sometimes a way could be deliberately blocked. The account of the court for November 1440 states that John Walloppe had 'blocked up the highway from Hackwoode towards Kempshott'. For this offence 'to the common detriment' he was fined 12d.

Matters involving health and safety were also brought to the court's attention. In November 1464, Ralph Digon was charged with causing danger to his neighbours by leaving a well unenclosed. He was fined 4d. and was ordered to see to it that the well was covered without delay.

Some cases were concerned with persistent anti-social behaviour. In November 1455, the tythingman presented that Isabella Clapsho was 'a common scold and a disturber of the King's peace to the detriment of the whole neighbourhood of Basingstoke.' It was decided that she should be punished by means of the 'tumberall' (ducking-stool). The court deferred sentence but said that punishment would be 'inflicted upon her without delay', if she relapsed into her 'evil ways'.

Office-holders were liable to be fined if they neglected their duty e.g. by non-attendance without good reason, or by failure, from whatever cause, to ensure the attendance of offenders at court. In November 1455, Thomas Brygthwyse, one of the tythingmen for Basingstoke, was at mercy 'because although duly summoned he has not come here to receive his oath and to present as he ought to do.'

In July 1440 the report of the Court Leet was that 'the bailiffs are at mercy, because they have not here the Lord of Basing (John Paulet, Esq) to render suit.' It is disappointing that we do not know why a member of one of the leading local families was required to attend the court, but it is pleasing to see that the court showed no favouritism, giving instruction that both he and the bailiffs should be 'distrained'.

Fields and pasture

The medieval countryside consisted of relatively small islands of cultivation separated from each other by large expanses of waste or forest. Habitation was in the form of small village communities joined to their neighbours by tracks, rutted and muddy in winter, but dry and dusty in summer.

Medieval Basingstoke was such a village, surrounded by its large open fields, originally probably three in number. Although their total area remained very much the same over a long period, coinciding more or less with that of the parish, they underwent subdivision and change of name at different times, so that it is difficult to be definite about their precise pattern.

By the time of the Enclosure Award in 1788 there were six of them: North Field (116 acres); Hackwood Field (422 acres); Hatch Field (541 acres); Winchester Field (560 acres); Salisbury Field (406 acres); and Chapel Field (1006 acres). These took up 80% of the parish, with the Common land or Down in the extreme south-west making up the remainder of the farm land. As the Plan of Basingstoke - New Allotment 1788 *[see page 46]* – shows, the greater part of the area of the Award lay west of a north-south line running through the centre of the town.

The fields were sub-divided into holdings of varying size, these being further divided into strips, not grouped together but scattered throughout the fields. The manner and degree of subdivision can be illustrated from the holding of William de Bentworth (c1300) *[also spelt Binteworth]*. He held 61½ acres, divided into 46 plots, distributed in four fields. In the early years of the 15th century, Thomas Gregory held 185½ acres: in Northfield 36½ acres, in Westfield 23 acres, in Southfield 60 acres, in Eastfield 18½ acres, beyond the Herepathe (the Harrow Way) 30 acres. Separately 12½ acres; and in Wildemore 5 acres of meadow. We should remember that change in ownership of holdings was a constant process, leading to some degree of consolidation.

In 1762, when the Duke of Bolton decided on a survey of his estates in Basingstoke, his properties were so scattered about that he needed a map of the whole town to make sense of it all. The result was 8 maps covering the town centre, the six Common Fields and Basingstoke Down, together with a book of reference listing all his properties and tenants. It is a treasury of information on land ownership just before enclosure swept the old field strip system away, and also a work of art.

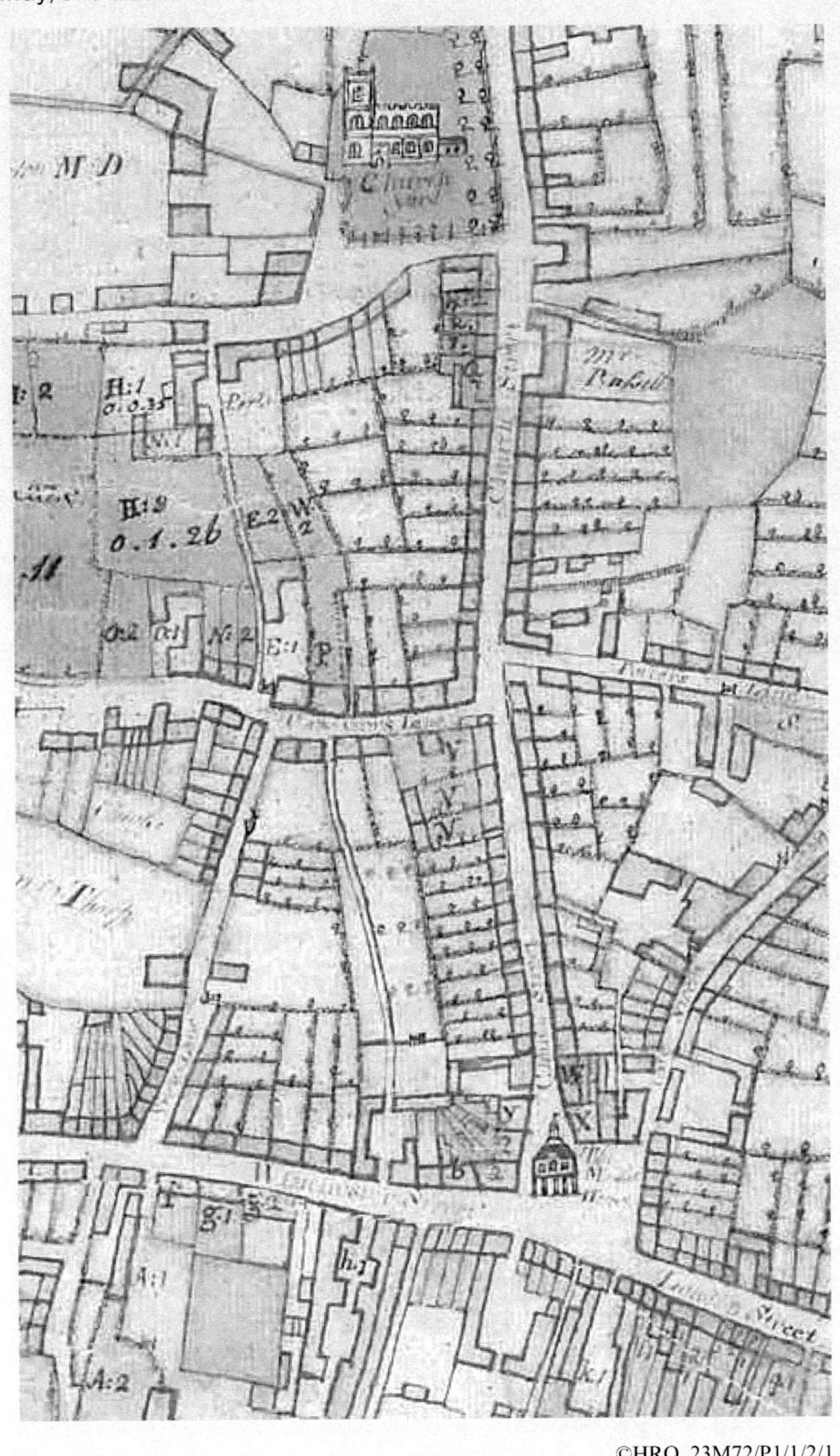

©HRO 23M72/P1/1/2/1

The map on the previous page, the text accompanying it and the three maps below are reproduced by kind permission of the Hampshire Records Office.

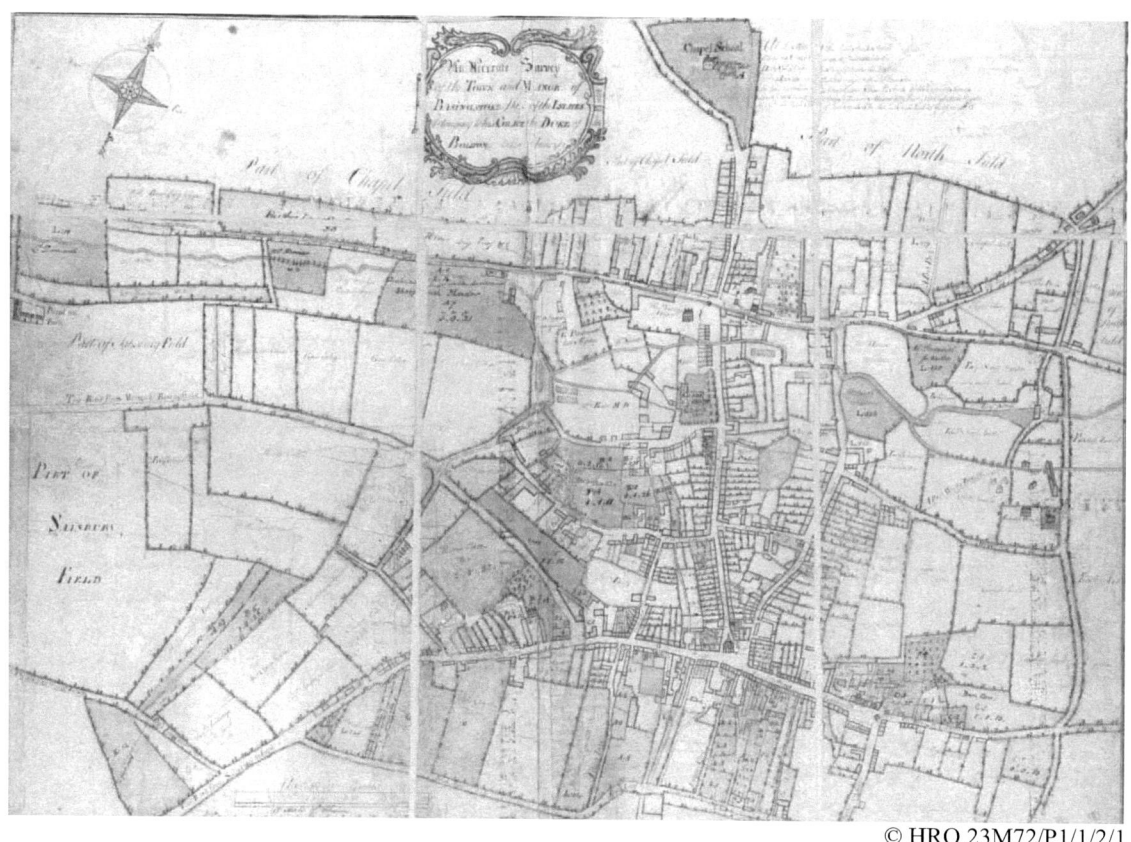

© HRO 23M72/P1/1/2/1

An extract from the Duke of Bolton's map of 1762
It shows much of the medieval layout surviving

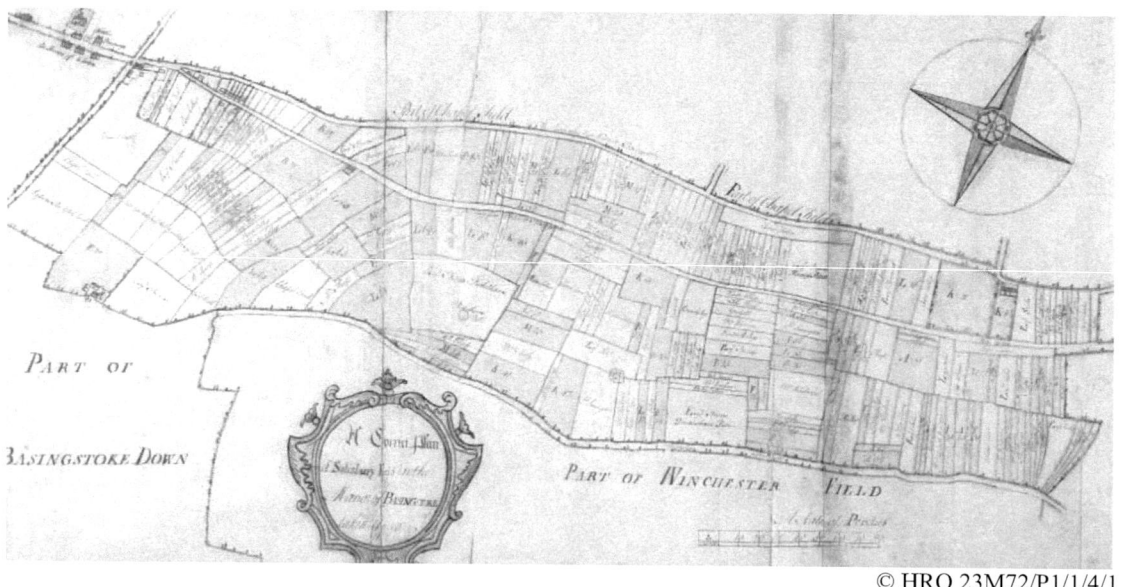

© HRO 23M72/P1/1/4/1

Extract from the 1762 map of the Basingstoke
showing the land holdings in Salisbury field

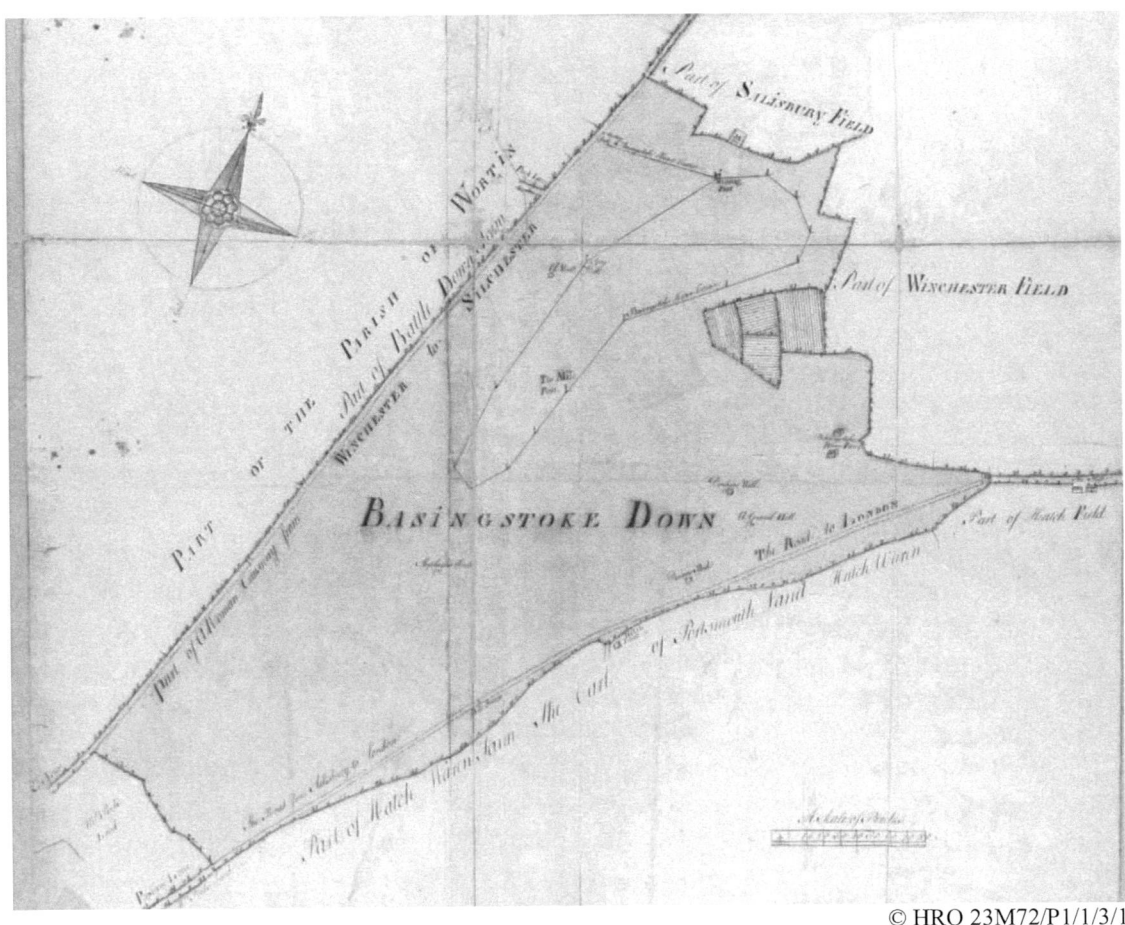

© HRO 23M72/P1/1/3/1

Extract from the 1762 map of the Basingstoke, showing Basingstoke Down

Besides the arable of the open fields, there was common grazing land (631 acres) at Kempshott, known as The Down. Out to the north-east of the town there was meadow-land at Wildmoor, also used for grazing, as a source of hay and for fishing. 'The Custom of the Manor' governed the use of all land in quite considerable detail. *The Regulations and Constitutions of the Manor of Basingstoke* referred to above set out the duties of two officials - the hayward, who was responsible for the maintenance of hedges, etc. and the swine-herd. For their services they were paid partly in money and partly in kind. Between them they ensured that livestock belonging to the tenants did not cause damage by trespassing on land where they should not be. They had the authority to impound any animals until the aggrieved parties received compensation. There were two pounds, one on Holy Ghost Hill, the other in Winchester Road.

They were also responsible for regulating the numbers of livestock allowed on the land of the common pasture, in order to limit damage by over-grazing. Entry on to the stubble land, for grazing after harvest, was also strictly controlled; a fine could be levied if a tenant's stock was found on such land before the appointed day. Harvest-time was not without its problems. A tenant had to be careful not to damage his neighbour's corn crop: 'No man, of whatsoever condition he may be, shall drive his cart through anyone's corn in the harvest-time to his own land, to the damage of anyone.' These detailed regulations included one which laid down the conditions under which gleaning was allowed.

There was a protectionist element in at least one of the regulations. Pasture-land should not be let to 'any stranger dwelling outside the aforesaid town'. Anyone doing so was obliged 'to pay to the use of the church of St Michael double the sum he receives for the aforesaid pasture so let.' As the following extract from a court roll shows, strangers did sometimes cause trouble. 'John Wallop, Esquire, dwelling and residing at Farley [Farleigh Wallop], which was outside the said town of Basingstoke and not having a tenant of his holding dwelling within the town, on the second day of October, in the third year of the reign of King Edward IV [1463] entered the field of the proved men and tenants of the Lord King at Basingstoke called Winchester Field, contrary to the said custom, with 700 sheep, which then fed upon and trod down the stubble and herbage of the aforesaid men and tenants to their great injury.' He continued to offend on several other days of the month. He was fined 27 shillings. This was not an isolated incident. He had on a previous occasion (8 March 1456) 'entered the aforesaid common pasture of the Lord King Edward and of his aforesaid proved men, called Basingstoke Heath, alias Shepedowne, with saws and instruments - cut down, disbranched, prostrated and altogether laid waste many thorn and other trees - carried them off to his lordship of Farley and there of his own will disposed of them to the great damage of the same proved men, their heirs and assigns - at mercy. Fined £10.'

At a later date it was found necessary to confirm the provisions of the 1389 Regulations and Constitutions. It is not known by what stages it came about, but the disagreement between the town and Wallop appears to have been settled to the satisfaction of both parties.

In 1455 we learn of another official. The View of Frank-pledge of November of that year elected Henry Mulward to 'the office of mower, alias keeper of le Wyldmore'. It was his responsibility to see that the meadowland there was properly used in the interest of all. In the following year, he was carrying out his duties by making presentment to the View of Frank-pledge that the stream called Rotherwykes Broke [Rotherwick Brook] was unscoured so that the meadow called Wyldmore [also spelt Wildemore] was overflowing with water. The two tenants were ordered to clean out the stream 'against the next court day under the penalty of 3s.4d. each.'

Chapels, Hospital and Guild

Thomas Hardy, in *Jude the Obscure,* refers to 'picturesque Medieval ruins' standing beside the railway at Stoke Barehills, his name for Basingstoke. These are commonly known as the Holy Ghost Ruins. Strictly speaking, this term refers only to the remains of the westernmost of two buildings situated in the area known as the Maiden Acre, part of which is the Liten (or Corpse land). The other building - damaged, but less so - is the Chapel of the Holy Trinity, a chantry chapel built in 1542 by Lord Sandys of the Vyne.

It was in the Liten that the townspeople buried their dead, when the papal interdict, imposed by Pope Innocent III in 1208, forbade them the use of the parish churchyard. After 1214, the ground of the Liten was consecrated. Some time later, a chapel was built here - the Chapel of the Holy Ghost. It is assumed that from then on a chaplain was appointed to perform the services of the chapel. It is possible that he also undertook educational duties.

At a later date, a Guild, described by Baigent and Millard in their *History of Basingstoke* as 'a voluntary association of certain inhabitants of the town', was established in connection with the chapel. The members of the Guild (both brethren and sisters) elected annually an alderman and two wardens to administer its affairs. It obtained a legal, corporate status in 1524, when Henry VIII at the request of Richard Fox, Bishop of Winchester, Lord Sandys of the Vyne and local citizens, granted it a licence, by which it was permitted to hold land and other property and derive income from them.

The History of the Brotherhood or Guild of the Holy Ghost in the Chapel of the Holy Ghost, by Samuel Loggon (dating from 1742) gives details of the properties held - houses in Wote Street, Northbrook Street and Holy Ghost Street, as well as 100 acres in the common fields.

Since there is no evidence to show otherwise, it must be assumed that it was for mutual self-help that the members originally came together. There is, for example, no mention of charitable works to assist the population at large. It must not be forgotten, however, that some of the Guild's revenues came to be devoted to educational purposes. It is from this that we trace the origin of the Holy Ghost School, more recently known as Queen Mary's School (see Chapter 18).

The town had another religious foundation - the Hospital of St John (or St Mary and St John). It was situated 'on the north side of the town brook, a little below the bridge' i.e. opposite Chute House at the bottom of Church Street. It was re-founded some time between 1230 and 1240, at the instance of Walter de Merton, who was born in the town and inherited property here from his mother. It was to be 'for the support of the ministers of the altar of the Lord, whose strength is failing and the wayfaring poor of Christ'. In 1262 (8th June) Henry III declared it to be a royal hospital 'for the perpetual support of ministers of the Lord and of poor men sojourning there in sickness'.

Walter de Merton later rose to be Lord Chancellor of England; in this capacity he served two kings, Henry III and Edward I. His political career came to an end in 1274, the year in which he was consecrated Bishop of Rochester. Besides carrying out his duties to the See of Rochester, he devoted much of his time to advancing the interest of the college which he founded in 1264 - Merton College, Oxford.

The Warden of the College was, as Warden of the hospital at Basingstoke, responsible for ensuring that the intentions of the founder were carried out. In 1401, because it was apparent that the terms of the endowment were not being fully met, the Crown confiscated the hospital's revenues, which were not restored until 1405. It must be said that at a later date also the College seems to have been rather casual in its administration, in particular in its failure to maintain a Chaplain for the hospital. In course of time, the building, as well as the institution itself, decayed and the site became Merton Farm. In 1887 the site of the hospital was cleared of its buildings 'owing to Mr Portsmouth having purchased the ground from the College authorities, whereof he had been tenant for many years'. (Baigent & Millard's *History of Basingstoke*, page 640.) We are forced to the conclusion that the foundation did not have the lasting influence its benefactor would have wished.

The end of the Open Field system in Basingstoke. Contributed by Derek Spruce

> *As Eric Stokes makes clear, the 'men of Basingstoke' not only regulated the trading activities but were Lords of the Manor of the large farming parish. The map on the next page, based on a 1762 plan (HRO 23M72/P1/1) and the 1788 enclosure award, shows the six open fields of varying sizes referred to on page 40. The small extent of the Old Enclosures separated from the open field strip system shows that the Manorial Court had been successful in resisting pressure to allow enclosure. Note that there were very few houses outside Basingstoke town, all farm houses were in the compact urban area, with workers trudging out to a scatter of strips in the open fields. Note also that the common grazing (The Down) was on the south west edge of the parish.*
>
> *The radical extent of the resulting change is shown on the 1834 map. Within 46 years seven new large farms had been established away from the town. The map shows the large extent of land rented by maltsters and brewers. The Curtis brothers of the Angel Inn owned only 22 acres but rented 564 acres for barley growing and also horse grazing, for they owned the largest coaching inn. Four other innkeepers and horse dealers rented 400 acres. The revised borough boundary suggested by the Municipal Corporations Commissioners in 1836 shows that they did not envisage the urban areas growing very much. [See maps on pages 122 & 123.] In 2008 the whole of Basingstoke parish is now urbanised.*   DS

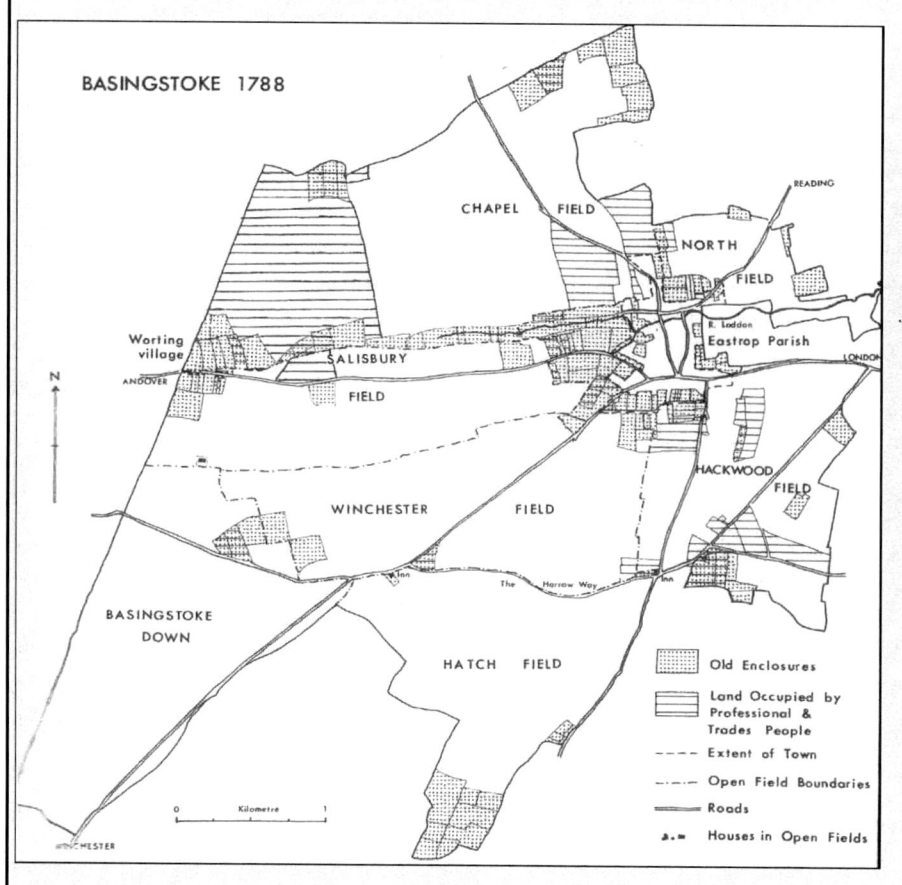

This map is based on the 1762 plan (HRO 23M72/P1/1) and the 1788 enclosure award. It shows the six open fields of varying size.

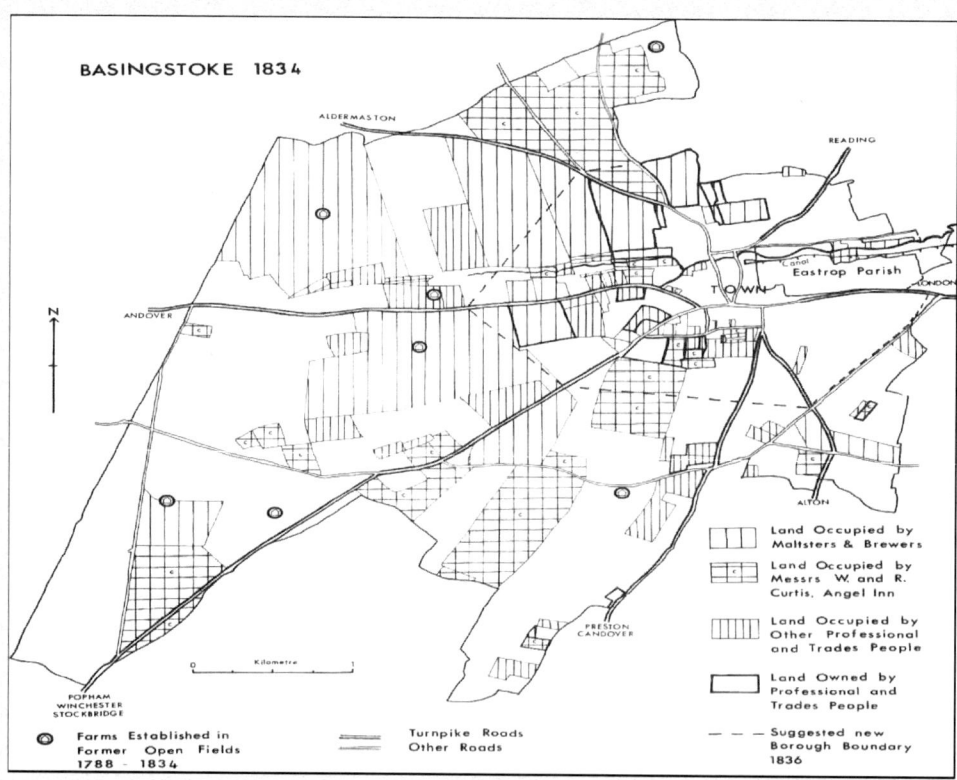

Map showing the distribution of land occupation in 1834 Both maps ©Derek Spruce

6   MARKETS AND FAIRS

A mercate town well frequented upon the descent of an hill.

Camden's Britannia 1586, translated by Philemon Holland – 1637

Markets

We are accustomed to wide variations in the spelling of words. The use of the spelling 'mercate' is particularly appropriate, since it shows that our word 'market' is derived from the Latin *mercatus*, meaning trade and by extension 'a place of trade'. We need to know why and how a place becomes a market-town. It will perhaps help if we start with the statement, 'Markets grow up where it is convenient - and profitable - for commodities to be assembled for sale.'

Under the manorial system, everything was regulated according to the custom of the manor. Crops were grown, goods were produced, and services were performed to meet the needs of the manor.

The aim, particularly at an early stage, was self-sufficiency, the need to produce enough food being most important, vital even, to a community whose fortunes could fluctuate widely from year to year. One place might be favoured by natural conditions - better soil would be one of these - and so be able, if only from time to time, to produce a surplus, which could be disposed of elsewhere in the district. Given the increasingly reliable availability of a surplus, combined with a growing demand from communities whose inhabitants were becoming more specialised and therefore devoting less time and effort to growing their own food, regular trading links would develop and a market could be established. The lord of the manor could turn this to his advantage; he could derive income from levying tolls on those who frequented the market. Once established, the market would attract more suppliers from round about and eventually also merchants coming from further afield, able to supply goods not available from local sources.

What factors operated to make Basingstoke a market centre serving a considerable area round about? We can suggest three possible reasons for its success (at the expense of other places having market rights). Firstly, it was located on the margin between two contrasting types of country - chalk downland and clay lowland, each with its characteristic agriculture, thus providing the opportunity for profitable mutual exchange. Secondly, it had the advantage of a natural nodality; the meeting of a number of routes facilitated the coming together of people and the assembly of goods. A third advantage derived from the fact that the manor of Basingstoke was a royal one, and was also of considerable extent. This gave the town an importance (a 'political' one) greater than that of its neighbours and made it a place of much greater 'thoroughfare', with many more people than was the case elsewhere coming and going about the affairs of the manor and hundred.

The growth of the town into a centre serving a hinterland of smaller places within a radius of four or five miles would have been very gradual. It was obviously well advanced by pre-Conquest times. Christopher Hibbert, in his *The English - a Social History - 1066-1945*, gives the number of markets recorded in Domesday for England as fifty. Basingstoke was one of these. It was assessed as being worth thirty shillings. Compare this with another early market at Titchfield worth forty shillings. Its nearest rivals were Overton, Whitchurch, and Alresford. All of these had, by late medieval times, achieved market rights (Overton in 1217 and Whitchurch in 1241) as well as rights to hold fairs. It is assumed that, although they do not appear to have been given official status as markets, Odiham and Kingsclere would, to some extent have shared in local trading activities.

The market at Basingstoke was originally held on a Sunday, but in 1203 the day was changed to Monday. Later, in 1214, Wednesday became market-day, as we learn from the following announcement (Baigent & Millard's *History of Basingstoke*, page 65): 'Peter [de Rupibus], by the grace of God, Bishop of Winchester, to the Sheriff of the County of Southampton sends greetings. Know ye, that we have granted, on behalf of the Lord King, that the market, which was wont to be held at Basingstoke, is to be held there on Wednesday throughout the day, in order that this market may not be injurious to the neighbouring markets. And therefore, we command you to make proclamation that this market shall be held on that day. Witness ourself at the Tower of London on the twenty-ninth day of June in the sixteenth year of the reign of our Lord John the King.'

The inhabitants of the growing town were not only consumers buying from suppliers coming in from the country; they were also producers of goods and providers of services for those same country people. In course of time, a number of inhabitants would have developed particular skills and become specialist craftsmen, making things in their own homes. Eventually, further specialisation produced a separation into two distinct functions: the 'maker' in his workshop, the 'seller' in his shop.

It is fortunate for us that not all the town's shopkeepers conformed to the agreed 'trading standards'. Their infringement of these and the amercements they had to pay are recorded in court rolls of the time. An amercement was a fine awarded at the 'mercy' of the court. It was arbitrary, not a fixed penalty, subject to assessment according to the circumstances of the case. The affeeror would assess what was a reasonable amount to pay. From these records we can learn what trades were represented in the town.

The court rolls for 1456 (17th April) and 1464 (17th November) are useful for this purpose. It is convenient to divide the trades into four groups:

1. To do with food and drink: Bakers, Brewers, Butchers, Fishmongers, Grocers, Millers.
2. To do with clothing and footwear: Drapers, Dyers, Haberdashers, Mercers, Hosiers, Shoemakers.
3. Working in leather, metal, wood, wool, etc: Braziers, Carpenters, Coopers, Curriers, Dubbers, Fullers, Ironmongers, Joiners, Saddlers, Smiths, Tanners, Tilers.
4. Other: Tapsters, Chandlers, Innkeepers, Labourers.

A roll of 15th November 1516 showed that the following trades were also being carried on: Barber, Capmaker, Fletcher, Glover, Mason, Tailor and Weaver.

Whereas in Andover, for example, these trades were organised into guilds of a commercial nature (Merchant Guilds), there was no corresponding organisation in Basingstoke. The Guild of the Holy Ghost was primarily a religious one.

The Assize

There is frequent reference to 'breaking the assize'. This meant that, either by providing goods of inferior quality or by giving short measure or by overcharging, the trader had departed from the standard laid down. In the assize of bread, the price of a loaf was related by statute to the price of wheat. Likewise, the price of ale was regulated by the prevailing price of barley. Brewers seem to have been frequent offenders. The roll of 17th November 1464 records that 17 brewers had broken the assize. Ten tapsters (sellers of ale) were also guilty of the offence; having sold ale 'by cups and other measures less than the standard of the Lord King.' The previous court (10th November) had heard from the ale-conner (ale-taster) that two tapsters had sold newly brewed ale before he had approved its quality by tasting it.

Bakers in the town did not always conform. In 1516, the following presentment was made by the jurors at the court (of 15th November), 'We find that such as are common bakers do not keep the assize in their baking, but their bread is too small, for as much was the bread in quantity when wheat was at fourteen pence the bushel, as now that it is at eight pence the bushel, which is deceiving the King's people and a special [hardship] for the poor people; and we hear many strangers say that the bread is much more [in quantity] in other towns than here, whereas they buy their wheat quite as good and cheap in this town as in any town in this shire.' An interesting illustration of consumer protection at work. The fines levied ranged from 20 pence *[1s.8d.]* to 5s.8d.

'Breaking the statute' (another phrase used) seems to have been a quite common occurrence. It was certainly not confined to the brewers and bakers, as we can see from a roll of November 1464. Here we find, among other law-breakers: Thomas Cordale, brazier, selling copper as well as brass vessels, etc; William White, tanner, selling leather at an excessive price; John Russell, joiner, overcharging for his work; and Edward Hayne, fishmonger, exceeding the assize in selling fish.

We have already mentioned in Chapter 5 another form of sharp practice in November 1390 when John Wortynge and John Reynald each had two bushels, a greater and smaller one, buying by one and selling by the other.

The market was intended to be an 'open' one - accessible to all during stated hours of opening and held in an officially appointed place. Unscrupulous traders made the market less open by 'forestalling'. They would buy up goods from merchants on their way to the market. By thus gaining control of some part of the supply of a particular commodity, they could force up the price and make an unfair profit. Another method, known as 're-grating', was also common; this involved the trader in speculative buying and selling in the market place itself, exploiting to his advantage variations in supply and demand. A merchant could also engage in 'engrossing'; he would purchase the entire supply of a commodity (or a large part of it). By 'cornering the market', he could regulate it, to enhance the price he could command. It was the responsibility of the bailiffs or their representative, (at a later date known as the clerk of the market) to take appropriate action to punish those who broke the statute. It has to be said, however, that the fines that were levied do not appear to have been the deterrent they might have been.

Fish was a commodity much in demand, and so among the merchants regularly visiting the town from a distance were the sea-fishermen, sometimes referred to as 'rypyers'. The innkeepers took advantage of the fact that they provided accommodation for these and other travellers. We read in a court roll of November 1519, 'The innkeepers doth re-grate and take up the fresh fish and keepeth it and chooseth the best for themselves, and the poor people cannot have any fish but as they will.' In 1521 there is again a complaint, namely 'that the innkeepers, as soon as the fishers come, they will take it all secretly, between them, and no man shall have none of the fish. And if they may spare any fish, we must buy it at their price.' This was accompanied by a request that a place be set aside in the market-place where the fish could be displayed openly for sale to anyone. An order was made that no innkeeper was to buy any fish before the bailiffs had inspected it and allowed it to go on sale. This was a pious hope; in October 1543, the innkeepers were still exploiting their position, by allowing the sea-fishermen to sell to their guests privately.

Such practices were not confined to the trade in fish. A roll of November 1511 names Robert Pytter as a forestaller of the market. It says of him that 'he buyeth both butter, eggs and cheese and will not let them come to the market place.' He was amerced 12d. A later roll (10th May, 1550) names Christopher Thacker and John Blounden as re-grators and forestallers of eggs and cheese. Each was fined 12d.

The weekly market continued to be an important contribution to the commercial life of the town, since it added to the variety and volume of goods available. On market days there would be increased hustle and bustle as merchants arrived and set out their wares in the market-place, at or near the market house (in some cases, underneath it). The right of merchants to frequent the market was confirmed by charter. The Charter of 1622 stated clearly that 'all and everyone shall be allowed to assemble there who may wish to do so, to sell, buy, and expose for sale their wares, goods, merchandise, grain, wool, and all other things whatsoever, as well as all and every kind of oxen, sheep, pigs, yearlings, horses, mares, geldings and colts, and other beasts, goods and chattels, at their free will according to the laws, customs and statutes of the realm.' Tolls were charged 'towards the exoneration of the burdens and expenses of the town.'

The charter also mentions the authority of the bailiffs to hold 'a court of pie-powder' (*pie-poudre*). Both plaintiff and defendant were brought in haste before the court and so had 'dusty feet' (*pieds poudreux*), particularly true of merchants who had travelled from a distance. This was intended as a means of dealing immediately on the spot with disputes which might arise between buyer and seller. The Charter of 1641 gave renewed confirmation of the town's right to hold 'a market on Wednesday every week every year for ever'.

In 1764 we are given a reminder of how necessary it was to regulate the market. At a meeting of the Vestry, on 10th December, we find Thomas Wigg, one of the two sergeants-at-mace, being appointed Clerk of the Market. It was his responsibility to ensure that all goods brought into the town were 'pitched' in the market. Anyone failing to conform would be proceeded against as the law directed. Five years later, also at a Vestry (on 27th November 1769), William Jeffrys, Cordwainer (worker in leather, shoemaker) was appointed to fill the same position. The minute gives a clearer idea of the Clerk's duties. He was 'to inspect into' the prices of corn and other provisions and report his findings to the magistrates 'in writing'. His duties also included the inspection of 'waits [sic] and measures'. The same minute expressly forbids forestalling, engrossing and re-grating, the practices we have met with earlier.

Some time early in the nineteenth century it had occurred to those in authority that it would be advantageous to the town to have a larger market-place and to establish the market for live cattle elsewhere. Its small size seems to have been for a long time the cause of its activities overflowing into the streets leading from it. It had been stated in 1510 (20th April): 'They findeth that the market folks set their wares in the Ote strete [Oat Street], whereby children and many others standeth in great jeopardy.' On 10th May of the following year we find it being reported that 'the men of the country tie their horses and mares in the Ote Street - and we be loath to have that street encumbered more than others, and such mishaps as may befall.'

The necessary changes could not be made without the authority of Parliament. The act '*for enlarging the Market Place in the Town of Basingstoke, in the County of Southampton; and for fixing and regulating the Markets of the said Town, and for establishing a Market for Live Cattle adjoining the same*' received the Royal Assent on 14th May 1829. The list of 49 country gentlemen and farmers, who were appointed Commissioners to put the Act into effect, included such names as William Apletree and the Mays; they farmed in the borough itself, on Goldings and Glebe farms respectively. Other Commissioners, William Chute, George Jervoise, William Portal and Thomas Terry, were important landed gentry of the neighbourhood. Other interests, including those of the town, were represented by John Birnie, Charles Headeach, Charles Shaw Lefevre (Recorder of Basingstoke), William Anthony Lewis and James Warne. These were responsible for deciding that certain existing properties in the market place should be 'taken down' and that the new cattle market should be established on a site at Fairfields. The 1851 map of the town shows it forming part of Fair Close, the area allocated to the town under the Enclosure Award of 1786. We could usefully recall that what is now *The Bounty* public house was originally *The Cattle Market Inn*.

It was in October 1880 that the following reference was made to the cattle market in a comment in the local newspaper, 'It is almost a pity that the gallant captain did not buy up the old cattle market over the Folly wall.' The account went on to say that the cattle market was overrun with weeds and that it was no longer used for its original purpose – 'The glory of this place hath indeed departed, in all probability never to return again.' Local auctioneers had already in 1872 established a weekly auction market on a site near the railway station, where weekly auctions occurred until 1966; the official closure took place on 4th May. The increasing role of auctioneers' markets and the decline of the statutory weekly market in grain and livestock was mentioned in 1888 at an inquiry, in September of that year, into the town's markets and fairs. This was conducted by the Markets and Fairs Commission. One firm, in particular, was mentioned at the inquiry - Messrs Raynbird.

The 1829 Act also charged the Commissioners with the further task of 'regulating the market'. This required them to decide what tolls should be paid. A scale of charges, which was thought to be 'just and equitable', was drawn up and published as a schedule to the Act. An interesting provision was included, namely 'that no rent, tolls, duties, sum or sums of money shall be demanded to be taken for any corn, grain or agricultural seeds for the period of fourteen years from and after the passing of this Act.' This was to cause a certain amount of trouble in 1850, when the Council wanted to levy tolls and insisted on the legality of its right to do so. A number of farmers objected and signed a remonstrance, which they addressed to the Council. The Council's reply (on 11th February 1851) was that the Act had been 'sanctioned by the whole neighbourhood, and no less than 49 country gentlemen and farmers appointed Commissioners for carrying the same into effect.'

The notice sent to all who had signed the remonstrance appears not to have satisfied them, for, as a result of a meeting held on 10th March, a request was sent to the Mayor, asking him to meet a deputation. On 18th March 'the agricultural interest' presented a petition to the Mayor, saying that the 1829 Act was not in the best interest and asking for the tolls to be withdrawn. Some rebel farmers even attended their own toll-free market at Basing, announcing their intention in the *Reading Mercury*.

The ratepayers of the town also approached the Council, pointing out that they too were, as consumers of agricultural produce, interested in the level of tolls charged. The attitude of the Council was that the tolls were necessary for meeting the cost of improving the market. Improved facilities would attract dealers from further afield: '...there is no doubt that our market will attract the attendance of many London and other large buyers, which must ensure for our neighbouring agriculturists a better price for their produce.'

In 1832, the Market Place underwent another change. Samuel Attwood *[see note on page 82]* included in his diary a reference to the 'taking-down' of the old Town Hall and the laying of the first stone of the new building. A print of 1835 shows its appearance well and *White's Directory* for 1859 gives the following description, 'The Town Hall is in the upper storey. The Corn Exchange occupies the ground storey, under the Hall - and behind it is the Market Place, for the sale of meat, poultry, fish, vegetables, etc.' Although a market house is mentioned, there appears not to have been a separate building having that function. The ground floor was enclosed in 1866. The market place referred to above was the Lesser Market, which was opened for business on 1st April 1835. It was partially roofed over in 1878, eliciting the comment in the local newspaper that better market accommodation had been wanted for several years. The writer continued, 'Over £200 expended, but a poor do by no means worthy of the town.' However, he thought that the changes made would be a great benefit to all. Further change occurred in 1895, when a row of small shops was built.

In 1865 a development took place which provided increased facilities for farmers and merchants. It was in March of that year that the new Corn Exchange (now the Haymarket

A print of the new Town Hall as built, drawn in 1835

The Town Hall after enclosure of the market hall, 1866
Also shown are the entrance to the Lesser Market and the Corn Exchange

Theatre) was opened for business. St Michael's *Parish Magazine* commented favourably on the occasion, 'A very successful day ushered into active life the Basingstoke Corn Exchange. Suffice it to add that in a short six months energy and perseverance have raised a building much wanted, substantially built, well proportioned and an ornament to the town....' The enthusiasm with which the opening was received is a reminder to us of the dependence of the town on the health of the farming of the surrounding district.

The steady growth of the town as a market centre of more than immediately local importance had already been recognised in the Report of the Commissioners for Municipal Corporations Boundaries of 1837: 'The town is represented to be gradually increasing in size and importance. It contains no manufactories but is a place of great thoroughfare and is situated in the centre of a rich agricultural district. The markets held here are well attended, being resorted to by persons from Andover, Winchester, Newbury and Reading.' The coming of the railway was to extend still further the town's sphere of influence.

Fairs

The right to hold a fair was first granted to the town by Henry Vl. According to the charter of 1449, it was to be an annual event, held near the Holy Ghost Chapel, lasting from Wednesday to Friday in Whit Week. Two fairs are mentioned in the 1622 Charter: one at Whitsun, the other on the feast of St Michael. The right to hold these was confirmed by the 1641 Charter. In 1671 Charles ll granted the town the right to hold two additional fairs: one on the Tuesday and Wednesday after Easter, the second on the 10th and 11th September. The venue for these was the Down at Kempshott.

In the early part of the nineteenth century, another venue is mentioned. A report in the *Hampshire Chronicle* in September 1840 refers to the use of the Common (just east of the town centre) for this purpose. The report reads, 'The sheep and cattle fair, formerly held on Basingstoke Down previous to its enclosure, and since that period held in a very limited field set aside for that purpose, took place by permission of the Trustees, on the Common last Wednesday, and was attended by dealers and breeders, the supply of sheep being very considerable, which went off readily at prices similar to those at Wilton. The revival of this fair in the midst of so extensive an agricultural district as that which surrounds Basingstoke appeared to give universal satisfaction to the numerous breeders and dealers attending it, who expressed the determination to support the same by every means in their power...' Wilton was a much larger affair in the 19th century, with as many as 10,000 sheep penned for sale. The Common continued to be used for the September fair. The number of sheep penned in 1841 was 5,000, of which 4,000 were sold; in 1852, the reported number of pennings was 'only 2,000'.

From at least 1878 onwards the pattern seems to have been to hold two fairs, in July and October, the July one being mainly a sheep fair, the October one being mainly a hiring and pleasure fair. At no time during the period 1878-1888 did the number of sheep penned reach the relatively small total of 10,000. For 1879 the figure was 8,760; for 1884 the number was given as 'considerably over 7,000'. In 1888 the number of pennings was less than 1,000. Figures for the July fair at Overton for roughly the same period give a useful comparison: 1887 - 25,000; 1890 - 8,000; 1894 - 24,000.

Discussions about the future of the town's fairs took place in 1888. In May a meeting of the Town Council discussed the value of the annual sheep fair to the town. The question of the contribution it made to the economy of the town arose when consideration was being given to the award of prize money for competition among farmers. Alderman Wallis said the fair should be encouraged, if it could be proved to be of benefit to the town; Alderman Portsmouth's view was that the fair was dying out, that people came to the fair for a mere nothing. It made little contribution to local farming; prizes would not bring extra sheep to the fair.

In 1889 came the statement that the July fair would be abandoned; this was said to be for one year only. However, there seemed to be no chance of giving it a new lease of life. Sheep fairs were held after that date; there was one in 1890. If only because of the reduced area of the fair field, (Fairfields School had been built on part of the site, and housing development was already taking place there) it cannot have been a very large one.

The Michaelmas fairs continued, but there had already been an intimation that times were changing, As long ago as 1868, a petition had been presented to the Borough Council in the names of 81 householders and 54 farmers, requesting the abolition of the fair. The decision to accede to this request was taken on 3rd August and a public notice was published on 25th September 1868, stating that the fair would be abolished 'next year'. In fact, although they changed in character, the Michaelmas fairs were not discontinued. Traditionally, they were hiring fairs, the occasion when farm-workers, in search of a new situation, appeared wearing in their hats an indication of their particular calling. A carter would wear a piece of plaited whipcord; a shepherd would sport a tuft of wool, while a cowman would display some hairs from a cow's tail.

Some time in the 1880s there was, to judge from newspaper accounts, the gradual onset of a feeling of disenchantment on the part of some of the inhabitants of the town. Early on in this period the accounts are not at all critical. One reads of a very large attendance, the town wearing 'an unusual aspect of business and excitement'. Gradually a note of criticism comes in - a reference, for example, to the harvest reaped by the publicans: 'If the labourer could be persuaded to spend more money on clothing, boots and home comforts, and less upon that which makes a fool of him, the Michaelmas fair would remain an institution worthy of respect.' Some expressed outright displeasure at the bustle, noise and drunkenness that accompanied the 'invasion' of the town by 'hundreds of rustics', while others were slightly more tolerant of the behaviour of 'Hodge and Mary', conceding rather grudgingly that the trade of the town probably benefited.

It would be by about the mid-1880s that the old system of hiring was beginning to die out. Now it was possible to see jobs being advertised in the local paper. In 1888, for example, the following appeared early in October: 'Wanted. - Single man as carter - for four-horse team. Also two strong lads as under-carters, Milsom. North Waltham.' Sometimes the farm-worker advertised for a position:

'Wanted - By married man - a situation as cowman or farm labourer.
Apply Gazette Office, Basingstoke.'

Fewer of our 'rural friends' may have come in order to hire themselves out for the coming year; they did all come, however, to make purchases and to enjoy themselves, for the fair was also a pleasure fair. In the evening, particularly, country- and town-people mingled in the different parts of the town given over to the fair: the Wheatsheaf meadow, and the Market Place with Winchester Street linking the two. The vacant ground 'at the bottom of Church Street' (i.e. the land belonging to Merton Farm) was also sometimes used. In 1888, the fair featured on this site, not only 'Rose's Patent Galoping [sic] Horses' but also swings, shows, shooting galleries, coconut shies and other attractions, all accompanied, to the great regret of some of the inhabitants, by the 'fortissimo blast of the showman's organ'.

The account of the fair in 1887, referring to the usual large number in from the country, says that they caused little trouble. Many of them showed 'a fondness for John Barleycorn', but 'drunkenness was confined to a few and this few did not reach the advanced stage. The number of street quarrels was likewise very small.'

It was customary for the town's shops to take advantage of this rural influx, by holding Michaelmas sales. At the time, the local paper would contain advertisements for 'Michaelmas clothing'. The report on the fair of 1887 referred to the fall in agricultural wages and said that this had a considerable influence on the trade of the town: 'complaints of the want of ready-money purchases are general.' The account concluded by saying that the farmer was himself feeling the pinch of hard times and could hardly be expected to pay more for his labour.

Mr Thomas Burberry's shop was one where Michaelmas clothing could be purchased. In 1890 we find the following details of prices:

Men's overcoats	12s.11d.
Men's cord jackets	6s.11d.
Men's cord trousers	3s.11d.
Long leather gaiters	6s. 6d
Heavy watertight boots	6s.11d

These should be set against details of average agricultural wages for Southern England (including Hampshire).

1875	11s. 8¼d.	weekly
1880	11s. 8¼d.	weekly
1885	12s. 1d.	weekly
1890	12s. 4¾d	weekly

Although not strictly comparable, since they do not apply specifically to the Basingstoke area, it is useful to quote the joint annual earnings of a head carter and his wife, employed on a Hampshire farm in 1873-74. The figure given is £51.7s.6d. They had one child, they lived rent-free and, as usual, received certain payments in kind. For comparison, the earnings of an ordinary labourer, a single man, were just under £41.0s.0d. (figures from *The Farm Labourer at home and in the field: a short account of the North Hampshire labourer in his cottage, wages, and in his schooling; with a review of the emigration question, strikes, etc.* Joseph Stevens, Wyman 1874.)

7   ENCLOSURE 1786 - 1788

An Act for Dividing, Allotting and Inclosing, the Open and Common Fields, Common Downs, Common Pastures, Common Meadows, Wastelands and other Commonable Places within the Parish of Basingstoke in the County of Southampton

26 Geo. 3

'Hedging in'

Documents known as 'terriers' are records kept by individuals and 'corporations' to show the location, boundaries and area of their holdings. They show that the process we call 'enclosure' had been taking place long before the large-scale schemes of 'parliamentary enclosure' occurred. Separate, small parcels of land had, in course of time, been consolidated to form larger holdings, either by agreement between two owners or by an owner arbitrarily incorporating other land into his own holding. The records of meetings of the Court Leet (see Chapter 5) provide some illustration of the latter. On 10th May, 1511, Richard Hogges was at mercy for having 'hedged in part of an acre from the common field'. The same court was concerned at the example set by 'Master Vicar' (Richard Gosmer, the vicar of Basingstoke 1499-1541, who held lands in both Westfield and Hatch Field) who 'hath part of an acre hedged in that was sometime Baron's land, and of the common field, that first was hedged in by Thomas Andrew, and if this be right, others will close in much more which is as yet common field.'

Details of the ownership of land in Basingstoke and its neighbourhood can also be found from a map in Hampshire Record Office entitled *An Accurate Survey of the Town and Manor of Basingstoke. Part of the Estates belonging to His Grace, the Duke of Bolton, Taken Anno. 1762,* (HRO23M72/P1/1). *[See pages 41 to 43].* The Duke of Bolton was the largest landowner in the parish, with 12 farms divided up into 600 plots. This map shows the town, with its crofts, closes, meadows and gardens, surrounded by six large open fields: Hither and Further Long Croft, Chequers Close, Sheepwash Meadow etc. Although changes had occurred from time to time, resulting in the ownership of the land becoming concentrated in fewer hands, we can see that the layout of the fields remained much as it had been in medieval times.

Towards the end of the eighteenth century schemes of parliamentary enclosure were becoming much more common. By means of a private members' Bill presented to Parliament, a group of interested landowners could gain authority to undertake the deliberate, comprehensive enclosure of the lands of a district. Provided that the promoters of the scheme could show that the owners of at least 75 % of the land supported the proposal, there was little or no difficulty in getting a Bill through Parliament. The remaining owners, probably less wealthy, less influential, were obliged to go along with the change proposed. This involved the 'pooling' of the existing separate parcels of land for subsequent division and re-allotment to the owners in larger units.

It was the more influential landowners who took the initiative in putting forward these schemes. They were able to argue that, with their newly-acquired larger fields, they would be able more readily to introduce improvements in husbandry.

J R Plumb in *England in the 18th Century* states that nationally, during the second half of the 18th century, 2,015 Acts were passed. The enclosure of Basingstoke's fields was one of 287 such enclosures that took place during the decade 1780 to 1790. Enclosure also took place in neighbouring parishes: Dummer in 1743; Monk Sherborne in 1792; Basing and Mapledurwell in 1796. Some parishes, however, retained their strip fields for a much longer period. For example, enclosure of the fields in the parish of Sherborne St John did not occur until 1829.

The preamble to the Bill includes the following justification for the petition to Parliament: 'Whereas the said Open and Common Fields, Common Downs, Common Pastures, Common Meadows, Waste Lands, and other Commonable Places are, in their present situation, incapable of any great improvement [and] it would be very advantageous to the Several Persons interested therein, if the same were divided and inclosed, and specific Shares thereof allotted and set out to them according to their several and respective Rights and Interests in the same ...'.

The Duke of Bolton's name does not appear in the preamble to the Bill, but it is thought probable that he was the leading promoter of the scheme. He would have received support from the other leading landowners: the Earls of Dartmouth, Northington and Portsmouth. The petition was presented to the Commons on 2nd March, 1786.

The proposal met with strong opposition. The clearest expression of this was contained in a letter written by Henry Barton, Warden of Merton College, Oxford to the Reverend Thomas Sheppard, Vicar of Basingstoke from 1768 to 1814. The letter, dated 29th March 1786, refers to the petition of the previous year (25th February 1785), which had been signed by eighty inhabitants consisting of the Mayor and seven other members of the Corporation, 40 freeholders and 32 leaseholders. The opinion expressed was 'that if such inclosure was to be carried into execution, the same would be very detrimental to the Parishioners and Inhabitants'.

Henry Barton, drawing on the College's experience of three other enclosures, doubted if much in the way of improvement was achieved by exchange of lands, even when determined by Commissioners of approved ability and integrity. Their decisions were arbitrary, favouring some, while failing to meet the legitimate claims of others. He asks the question, 'Can anyone be surprised that we wish to preserve it [our estate] intire, not to have our landmarks and fences levelled and destroyed by the arbitrary distribution of Commissioners of inclosure, our Terriers rendered quite useless, and even our property exposed to some hazard and uncertainty by the projects of innovators?' His concluding paragraph reveals his distrust of those who are promoting change: 'I am sorry that the influence of Lords in your neighbourhood is likely to disturb us in our ancient possessions.' Those Lords were able to ensure an easy passage for the Bill, which seems to have been a mere formality. It received the Royal Assent on 16th June, 1786.

It was now possible for the five Commissioners (they were named in the Bill as John Poore of Andover, Thomas Hasker of Chineham, John Ewen of Froxfield, Richard Bloxham of West Dean in Wilts*[shire]* and John Carter of Kingsclere) to proceed, with the authority of Parliament, to make considerable alterations to the local landscape. A surveyor, George King from Northampton, was appointed to assist them. They probably started their work with a perambulation of the area, to ascertain the existing boundaries. This would have been followed by a detailed survey of the various portions of land, so that these could be 'qualitied' and their value assessed. Then it would be for the Commissioners to decide what the 'allotments' should be. The whole process took two years to complete; the award was signed in September 1788. The result was that the six great open fields were divided up into over 150 new fields, more or less rectangular in shape, the majority of them being from 2 to 20 acres in area. The Act laid down that the boundaries of the new allotments had to be 'quicksets' or 'sufficient stake hedges'. It also required that convenient roads should be provided. Attention had also to be paid to other features of the infrastructure - drainage ditches, bridges, gates, etc. as might be necessary. The Act specifically mentions the need to attend to the drainage and watering of Wildmoor, the detached area of meadowland lying to the north-east of the town.

The total area affected by this exchange of lands was 3,519 acres, 3 rods, 8 perches. The largest allotments were of just under 750 acres to Lord Bolton; about 470 acres to the Earl of

Dartmouth; 262 acres to the Vicar of Basingstoke (the Rev. Thomas Sheppard) *[Interestingly, the Rev. D Sheppard was an enclosure Commissioner for nine places in Hampshire and five elsewhere. DS]*; 215 acres to Pembroke College; and 207 acres to Harriet Brocas (the Brocas family had long held land, not only in Basingstoke but also in several places to the north of the town, such as Sherborne St John; Beaurepaire, near Bramley was the chief family residence in the area.) Three other colleges received allotments, ranging from Merton College's 155 acres to the 12 acres awarded to Magdalen *[Oxford]*; Winchester College's allotment was 112 acres. Lord Portsmouth was allotted 70 acres. The smallest allotment was made to Mary Cooke - 32 perches (about one fifth of an acre).

Other allotments were of land for a pesthouse and for enlarging the garden of the workhouse; chalk pits and gravel pits were provided for, as sources of material for road repair. An area of land was also allocated to the Corporation as 'owners of the soil'. This is shown on the 1851 map as Corporation land and described as adjoining the parcel of land allocated for holding fairs upon (Fair Close on the 1851 map).

The Common

The map of the 1788 Award showed an area to the south-east of the town centre as being land belonging to 'the proprietors of houses and tenements'. This was the Common, an area of 107 acres, allotted to the inhabitants in lieu of common rights, which they had held 'time immemorial'. These were the right to graze their animals on the stubble fields and the one which permitted them to cut furze for firewood, a right known as *firebote*. The area allotted by the Commissioners was in 'one intire plot, at or near a certain place called Newram Springs, within one of the said Common Fields, called Hack Wood Field.' It was provided that trustees, who were then, as now, the Mayor, two justices of the peace and four churchwardens, should be appointed to manage the Common.

Besides fulfilling its original purpose, the Common has been used in other ways: as a venue for sheep and cattle fairs (*Hampshire Chronicle,* 28th September, 1840), for horse-racing (*Hampshire Chronicle* 19th September, 1849) and for military camps during the 1914-1918 War. A slight modification was made when the Basingstoke By-pass was constructed in the 1930s. To replace the six acres lost through this, an area of slightly more than six acres was provided on the south side of the road (the A30) in Newrams Close (Rucstalls Hill).

Under the plan for the expansion of the town, approved by the Minister for Housing and Local Government 1965, 85 acres of the Common were scheduled to become part of a major residential area. In the event, that development did not take place. However, there have been some encroachments: by the extension of the Harriet Costello School (formerly the Girls' High School); by the building of a hotel; and through the alteration in the road pattern linking the town's expanded road system to the M3 Motorway.

The road proposals included the replacement of the existing Common with a new one. There was strong opposition to the idea of losing the original Common and also part of the neighbouring Memorial Park. Opposition was expressed in letters to the *Basingstoke Gazette* and during the Community Conference from 26th June to 2nd July 1971. Eventually altered proposals were put to a public inquiry in August 1971. Approval of the scheme was given in 1972. Basingstoke now has 'the substitute Common', situated to the east between the town and Old Basing.

8 COACH, BARGE AND TRAIN

The Coaching Era

Salisbury Coach stops at the Three Tuns in going to London every night about ten; and in returning every morning about two; stops likewise at the Red Lion..

Hampshire Directory, 1784

[See Appendix 1 for the current (2008) names or occupiers of the sites, where these are known and have changed, of the Basingstoke inns mentioned below.]

The earliest recorded reference to wheeled traffic passing through Basingstoke appears in *Angliae Metropolis* of 1690. In that year we find mention of William Goodwin operating a coach service from *The King's Head* in The Strand to Basingstoke on Mondays, Wednesdays and Fridays, with journeys in the reverse direction on the alternate days. At the same time, wagon services were being run from London (where one busy starting-point was *The King's Arms*, Houlborn [sic] Bridge to Basingstoke (by Lawrence Wardner), to Andover (by Roger Bird) and to Exeter (by John Lowry and others). Other destinations served were Kingsclere, Winchester and Salisbury. At this time goods traffic may well have been more important than passengers.

The *Hampshire Directory* for 1784 gave details of the services then operating. We learn that there were at that time coach services between London and Southampton, Salisbury, Exeter, Taunton, Bath and Bristol; wagon services ran to Salisbury, Exeter and Taunton. In 1836 Monk's Basingstoke Coach, leaving Basing Lane in London at 8.45 a.m., was timed to do the journey in six hours. From London to Southampton took eight hours, and to Salisbury fourteen hours. The Royal Mail Coach was expected to do the journey to Exeter in about the same time. *The Traveller,* operated by R Fagg & Co, was allowed 25 hours for that journey, one of 175 miles.

Pigot's *Hampshire Directory* for 1824 states that the town is 'situated 45 miles from London and that its trade and commerce is much increased by contiguity thereto.' It adds that it is 'the principal thoroughfare to all parts of the West of England.' There might have been some disagreement about this, but the town undoubtedly became a very busy staging-point for coaches and wagons passing to a number of destinations.

The inns of the town contributed to and greatly benefited from this 'busyness' by supplying meals and accommodation for the traveller. They also provided stabling for the relays of horses required for the reliable operation of coach services. As would be expected, they were located at or near the 'high road' through the town. Besides *The Red Lion* (London Street), they were the *Angel* (Market Place); *The Crown* (Winchester Street); *The Feathers* (at the top of Wote Street); and *The Wheatsheaf* (Winton Square), where the road divides into two, one leading to Winchester, the other going to Salisbury, via the appropriately named Sarum (Salisbury) Hill. A notice of an auction sale in the *Hampshire Chronicle,* 28th September, 1850, describes *The Angel Inn* as 'an hotel of the best repute, doing an excellent trade, with ample accommodation, a capital brewery, stabling for nearly 100 horses, granaries, barn, farmyard etc.'

Some idea of this activity can be gained from the details given in the directory. Wagon services included those to London on Mondays, Wednesdays and Fridays, provided by H Jones & Co. These were complemented by the wagons of Dawes & Co. on Tuesdays, Thursdays and Saturdays. Their services left from their respective warehouses. J & G Jones and Lye ran similar services from *The Feathers* and *The Wheatsheaf.*

The firm of Woolcot, Russell and Brice provided wagon or van services to various destinations in the West of England, which included Salisbury, Sherborne and Taunton. Besides these long-distance services there were those to more local destinations, mostly once weekly. Among the consignments carried were those which arrived at the Wharf by canal. A billhead of 1814 for Bagnall & Foyle (*Hampshire Museums & Archives Service*) describes them as 'Bargemasters, carriers and coal merchants ... Goods immediately on their arrival at Basingstoke are forwarded by wagons to Sarum, Southton, Winton, Andover, Romsey and all places adjacent.'

The section on coach travel in the *Pigot's* 1824 directory starts with the Royal Mail service. We are told that the Royal Mail leaves *The Angel Inn* for London every night at half past twelve; its companion service in the opposite direction, leaving for Exeter and Plymouth, departs from *The Angel* every morning at two. Light coach services are mentioned. These left *The Angel* for London 'every morning at 5, 8, 11 and half past twelve in the day, and quarter past two in the afternoon.' The service to Exeter left every afternoon at two o'clock and at ten o'clock at night. The London to Barnstaple coach, leaving *The Wheatsheaf* 'at a quarter before 5', used to go via Salisbury on Monday, Wednesday and Friday evenings, and via Amesbury on the alternate days. Regular services are also shown as running to Weymouth and Southampton. A busy cross-country route was the one from Southampton to Reading, providing the traveller with a means of reaching Birmingham.

An advertisement appeared in the *Hampshire Chronicle* of 23rd May, 1822, for 'A light post-Coach, 4 horse. *The Trial*. To carry 4 inside only. Southampton to Reading.' To judge from a notice which appeared on 10th July, 1824, the operators, Rogers and Co, were pleased with the support given by the 'discerning public'. The notice also says that the firm will 'charge as low as any coach on the road'. There was competition there from at least August 1822, provided by *The Rocket*. (*Hampshire Chronicle*) Proprietors of coaches chose such names to demonstrate the speed and/or reliability of the service they provided. The names, *Flying Machine*, *Swiftsure*, and *Quicksilver* are characteristic.

The first of these names appears on a notice advertising a service between Salisbury and London:

> 'The old, original Salisbury Flying Machine
> Hung on steel springs
> Thro' Andover, Whitchurch and Basingstoke.
> Will, for the more speedy and better Conveyance
> of Passengers and Parcels, set out from the
> Bell Savage [sic], Ludgate Hill, London, and
> from the Red Lion, Milford Street, Salisbury, every
> night at Ten o'clock, and arrive at each of the
> above places by one o'clock the next Day . . .'

The notice explains that the service is intended for the convenience of those who wish to travel further the same day. It names *The Red Lion* at Basingstoke as one of the inns where a change of horses occurs. It is here too that breakfast is taken on the 'down' journey from London. The notice hints at the risks facing the traveller. It is headed by the words 'With a Guard'. Near the end of the notice comes another comforting statement, 'Care will be taken not to stop at unnecessary places.' The operators, Anthony and John Cooke, took the precaution of saying that the journey would be 'performed if God permit'. A very appropriate observation, given the poor state of the 'roads' before improvements were brought about by turnpiking.

[The following account of the coaching era in Basingstoke, is taken from an unpublished essay, **Turnpike roads from Basingstoke**, *by Andrew Duckworth, produced as coursework for a WEA Local Studies course in the 1980s. It gives a vivid portrait of the effect of the*

coach traffic on the centre of the town. A full copy of the essay has been deposited with the Willis Museum's Resources Room.]

During the period under review, [c1750 – 1850] with the gradual improvement of the roads, people began to travel more, and this created a demand for public transport. To use one's own vehicle and horse was a slow way to travel, as a horse could not do more than fifteen miles a day, day after day, on surfaces which were still poor. The first passenger-carrying coaches were modifications of private coaches, and extra travellers were accommodated by sitting them on top, or even in the wicker basket slung behind the coach, intended for baggage.

The first regularly operated coach services began in 1706 between London and York. In 1754 a regular service was set up between London and Edinburgh. In 1784 the Post Office entered the scene with their own coaches. Superior coaches, horses, organisation at changing places, and free passage through the toll gates made travel in their coaches faster and more comfortable, although the number of mail coaches on a route was determined by the amount of mail carried rather than by passenger demand.

The prosperity of Basingstoke at the beginning of the 19th century was largely attributable to its felicitous position on the network of roads leading to the West Country and the major maritime towns of the South Coast, which were of prime importance in the war with France. A gazetteer called Paterson's Roads (1826, 18th edition) details 'all the Direct and Principal Cross Roads in England and Wales' and was published in many editions over the period we are considering. It states: 'Situated on the line of road from London to Southampton, Winchester and Poole, and also at the point of division, on the road to Salisbury, Exeter, Plymouth, and the Land's End, Bridgewater[sic], Barnstable and the Northern part of Devonshire, Basingstoke is consequently a very great thoroughfare, and participates not only in the advantages resulting from the expenditure of travellers, but also from large establishments of horses and men in the employ of the several coach proprietors, engaged in working the western mails and other stages, and whose several concerns in the town are worked on an extensive scale.'

In addition to the main roads mentioned, three important roads went through the town: from Reading to Alton; from the London Road to Aldermaston, linking with the Bath Road; and to Kingsclere, an important farming and brewing community.

Every night coaches from London, Exeter, Bridgwater, Devonport, Salisbury, Taunton and Weymouth came into the town to change horses and set down and pick up passengers and mail. A four-horse coach was not a silent conveyance. The coaches from London, with horses changed at Hartley Bridge, passed through the turnpike gate at the foot of Wellocks Hill. When they had climbed slowly up the hill along the edge of the Common, the guard sounded his coach horn at the toll gate by The White Hart Inn to warn the ostlers there to have the replacement horses ready. Coaches from Southampton had an easier run into the town past Kempshott Down into Winchester Road, but the horses pulling the coaches from the west, after a stiff and hilly run from Andover via Whitchurch, had a slow climb up Sarum Hill. Much of this activity took place in the early hours of the morning, and London Street, Winchester Street and the old Market Place would have been clamorous with the rattle of wheels and harness, the sound of coach horns, the clatter of horses' hooves, the neighing of the horses, and the cries of the ostlers, all in a very small area of the town.

The demands made on the town's resources by this heavy coach traffic have never been fully evaluated. On the negative side it would seem likely that the parish was responsible for the maintenance of the roads in the town between the turnpike gates. They would probably have used crushed chalk, gravel or flints, loosely spread for the traffic to consolidate, and this may well have been a factor in the proposals for the Pavement and Paving Act which came to fruition in 1815.

Thirty-seven coaches a day changed horses at the six coaching inns (The Angel in Market Square, The Crown in Winchester Street, The Wheatsheaf and The Three Tuns in Winchester Road [Street], and The George and The Red Lion in London Street and at one coaching office. Stabling had to be provided for a minimum of 148 horses, not counting reserves. This is the number that were changed every day. Other spare horses would be grazed in the water meadows.

The innkeepers responsible for servicing the coaches were known as contractors, and worked an exchange system with those at the end of each stage on the routes through the town. This contracting system also covered the mail coaches. The Post Office was active in improving the design of coaches to increase their speed and comfort and they sub-contracted the operation of the services to the large stage coach proprietors, who included one redoubtable lady, Sarah Ann Mountain. The Angel Inn handled the largest number of coaches. For most of the period under review it was owned by the Curtis family, who were also large owners or tenants of land around the town [see the map on page 46]. The other inns were also heavily involved in this traffic, and the life of these inns must have been almost completely organised around the coach schedules. There is no indication from timetables that there were any meal stops, but each coach would be met by serving girls, carrying drinks for passengers who were often stiff and cold from the tiring journeys.

It is, however, the organisation around the handling of the horses which was of most importance in ensuring regular employment in the town. Just one example of what was required is the matching of horses in sets of four. Stage coach proprietors placed great importance on this. Each horse had its own collar, with its number stamped on it, and would normally be stabled with the other horses in its team. Changes, which could be carried out in three minutes with a skilled group, needed two horse handlers, the coachman and two ostlers whose job it was to lead the horses from the stables and hold their heads at the change, as well as the other stable duties. A farrier was in attendance at each change, also a harness maker for repairs or changes. A wheelwright had also to be close at hand throughout the 24 hours. Carriage makers in the town profited from the need to keep the coaches in good repair, and the innkeepers had to have food ready in case breakdowns or bad weather conditions caused enforced stops. Day and night the scene was the same, with the men catching a few hours sleep when they could.

The town lived with the clatter of hooves, the rattle of harness, and the activity around the extensive stabling. Wagons of straw, grain and fodder lumbered through the streets. The ring of metal from the forges and the wheelwrights, and the cries of the horse handlers did not cease, even on Sundays. A very different town from the Basingstoke of today; for over a hundred years the mail and stage coaches dominated its life.

In addition, the inns were busy servicing the travellers who came into the town in their own or hired carriages, or on horseback, to pick up a coach, or to meet travellers alighting in the town. This cross-country traffic increased still further the need for stabling and services, from which the smaller inns in the town also benefited. In addition to the passenger traffic, Pigot's 1828 Directory lists 20 carriers who took goods and the humbler travellers to the surrounding villages and towns from The Feathers, The Wheatsheaf, The Harrow and the Canal Wharf, making further demands on the servicing businesses in the town.

The town grew in size from 2,589 in 1801 to 4,263 in 1851, less than the national average. So one cannot determine from this statistic the effect of the coaching business on population growth. There is no doubt that, while it lasted, it gave steady employment to a large part of the town's population.

AD

The Basingstoke Canal

A Canal called the Basingstoke is made from the town, passes near Odiham, and joins the River Way [sic] *a small distance from the Thames.*

Cary's *New Itinerary*, 1810

- however injurious to many estates through which it passes - a disappointment it may have been to many of the first adventurers – [it] is regarded as a valuable acquisition to the northern part of the county.

Charles Vancouver, *General View of the Agriculture of Hampshire and the Isle of Wight*, 1813

At about the same time as the Commissioners for Enclosure were at work, re-drawing the map of the local area, a scheme was being put forward which would also bring change to the appearance and character of the town. This was a proposal, first put forward in 1769, to provide a link from the town to the Thames via a new canal which it was proposed to construct between Maidenhead and Reading. A meeting of interested parties, at the Town Hall, Basingstoke in 1770, gave its approval to the scheme, as being one of great public utility. (*Salisbury and Winchester Journal*, 29th October, 1770). However, opposition from landowners and various Thames interests caused the scheme to be abandoned.

A new proposal came forward in 1776; this involved a link to the Thames via a canal from Basingstoke to a junction with the River Wey. It met with less opposition and a petition in support of the scheme, presented to Parliament in February 1778, resulted in the establishment of 'The Company of Proprietors of the Basingstoke Canal Navigation'. The enabling legislation, 'An Act for making a navigable canal from the town of Basingstoke to communicate with the River Wey in the parish of Chertsey, County Surrey, and to the south-west side of the turnpike road in the parish of Turgiss, County of Southampton. 18 Geo.III' received the Royal Assent on 15th May, 1778.

Because of the problems facing the country, resulting from its involvement in war (the American War of Independence), the Company found it difficult to raise the necessary capital to finance the scheme. In a statement which the proprietors thought it appropriate to address to the public in 1783, reference was made to the country's need for 'every resource of men and money for the extensive war in which it was then engaged.' Peace having been restored, they proposed to go ahead with the work.

By March 1788, a capital sum of £86,000 had been raised. The subscribers included members of the local nobility and gentry - the Earl of Northington, the Earl of Portsmouth and Joseph Portal - and also members of the Corporation of Basingstoke - John Covey, Thomas May, John Ring, William Ring, Thomas Robbins and the Rev. Thomas Sheppard. The Corporation itself, as a body, also subscribed to the funds, 'from a belief that the canal would benefit the town.'

As would be expected, investment did not come only from the immediate local area; those with business interests in London and along the route of the canal were also prepared to invest in the enterprise.

Following the appointment of a Surveyor and Chief Engineer, William Jessup, and the awarding of the contract to John Pinkerton, work started in October 1788, at two places: at the point where the canal would join the River Wey and also, about six miles from the proposed terminus of the canal in Basingstoke, at Greywell, where the construction of a tunnel was to prove something of a problem. Good progress was made with the work, as can be seen from the minutes of a general meeting of the proprietors at the Town Hall,

Basingstoke on 4th June, 1792 where it was stated that 'From the report of the resident Engineer, it appears that 32 miles of the canal (out of a total of 37½) are finished or nearly so; that the parts under immediate execution are in a forward state, and that half a mile only remains to be begun upon.' The Greywell tunnel, 1,200 yards long, was stated to be well on the way to completion.

Unfortunately, however, the company found that the work was costing more than had been anticipated. It was necessary to raise more capital. For this, new legislation was necessary. This was forthcoming in the form of 'An Act for effectually carrying into execution an Act of Parliament of the 18 Geo.III for making a canal from the town of Basingstoke to communicate with the River Wey in the parish of Chertsey. 33 Geo.III.' This provided authority for the borrowing of an additional sum of £60,000 and it received Royal assent on 28th March, 1793.

The work was sufficiently advanced by the following year for the proprietors to be able to announce that the opening of the canal would take place on 4th September, 1794. The public were informed 'That Barges will begin to be Navigated on that day, from Basingstoke Wharf to the Hambro Wharf, Upper Thames Street, London, and from London to Basingstoke, every Thursday.' The notice also listed the other wharves along the line of the canal. The rate for the through transit of goods between Basingstoke and London was given as 12 shillings per ton.

The canal was not as successful an enterprise as had been expected. Investors were told in a letter dated 21st December, 1797 that 'when the Company was first formed, some of the more intelligent of the Members, with great Industry, collected an Account of the Quantity of Goods that was carried from London to or through Basingstoke, and that was brought down from Basingstoke to London by Land Carriage. This was found to amount to about 30,000 tons per annum, and the Produce of it, supposing it were carried on the canal, paying at the Rate of 2d per Ton per Mile, was estimated at £7,700 per Annum.' This estimate proved to be unduly optimistic, probably because the analysis of the potential traffic was not detailed enough.

The failure of the canal's traffic to reach the expected volume is shown by figures of tonnage carried and the net revenue earned (excluding payments on the bond-debt): (*Figures from Vine, 1994.*)

Year	Tonnage	Revenue
1799 - 1800	17,877 tons	£1,345
1800 - 1801	18,638 tons	£3,038
1805 - 1806	17,000 tons	£1,500
1810 - 1811	23,809 tons	n/a
1815 - 1816	20,106 tons	£1,511
1820 - 1821	20,050 tons	£1,784
1825 - 1826	15,258 tons	£1,002
1830	19,845 tons	£419

The explanation for this must be sought in changing political and economic circumstances. During the Napoleonic Wars it was not safe for coasting vessels to use the Channel, so goods in transit to Portsmouth and Southampton went by way of the canal. The ending of hostilities in 1815 made this no longer necessary. On 21st October, 1816 the Company recognised 'that, from the facilities afforded in peace to the conveyance of goods by sea, some considerable injury must be sustained by the canal'. Already in 1802 it had been stated that 'a considerable quantity of the goods conveyed to the Isle of Wight, Jersey, Guernsey, etc., which used to go up the canal to Basingstoke and thence by wagon to Southampton are now sent directly from the Thames by vessels trading to those islands'.

There had been discussion of the idea of a canal linking London to Basingstoke being extended to provide a route to towns in the 'West of England', such as Salisbury and Bristol. This would have been an alternative to that provided by the Rivers Thames, Kennet and Avon. Such a scheme, which would have been difficult to implement, was rendered null and void when the Kennet and Avon Canal was opened to traffic in 1810. Given the poor state of its finances, the Basingstoke Canal was in no position to compete. A proposal, made in 1825, to replace competition by co-operation, by linking the two canals by means of the Berks and Hants Junction Canal, from Old Basing and Newbury, met with strong opposition and came to nothing. It was about this time that increased competition from operators of wagon services was causing concern to the canal company. Attention was drawn to this in a letter from a member of the Management Committee on 11th October, 1822. He wrote that increased competition between wagon-masters had brought about a lowering of the rates charged for transport by road. There was now so little difference between the charge by wagon and that by canal that it was to be expected that traders would prefer to use wagon transport because of its greater speed. Just under 12,000 tons is the total given for 1822-23.

There was a hint of stronger competition to come. On 22nd September, 1831, a meeting of the company was held, at which it was decided 'to adopt such measures as may be necessary for the interests of this company, in regard to the proposed railway from London to Southampton.' With the arrival of the railway in 1839, the threat became a reality; the canal company was obliged to lower its charges to an uneconomic level, in an attempt to compete. The canal contributed to its own decline by carrying materials used in building the railway; in 1838-39 the total tonnage handled was 39,000 tons.

Barge traffic continued for some time. Records in the possession of Wallis & Steevens Ltd showed that barges with names such as *Defiance*, *Rapid*, *Independent* and *Britannia* were in use in 1844. An entry for 10th May of that year shows the *Independent* bringing a cargo of 68 tons, consisting entirely of timber for three Basingstoke firms. Much more usual were mixed cargoes (some of them very mixed). In the following month the same barge brought a cargo of 55 tons, consisting of 28 tons of coal, a large quantity of building timber, 131 iron pipes, cement; bars of iron, bricks, bags of nails and an iron retort (for the Gas Company). The remainder of the cargo consisted of 2 hogsheads of sugar, 5 chests of soap, 10 firkins of butter, bacon, 2 hampers of wine, 1 cask of vinegar. Also, fruit in barrels and bags, not to mention the various bags, bottles, casks and hampers, the contents of which were not specified. Some of the items were taken off at Odiham; the remainder was unloaded at Basingstoke Wharf, most to go to destinations in the town, some to be taken on by wagon to Laverstoke, Whitchurch, Andover and Salisbury.

The canal made a useful contribution to the commercial life of the town and its neighbourhood, but its route through a mainly rural area could not be expected to generate the volume of bulk traffic characteristic of the canals of the North. Hadfield (*Hadfield, 1968*), called it 'the first of the agricultural canals'. As we have seen, bulk cargoes of coal and timber were carried, but perhaps more important was the transport of agricultural produce from the region, including malt (one of the chief manufactures of the town), manure and chalk (for use in improving the heathlands to the east of the town).

The Wharf, where the canal had its terminus, provided warehousing for goods in transit. A contemporary writer, Robert Mudie *(Mudie, 1838)*, having discussed the possibility of extending the canal westwards, to link up with the River Test, came to the conclusion that Basingstoke did not suffer from being the terminus of the canal 'because it thereby becomes a place at which the canal-borne goods both to and from the Metropolis are stored, and this gives a good deal of bustle and employment and consequent profit to the inhabitant.'

Individual traders may have prospered from the service provided; the canal itself did not. It continued to lose traffic, firstly to better wagon services (which benefited from improved roads) and later to the railway. Although there was occasionally some recovery in the volume of traffic in parts of the canal, there was no real prospect of it ever becoming a financially viable concern. The result was that in 1866 the company went into liquidation and was wound up three years later. It was re-established in 1874 as the Surrey and Hampshire Canal Corporation. In an attempt to revive the fortunes of the company, the owners caused a notice to be placed in the *Hants & Berks Gazette* of 22nd December, 1880. This stated, 'The business of the [above] canal system of navigation will be resumed on and after the first day of January next for the conveyance of every description of goods from and to Basingstoke and the River Thames, including the intermediate stations.' The notice went to say that 'new and commodious barges' had been built to provide a service from Barnes Walls, Bermondsey and Basingstoke Wharf. Three years later (13th July, 1883) the canal was again put up for sale. New owners took the concern over in 1896 and operated it until 1900 as the Woking, Aldershot and Basingstoke Canal and Navigation Company. During this period there occurred the final flourish of commercial activity, so far as the upper part of the canal was concerned. It resulted from the operation of a brickworks at Up Nately, by the Hampshire Brick and Tile Company.

Dubious financial dealings accompanied some of these changes in ownership. Perhaps the best-known are those associated with the name of Horatio Bottomley, MP, who, in 1905 fraudulently promoted a newly constituted company, the London and South-Western Canal Company. This went into liquidation in 1911. Eventually, in 1923, the ownership passed to Mr A J Harmsworth, who did much to maintain the canal as a going concern. Two years after his death in 1947, the canal was again put up for sale on 1st March, 1949.

This time the buyers were the members of a 'Purchase Committee' who wished to ensure that it was not sold off piecemeal. The company which then came into being - the New Basingstoke Canal Company - accepting that the canal no longer had a commercial future, turned its attention to an examination of its potential amenity and recreational value. Its conclusions were presented in *Basingstoke Canal - the case for restoration*, which was published in 1968 *(Jebens, H D, 1968)*. The members of the Surrey and Hampshire Canal Society, founded in 1966, supported the company so successfully in its restoration aims that the County Councils of both Surrey and Hampshire were prevailed on to buy the canal. Intensive restoration work, to a large extent by voluntary labour, has taken place, especially since 1973. The canal is now open as far as the eastern end of the Greywell tunnel. This has turned 'a virtually useless waterway' into a feature of great recreational value, Although the visitor to places along the canal will no longer see the *Independent*, with its very mixed cargo, making its slow way along, he or she may see - or perhaps, be a passenger on - the *John Pinkerton*, named after the man who was responsible for the construction of the canal.

The coming of the Railway

'That the committee have shewn, that an adequate return may reasonably be expected from the conveyance of the number of passengers and quantity of traffic now annually passing along the route of the intended line; as the railway will greatly increase the facility of communication between the Metropolis and southern and western parts of England, at a considerably diminished expense, an important additional return may fairly be anticipated. At the same time, it will provide employment for numbers of the labouring classes, and be productive of great local and national advantage.'

Extract from *Notice of share issue Southampton and London Railway*, 23rd January, 1832

The construction of the railway line from London came about as a result of a meeting which took place on 26th February, 1831 at the house of Mr Duttin, the MP for Southampton. Those present discussed an ambitious project which was to be of great significance, not only for Basingstoke but also for other places in Hampshire and the south of England generally – the proposal for a railway to connect Southampton with London. This had been put forward in a prospectus issued on 2nd October, 1830. Associated with this was the idea of constructing a branch line from Basingstoke to Newbury to provide a route to Bath and Bristol, alternative to the one being proposed from London via Maidenhead and Reading. A further proposal involved the 'line of railway' being connected to docks which would be constructed on Southampton Water. A public meeting was held on 6th April, 1831 to set up a company whose name clearly epitomises the threefold intention of the promoters - The Southampton, London and Branch Railway and Dock Company.

It was to be expected that any proposal to provide a railway would meet with opposition from two sources: landowners whose property was likely to be adversely affected and the proponents of alternative routes. In the rivalry between two companies competing for actual and potential traffic, it was necessary for promoters to gain as much support as possible by convincing people, especially influential ones, of the advantage of their particular scheme and thus persuading them to put up the necessary money. Hence, in August 1832, we find William Anthony Lewis (formerly Town Clerk *[of Basingstoke]*, but here, as a solicitor, acting as agent for the railway company) sending out a letter notifying local residents of a public meeting to be held on 29th August. Its purpose was to 'take this important subject into serious consideration'. Pointing out that 'ruinous consequences' could follow from the construction of a direct line from London to Bristol via Newbury, his letter advocated support for the Southampton and London Railway, which saw Basingstoke as the junction at which two lines, one from Newbury, the other from Southampton, would converge to form a 'trunk' line to London. He argued that the Southampton, London and Branch Railway would not only safeguard Basingstoke's existing advantages, but would 'incalculably increase' them; a display of well-founded optimism. The most obvious advantage would be 'an immediate influx of trade'; there would also be an enhancement of property values and an increased volume of heavy goods carried by the canal (railway companies did not always remain so kindly disposed to canals!)

The letter tactfully suggests the need for 'a little energy on the part of the town and neighbourhood'. It concludes by describing the Southampton, London and Branch Railway as 'the cheapest and most practicable, perhaps, of any line of equal extent in the Kingdom', contrasting it with 'the upper line' with its 'numerous obstacles and heavy expense'.

In the event, nothing came of the branch line element of the proposed scheme. Towards the end of the century there was to be a revival of the idea of joining Basingstoke to Newbury via Kingsclere.

The necessary Act of Parliament (for the Southampton to London line alone) received the Royal Assent on 25th July, 1834. Work began at once, under the direction of the engineer Francis Giles. Progress was slower than anticipated and it was also found that Giles had seriously under-estimated the cost involved. He was forced to resign his appointment.

More rapid progress was achieved under his successor, Joseph Locke. Even so, the section between London (Nine Elms) and Woking was not ready for opening until 19th May, 1838. The official party was entertained at the end of their journey with a cold collation, accompanied by champagne. It is said that the return journey was retarded by a head wind and by the behaviour of gentlemen 'on the roof of the train', who were 'mellowed', by the cold collation.

Public traffic began two days later, with five trains a day each way. By 24th September the line had reached Shapley Heath (Winchfield), a distance of 38½ miles. The formal opening of the line through to Basingstoke came on 10th June, 1839. The event was recorded in the *Hampshire Chronicle* in the following words:

'On Monday the line of road from the Winchfield and Hartley Row Station was opened as far as Basingstoke, a distance of eight miles, and on the same day from Southampton to Winchester, leaving only eighteen miles to complete the undertaking. A party of directors and their friends left the terminus at Nine Elms, Vauxhall at 11.30 and arrived at the Winchfield Station at about five minutes to one, where a crowd of spectators was assembled and greeted them with hearty cheers. After a short delay the train proceeded over the new ground to Basingstoke while upon every height and at every place where a view could be obtained groups of admiring and anxious spectators were stationed to watch and applaud the progress of the engine and its bulky train upon its maiden excursion. At about 2.30 p.m. the train started from Basingstoke on its return to Winchfield, accomplishing the distance without the slightest accident or annoyance to mar the pleasures of the day. A cold collation was provided at a cottage in the vicinity of the station to which about 60 ladies and gentlemen sat down, including Mr Easthope MP, the Chairman of the Company, Mr T Dunscombe, MP, Mr Bainbridge, etc. At 7 o'clock the party broke up, and the train finally reached Vauxhall at 8.10.'

Six trains per day from Nine Elms to Basingstoke and return was the service provided at this time. The single fare was 11s.0d. First Class and 7s.0d. Second Class. Pending the completion of the line through the relatively difficult country south of Basingstoke, passengers were obliged to 'leave the railway carriages and proceed along the turnpike to Winchester', as the 1839 *Railway Directory* states. An observer of the scene would have noticed some resemblance between the railway and the horse-drawn carriages.

The line between Basingstoke and Winchester was officially opened on 11th May, 1840. Directors and bands of music left Nine Elms at 8 a.m. and arrived at Southampton at 11 a.m., to be greeted with a 21-gun salute. On the return journey, there was the by now inevitable cold collation; laid on by Thomas Brassey (who was responsible for the construction of the Basingstoke to Winchester section), at Warren Farm, near the Andover Road Station (Micheldever).

In 1844, there was an important development, which was eventually to increase the volume of traffic passing through Basingstoke. In that year Parliament authorised the construction, by the Berks and Hants Railway, of a line from Reading to Basingstoke. Since the Berks and Hants Company was sponsored by the Great Western Railway (GWR), the line was a broad gauge one. The two towns became linked on 1st November, 1848. A train left Reading at 9.05 a.m. and arrived at Basingstoke at 9.50 a.m., passing the only intermediate station at Mortimer on the journey.

The *Reading Mercury* said of the opening of the new line, ' ... graziers attending the large fairs in Hants, Wilts and Dorset will find this branch a great benefit, enabling them to send their stock in a more safe and expeditious manner than driving them for many miles across country.' More people than ever before attended Basingstoke Markets - corn dealers, millers and farmers. To begin with, the service consisted of four trains each way on weekdays and two on Sundays. Bramley Station appeared in *Bradshaw* as the second intermediate stop in 1895.

The new line had its own separate terminus; this meant that the convenience of through train travel was for the time being denied to the traveller. He could, however, while waiting for his train, fill in the time by availing himself of the facilities provided by the London & South Western Railway's station refreshment room, which was highly praised in their 1845 guide: 'We can assure the stranger to the line that every article of excellent food, from a bun or a sandwich to mock turtle or a cold fowl, every assuager of thirst, from tea or bottled beer to iced lemonade or aristocratic champagne is provided with express train rapidity by civil, efficient waiters.'

It was soon realised that the movement of both passengers and goods could be more conveniently and cheaply effected if a direct link were to be established between the two systems.

The Great Western Railway Station in the mid 1960s.

Photo © Sid Penney

This was done in 1856. After 22nd December of that year, through travel from Birmingham to Southampton without changing trains became a possibility. No consideration had as yet been given to 'opening-up' the country to the west of the town. The London and South Western Railway (L&SWR) appeared to be reluctant to undertake the construction of a line to Salisbury, and it was only after the inhabitants of places along a possible route brought pressure to bear that the work was begun. Andover people were well to the fore in this, but 25 leading citizens of Basingstoke also made their contribution; on 9th May, 1845, by presenting the following notice to the Mayor: 'We, the undersigned, inhabitants of Basingstoke, convinced of the advantages of railway accommodation, respectfully invite you to convene a public meeting to consider the propriety of adopting some measures for promoting the intention of the London, Salisbury and Yeovil Railway Company, which from the proposed junction of their undertaking with the South-Western Railway at or near Basingstoke must, We believe, contribute to improve the trade and prosperity of the town.'

A single line was eventually opened as far as Andover and regular services began on 3rd July, 1854. By 1st May, 1857, it was possible to travel to Salisbury (Milford Station). Two years later the line reached Fisherton, where a new station had been built next to the station of the Wilts, Somerset and Weymouth Railway Company (the GWR), whose line had reached Salisbury in June 1856.

Later on, enthusiasm was shown for a line from Reading to Portsmouth via Alton that would follow a route through the local area but without effecting a junction at Basingstoke. A suggestion for such a line was put forward in 1885 by Mr Robert Mulford, a resident of Greywell. It would be, in his opinion, 'for the benefit of those living in isolated villages'. The route he suggested was Shinfield, Swallowfield, Eversley, Bramshill, Heckfield, Hazeley, Mattingley, Rotherwick, Newnham, Odiham, Up Nately, Nately Scures, Greywell, Upton Grey, Long Sutton, South Warnborough, Shalden. Three years later, the area to the east of the town was again in the news, when a proposal was made to link the main line at Hook with

Farnham via Odiham and Crondall. The supporters of this scheme optimistically stressed the potential of this area. One of them, concealing his identity under the pseudonym, 'Hop o' my Thumb' wrote in a letter to the *Hants & Berks Gazette* in August 1888, of the 'considerable and increasing population' (anticipating by just 100 years the pressures on this part of the county). He also suggested that there were 'various industries that would no doubt be only too glad to avail themselves of' the opportunity afforded by the railway.' Another writer, signing himself 'Progress', thought that other smaller places in the area - Rye Common, Well and Long Sutton - would find the line of great advantage. On 8th September 1888, those present at a public meeting expressed the collective opinion that the line would be 'of great practical utility to the district and an accommodation much required by the public.'

Proposals for yet another 'line of rail' were being put forward. In this year, on 30th November, a report headed 'Proposed Railway - Basingstoke – Wokingham' appeared in the *Hants & Berks Gazette*. The report said that plans and sections for the proposed line had been deposited. The promoters argued that it would be 'the final link in the alternative route from Basingstoke to Waterloo.' It would run from 'near Basingstoke Station via Basing - Sherfield - Rotherwick - Hartley Wespall - Stratfield Turgis - Stratfield Saye - Heckfield - Mattingley - Hazeley - Bramshill - Risley - Eversley - Finchampstead - Barkham to Wokingham, where it would effect 'a junction with the L and SW Railways.' The engineer for the scheme (Mr Arthur C Payne) said that the route had been 'approved almost unanimously by the landowners whose property it will intersect.'

Some of the arguments put forward in support of the new line seem to be rather thin. It was stated that it would be invaluable as a relief line, necessary in view of the increase in traffic on the L&SW Railway. It would enable those who lived in the extensive residential districts of Richmond, Staines and Wokingham to proceed directly to 'watering places on the Southern and Western coasts.' For passengers from Wellington College, the Royal Military College and the Staff College it would provide a route 'better than the present inconvenient one via Farnborough.' It would also help to reduce the inconvenience caused in the 'heavy press of traffic during the Ascot Races.' The hope was expressed 'that those in authority in town and village [will] do all they can to further the project.'

Of all the proposals to increase the network of railway routes involving Basingstoke put forward in the last years of the 19th century, only one became a fact - the route via Cliddesden and Herriard to Alton, and then on to Portsmouth. It was first proposed in 1887. A notice under the heading 'Proposal to present a Bill to Parliament. Basingstoke - Alton - Portsmouth Railway' appeared in the *Hants & Berks Gazette* on 8th October of that year. It was worded, 'The people of Basingstoke are doubtless considerably interested in the proposal to authorise the construction of a railway, so long talked of, which is to connect the town with Alton and Portsmouth. The Mayor and Corporation of Basingstoke have been informed, on behalf of the promoters, that the preliminary surveys have been made and the route of the proposed railway approximately fixed.' After naming the sponsors of the Bill - Jeffreys of Burkham, Jervoise of Herriard, Woods of Warnford, Crowley of Alton, together with Nicholson of Basing Park - the item concluded, 'There is no doubt that the line, if constructed, will be of considerable benefit to the town and trade of Basingstoke.'

The Bill did not obtain the sanction of Parliament, on the grounds that the line was unlikely to be financially viable. The promoters, however, were not deterred by this. In 1895, we find it being reported on 2nd November that the Portsmouth - Alton - Basingstoke line was again under consideration. The solicitor for the promoters (Mr A M Downie) reported that various landowners had agreed to raise finance for the scheme; but some of the Portsmouth promoters wondered whether a spur line from Winchester to Portsmouth, eliminating Alton, might not be a better solution. The financial support of Basingstoke was reported as being necessary for the success of the proposal; in fact, the solicitor hoped the town would be able to prevail on the Corporation to 'pass a resolution to the effect that the line would benefit the town of

Basingstoke.' He also hoped that the town would contribute to the preliminary costs! To the fear expressed that Basingstoke might be left out, he said, 'People in Portsmouth consider that coming to Basingstoke is a most important part of the whole scheme - and are committed to it.' Interesting, in view of the way the lay-out of the town would have been changed, was the site proposed for the terminus of the new line - Dark Lane (Eastrop Lane) near the Common. It was argued that one larger station for the town would be preferable, but this was not thought to be possible because of the proposed changes in 'railway accommodation' already being planned by the L&SWR. These were the subject of a Bill going through Parliament in March, 1895.

The proposal was to widen the tracks between Basing and Worting Junction and to enlarge the station itself: 'The Station will be entirely rebuilt on a scale which will be commensurate with the growing importance of the town, and with the increasing demands of the traffic.' The construction of 'a commodious goods yard on the Chapel Street side of the line' would involve the loss of allotments in May Street and also take up land to the rear of May's Brewery; it would also require the destruction of the 'Infectious Hospital'; a good slice of cottage property in Chapel Street and Junction Road would also be affected by the proposed changes. These were apparently thought to preclude the provision of a junction with the main line. Arguments advanced in favour of the Dark Lane Station were that proximity to London Road would prove 'an advantage to the town generally', and that it would increase the value of property in the neighbourhood! It was thought that, although they would be involved in expense, travellers wishing to transfer from one station to the other would not be too inconvenienced.

A new proposal for the line was made in 1897 under the 1896 Light Railways Act. This application was successful and construction began in July 1898, starting from the existing station. The service of three trains a day in each direction was inaugurated on 1st June, 1901, 'quietly and unostentatiously'. By October 1914 there were six trains daily in each direction.

Although it considerably improved travel between Basingstoke and Alton, shortening the journey time by three-quarters of an hour, this ambitious line, serving a mainly rural area, could never have expected to handle a large volume of traffic. This proved to be the case; consequently it ran at a loss; estimated at about £4,000 a year up to 1916.

The line was, in fact, closed on 30th December, 1916, the rails being removed for use in France. It was naturally assumed that the end of the 1914-18 hostilities would bring the restoration of the line. The L&SWR was unwilling to do this, and in 1923 sponsored a Bill in Parliament to abandon the line. There was opposition to this from local public bodies, traders and farmers, and particularly from two leading landowners, Major General Sir George Jeffreys (of Burkham) and Major Jervoise (of Herriard). A committee of the House of Lords was convinced by the argument put forward and authorised the re-opening of the line. This occurred on 18th August, 1924, but the results were just as unpromising as they had previously been.

Eventually the Company had its way and the line was closed to passenger traffic from 12th September, 1932. A service for goods traffic was continued until 30th March, 1936.

Two occasions are recalled when its normally uneventful existence was temporarily disturbed. The first was on 19th August, 1928, when a collision between a train and a lorry was deliberately arranged, to meet the requirements of those who were making the film *The Wrecker*. The second was in June 1937, when there were amusing, unlikely happenings on the 'Southern Railway of Northern Ireland' at 'Buggleskelly', otherwise known as Cliddesden in the film *Oh, Mr Porter*.

The impact of the railway on the Turnpike Trusts - Contributed by Derek Spruce

The two following charts show the impact the arrival of the railway had on road traffic as shown in returns published in Parliamentary Papers.

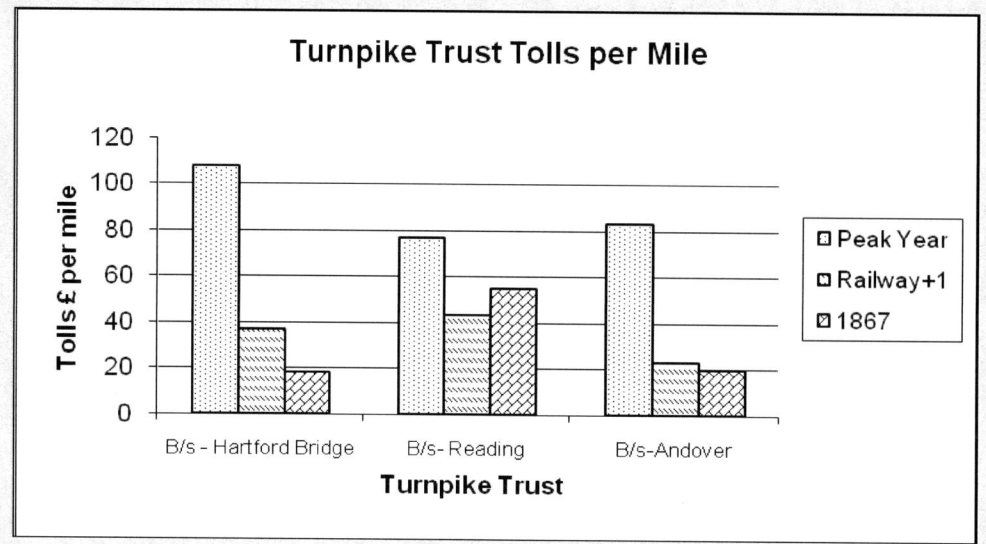

The chart above shows three turnpike trusts that ran parallel to new railways. The Basingstoke Hartford Bridge paralleled the London Southampton line from Winchfield and was greatly affected from 1839. The trust to Andover had an even greater decline after the direct line was opened in 1854 but the Reading route, surprisingly, suffered only a modest decline after the Great Western broad gauge branch reached Basingstoke in 1848.

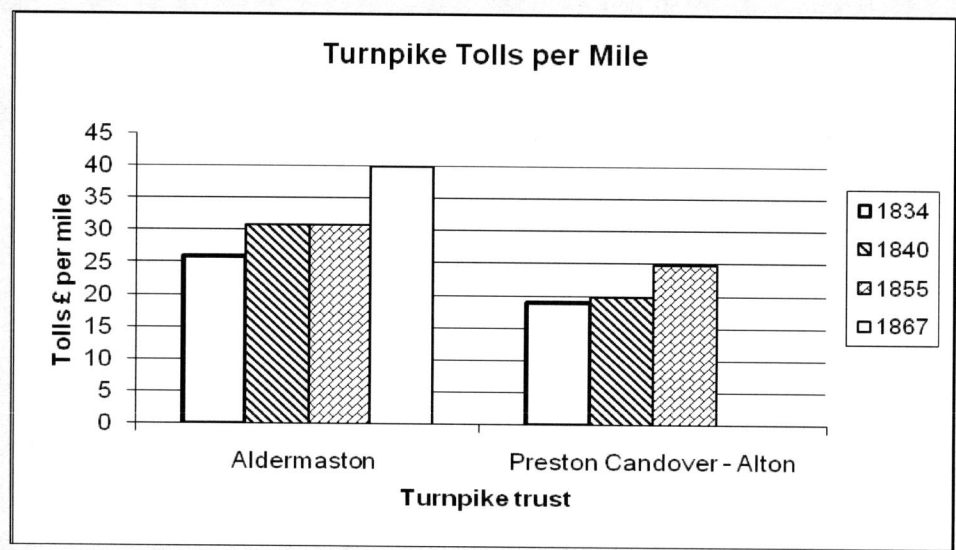

The two trusts in the second chart had much smaller incomes and served areas from Basingstoke where railways did not compete. These continued to be used by carriers and others making journeys to the railway and shops in Basingstoke. Their income showed modest growth after the opening of the railways.

The last Turnpike trust ended in 1885 and in 1889 the newly founded county councils took responsibility for main roads

DS

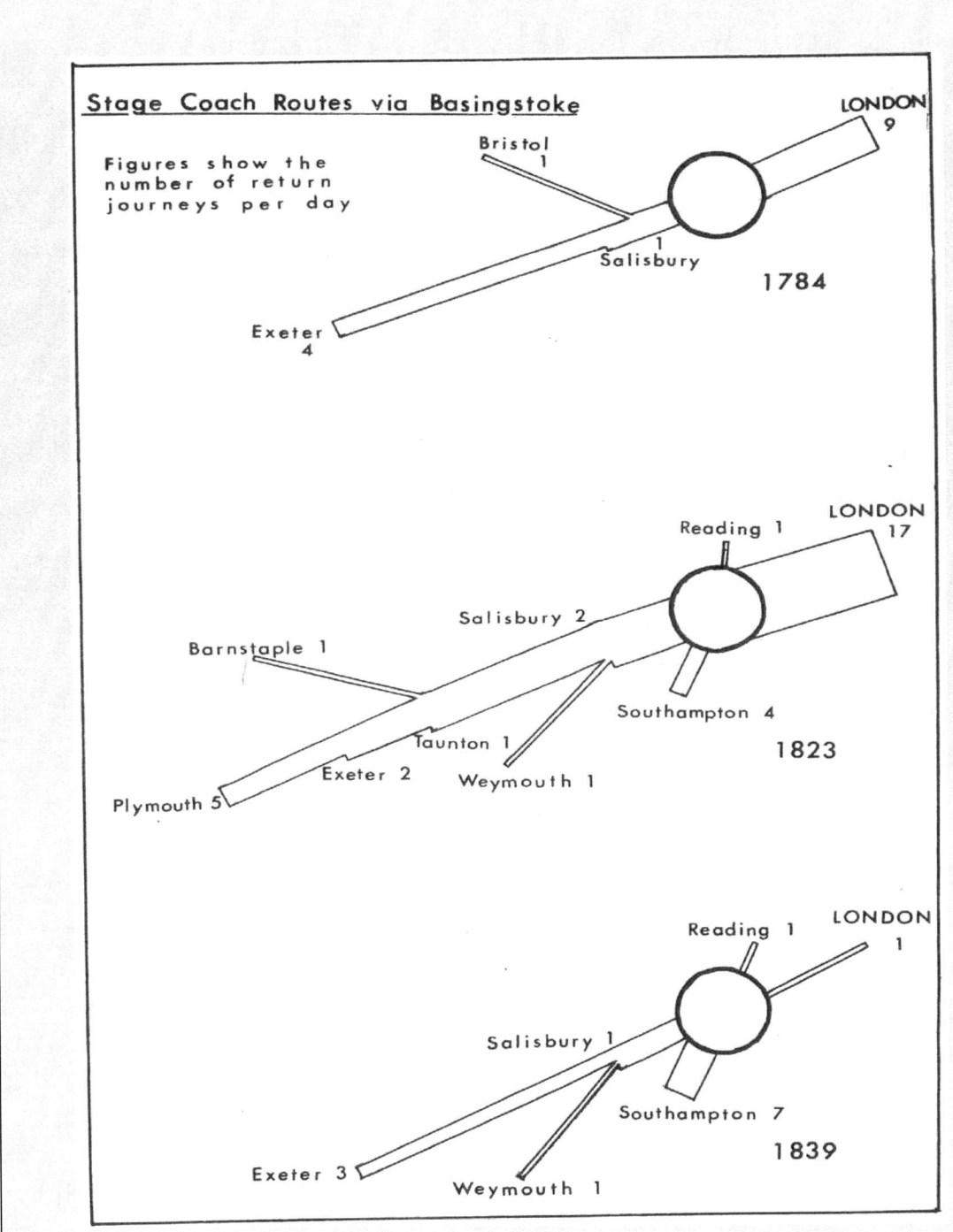

A schematic representation of the effect the arrival of the L&SWR had on the coach trade through Basingstoke.

The railways had a dramatic effect on the number of coaches coming through Basingstoke as can be seen on the distribution diagram, above. This would have had a severe knock-on effect on the number of people employed servicing the coach trade. This may, in part, be the reason for the low population growth shown in the 1841-1851 figures in the table below (taken from Table 1, Chapter3).

Table 4

POPULATION GROWTH - BASINGSTOKE BOROUGH AND ENGLAND WALES 1801 – 1851   Source: *Census of Population*

YEAR	BASINGSTOKE	DECENNIAL % INCREASE	ENGLAND & WALES 000s	DECENNIAL % INCREASE
1811	2,656		10,000	
1821	3,165	19.2	12,000	20.0
1831	3,581	13.1	13,897	15.8
1841	4,066	13.5	15,914	14.5
1851	4,263	4.8	17,928	12.7

EDITORIAL UPDATE

The last steam trains ran in 1967. What was already an important junction with busy lines has become even more so. The growth of daily commuter traffic to London from as far away as Bournemouth after electrification, the introduction of modern diesel electric units on the Salisbury line, the changes after privatisation and the container traffic from Southampton to the Midlands have all contributed to making the railway through Basingstoke one of the busiest in the country.

The GWR eventually got their route to the South Coast by sponsoring the company that built the Didcot, Newbury and Southampton line which joined the L&SWR near Winchester, opened in 1885. The route was upgraded to a heavy duty line in WW2 to service the build-up to D-Day; it was closed in the 1966 as part of the Beeching cuts. Had it remained open, it would have been ideal for the container traffic that is now routed through Basingstoke and Reading.

9 GOVERNMENT BY VESTRY

At a Publick Vestry of the Inhabitants of the said Town and Parish held at the usual Place pursuant to Notice given the preceding Sunday in the Church of the said Parish and from thence adjourned to the Town Hall in the said Town ......

Basingstoke, January 7th 1783

From the middle of the 16th century almost to the end of the 19th, much of the town's business was transacted, not by the members of the Corporation but through meetings of the Vestry, so called because it met in the vestry of the parish church. To its responsibility for the upkeep of the church and related matters (see Baigent & Millard's *History of Basingstoke*, pages 499-531) was later added the task of carrying out the regular maintenance of the roads within the parish. The Highways Act of 1555 gave the parish the authority to appoint 'Surveyors of Highways' or 'Waywardens' to supervise this work. Its powers were further increased in 1601 when the Poor Relief Act authorized the appointment of 'Overseers of the Poor'. To meet the expenditure involved, the parish was allowed to levy a rate, which eventually came to be known as 'the Poor Rate'.

These officials, together with the churchwardens, formed the executive body of the parish, and were responsible for the routine day-to-day business. The local Justices of the Peace exercised supervision of the way in which these did their work, approving the rate levied, and certifying the accuracy of the overseers' accounts. From time to time they were required to give their attention to settlement matters, when disputes arose between parishes, each being determined to ensure that individuals and families did not receive 'welfare' to which they had no claim.

This system of managing local affairs has been called 'government by public meeting'. Although the meetings continued to be called Vestries, they were frequently adjourned to the Town Hall, latterly almost always so. This, together with the occasional attendance of the Mayor and the Town Clerk, may be taken as recognition that most of the business concerned not only church matters but affairs of importance to the town as a whole – 'the inhabitants at large'.

Two facts are apparent from a study of a Vestry minute-book covering the period 1755 to 1797. The first is that, for much of that period, meetings took place at irregular intervals. Secondly, the size and make-up of the meetings varied. During the above-mentioned period, the largest number recorded as attending was 36, on 10th May, 1756, when those assembled decided that there should be no change in the way help was to be provided for the poor. Normally, the recorded attendance was much smaller; in about half the cases, ten or less were present. Decisions were recorded in the following terms: 'Agreed by the major part of the inhabitants then assembled' or 'Agreed by the majority of the persons present, inhabitants of Basingstoke who pay to the poor rate.'

Irregularity of meeting and variability of membership cannot have made decision-making easy or satisfactory. Although not so stated, perhaps this was the reason for the change proposed by the Vestry of 12th October, 1789. Those present resolved unanimously that there should be 'a regular Vestry the first Tuesday in every month.' It was further proposed that 'a committee [should] be elected, which would be impowered to attend every Vestry to inspect, settle and direct the full management of the poor in every respect whatever.' The committee was to consist of the magistrates, the churchwardens and the overseers, together with thirteen leading townsmen. Another change was proposed five years later; it was that one of the overseers should be 'perpetual' and paid for his services. He would perform 'the laborious part of the office but subject to the control of the other three overseers.' In May 1795, Mr Robert Cooper was so appointed, at an annual salary of £25.

'Farming the Poor'

Two words commonly occur in the Vestry minutes when provision for the poor is being considered – 'farming' them or 'managing' them. The job of looking after the poor was 'farmed out' to an individual who undertook to provide for them at a fixed sum per head for a specified period – the word 'farm' or 'firm' is derived from the medieval Latin *firma*, a fixed sum. Both terms refer to the responsibility which the 1601 Act placed on the parish to give relief to poor people, either by accommodating them in the poorhouse or by providing out-relief.

There was always one important consideration - that the cost of providing relief should be kept as low as possible. Relief was for the deserving poor only. We do not know when the town first had its poorhouse; we do know that it was much in demand in the eighteenth century. We also learn that the town had its pesthouse. We are reminded by the minutes of 19th August, 1755 that both needed repair.

The 'farmer' was responsible for the day-to-day running of both the workhouse and the pesthouse. He was expected to do so, according to terms and conditions that were set out by the parish. The minutes of the Vestry of 11th February, 1782 show clearly what he and others had to do:

> 'Mr White, having delivered in his proposals for farming the Poor the ensuing three years, it was resolved that the said Mr White shall take the Poor to Farm on the following conditions: the Farmer to enjoy the Workhouse and Pesthouse with the apparts with the Household Goods Linen and Furniture and have the benefit of the Labour from the 5th day of April next for three years if the Farmer shall so long live. Consideration £480 per annum payable monthly.
>
> Farmer to provide for and keep the poor lawfully intitled to relief, teach the children to read and learn the Church Catechism and to attend Divine Worship.
>
> Also to relieve the Poor out of the House to prevent their coming wholly chargeable.
>
> Also to find a skilful Surgeon to be approved of by the Magistrates.
>
> Also to Pay the Funeral Expenses of the Poor.
>
> Also to relieve Indigent Travellers.
>
> Also to pay the Town Clerk's Fees relating to the Poor.
>
> Also to pay the Annual Charge for the County Rate.
>
> Such Intruders as are now in the Town to be removed at the Town's Expense or Security provided for them except such as may be objected to by the Justices and officers.
>
> The Farmer, after the present Intruders are removed or Security obtained except as in the last article, to remove Intruders at his Expense, according to the direction for that purpose in Mrs Burridge's last article. [Mrs Burridge was the farmer from March 1745 to December 1781.]
>
> The Town to keep Workhouse and Pesthouse in repair and pay the Insurance from Fire.

Inventories to be taken as in Mrs Burridge's article. As mentioned, the difference to be paid by either Party to which the same shall apply.

Inhabitants to have liberty to enter the Workhouse and Pesthouse. Inspect the same and see the condition thereof. If any Mismanagement the same to be rectified in the manner as mentioned in the late articles.

Farmer to take no Person into the House without consent of the Justices nor remove any Person out of the same without such consent.

The Poor not to be corrected without the approbation of the Magistrates and Officers.

Farmer not to be liable the expense of Law Suits.

To receive Persons Infected with Small Pox into the Pesthouse upon an order from Justices or Officers as in the last article, Except more than fifteen should be down at any one time, in which case the Town is to bear the Expense of the Surplus.

Farmer not to be liable to pay the Bounty money to Militia Men drawn during the term.

Poor Children to be placed out Apprentices at the Expense of the Town as often as the Officers should see occasion, the Farmer to clothe them. No order for Relief of the Poor out of the Workhouse to be granted for longer than one week, except it be made at the Town Hall of a Court Day and signed by one or more Justice or Justices.

That the Town Clerk do draw the Articles as soon as possible for the Inspection of the Magistrates Officers and Farmer previous to being ingrossed.

Mr Charles Knight and Mr Robert Cooper have offered themselves as Security jointly with the Farmer to be bound in a Bond Penalty £200.

Witness the hands of the Inhabitants, Farmer and Sureties the day and year aforesaid.

Thomas Sheppard	John Lyford
Simon Throrogood	Thomas Metcalfe
William Glover	William Best
Robert Cooper	Charles Knight
John Butterfield	Jonathon Davies
William Brambly	
John Gale	
John White	

Sometimes, in these minutes, when the matter of dealing with the poor is under discussion, we read of a proposal 'to employ them under a manufacture'. The Vestry of 21st March, 1785 resolved that 'some form of manufacturing should be established in the workhouse.' However, no serious attempt to find a suitably qualified person appears to have been made until in February 1789 it was resolved that the Vestry should advertise for someone 'capable of undertaking the poor, provided he understands some manufactor.' A suitable appointment was made in November 1788 - Mr George Goves, of Farnham. It having been stated that he had been employed in the business of blanket manufacture for many years, and his character having been reported on as 'in every way deserving the confidence of the parish', the Vestry resolved that his services should be immediately retained to instruct the poor in 'the said mistery'.

Overseers' Accounts

In 1755-56 there were four overseers: the Rev. William Henchman (vicar from 1745 to 1768), Henry Craft, Daniel Jackson, and John Woodstock. Between them they were responsible for collecting payment on 326 properties in the town. At a rate of 2d. in the pound, this brought in about £400. The rates were 'made' not at fixed, regular intervals but when it was considered necessary. In all, these overseers levied 16 rates during their year of office.

Two entries regularly occur in the accounts. On 7th April, 1755 we read in the joint account of the Rev. Henchman and Henry Craft: 'Paid Mrs James her weekly payment of £2.3s.6d.' followed by 'Paid the weekly payment out of the house £1.12s.6d.' The first of these shows that there were 29 inmates in the poorhouse at this particular time, the payment per inmate being 1s. 6d. per week. Between them the four overseers paid over to Mrs James (the farmer of the poor) the sum of £115.14s.0d. to cover the cost of maintaining the inmates for a year. The second entry refers to regular expenditure on 'the weekly list', by which the farmer was 'to relieve the poor out of the house to prevent their coming wholly chargeable.' At this time the sum of £1.12s.6d. weekly was being shared out among 26 people, 13 of whom were widows. The amounts ranged from 9d. to 4s.0d. It can be seen that the total for the year under this heading would be about £90. The farmer was thus responsible for spending slightly more than £200 on the poor. Extra payments were made if it was necessary to look after persons in the pesthouse; an entry for 24th February, 1754 reads 'To Mrs James for 8 weeks nursing and maintenance of a woman with the smallpox - £2.0.0.' At different times during 1753-1755 the number of inmates varied from 20 to 32. Ten years previously the number was on one occasion as high as 41.

The accounts record expenditure under a number of other headings: the provision of materials such as cloth and yarn for use by inmates of the workhouse; food and drink; doctors' services, etc. Occasionally there is mention of repairs to the pesthouse or other parish houses, and of repairs to the spinning wheels at the workhouse - a reminder that the inmates were expected to do useful work. The farmer, it should be remembered, was entitled to receive 'the profits of the labour of the poor'. Another kind was the purchase of two gallons of aqua vitae for the inmates; we presume that this was for medicinal purposes only, the refreshment normally supplied being beer.

Another entry, made by overseer Oliver Hern for 5th February, 1734, reminds us of one of the ways in which paupers were regarded, as nuisances who must be discouraged. So that they could be easily distinguished, they were obliged to wear a badge (the letter P) on their right shoulder. This is the explanation of the entry, 'Paid Matthew Cleeve for sewing the Badges on the Poor at the Workhouse - £00.00.08d.'

Many entries are of 'welfare' payments to individuals, not always named. Some of these were for clearly stated purposes, but sometimes the entry appears as 'by the Mayor's order', no reason being given. John Watteridge received 1s.6d. in this way. We are to assume that his was a deserving case, for he received other payments of the same amount later on. In May 1754 Edwin Mitchell was paid 3s.6d. for a pair of shoes for Elizabeth Bignal. On 18th September of the same year occurs the entry: 'Allowed Mary Knight cloaths to fit her out for service - 18s.3d.' This was in accordance with common practice, as laid down by the Vestry – 'poor children to be placed out apprentice at the expense of the town, as often as the officers should see occasion, the farmer to clothe them.' Accommodation was sometimes made available other than in the workhouse. In June 1755, for William Wyeth, Jnr, it was 'agreed that he should go into a parish house in Stew Lane (New Street), the overseers to buy bedding and other necessarys which he is to be allowed the use of.' Arrears of rent could be met by the parish; this happened in May 1755, in respect of Widow Paice, who owed £1. 6s. 0d. from two years previously.

People who were ill received assistance. In overseer William Blackman's account for 1754 we find the entry for 6th November: 'Relivd John Hannington in his illness 8s.1½d.' Benjamin Knight received several smaller payments during his illness in June and July 1754, to no avail; from another entry we learn of his death. The overseers were prepared to meet the cost of funerals. William Porter's account for March 1736 shows us this:

' Paid for carrying Wm Fletcher's wife to the grave	0. 4. 0.
Paid for grave and knell	0. 1. 6.
Paid for bere	0. 2. 0.
Paid for shroud	0. 3. 5.
Paid 1s 6d for ye affidavit and 5½d for a pd. of candles	0. 1.11½.'

From a previous entry we learn that the coffin cost 7s.6d.

Travellers

Although most people never travelled very far from their home town or village, there was some movement about the country. Some travelled by coach or wagon, some on horseback, the majority on foot. There are occasional references to travel expenses being paid. In March 1756 we read 'carriage and maintenance of three children to London. Horses, etc. £4.15.0.' When Ann Buckler was going into service in April 1756, 3s.6d. was paid for 'her carriage to London'. Some people went less willingly. There are several references in the 1736 accounts to the affairs of 'the Yorkshire family'. The conclusion of this matter was reached in May of that year, when the family was transferred to Yorkshire. For the move, the parish was reimbursed the sum of £40. It had involved the cost of hiring horses and a cart, expenses of the overseers and payments to a nurse for the children.

Many travellers passed through the town on their way to a variety of destinations. Many of these fell into the category of 'indigent travellers'; as such they could expect to receive relief, however slight, from the parish. One helped on his journey was a drummer who, with his wife and three children was on the way to Plymouth in December 1754. The sum paid was 3s.6d. Some were less deserving; any financial assistance they received was to persuade them to 'move on'. In 1754 payments were made by overseers Nathaniel Kendrick and William Blackman. In June of that year the sum of 1s.10d. was paid 'by several orders by Mr Mayor to vagrants'. It would seem that the amount per vagrant was not meant to be very large, perhaps just enough to urge them on their way, to try their fortune elsewhere. There were several occasions when payment was made to seamen. Mostly they received 4d. each, but on 2nd November, 1754, four of them had to share 9d! Some accounts show payments made to 'saylors'. In 1744, 80 seamen passing through the town on 12th, 13th and 14th December were paid 2d. each, while 21 sailors received 3d. each. The reason for the distinction is not known.

More evidence of 'helping travellers along their way' comes from previous years. In 1740 we find an entry 'Gave a family 1s.6d. to go out of town.' The year 1743 (September) shows a payment of 2s.6d. 'to a man with wife on the tramp.' In June 1747 the sum of 3s.6d. is entered as 'expense in conveying a woman out of the town being with child.'

These cases show the understandable reluctance of the parish to accept responsibility for looking after all and sundry. This was particularly true when the health of the inhabitants could be at risk from disease brought in from outside. So it is no surprise to read that on one occasion 4s.6d. was given to a man 'to go away with his children that had the smallpox' or that on another occasion (August 1756) there is the entry 'Gave a woman and two children to go out of the town on suspicion of the smallpox 1s.0d.'

Intruders

Although the overseers accepted with varying degrees of willingness the responsibility for providing assistance to 'indigent travellers', they were less kindly disposed to 'intruders', those who moved from their own parish to try to settle elsewhere. Settlement matters were from time to time causes of trouble and expense, sometimes making it necessary to have recourse to the law. To quote the 1782 terms and conditions of the farmer's employment, 'such intruders as are now in the town to be removed at the town's expense or security provided for them except such as may be objected to by the justices and officers.' The accounts show that the overseers, churchwardens and justices met together, when it was necessary, at one of the town's inns 'to examine intruders'. The examination sought to establish the parish of origin of the intruder, in order that he or she could be removed there and so cease to be a charge on the parish of Basingstoke. On 16th January, 1746 overseer Samuel Hay made the entry 'Expense - meeting the officers to take a list of ye intruders - 3s. 0d.' This was followed on 27th of the month by the entry 'Pd Bellman for warning in *(sic)* intruders - 1s.0d.' We do not know how many intruders were examined on this occasion, but the proceedings lasted 'from three in the afternoon till 11 at night.' Unfortunately there is no record of the action taken in these cases, but it seems likely that most examinations resulted in intruders being sent away from the town. We know this happened to Ruth Withers. The overseer recorded on 16th March, 1736 that the sum of 1s.1d. was paid to send her to her parish.

The account of one of the overseers in February 1760 includes another example of the 'sending away' process:

Pd Thomas Standly for leading the soldier's wife from ye workhouse to Mr Russell's to be examined	0.0.6.
Pd Thomas Standly for leading ye said woman from the workhouse in ye morning before day to take a wagon	0.1.0.
Pd ye wagoner for her carriage to London	0.3.0.
Expenses in ye morning at Fullers	0.2.8.
Pd ye woman to support her on her journey	0.6.0.

The 'Union'

Various pieces of legislation and generally changed circumstances led to Vestries being deprived of the powers they once exercised. A major change occurred in 1834, with the passage of the Poor Law Amendment Act. The administration of all poor law matters passed to locally elected Boards of Guardians. Parishes were amalgamated into unions; new, larger buildings were erected. Such a building was opened in Basing Road on 7th October, 1836. It was to serve Basingstoke and 38 other parishes (corresponding to the subsequent Basingstoke Rural District Council area). *White's Gazetteer* for 1859 tells us, 'Basingstoke Union Workhouse is in Basing parish, and has room for about 420 inmates, but it had only 293 in 1851, when the Census taken.' It replaced Ford's Buildings in Brook Street.

Law and Order

The parish also took action to deal with other aspects of law and order. Those present at the Vestry of 27th April, 1775 agreed that the constables should hire 'two proper persons . . . . . .

to watch the town the whole year, one person each night, and to cry the hours of the night the town through.' There is no detailed statement here of the duties of 'the watch' but it is reasonable to suppose that these were 'to apprehend and secure . . . all such malefactors, disturbers of the King's Peace and all such suspected persons as shall be found wandering or misbehaving themselves.' The wording is that of the 1815 Act (see Chapter 10), by which the Paving and Lighting Commissioners were authorised to appoint watchmen (as many as they thought necessary).

Cage and Bridewell

Lawbreakers were liable to detention in the 'cage' or the 'bridewell' or they could be whipped by the bellman (beadle). The cage is frequently mentioned in the overseers' accounts. From its very name and the fact that it was floored with straw (the bellman was paid to provide fresh straw from time to time), it cannot have been a very comfortable place in which to be imprisoned, even for a short time. In November 1745 we learn of John Silver being paid one guinea for going to London to apprehend a money coiner. Pending his removal to Winchester, where the County Gaol and House of Correction was located, the coiner was held in the cage, where he was 'watched' by Joseph Butler and Thomas Taylor. They were paid 19s. for doing so. Having been seized in London on 9th November, he was transferred to Winchester on 13th. Thomas Wigg one of the Serjeants-at-Mace, received £2.1s.2½d. 'for keeping the money coiner in the Cage and having him to Winchester by the Mayor's order.'

The term 'bridewell' (from the house of correction in St Bride's Well in London) was commonly used to mean prison. We do not know when the town first had use of such a building; we do know that it was in use in the 18th century. We learn, for example, that the Vestry of 17th April, 1786 resolved 'that, as Thomas Daker has left his family chargeable to this town, proper steps be taken to convict him to the bridewell for such offence.' In June 1790 there was discussion about building a new pesthouse and airing house. At the same time the parish considered how a new prison might be provided. The overseers were in no doubt about the need, but they were, as ever, concerned to keep costs low. They asked themselves 'whether it may be contrived to fit up, the present pesthouse or part of the same for that purpose.' Decision was postponed to a future meeting.

The matter was taken up again at a Vestry on 1st May, 1792, when those present were asked to take into consideration and determine the propriety of enlarging the common prison of the town or of erecting a new one. In June of the same year the Vestry approved the plans for the new pesthouse, to be erected 'on the spott [sic] allotted for that purpose by the Commissioners under the late Inclosure Act', but no mention was made of the prison. However, the minute of the 11th September meeting referred to 'estimates for the compleating [sic] a Bridewell at the old pest-house as well as estimates for enlarging the present common prison of the town' having been received. A decision on the matter was postponed to 18th September, but this meeting did not take place.

There is in fact no record of any decision to provide these buildings having been made. We next hear of the matter on 4th April, 1793; on that date it was 'Resolved that the two Prisons or Bridewells already erected (one in 1817 at a cost of £618.15s.2d.) meets [sic] with the approbation of the Vestry . . . . .'

Bellmen and watchmen

Besides being imprisoned, those who broke the law could be punished by receiving a whipping. This was usually administered by the bellman, to women as well as men. His regular 'fee', which seems not to have varied with the years, was 6d. per wrong-doer. Mr Overseer Blackman's account for 26th October, 1754, has the entry 'Paid the Bellman for Whiping [sic] 10 people - 5s.0d.'

As we shall see in Chapter 10, the Paving and Lighting Commissioners had, with the authority of the 1815 Act, the power to appoint watchmen. On 30th December, 1817, the Vestry resolved that a watchman should be appointed 'in consequence of the late depredations and mischief committed in the town at night.' John Hacker applied for the post; the Vestry, thinking him 'a proper person to fill the situation', recommended that the Commissioners should appoint him. He was to be provided with a watch-bill and a double rattle. He was to walk the town during the hours of darkness to make sure that all was well. His base was to be (with the permission of the Mayor) a watch-box (appropriately enough made by John Carpenter) underneath the Town Hall. It is clearly stated that he had an additional duty 'to be on the alert every Sunday evening at 8 o'clock, to prevent disorderly assemblages of people.' His pay for these duties was to be £15.0.0. a year.

It seems that in 1823 'the nightly depredations and mischief' were more than one watchman could handle by himself, for we find the Vestry recommending on 30th December of that year, the temporary appointment of four additional watchmen (John Ballard, John Sutton, John Spencer and James Champion). A new development was that John Hacker was expected 'to attend at the Town Hall every Tuesday to give an account of the week's proceedings.' To which of his possible masters did he directly report? Unfortunately, we are not told if it was the overseers on behalf of the Vestry, the 'Pavement' *[see page 87]*, the Corporation (in the person of the Town Clerk) or the Justices of the Peace. It was most probably the last-named, for they met at the Town Hall every Tuesday. John Hacker was still performing these duties in 1829.

This body of watchmen was not mentioned in the report of the Commissioners for Municipal Corporations of 1835. Law and order was said to be maintained by a force consisting of two constables, two tythingmen and one beadle. It was stated to be 'not sufficient for the protection of the town.' Were the Commissioners influenced in any way by the troubles which had occurred locally during the 'Swing Riots' of 1830? We are told that Down Grange Farm was the scene of a disturbance in that year. A mob, armed with sticks, came demanding money and saying that they were going 'to rise in a body to have their wages risen.' The owner, Cassandra Hankey, gave them money and they went away, but not without breaking her winnowing machine. In his diary Samuel Attwood *[see the end of this section,]* recorded the occasion with an entry dated 21st November, 1830; 'a great number of riotous persons assembled in a disorderly manner breaking all machines, committing robberies and demanding money. Two hundred special constables sworn in, the military sent for, the 9th Lancers arrived, shops shut in the evening; a number of prisoners brought in and all the town and neighbourhood in confusion.' Of the 55 rioters who were apprehended, 20 were committed to Winchester Gaol; the remainder were discharged 'after being suitably admonished.'

The Municipal Corporations Act of 1835 made a permanent, full-time force a statutory requirement for all boroughs. Continuity with the past was maintained by naming the corporation committee having oversight of police matters 'the Watch Committee'.

[Samuel Attwood, a distant relative of the town's second Freeman and local historian Arthur Attwood, was a tailor who kept a diary between 1816 and 1870. He recorded his work and leisure activities and some events of local and national significance. It is not a daily or weekly diary, but a record of what he thought noteworthy at the time. The diary is held in the Hampshire Records Office (HRO reference 8M62/27). A copy may be consulted in the Resources Room of the Willis Museum.]

TOWN OF BASINGSTOKE.

The following Rules, Orders, and Regulations have been made by the WATCH COMMITTEE for the Guidance and Government of the *Night* and *Day Police Establishment* of the Town; and such Orders, Rules, and Regulations are published for the general information of the Inhabitants. It is particularly requested that any Inhabitant who has, at any time, cause of complaint against either of the Police Constables, do forthwith apply to the Town Clerk, that the same may be immediately investigated, and that the Party found offending may be admonished, or forthwith discharged.

The Duty of the Chief Policeman is to patrol the Town by Day, from Six o'clock in the Morning until Nine o'clock in the Evening; to apprehend all loose and disorderly Persons, to clear the Streets of Beggars, of crippled and maimed Persons exposing their Deformities, and of lewd and common Women; to prevent Persons from congregating and loitering at the Corners of the Streets; and to obey all orders of the Council and the Magistrates of the Town. His residence is at the Bridewell, in New Street, which is the Police Station House of the Town, and it is his Duty to receive any Night Charges which may be brought to him during the Night, by either of the Night Policemen, and enter the same in his Charge Book, and not to release a Charge without bringing the same before the Mayor or Magistrates for the Town. He is also expected to visit the Night Police at uncertain intervals at Night, during the Week, in order to ascertain if each man be on Duty, and on his proper Beat.

The Night Policemen are particularly enjoined to stop all suspicious Persons with Sacks, Baskets, and Bundles, and to examine the Contents of the same; to prevent Nightmen from executing the duties of their calling, excepting between the hours of Eleven o'clock at Night and Three o'clock in the Morning; and they are also to be in readiness to give their assistance during the Day, should any circumstance arise in which their services may be required.

No Policeman is to appear in Public without his uniform.

Police Establishment.

STEPHEN FRANKLIN, *Chief and Day Police Constable.*
JACOB PIDGEON, } *Night Police Constables.*
WILLIAM FRANKLIN, }

Other Officers of the Town.

JOHN RENOUF, } *Constables.*
RICHARD HALL, }
WILLIAM WOODBRIDGE, } *Tythingmen.*
HENRY LUNN, }
JOHN HACKER, - - - *Town Crier.*

APRIL 2, 1836.

JOHN SIMMONS,
MAYOR.

R. Cottle, Printer, Basingstoke.

'The Small-pox or any other pestilent Distemper'

The farmer of the poor, besides being responsible for administering the poorhouse, also had charge of the pesthouse. From the Vestry minute of 11th February, 1782 we learn that he is 'to receive persons infected with the smallpox into the pesthouse upon an order from the justices or officers.' The townspeople had a constant fear that travellers would bring with them epidemic disease, which might do great harm. The town had experienced a serious outbreak of smallpox in 1714. In that year there were 76 burials; of these 52 were of persons who died of the disease. There was a similar occurrence in 1781. At the Vestry of 28th May, 1781 it was resolved 'that no people out of other parishes shall in future be permitted on any pretence whatever to be brought within the parish to be aired after the small-pox.' Legal proceedings would be taken against any person or parish found to have conveyed into the town anyone suffering from the smallpox. This was a re-statement of a decision taken at a previous Vestry, on 10th June, 1765. The situation was sufficiently serious in 1781 for the overseers to be directed 'to look out for a proper house as soon as possible for the use of airing the people of the parish.' Later on in the same year (6th August) those present agreed 'that the proper officers should be empowered to treat with Mr John Pink, the brewer, or any other person for such a building as shall be convenient for the purpose of receiving such of the inhabitants as now are, or may be, taken with the smallpox, or, for the purpose of airing the same.' As an alternative, they could put up a temporary building for the purpose.

The threat of prosecution appears not to have been the deterrent it was intended to be. The Vestry of 24th March, 1788 was told that Richard Matthews of Winchester Street had been taking in persons to air; 'he now has many in his home and has declared he will continue the practice.' The meeting resolved that the Town Clerk be asked to give notice that Mr Richard Matthews and others would be proceeded against, if they did not immediately mend their ways.

The Vestry of 5th May, 1793 also shows the seriousness with which the town was obliged to regard the disease. It was called to consider 'a proposition of Colonel Rolle of the South Devon Militia, billeted in the town, regarding the inoculation of such of his men who had not had the smallpox.' It should be remembered that vaccination was a new idea, not yet fully accepted by the medical profession, despite the work of Edward Jenner. There was anxiety that inoculation would increase the risk to health rather than diminish it. Those present at the Vestry, eighteen of the town's leading citizens, 'resolved *nem. con.* that if such inoculation was to take place in this parish, it would be highly injurious to the trade of the town, as well as dangerous to the lives of many of the inhabitants.' It was further agreed that a letter should be sent to Colonel Rolle, expressing the hope that he would not attempt to carry out the inoculation. One of those present, Mr John Lyford, Surgeon, represented that 'Colonel Rolle's intention was for the general good of the town, in proposing such an inoculation, as one of the men had now got the small-pox, and being apprehensive many more of them are infected, that the thanks of the meeting be given to the Colonel for his good intentions, and that he be informed if any more of his men should fall in that disorder during their stay here the pesthouse will be at their service.'

As time went on, outbreaks of smallpox occurred less frequently; even so, it was possible for the Medical Officer for the town to record in his annual report of 1877 three cases of the disease and one death from it. It is interesting to notice that the term 'pesthouse' was still in use in 1878, when it was reported that the Works Committee of the Borough Council had met with the Churchwardens to discuss a proposal for the establishment of an 'infectious diseases hospital'. As we shall see in Chapter 10, Dr Ballard, reporting on the sanitary condition of the town in 1871, had recommended that 'The Local Authority should further carry into effect the provision of the Sanitary Act 1866 ... by making proper and sufficient hospital provision for the reception of cases of infectious diseases, so as to secure the separation of the sick from the healthy.' The need for such provision became only too evident when, in 1905, the town had to deal with an outbreak of typhoid. *[See pages 101-103]*

Highways

With the passage of the Highways Act of 1555, the parish became responsible for maintaining the roads of the town in good repair. The Act made all inhabitants liable to contribute to this work, either by providing materials and the means of transporting them or by supplying their labour (this requirement was ended by the General Highways Act of 1835.) A 'Surveyor of Highways' was appointed annually to perform the unpaid, thankless task of ensuring that the work was done. He may or may not have had any particular expertise that would fit him for his appointment.

At the Vestry held on 10th November, 1789, attention was drawn to the ruinous state of the new public roads provided under the Enclosure Award of 1788. Consideration of the matter was postponed to the next Vestry, when it was hoped that a decision would be taken 'to prevent as far as possible the ill-consequences likely to ensue to the parish at large.' At its meeting on 1st December, 1789, the Vestry resolved unanimously that it was advisable 'to appoint persons of skill and experience to be surveyors.' Mr William Windover and Mr John Adams were appointed at a salary of £15 per annum each, 'for their trouble'. Unfortunately, we have no record whether or not these two gentlemen were able to do anything to put right the problem of these roads.

In September of the previous year the question had arisen as to whether the 'inclosure of a certain watery lane leading from Flaxpool to Round Mead' would result in any inconvenience to the inhabitants. The Vestry meeting decided that it would not, and so Mr Jackson was allowed to close it. The matter came up again for discussion at a Vestry in September 1795. It was then agreed that 'the intire shutting-up of the said lane would be detrimental but that erecting gates at each end may not be of any inconvenience to the public at large.'

In 1776 the Vestry had to deal with a highway matter of a different kind. The meeting of 6th July considered the problem presented by 'a stoppage [being] erected in a lane commonly called Woodroffe's, alias Bishop's, alias Rolfe's Lane, leading from the Market Place to Rack or Rutts Lane.' In erecting this obstacle, Thomas Adams had created 'a common nuisance by depriving the inhabitants of this town and parish and others from a passage which time out of mind they have enjoyed.' It was resolved that Mr Adams should be informed that he must remove the obstacle within 20 days, otherwise the surveyors were authorised to pull it down.

The Basingstoke Vestry continued to exercise its highway powers into the early 1870s. In 1870 it authorised the repair of Bunnian Place. For this purpose, 50 tons of flints were provided by the L&SWR and £50 was given by the GWR. In the following year the Vestry gave the Basingstoke and Eastrop Waterworks Company permission to lay mains in the public roads on condition that all damage was repaired and the public were inconvenienced as little as possible. In 1872, the last year in which a Highways Surveyor was appointed, the Vestry sanctioned the removal by the Andover and Basingstoke Turnpike Trust of the toll-house at Worting.

Men for the Navy

There was one occasion when the Vestry met to take a decision in connection with special national circumstances. The meeting was called at short notice in March 1795, during the war against France. The Government had passed 'An Act for raising, a certain number of men in the several counties in England for the service of His Majesty's Navy.' The County Justices, meeting in Winchester at a General Session of the Peace, passed on the order to the parishes. A joint Vestry was held on 25th March, attended by churchwardens and overseers from Basingstoke, Eastrop, Basing and Cliddesden parishes. Between them the four had to 'find' four men; three would come from Basingstoke, while the other three parishes would share the provision of the remaining one. The number was arrived at by relating 69 ('the proportion of houses to find a man') to the number of assessed houses, in this case 273, of which Basingstoke had 221. The decision of the Vestry was that they would give 'a bounty of fifteen guineas but not to exceed £20 to such volunteer so to be raised being fit for a seaman, able-bodied and not less than 16 nor more than 45 years of age, and five shillings to drink His Majesty's health. One third of the bounty to be paid on being approved of and the remainder on being mustered on board of any of His Majesty's ships of war.' The minutes make it clear that the parish officers would have to be 'vigilant and active in the business so that such men be raised, approved of and inrolled in His Majesty's service on or before the first day of April now next ensuing being the time appointed for raising such men.'

10 PAVING, LIGHTING AND DRAINS

To modern eyes, the picture of local government in the middle of the 19th Century is an administrative nightmare, a tangle of authorities unrelated to each other, either in area or function and with little uniform direction from above.

Local Government in England and Wales W. Eric Jackson, Pelican 1945

Paving and Lighting

One such authority came into being on 23rd March, 1815, when the Royal assent was given to 'An Act for paving the footways and crosspaths and lighting, watching, cleansing, widening and otherwise improving the streets and other public passages and places in the Town of Basingstoke in the County of Southampton.' As its various clauses show, the Act provided a framework within which change could take place in the future, and as such it can be regarded as the first piece of local legislation to be concerned comprehensively with what we today call 'the environment'. It had a strong public health element. Our interest lies in the fact that it gave authority, not to the Corporation, but to an *ad hoc* body of 'Commissioners', whose chief qualification was one of financial standing. They (there were 83 of them!) were men prominent in business or in the professions; a minority were active in the government of the town. The names of brothers or of father and son appear in the list, William and John Attwood, Thomas and Aaron Caston, John and Charles Lyford, Thomas and Charles May, John and Charles Simmons and James and Richard Wallis, as do those of important near neighbours of the town, men such as William Chute (of the Vyne) and George Jervoise (of Herriard).

The minutes of 'the Pavement' which held its inaugural meeting on 9th May, 1815, give some idea of the way in which this unelected body of Commissioners set about dealing with matters which we today regard as being more properly the responsibility of the local authority. Some set out the stages by which the Act was put into operation; some record the failure of individuals to conform. More than one show the continuing financial problems. Others are concerned with weightier matters of policy and plans for the future. Among these was the proposal for a drainage scheme for the town, but it was with 'the Pavement' that the Commissioners began their work, in May 1815. They advertised in the *Hampshire Chronicle* and the *Reading Mercury,* requesting tenders for paving the town with 'Yorkshire stone not less than 2" thick'! They accepted the tender of William Yates Gibbs, stonemason, of Basingstoke. He was to begin his work in Winchester Street and London Street, the main route through the town. Some progress was made with the work, but by December, owing to the approaching winter - and for other reasons - it was decided that 'it would be prudent if the Pavement was and is suspended till the approach of the ensuing Spring.' Could it be that the other reasons had something to do with money - or rather the lack of it? Certainly this appears to have been the case in the following year, when reference is made to 'the pressing claims of creditors'. It was agreed that subscribers should be asked to make immediate payment, not only to enable the Commissioners to satisfy their creditors, but to enable them to 'resume the pavement'. Gradually the work was extended to other parts of the town, parts of Hackwood Lane, then the footways and crossways of the Market Place, followed by Church Street. The minutes of the July 1817 meeting say that Potters Lane was to be paved 'as soon as the funds of the Commissioners will permit.'

'Setting Up Lamps' – the Gas Company

An important provision of the Act was the power given to the Commissioners to set up lamps. Once these had been provided, the Commissioners were 'to cause the same to be lighted at such seasons of the year and such hours of the evening, and to be kept burning for so many hours as to them shall seem necessary or proper for the well and sufficient lighting, of the different parts of the town.' Some time was to elapse before this could be done.

The decision to establish a Gas Company was taken at a public meeting held on 18th December, 1833, on the initiative of Mr George Caston, ironmonger. One of the sponsors of the scheme was Aaron Caston, one of the Commissioners. In attendance at the meeting were Mr T Barlow, a gas engineer from London and Mr Byng, from the Staines and Egham gasworks. It was officially established as the Basingstoke Gas and Coke Company on 22nd May, 1834. Now it was possible to make a real improvement to the lighting of the town. It is pleasing to report that the Commissioners were concerned to save money where possible; no lighting was to be provided during the five nights of each full moon.

The town was first supplied with 'inflammable air' in 1834, when the gas works were opened in a lane which later became Gashouse Road or Lane, between Basing Road and Reading Road. Samuel Attwood recorded the occasion in his diary for October 1st 1834: 'A partial illumination two nights - the Band paraded the town - public dinners, suppers - bells ringing on the occasion.' It is perhaps of some significance that the contract for installing the plant went to T Barlow and Sons; local firms undertook the laying of distribution mains. Originally there were 150 consumers, among whom were the Paving and Lighting Commissioners, who were responsible for lighting the town with a number of public lamps, for example, at Flaxfield and in the Market Place. A short history of the Gas Company records that consumption increased with the coming of the L & SW Railway and also with the increasing appreciation of the value of gas as a means of providing illumination. The Mechanics' Institute made its contribution. In 1841, members were able to hear a talk by a Mr Sharp, of Winchester, on 'The Principles and Practice of Cooking by Gas'.

'Laying The Dust'

Keeping the pavements and streets clean was provided for in the Act. Occupiers of houses were obliged 'to sweep and cleanse or cause to be swept and cleansed the said foot-pavements before their respective houses or other tenements or offices every day before ten of the clock in the forenoon.' In December 1817 the Commissioners accepted Mr George Porter's tender for street cleaning. Later the provision of a water-cart for watering the streets to lay the dust was an essential item of expenditure by the Corporation. The Basingstoke and Eastrop Water Company in its prospectus undertook to provide hydrants throughout the district, available in case of fire and for watering the streets, flushing drains, etc.

'The Watch'

There had always been a need for the town to be watched (see Chapter 9). Originally the ordinary householder could be called upon to take his turn at 'keeping watch and ward' (guard). In 1544, there is a record of one Nicholas Hore being fined 6d. 'because he failed to keep the night watch'. It would be wrong to take too literally Shakespeare's portrait of the Watch in *Much Ado about Nothing*, but he appears to have known that the system was not without its faults. The 1815 Act included power to appoint watchmen, particularly to walk the town at night. One such appointment was made in December 1817. John Hacker, who took up the post, was still performing his watchman's duties in 1829.

'Widening and otherwise Improving'

The Act provided the Commissioners with the necessary powers to improve the town by opening up its 'narrow parts'. They were authorised to contract for the purchase of any properties whose removal might be necessary to enable the proposed work to be carried out. It was lawful for them 'to take down such houses, buildings or erections and throw the site thereof … into the said streets, lanes, public passages and places.' In May 1832 the Market Place underwent alteration when the 'taking down' of the Old Town Hall and other buildings occurred under the terms of the 1829 Act. *[See page 51.]*

'Preventing Annoyance in the Street'

The clause in the Act titled as above gives good guidance as to what is meant by 'annoyance'. In the fairly comprehensive list of what the citizen might not do are the following: he was not allowed to
- drive a vehicle on any of the footpaths or pavements
- make or repair the wheel of any carriage in any of the streets
- make bonfires
- let off fireworks
- permit/allow any household or business rubbish 'to lie in any of the said streets, etc. for any longer than shall be necessary for the loading and carrying away of the same.' *[See page 30.]*

Drainage

There is no specific mention in the Act of power to undertake any drainage scheme for the town. As we shall see in Chapter 12, the new Corporation had been set up in 1836 but from 1837 onwards, it was still the Commissioners who concerned themselves with this matter. On 31st August, 1837, Robert Cottle reported in a letter to the Commissioners the findings and recommendations of a Committee formed 'to ascertain the best and most effective means of carrying off the great torrent of water which flows out of Winchester Street and Allens Lane [the former name of Victoria Street] down New Street into Church Street at certain periods of the year, more particularly during heavy storms of rain.' Reference is made to the torrent of water being added to by a similar flow down Church Street from the Market Place, causing flooding of houses in Church Street.

The solution proposed was an underground barrel drain or common sewer, 'from the lamp-post near Mr Paice's to Ring's cottage at Flaxpool' - i.e. down New Street. The letter concludes by referring to 'the above desirable object [which] will greatly tend to promote the cleanliness of the streets - and very materially add to the comfort of the inhabitants.' The proposed work was carried out and its completion was reported to the Commissioners at their meeting on 10th January, 1839.

The possibility of a more thorough-going scheme was looked into a few years later. On 10th January, 1850, the Commissioners held a special meeting 'to take into consideration the best method of draining the town.' The meeting considered the views and recommendations of two gentlemen, Messrs Davis (Archer Davis, whose map of the town dates from 1851) and Briggs, who had made a survey of the town for this purpose. Unfortunately, the same meeting was told of the embarrassed state of the Pavement Fund. For this reason the Commissioners 'deem it inexpedient at the present time to entertain the question of general drainage.'

The meeting was a pointer to the future: one Commissioner proposed that the town should conform to the provisions of the Public Health Act of 1848. This Act, the first of its kind, gave local authorities the power to set up local boards to deal with matters affecting drainage, housing, health, etc. (Later legislation such as the Nuisances Removal Act of 1855 and the Local Government Act of 1858 increased these powers.) Had the proposal been adopted, it could have meant the Town Council assuming responsibility for the work currently being done (or rather, not being done) by the Commissioners. The proposal was negated by a large majority. Basingstoke was only one of many authorities which were slow to put this permissive legislation into effect.

Dr Ballard's Report

A report on *The Sanitary Condition of Basingstoke* by Dr Ballard for the Medical Department of the Local Government Board in 1871 brought pressure for change. He detailed the causes of the insanitary conditions found in a large part of the town and made ten recommendations, the first of which was: 'There should be only one Authority in the town for all sanitary purposes.' The need was for all such matters to be 'concentrated in one public board.' Elsewhere he pointed out that the Commissioners had been unable to do all that was necessary because they had long ago exhausted their borrowing powers and could raise only a relatively small sum by means of an annual rate. By the time they had met interest charges and the cost of lighting the town, they had too little to spend on drainage works.

The Corporation appears to have taken note of the Ballard report, for in March 1872 they invited the Commissioners to join them in removing nuisances. The Commissioners agreed to cooperate 'with a view to the effectual removal of the evils complained of.' By August, 1872 they seemed to be having doubts about their future rôle, for, on the 29th of that month they resolved, with reference to the Public Health Act of 1872, to find out from the Local Government Board what their future powers would be. The reply must have been discouraging for, at their meeting on 20th December, 1872, taking all their difficulties into account, they decided 'that all the powers and duties hitherto exercised and performed by this Board should be in the future undertaken by the Urban Sanitary Authority' (set up under the Public Health Act of 1872) i.e. by the Corporation. The final act of the Commissioners, (only six were present at their last meeting), on 21st February, 1873, was to pass a resolution that all their property, books, papers, etc. should be transferred to the Town Council.

So came to an end the work of an *ad hoc* body of public-spirited persons. It had done much of use towards ensuring 'the benefit, convenience and safety of the inhabitants [of the town] ... and all persons resorting to and travelling through the same' but it was no longer equal to the task of dealing with the problems arising in a town rapidly increasing in population and area.*

[* *It probably never was, as it was too weak financially – its borrowing powers were too restricted to deal with large projects. DS*]

11 THE CORPORATION OF BASINGSTOKE

The most common and most striking defect in the constitution of the Municipal Corporations of England and Wales is, that the corporate bodies exist independently of the communities among which they have been found. The Corporations look upon themselves, and are considered by the inhabitants, as separate and exclusive bodies; they have powers and privileges within the towns and cities from which they are named, but in most places all identity of interest between the Corporation and the inhabitants has disappeared.

Royal Commission on Municipal Corporations, 1835

Before the Municipal Reform Act

Places grow in size and importance. While they remain small they are relatively easy to administer. As they become larger, relationships within them become more complex and there is then a greater need for an overall controlling authority. The affairs of the small rural community were regulated according to the manorial system, in which the tenant owed allegiance to his lord and performed clearly defined duties to him and the community. The inhabitants of the growing town - the burgesses - no longer performed services for their lord; instead, they paid him an annual rent for a 'tenement' or holding. If the castle and the manor symbolize the feudal system, it is the Town Hall that represents the increasing responsibility of the 'proved men' of the town for looking after their own affairs. Towns gained their powers through charters granted by the Crown. We have seen in Chapter 5 how the granting of the charters of 1256 and 1392 contributed to the evolution of the government of the town.

We need to see the part played by more recent charters. In the 17th century the town received three charters. The first, granted by James 1 on 1st July, 1622, set out the way in which the town was to be governed. Two burgesses, called bailiffs, were to be elected annually as the leading men in the administration of the town's affairs. James Deane and his fellow-townsman George Baynard were the first to hold office. They were to be assisted in all matters by 'fourteen of the best and most upright burgesses, who shall be called capital burgesses.' Those appointed were William Hearne, John Smith, George Goringe, John Hall, John Stoker, Richard Spicer, Thomas Hall, William Blunden, John Blunden, Thomas Bunney, John Normanton, Thomas South, Henry Purchis, Richard Cloffe and Adam Reeve (*vice* Richard Cloffe deceased). As a common Council, they were to have authority 'to constitute and ordain from time to time laws and ordinances which shall seem useful and necessary for the good government of the town.'

The charter also provided for the selection of 'a discreet man' to be High Steward. The first holder of this office was William, Marquis of Winchester. He was to be assisted by an Under-Steward, John Foyle being the first to occupy the post. The position of Common Clerk to the town was created and Henry Osey became the first Town Clerk. Two other officials were the Sergeants-at-Mace, whose function was to execute all processes of the Court of Record. The court was to meet weekly on Tuesdays for the purpose of hearing 'complaints about all manner of contracts, trespasses by force and arms, contentions, contempts, deceptions and other personal actions within the town of Basingstoke, provided that none of them exceed the value of £10.' Judgements in these matters were made by the Justices of the Peace, namely the Bailiffs, the High Steward and the Under-Steward. The policing of the town was to be carried out by 'constables and other inferior officers according to the former customs of the town.'

Guidance was given in the charter as to the way in which the commercial life of the town should be carried out. The regular weekly market (held on a Wednesday since 1214) was to continue, as were also the two annual fairs, one at Michaelmas, the other at Whitsuntide. The regulation of trade in the interest of the merchants of the town was ensured by another provision of the charter: 'No stranger unless he be a freeman of the town may henceforth sell any goods within the town other than in gross or that is necessary for the victualling of the town unless at times of the fairs and markets.' Strangers were not allowed to keep 'any shop, place or stall nor use any occupation or manual art without first obtaining special licence of the Bailiffs and Burgesses in writing under the seal.'

[Interestingly, Romsey had received a charter from James 1st in 1607 with almost identically worded clauses. This is held by HRO (97M81).]

There is no mention in the charter of a regular meeting of the Corporation but in 1630 (16th September) a decision about this was taken: 'It is ordered and agreed That the Bailiffs and Burgesses of the town of Basingstoke shall henceforth assemble themselves and meet together in the town hall in Basingstoke aforesaid, on the first Monday of every month, at the hour of nine o'clock in the morning to conduct and confer on such matters as shall concern the government of the town.' They were to be reminded of their duty to attend by the ringing of the market bell; for non-attendance they were liable to a fine of 2s.6d.

There was an interesting development in 1633 - a division of the town into 'circuits' – for instance, 'From Reading corner in the Oate Street to Northbrooke Street, and in Northbrooke Street to Weavers tree, and From Weavers tree to Rowdens and all Holy Ghost Street.' These descriptions of the circuit, and the summoning of the market bell are a reminder that 17th-century Basingstoke was a very small community. On 3rd March, 1633, it was agreed by and between the bailiffs and burgesses, that 'they should henceforth at convenient times divide themselves into several companies (as hereafter mentioned) and frequent such parts of the town respectively assigned to them.' They were 'to take notice of the carriage and behaviour of such as do reside and dwell within their several and respective limits and circuits; survey and note the number of persons in each poor family, and how they are employed and set to work, that such course may be taken for the reformation of the ill-mannered behaviour of such persons as are of lewd conversation as to justice appertaineth, and care taken for the relief of such persons as are in necessity and poverty.'

In 1641 Charles I granted the town a new charter, which confirmed the rights and privileges conferred in previous charters: 'Of our special grace, we order and declare that the Bailiffs and Burgesses of the said town of Basingstoke by whatever name they were formerly incorporated, henceforth may be a body corporate and politic in fact and in name by the Mayor, Aldermen and Burgesses of the town of Basingstoke in the County of Southampton; and by this name they may be persons capable in law to have, acquire, relieve and possess lands, tenements, liberties, jurisdictions and whatsoever hereditaments for themselves and their successors in fee and perpetuity or for lives or years, and also goods and chattels, and all other thing of what kind soever, and to give, lease and assign the said lands, tenements, hereditaments, etc.'

It will be noticed that for the first time, we have the use of the term 'Mayor' and 'Aldermen' in respect of the government of the town. George Baynard, who was one of the two bailiffs appointed in 1622, was nominated as first Mayor of the town, while John Aylwyn, William Blunden, Richard Spyer, Andrew Butler, Richard Brackley, and Robert Stocker junior, were appointed Aldermen. Those nominated Burgesses were Thomas South, William Herne, William Greene, John Holmes, James Whyte, Edmund Pitman and Richard Woodroffe. John Aylwyn became the Common Clerk of the town.

The charter went on to nominate Sir Henry Wallop to the office of High Steward, and to create the new post of Recorder, which was to be filled by Thomas Willys, 'Clerk of the Crown of our Court of Chancery'. The Mayor, the High Steward, the retiring Mayor and one alderman chosen annually were, as Justices of the Peace, to be responsible for the local administration of justice, hearing cases which were brought before them weekly. Besides the weekly Court of Record instituted in 1622, they were empowered to hold occasional Sessions of the Peace, at which 'to hear and determine according to the laws and statutes of the realm of England all felonies, contempts, transgressions and lesser offences as other justices in other counties, cities, boroughs and corporate towns without other warrant or commission, provided that they do not proceed to the determination of any treason, misprision of treason, murder or felony or other offence concerning loss of life or members.'

A close Corporation and Municipal Reform

The form of government prescribed in 1641 continued until 1835. On 9th September of that year the Municipal Reform Act was passed in Parliament. The Act put into operation the recommendations of the Commissioner for Municipal Corporations. Basingstoke had come under the scrutiny of the Commissioners some time in 1834. They reported that, as with most other boroughs, the members of the corporation came from just a small section of the population. It was a situation that encouraged self-perpetuation and nepotism; it was likely not to be sufficiently representative of the interests of all the inhabitants of the growing town; it might easily fail to meet the demands of changing times. The Commissioner's report states, 'The corporate offices are objects of ambition to the respectable inhabitants, who are desirous to have the power of electing their own officers. It is felt to be a grievance that the Corporation allow non-residents to remain members of their body, and that they have elected strangers to fill up the vacancies in the corporation to the neglect of the native inhabitants of the town.'

Once elected, the members of the Corporation held office for life. They could be removed from office for misconduct or if 'some other sufficiently reasonable cause should arise.' Baigent and Millard in their *History of Basingstoke* say, 'Under the charter it was not only a close corporation but in course of time became a family party, all its members being allied to one another either by kinship or marriage.' There is no doubt that there was slackness in the affairs of the Corporation. The Rev. John Ilsley (Curate of Ellisfield and Herriard and also usher of the Holy Ghost School) was an alderman from 1796 until his death in 1806. Four years were to elapse before his place as alderman was filled. We are also told that John Simmons was elected alderman on 4th October, 1824, to take the place of the Rev. Dr Sheppard, deceased. Dr Sheppard had been dead for more than ten years. The 'family party' theme is well illustrated by the following: Thomas May, junior, was elected a burgess on 3rd May, 1794 and an alderman on 7th April, 1795, becoming Mayor for 1796-1797. Thomas May, senior, was elected a burgess on 6th October, 1783, but, on account of non-residence, was not sworn in. On 10th May, 1795, Charles May was elected and sworn a burgess in his place.

When the Commissioners reported (1834), the make-up of the Corporation was:

Aldermen

Thomas May (common brewer)
Robert Hulbert, senior, Esq
Charles May, senior (common brewer)
Charles Hawthorne, Esq
Richard Eyles, Esq (landowner)
* James Warne (attorney-at-law)
William Anthony Lewis (attorney-at-law)
John Simmons (banker

* James Warne was Mayor at this time

Burgesses

Charles May, junior (common brewer)
Thomas Workman (surgeon)
Charles Headeach (gentleman)
Robert Hulbert, junior (chemist)
John Osmond Nicholls (schoolmaster)

The Commissioners drew attention to the fact that Messrs May were related, as were also Messrs Hulbert, likewise Mr Headeach and Mr Workman.

At the very end of the year, on 26th December, election for the new Corporation took place, the election of aldermen and Mayor following on 29th December. The members of the new Corporation were:

*John Simmons (banker)   Thomas Workman (surgeon)
*Thomas May (brewer)   *Robert Cottle (printer, postmaster)
James Warne (attorney-at-law)   *Robert Skeat Hulbert (chemist)
Charles May, junior (brewer)   George Paice (auctioneer)
Charles Lyford (surgeon)   Charles Sissons
Edward Covey (surgeon)   William Houghton

* Elected aldermen

John Simmons was the elected Mayor, and William Anthony Lewis became the Town Clerk. A second election took place on 9th January, 1836, when five more councillors were elected: George Lamb (solicitor), Henry Brownjohn (wine merchant), Robert Curtis (coach proprietor), Edward Penton (maltster), and George Caston (ironmonger). Charles Headeach was appointed Treasurer, while James Cooper and Charles Cox, junior, were appointed Sergeants-at-Mace.

The new Corporation held its first meeting in January 1836; its first action was to appoint itself a Watch Committee. It is interesting to see from the minutes of the Council what constituted its business during the first few years of its existence. In doing so we must remember that it was only one in a 'tangle of authorities' dealing with 'matters municipal'. We have seen the contribution made by the Vestry and the Pavement Commission; by the Board of Guardians and the Turnpike Trusts. It was not until 1894 that the Vestry, for example, finally lost its civil powers.

Some items of Corporation business may perhaps appear rather trivial to us, but they were obviously of concern to the inhabitants of a small town undergoing change. Among the matters considered in its early years were a proposal to remove the turnpike gates; the control of the activities of hawkers, the cost of relaying the pitchings in the Market Place (an overlap here with the responsibility of the Paving and Lighting Commissioners); the repair of the pump at the Lesser Market; and, in an early case of 'municipalisation', the relocation of a weighbridge privately owned but used by the public, so that the tolls received for its use might 'in future be taken by the Corporation for the benefit of the town.'

More far-reaching and occupying more of councillors' time, including attendance at meetings additional to the regular quarterly meetings, was the question of levying tolls for the use of the Corn Market. As we have seen already (in Chapter 6) the Corporation, although legally entitled by the 1829 Market Act to take the action it did, met with opposition from local farmers. The disagreement, which began in 1844, was not finally settled until 1850. The interests of the farming community were certainly not neglected; the Corporation was active in encouraging the establishment of a wool fair, held for the first time in June 1851. It also had the physical comforts of the farmers and others in mind, when it proposed in 1853 the enclosure of the Corn Market under the Town Hall 'to keep out the weather and prevent the present draft [sic] through the same.'

At about the same time much discussion was taking place over the future of the Holy Ghost School. A wordy resolution, moved by Lord Bolton, at a public meeting on 6th December, 1849, requested the Corporation to take steps to ensure that more emphasis would be placed on the provision of a curriculum more appropriate to 'trade, agriculture and mercantile pursuits.' There were two accompanying concerns - the need to find a suitable site where a new school could be erected, and the delay in appointing a new headmaster. By 1855, both these concerns had been met, with the appointment of Rev. Lightfoot and the opening of the new school building in Worting Road. This outcome was the result of determined representation of the town's interests to the Lord Chancellor and other authorities. *[A fuller account of the Holy Ghost School and the succeeding Queen's School and Queen Mary's School is given in Chapter 18.]*

Before 1836 the rating of property was intended to provide the income to meet the many and varied items of expenditure. Under the new Corporation the same system persisted. At its February meeting in 1844, the Corporation decided that the sum of £300 would be necessary. It did not collect the monies itself. Instead, its method was to order 'that the parish be rated, taxed, and assessed in the sum required.' The Town Clerk had the authority, on behalf of the Corporation, 'to demand, collect and receive this sum from the churchwardens and overseers.' This procedure was a regular feature of the February meetings of the Corporation. In 1845 the sum required was again set at £300, but in 1846 it was agreed that the Borough Fund needed only £200. This sum was also considered sufficient for each of the years 1847-1850.

Some of the inhabitants were of the opinion that the Corporation was becoming extravagant, and in 1850 they passed the following resolution, 'that the attention of the Corporation at their next quarterly meeting be called to the expenditure of the Borough with a view, if practicable, to dispense with a Borough Rate.' A 'memorial' was presented to the Corporation in June of that year, in the following terms: 'We, the undersigned inhabitants in the parish of Basingstoke beg to represent to your honourable body that in our opinion it is not necessary or expedient with a balance of three hundred pounds and upwards in the hands of your Treasurer to levy a Borough Rate for any corporate purposes and respectfully desire that the rate now ordered be not collected.' The Corporation considered the matter in August 1850. Councillor William Challis, who presented the memorial, reinforced the argument by moving a reduction in the salaries of the Mayor and the Town Clerk. There was no seconder to the motion and so it failed.

Public health

As was discussed in Chapter 10, in the 1850s, as the Corporation was obliged to consider the implications of new legislation concerning public health, the question of drainage of the town was a constant item on the agenda. In 1848, the Government, concerned by the threat of an outbreak of cholera, had passed the Public Health Act and the Nuisances Removal and Diseases Prevention Act. The first of these provided for the setting-up of local Boards of Health. It was not until 1852 that the Corporation discussed the 'propriety of establishing' such a board. Pleading 'difficult and conflicting circumstances', it resolved not to present a petition on the matter to the General Board of Health. Was one of the circumstances the fact that the Paving and Lighting Commissioners already had 'public health' powers? In December 1853, the Corporation discussed the possibility of having an inquiry into 'the sanitary condition of the inhabitants of Basingstoke' but again it was considered not expedient to take any action beyond holding a public meeting of ratepayers.

Although steps had been taken in 1854 to prevail on the Inspector of Nuisances to undertake a more thorough cleansing of 'all ditches, gutters, drains and watercourses', still nothing was done to deal with the primary problem - lack of a satisfactory sewerage system. The year 1857 saw a more positive approach to the problem; the Corporation authorised the employment of an expert 'to view the streets of the town' in order to determine 'the general practicability of draining the town' and the possible cost of doing so. Not being certain of what its powers were in the matter of a drainage scheme, it also decided to take Counsel's opinion. In September that year it was resolved unanimously that 'it would not be expedient to move further at present in the proposed drainage but that it is desirable more effectually to scavenge the town.'

A special meeting was held on 8th February, 1859 to consider the provisions of the Local Government Act of 1858. The meeting did no more than propose regular cleansing and flushing of gutters, etc for the period of a year, the cost to be met from the Borough Fund. At the same time it was suggested that 'pecuniary aid' should be requested from the Surveyor of Highways for the Turnpike Trusts. This would appear to indicate that there was a reluctance on the part of the Corporation to find enough money from the rates to finance the necessary works. Shortage of money was also the problem of the other body, which had attempted to do something to alleviate the situation - the Paving and Lighting Commissioners. In May 1859 they reported that their funds were 'totally inadequate' to meet their responsibilities; they suggested that the Corporation should give early consideration to an Act for taking over the duties of the 'Pavement'.

By 1860 the Corporation was obviously thinking that it should take stock of its position and so in February 1860 it decided 'to examine into the actual requirements of the town and the several local and public Acts affecting the interests of the town.' Consideration would also be given to 'all the incumbrances under the local and general Acts on the Borough Funds.' This review soon confirmed what was already clear, that the fund was insufficient for 'purposes of any public improvement.'

When, in 1866, another outbreak of cholera was anticipated, 'a stir was made in the town' and several doctors formed themselves into a committee to inspect the town. This body reported very unfavourably on the conditions prevailing, but nothing in the way of permanent improvement came of this, and when the panic was over matters went on as before.

Dr Ballard, in his report on the sanitary condition of the town, presented to the Medical Department of the local Government Board in 1871, confirmed this unsatisfactory state of affairs (see Chapter 10). His attitude to what he found is well conveyed by the following: 'The organisation for the protection of the public health in Basingstoke is a subject soon disposed of. When I say that in this town there are two Local Authorities - one of which does nothing and the other next to nothing, except in spurts - that the Sanitary Act is to the Nuisance Authority as if it had never passed the legislature ... I have said almost enough.' He then mentioned the shortcomings of the Paving and Lighting Commissioners and the Town Council; he pointed out that the former body was unable to raise enough finance, while the latter had failed to use the 'abundance of powers' it already had under the Nuisance Removal Act.

It is as well to remind ourselves that the situation described by Dr Ballard was by no means unique. In Southampton the establishment of a local Board of Health was opposed on the grounds that its powers to levy unlimited rates would lead to a decline in property values (*Rance, A 1986*). In Winchester, 'fear of putting up the rates delayed main sewerage for over thirty years' (*Carpenter Turner, B 1976*). Basingstoke did not seriously attempt to provide satisfactory schemes of sewerage and water supply until the 1880s. The progress of these schemes is dealt with in Chapter 12.

Education

At the same time as it was showing a more ready acceptance of the need to provide solutions to public health problems, the Corporation was obliged to become involved in the question of elementary education (Chapter 18). Towards the end of the century, Basingstoke, in common with other places, was experiencing an increase in its child population. The voluntary bodies, mainly the National and British Societies, were failing to make 'adequate provision of places in their schools'. The purpose of the Education Act of 1870, which came into force on 8th August of that year, was to fill up the gaps in the education provided by the voluntary bodies. The idea was to urge them to put their schools in order, with the aid of government grants, if necessary, so that they could correct any deficiency. After much opposition to the idea of using rates for the purpose, the first Board School, Fairfields, was opened on 16th February, 1888.

The Corporation was still faced with the difficulty of finding a satisfactory solution to the related problems of water supply and sewerage.

12 WATER AND SEWERAGE

A wholesome supply of water should be provided from some uncontaminated source, and furnished to every house on the system of constant supply from a central source.

Ballard Report, 1871

Water Supply

The establishment of the Basingstoke and Eastrop Waterworks Company was the first step towards meeting the recommendations made by Dr Ballard in his 1871 report *The Sanitary Conditions of Basingstoke*. The Company, in its prospectus offering 700 shares at £5 each, stated that its aim was 'to provide the town of Basingstoke and the adjoining parish of Eastrop with an abundant supply of pure water, thus providing the health and comfort of the inhabitants, and at the same time offering a secure and remunerative source of investment of capital.' Messrs Raynbird and Co, corn merchants, were said to possess 'large unwanted steam power'. The Company contracted with that firm to use the surplus power to pump daily whatever quantity of water might be required. The water source was in a well in Steam Dell, a large chalk pit on the Reading Road. The prospectus went on to say that the reservoir for the system would be 'situated as to command the tops of the highest houses, and the service continuous and under pressure.' The site of the reservoir was in Darlington Road. Hydrants would be provided to meet the needs of the town 'in case of fire, for watering the sewers, flushing drains etc.'

Before long there were complaints that the company was failing to deliver an adequate supply of water. In particular, it was stated that the pressure in the mains was insufficient for fighting fires in some parts of the town. The complaints of domestic consumers that the supply could not be relied on at all times of the day and night were brought to the notice of the Corporation. In January 1879, the town's Health Committee discussed the problem. It allowed that the Water Company did not pump at all on Saturday nights and as little as possible on Sundays; the water level in the reservoir was sometimes too low to meet all demands satisfactorily. The purity of the water was sometimes questioned.

In September 1879 the Medical Officer of Health (Dr F Webb) was able to reassure the public that, despite its 'turbid and certainly unsightly appearance', it could, in the opinion of a consultant analyst, 'be safely used for drinking and all other domestic purposes.'

Matters came to head in February 1880: the Town Clerk, Mr W H Bailey, reported that he had visited the reservoir and found that there was 'insufficient supply for town purposes in case of emergency.' The Company declined to admit that they were failing to meet their responsibilities. Some councillors thought that they should withhold payment of sums due. There was some criticism of the management of the company's affairs, Alderman Wallis, a leading critic, going so far as to say; 'Our knowledge will bear favourable comparison with that of the directors of the company.' It came as no surprise that in May 1880, at the quarterly meeting of the Corporation, councillors discussed the possibility of purchasing the waterworks undertaking. Their argument was that, since it was the responsibility of the Urban Sanitary Authority to ensure a reliable supply of water for all purposes as cheaply as possible, the waterworks should be owned by the authorities, who could 'utilise the present waterworks and manufacture [sic] a supply considerably cheaper than the present company could do.' A water-rate could be levied and collected at the same time as the Urban Sanitary Authority rate. The meeting decided that a committee should be formed, to discuss with the directors of the Company the purchase of their enterprise. An agreement to purchase was signed on 22nd December, 1881, but some difficulties arose over the sum to be paid. The matter was submitted to arbitration and eventually a purchase price of £9,960 was agreed, 1st March,

1883. The Local Government Board gave its approval in May and the sanction of the Public Works Loan Commissioners was received in September of that year.

The acquisition of the Waterworks Company by the Corporation did not solve the town's problems. The growing population and the new sewerage involving the connection of more houses to the system caused an increase in the demand for water. It was becoming clear that new works would be required to ensure a dependable supply. In 1886, the provision of a new reservoir was being considered. The proposed expenditure of £1,200 for the purpose was opposed by a body of ratepayers, on the grounds that it was not immediately necessary.

There was also a need to find a new water-source. In October 1887 we find the Corporation considering the idea of taking water from a well at the sewerage pumping station in Basing Road. In the event, nothing came of this, because the related sewage disposal scheme intended for the site was successfully opposed at a public inquiry in February 1888.

In 1895, the water question was still concerning the authorities. On 14th October, a public meeting was held in the Town Hall 'to consider a scheme of water supply' to go before the inspector of the Local Government Board on the following day. It was estimated that about 400 attended the meeting; included were 'some of the largest ratepayers'. As was expected, in this exercise of local democracy it was the future indebtedness of the Borough that was the main point of concern. The works thought to be necessary would require the Corporation to borrow between £15,000 and £16,000. One councillor, who said that he would be opposing the scheme on the following day, asked why it was thought necessary to spend '£10,000 to take the water to Cliddesden for it to come back again to supply about 20 houses in Burgess Road, when the people were all asleep.' He said he was 'in favour of a new water-station belonging to the Corporation as soon as they thought the time was ripe for it.' The meeting concluded with the passing of a resolution that the scheme proposed was 'not required by the circumstances of the Board, and if carried out would inflict an unnecessary burden on the ratepayers, and that the Mayor was requested to present this resolution to the inspector tomorrow.'

At the inquiry, which opened on the following day, Mr Rofe, who had acted for the Corporation on previous occasions, for instance, in 1883 and 1887, argued that the scheme should be proceeded with. In support of his opinion, he provided figures of the average daily quantity of water pumped. These showed that over the period 1881 and 1884 there was an increase of between 3% and 4% a year. Given the figure of 400,000 gallons as the daily average for 1894, he foresaw the time when the demand might well be for 750,000 gallons daily. He suggested the need for a reservoir to hold 250,000 gallons; he proposed Cliddesden as a suitable location.

At a later stage in the inquiry, which was resumed on 15th November, various witnesses, some of them town councillors, argued against the provision of a new reservoir at Cliddesden. Mr W H Blatch, managing director of May and Co's brewery said that his firm were concerned that any large outlay would materially effect their business. He added that he had never had any water supply difficulties at his home, the Mount, in Winchester Road. One of the councillors put forward a proposal for a pumping-station on council-owned land at Flaxfield. His proposal included the laying of new mains to the Flaxfield area (in the process of being developed), but there was no provision for a reservoir. Mr. Rofe told the inquiry that he had made measurements of the pressure in different parts of the town at various times. He gave it as his opinion that the town would be left with an imperfect supply if the Cliddesden reservoir was eliminated from the scheme proposed.

The 'water question' which, it was admitted, had already been before the Council for a very long time, was again under consideration at two special meetings of the Council, in July and August 1896. On the first of these occasions, reference was made to the proposal, first put forward in November 1895, for the use of a site at Flaxpool (Flaxfield). This was described as a field, opposite the New Inn, at the bottom of Sarum Hill. Mention was made of springs rising a little to the south-west, to form a tributary of the River Loddon. The site met the requirement of low cost, since it was owned by the Corporation, but two other questions required to be answered. Would the site be able to provide an adequate and reliable supply? Would there be any risk of pollution? The experts disagreed. Mr C Isler (of Isler and Co), described as being 'one of the best water engineers in England', said that it would be possible to ensure a reliable supply of water, without risk of pollution. He recommended the sinking of what was called 'an artesian base tube well' to a depth of 150 feet. Mr Rofe was critical of this proposal, 'there is no site in this valley, on which a pumping-station could be put where you would not get a thickly inhabited and possibly polluted district.' He added that he could not think that any responsible engineer would advise sinking a well in that position.

At various times Mr Rofe had examined four other possible sites. Two were near the South Western Railway between West Ham and Bury farm; the third was described as being on the Winchester Road, half-way between the town and the White House; the fourth was one which had been under consideration for some time at Sherborne Bottom. A test well here had shown that the quantity required could be readily provided. There was little liability to pollution, but there were doubts about the probable cost, especially of laying the mains. Councillor Kingdon, chairman of the Water Supply Committee, thought the Corporation was taking too narrow a view. Cost should be a secondary consideration; 'the health and future prospects of the town depend on having a pure and sufficient water supply.' The town should not be put in danger because of increasing charge on the rates. He was joined in this by Councillor May, who spoke of the town increasing considerably in the next five or six years; the Corporation should look ahead and ensure an ample supply. The trustees of the Vyne Estate were prepared 'to treat with the Council' over the necessary land but were concerned that pumping would divert the flow from the natural springs in the area, possibly affecting the level of the water in the lake at the Vyne. This concern was reported to the Council in July 1898. Eventually it was decided not to proceed with this scheme, for reasons of cost.

The search for a suitable source continued, with three additional sites being put forward, as possibilities: near the junction of Cranbourne Lane and Viables Lane; at a point in Viables Lane itself, and later in January 1904 'at the corner of the common', a site similar to the one at Flaxpool, both being sources of tributaries of the River Loddon. There was some urgency in the matter, as we can judge from the reference above to danger to the health of the town. The authorities needed to find a source that could replace the Steam Dell well. Dr Webb, in his annual report to the council in 1891, had drawn attention to the potential threat to health. He wrote of 'the very serious and dangerous nuisances again and again recurring and immediately imperiling the purity of our water supply'. It is interesting that Dr Webb kept the Local Government Board informed of his actions and of the analyses of the well water. It is perhaps even more interesting that the Board assured Dr Webb that he would not be held responsible if the Council were to fail to take the necessary actions.

At a meeting of the Council in February 1904, Councillor Phillips drew the attention of members to the fact that the Water Supply Committee had made no clear decision about a site for a new well to serve the town. It was time for the Corporation to 'stop dragging its feet and get out of the habit of shelving the question.' During the discussion which followed, it was stated that 'a party of explorers under the captaincy of Mr Phillips would sally forth in the afternoon to survey certain sites believed to be suitable for waterworks.' The Committee would then meet at an early date to formulate a new scheme. Among the potential sites visited was one which had been referred to in 1896 as near the S W Railway between West Ham Farm and Bury Farm. On 14th May, 1904, a report appeared in the local paper under the heading 'Water Supply - a new beginning'. It stated that a letter had been received from Mr C F Simmons, auctioneer, offering to sell, on behalf of Winchester College authorities, 9 acres of land, near the Alton Light Railway.

As test-boring showed, the Corporation had at long last found a reliable source of water. It was now necessary to provide the required works. At a public inquiry held in mid-October 1905, the Town Clerk presented the Corporation's application for permission to borrow the sum of £19,450. After giving various statistical details, including the estimated population of the borough (11,000), the rateable value (£47,426) and the total rate (general, water and poor) 7s.7d. in the pound, he said that this was well within its borrowing powers. The Board of Agriculture had given its approval, the Basingstoke District Rural Council was prepared to allow pipes to be laid to a reservoir at Cliddesden. A provisional agreement to purchase the land at West Ham had been entered into; the cost would be £1,200.

The Borough Surveyor, who had prepared the plans for the new waterworks, then gave some technical details about the depth of the well (60 feet); the diameter (11 feet); the average daily yield during a 14 day test period (409,880 gallons); the extent of depletion and the rate of recovery; the current demand for water (360,000 gallons per day, of which 11,000 gallons were used by the railway companies). He forecast that within 30 years the waterworks would have to provide for a consumption of 800,000 gallons daily.

The Inspector was urged to try to prevail on the Local Government Board to make its decision known as soon as possible. In the request for a quick decision the Corporation referred to the contamination of the existing town well, long predicted by Dr Webb. Fortunately, the Board did not delay; sanction for the loan was received early in November and on 9th December it was reported that a pure water supply had been temporarily inaugurated.

The typhoid epidemic 1905 and Dr Farrar's Report

An outbreak of typhoid fever was caused by the contamination of the town well. This affected the town from mid-September to early December, 1905. The official report on the epidemic was made to the Local Government Board by Dr Farrar. It was published on 25th November.

The report refers to the sudden onset of the outbreak, which had reached its peak between 15th and 30th September. During this time there were 1,022 cases; between 1st October and 14th October 55 new cases were notified; the number reported during the period 14th and 30th October was 7.

After eliminating in turn insanitary housing conditions, contamination of the soil by the sewerage work then in progress, and foodstuffs such as ice-cream, shellfish and milk as possible sources of pollution, Dr Farrar concluded that the basic cause was water-borne infection. Pointing out that the epidemic affected all classes in the community, all ages over 5, every class of home and almost every part of the town, he stated his conclusion that 'such an incidence points strongly to impartially distributed infection which, in a town provided with a public water-supply, contaminated water was only likely to flourish.'

Although chemical analysis of the well water did not indicate 'any good volume of sewerage pollution', microscopic examination revealed 'pollution of organic matter, household refuse, fungus mycelium, cotton-wool fibres, etc.' He looked for a way in which such materials might find their way, not only into the water but into the supply generally. Could they have been washed in by a sudden heavy downpour of rain? Did infiltration occur into water mains fractured by sewerage work? There were instances of mains being broken in this way, but Dr Farrar looked elsewhere for the explanation. He referred to the works which had been taking place in the Basing Road - Reading Road – Goddard's Lane - Gashouse Lane area of the town, and more particularly to the testing of each section of sewer as it was completed. From his enquiries he found that the ultimate cause of the contamination of the supply was the failure of a workman to remove a plug which had been inserted into a manhole at the junction of Goddard's Lane with Reading Road, during the testing period on 29th July. This had remained *in situ* until 1st September, when its existence was discovered by the Borough Surveyor on return from his holiday. The effect of the plug had been to 'pond back' sewage in the lower part of the Reading Road sewer and in drains connected with it. The plug did not fit tightly. The result was a slow seepage into a storm-water sump at the rear of Steam Mill Terrace. From there it percolated into the chalk and so into the town well, situated only about 50 yards away.

Dr Webb's Report

The publication of Dr Farrar's report had been preceded, a fortnight earlier, by the report of Dr Frere Webb, the Medical Officer of Health for Basingstoke, to the Corporation. Whereas Dr Farrar concerned himself with events immediately connected with the outbreak, Dr Webb wished to show that the cause of the epidemic could be found further back in time, and more particularly that it need never have occurred if the Corporation had taken sufficient notice of his advice. To do so, he drew on the contents of annual reports which he had made to the Corporation over a number of years, especially from 1894 onwards. It can be seen that he had consistently warned of the liability to pollution of the town's water supply, but his warnings had not been heeded. In fact, it appears to have been in his report of March 1891 that he first mentioned the danger to the health of the town. His description of the Dell, with its four pig-sties, a large heap of manure and a quantity of rubbish, 'all foul and improper', and with the natural drainage towards the town well, which he described as 'the most important place in the whole town', showed that there was a high degree of risk of contamination by percolation.

In October 1894, samples of water from the well were sent for analysis. One was said to have 'a high degree of organic purity showing not the slightest admixture of rain or surface water, apart from slight turbidity.' Later on, the same month, however, another sample was found to be 'highly polluted with organic matter, a considerable amount of which is of animal origin.' Arising out of this report, an emergency meeting of the Council took action to reduce the risk to health in giving warning of the need to boil all water required for domestic use and to arrange to have one of the headings of the well blocked off.

In April 1895, Dr Webb, reporting on an outbreak of scarlet fever, said that he could find no possible cause other than contamination of the water-supply. In January 1896, we find him reporting, 'Boiling of water had saved the town from a serious visitation.' In November 1897, we read of 'the false security the town has been living under.' His report becomes more strongly critical of the Council, reference is made to 'the total disregard of all warnings, their absolute distrust of the results of analyses and their failure to take decisive action.' In fairness to the Water Supply Committee it must be said that analyses of water from the well did not consistently provide convincing evidence of pollution.

In his report for 1903, Dr Webb describes the well as being 'in an improper position'. It is here that he mentions a site on the north side of the Loddon Valley as being the best that could be chosen for a new well. This appears to the first reference to the West Ham site, later selected as the location for the new waterworks.

The Corporation cannot have been too pleased to be reminded of their shortcomings in such terms as: 'I have copied all this out from my report, so that the public may see the amount of difficulty and trouble I had to get the Council to take even the faintest interest in maintaining the purity of the supply. My fears were deemed unnecessary . . . I was complacently regarded as a water pollution fanatic, but my warning has come only too true. The book containing these reports appeared before you every month they were written since 1894, so that any of you could have seen the dangerous state the town supply was in, and how that since 1894 we have been expecting and vainly looking for the new supply which never came.' He concluded, 'It behoves you to bestir at once, to cease at the very earliest moment the use of water from this ever-polluted well, lay mains from your new well to the nearest point of your present service and supply the town from the new well, the water of which is unquestionable.'

In accepting Dr Webb's report, the Mayor commented that it contained much that required thinking about. He was sure that all would recognize that it had involved an immense amount of work by Dr Webb. The townspeople and the Corporation would be thankful to him for producing such an exhaustive report. Alderman Powell, Chairman of the Water Supply Committee said that a meeting would be convened to consider what still remained to be done. It was important that any outstanding work should be done so as to ensure that further contamination could not occur.

'No infection from the air'

Although during October 1905, there was a decline in the numbers affected by the typhoid outbreak, mainly because householders were advised, by public notice, of the need to boil water before use, the outbreak continued to affect the town. It was still necessary, on 24th November, to announce that 'An analysis of the town's water received on the 21st November proves it to be full of the more dangerous ingredients, dangerous alike to life and health.' Now householders were told that they should insist on thorough boiling of water used 'for any purpose whatever'. It was only after the reservoir and mains had been disinfected on 2nd to 4th December that the water supply could be declared free of pollution.

Although Dr Farrar reported to the Local Government Board and Dr Webb to the Corporation, no official public enquiry was held, and no attempt was made to allocate blame. However, although the Corporation disclaimed any responsibility for the 16 victims who died, they did pay compensation in two cases. Two widows, with the assistance of the Methodist Minister, the Rev. Barnes, sued the Council for £600 each. They were eventually awarded £150 each.

At their meeting on 15th December, members of the Council were told that the Health Committee had considered charging the typhoid patients for their hospital treatment. One of the Public Health Acts gave them the power to do so, but, following the policy adopted by other places, for example, Maidstone and Worthing, under similar circumstances, it was decided that no charge should be made.

The impact of the outbreak on the local community can be seen in reports of the reactions of different people. The Mayor thought it advisable to state at a Council meeting, reported under the heading 'No infection in the air' that people could come in from the country to shop, without any risk of catching the disease. The management of Messrs Thornycroft complained that the Corporation had failed to take proper precautions over the outbreak; the company had suffered loss and inconvenience owing to the absence of so many men from work. The Rev. J C Tarbolton, Minister of the Congregational Church, preached a sermon 'Is the typhoid a judgement on the town?' A letter from Lieutenant Crichton Maitland, R.N. (of Bolton Lodge) asked who should be blamed for the outbreak. The writer went through a list of those who in their various ways and in varying degrees might have had some responsibility. He concluded, 'Finally, are we ratepayers ever to know who is to blame? Are we to see our money mis-spent and incompetent persons receiving our support? Are we to continue to live under a cloud as to our safety in the future, due to such incompetence? If so, it is time to leave Basingstoke and let it wallow in its own corruption.' His letter ended on a more optimistic note: 'On the other hand, if the public is taken into confidence, blame awarded, future safety assured, under new and unbiased conditions, there is no reason why Basingstoke should not recover its former prosperous condition.'

Mid-Southern Water *[See up-date]*

Since 1906, when the waterworks at West Ham were officially opened, the town has been provided with a reliable source of water from boreholes there. In 1990, the average daily volume of water supplied was 4 million gallons. Four reservoirs form part of the distribution system. They are situated in Darlington Road (since 1886), at Cliddesden (since 1920), at Whitedown (since 1970) and at Ellisfield (since 1977).

The Basingstoke Borough Council sold the water undertaking to the Mid-Wessex Water Company in 1960. The Mid-Wessex merged with the Wey Valley Water Company in 1970 to form the Mid-Southern Company, supplying water to an area which extends from Maidenhead in the north to Petersfield in the south, from west of Basingstoke to the east of Aldershot.

Drains

'The drains of the borough demand our attention. They might be much better, might even be worse. But my doleful constituents desire me to mention that the drain they most dread is the drain on their purse.'

Un-named councillor quoted by Councillor Allnutt at a meeting held in January 1904, about the Basingstoke Corporation Bill.

With effect from February 1873, the Urban Sanitary Authority took over the public health duties for which the Paving and Lighting Commissioners had previously been responsible. It was to be some time before there was clear evidence that the Authority had decided to take any action.

Early in 1878 (26th January), however, there was a reference in the recently founded *Hants & Berks Gazette* to the acceptance of a tender to carry out a drainage scheme 'within the next nine months'. The names of two firms were mentioned, Small (of Gloucester) and Hookway (of Bideford). The contract went to Small, with another firm, Laidlaw (of Glasgow) supplying the pipes and the necessary pumping machinery. The *Gazette* provided a platform for protest: 'Is it possible that our good friends in authority have actually sanctioned and settled the contract for this wild pumping scheme! Can nothing be done to reverse a decision so disastrous to smaller ratepayers? Is there no spirit in this old town to agitate against this enormous outlay, ere it be too late?'

It is not known when the contractor started work, but, by 25th March, 1878, it was being reported that it had already begun at the site of the pumping station in Basing Road. By the middle of the year (29th June), 'no small inconvenience' was being caused by the fact that pumping that was taking place in connection with the laying of pipes, was lowering the levels of water in householders' wells. The Mayor was 'waited on' with a request that he should see what could be done to alleviate the situation.

In July, the Works Committee was told that only slow progress was being made with the work. The Contractor blamed two months of indifferent weather, with the additional difficulty that the workmen had struck for higher wages. However, he said he wished to press ahead with the work and would hope to employ more men. In September it was reported that 'astonishing' progress was being made with the drainage. By this time work was taking place in Church Street 'from below the parish church upwards.' In October the borough surveyor, reviewing the previous seven months as a whole, said that progress had been unsatisfactory.

It was apparent that there had been a serious underestimation by the contractor of the amount of work involved and consequently of the cost of carrying it out. He had not anticipated the difficulties that would be caused by the large volume of soil water, particularly in the lower part of the town, the valley of the Loddon. He argued that no contractor could have foreseen this.

Matters were brought to a head in a letter, dated 8th October, from Mr Small to the Corporation. The Drainage Committee considered it at its meeting that month. The gist of the letter was that the firm would be unable to continue the drainage owing to the excessive costs it had incurred through extra work in pumping and laying overflow and sub-soil drains. The Committee were being unreasonable in not voting 'a liberal sum for the extra work.' The firm also complained that persons had communicated with firms supplying materials, suggesting that it was unwise to do business with Mr Small. Mr Rowell, the Corporation Engineer, proposed that the firm be given three days' notice, after which the work would be continued by the Corporation itself, under the supervision of the Drainage Committee, the Engineer and the Clerk of Works.

In the course of discussion the members agreed that it had been wrong to employ Mr Small for such a large contract, worth in all about £12,000. The facts of the situation contrasted strikingly with the glowing account they had received about the competence of the firm. It was decided that the Corporation itself should take over from Mr Small and that the Drainage Committee should have the power 'to draw on the treasurer for such sums as may be required for the carrying out of the sewerage work.' This was on the understanding there would be greater care in overseeing the work done and that 'a good account of all transactions' should be made.

By 24th May, 1879, it appears that the laying of the main sewer for the town had almost been completed. It was also reported that the Drainage Committee had visited the pumping station to watch for the first movements of the engine recently placed there.

In November, the Drainage Committee reported, rather optimistically, that the work was drawing to a close. There had been serious difficulties, mainly to do with the large volume of water that had to be disposed of. Two parts of the town, both in the valley of the river, had been problem areas. The appropriately named Noah's Island was even more deserving of this name; it suffered from having too much water. The residents of Bunnian Place, described by Dr Webb as 'a comparatively crowded section of the community', complained that pumping operations elsewhere were interfering with the supply of water from their wells.

By February 1880, the work had so far progressed that the Medical Officer of Health was able to report to the Urban Sanitary Authority that, despite all the upset caused by the drainage works, the gloomy forecasts of likely ill effects on the health of the town had been proved wrong. 132 homes, roughly one tenth of the inhabited houses of the town, had been connected to the sewerage system. This was regarded as very satisfactory, given the unfavourable circumstances. Pumping continued to 'inconvenience' some parts of the town. The water supply maintained 'its wonted high state of purity'. Hopes were being expressed that 'speedily the mischief will be repaired and the connection generally commenced', the mischief being the need to replace defective portions of the main sewer in Brook Street. The year ended with some small disagreement about who was responsible for connecting homes to the sewers. One local builder, claiming that the regulations did not make this clear, thought that it should be done by the town's tradesmen. The view of the Corporation was that it should do the work itself, so as to ensure a thoroughly uniform system.

Progress was not rapid enough for Dr Webb, as we can judge from his report to the Public Health Committee of the County Council in 1900: 'It is understood that the Council are about to take into consideration supplying the WCs of over 800 cottages in the town with water. It is earnestly hoped that they will do so. The necessity has been urged in each annual report for years ... This matter cannot be fully gone into in a public report, but it thought that the Council can have no idea of the indecency that the lack of water entails.'

Meanwhile, because the existing sewage farm, described as being 'on the top of the chalk hill between the two railways', increasingly failed to measure up to the demands made on it, consideration was being given to a new scheme of sewage disposal. At the same time the Council were looking for a new source of water. In 1887 the idea was put forward that the two should be combined together on the site of the sewage pumping station in Basing Road. The well here, having been tested, had been found to provide a reliable yield of water of satisfactory purity. The committee charged with making recommendations had visited a number of towns, to see how they were dealing with the matter. One of the places visited was Salisbury, where they were able to see, on the estate of Mr F M E Jervoise at Britford, the effluent running directly into the stream (the River Avon), 'with no nuisance, so far as your committee can learn, arising therefrom.' The proposal was that the River Loddon should be used in the same way, if implemented, the combined scheme would result in the 'saving of some hundreds of pounds per annum in perpetuity.'

In considering this as a possible solution to their problem, the Corporation appear to have disregarded the likely reaction of their near neighbours down stream at Basing. They were unwise to do so. At a public meeting held at Basing on 12th December, 1887, with Lord Bolton in the chair, this 'injurious proposal' was discussed. After some reference to the existing method of treatment - at the sewage farm in Swing-Swang Lane at Basing - it was shown that the new scheme would involve 'irrigating the land with sewage'. The effluent would enter the Loddon 'in a more or less purified condition'! It was pointed out that the proposed scheme would infringe the Pollution of Rivers Act of 1876; it would be prejudicial to the health of Basing and the inmates of the workhouse; it would also depreciate the value of the surrounding land, which would otherwise be of great value for building purposes, and of the house and landed property generally in the village of Old Basing. Those present thought it incumbent upon them to use every means to prevent the adoption of this very injurious suggestion. They were supported in their objection by the Duke of Wellington and others living downstream. It was agreed that a 'Memorial' should be sent to the Local Government Board requesting that it should withhold its consent. This would effectively mean that the Corporation would be unable to obtain the necessary loan sanction and so would not be able to proceed with the scheme.

Opposition came from within the town itself. This was made evident at a meeting of ratepayers on 4th February, 1888. The main objection put forward was that the well at the sewage pumping station was 'not a desirable source of water, particularly since increased pumping would be likely to increase seepage into the well from the surrounding land.' This was described as consisting of 'low-lying meadows, generally saturated, and frequently overflowing with water.' It should be remembered that the proposal was to allow gravitational flow of effluent on to this area of land, shown on the 6 inch Ordnance Survey map as 'liable to floods'. (It now forms Eastrop Park, through which the River Loddon flows an altered course, linking new artificial water features.) Technical advice was available from Mr Latham, a civil engineer. He, having carried out his own investigation of the locality, gave the meeting a 'cost-benefit' analysis of the scheme. He came down on the side of those opposing it - it was quite impossible 'geologically situated as they were, to shut out impurities from the proposed well. He would ask them, as prudent men, was it right to make the waterworks in the very sink of the town?' The meeting resolved that the Local Government Board be requested not to consent to the proposed scheme.

A week later, the local paper, under the headline 'Collapse of Sewerage and Water Scheme', reported the Local Government inquiry into the proposal. The Corporation tried to make out a case for the new scheme, but, in the opinion of the Inspector, they were not able to produce sufficiently convincing evidence of the inadequacy of the existing sewage farm. The Local Government Board was unwilling to recommend any change where a scheme appeared likely to be successfully opposed in Parliament. Both sides of the argument were well served by technical experts, but the opposition to the Corporation's proposal was too strong, consisting as it did of local landowners, the Lords Basing and Bolton; the overseers, churchwardens and waywardens of Sherfield-on-Loddon and Stratfield Saye parishes; the Board of Guardians (for the Workhouse); and the Royal Sanitary Society. The ratepayers added their already clearly-expressed opposition.

Realising that they were most unlikely to get approval for their scheme, the Corporation requested an adjournment of the inquiry. Following a short consultation in the Council Chamber, the Town Clerk announced the abandonment of the scheme.

On 17th March, there was a meeting of Basing residents, to hear a report on the public inquiry. Reference was made to the 'overthrowing' of the scheme, which would have done 'a great injury to those who dwelt in Basing.' There were cheers when it was announced that 'the River Loddon was still, as might it long remain, a pure stream.' This was contradicted by someone, presumably anxious to ensure the accuracy of the record, who pointed out the inhabitants of the village were themselves polluters of the river. The general feeling of the meeting, was that, although there was 'much to rejoice over', there was also 'something to regret'. It was wrong to be fighting one's friends and neighbours. Applause followed the statement that 'The prosperity of these two places would never be helped forward by the placing of a sewage farm between the two in the valley of the Loddon.'

Wildmoor

The original sewage farm on Swing-Swang Lane continued in use until April 1967, when new treatment works came into operation at Wildmoor, situated on the eastern side of the Reading Road (A33) north-east of Chineham. The effluent, treated to the very high standard set by the Thames Conservancy Board, is discharged into the Loddon down-stream of Basing. Wildmoor also became the site of a new refuse incinerator completed in 1969. Previously, refuse for disposal and destruction was collected at the Town Yard in Basing Road, which was also the site of the original sewage pumping station, equipped with its 'handsome steam-driven beam engine'.

EDITORIAL UPDATE

Further consolidation in the water supply industry has produced the much larger South East Water Company that now supplies the town area. Thames Water operates the sewage treatment works, discharging into the River Loddon at Wildmoor. There is concern currently in some quarters that the growth of population and the associated housing and employment requirements, unless reined in, will outstrip the capacity of these utilities unless considerable infrastructure investment is made.

Also at Wildmoor is one of the County's main refuse incinerators. It is on the site of the incinerator built at the beginning of the town development. That was closed later because it did not meet modern standards. There was considerable local opposition to its reopening after a multi-million pound upgrading. 8 megawatts of electricity are fed into the National Grid from the energy recovered from the incinerated waste.

Having considered specific areas of civic responsibility in detail, the next two chapters step back in time to take a wider view of the small market town with an agricultural base, its natural growth and its evolution into a small manufacturing town.

13   THE SMALL MARKET TOWN

The town is represented to be gradually increasing in size and importance. It contains no manufacturing but is a place of very great thoroughfare and is situated in the centre of a rich agricultural district. The markets held here are well attended, being resorted to by persons from Andover, Winchester, Newbury and Reading.

Report of Royal Commission. Municipal Corporation Boundaries, England and Wales 1837

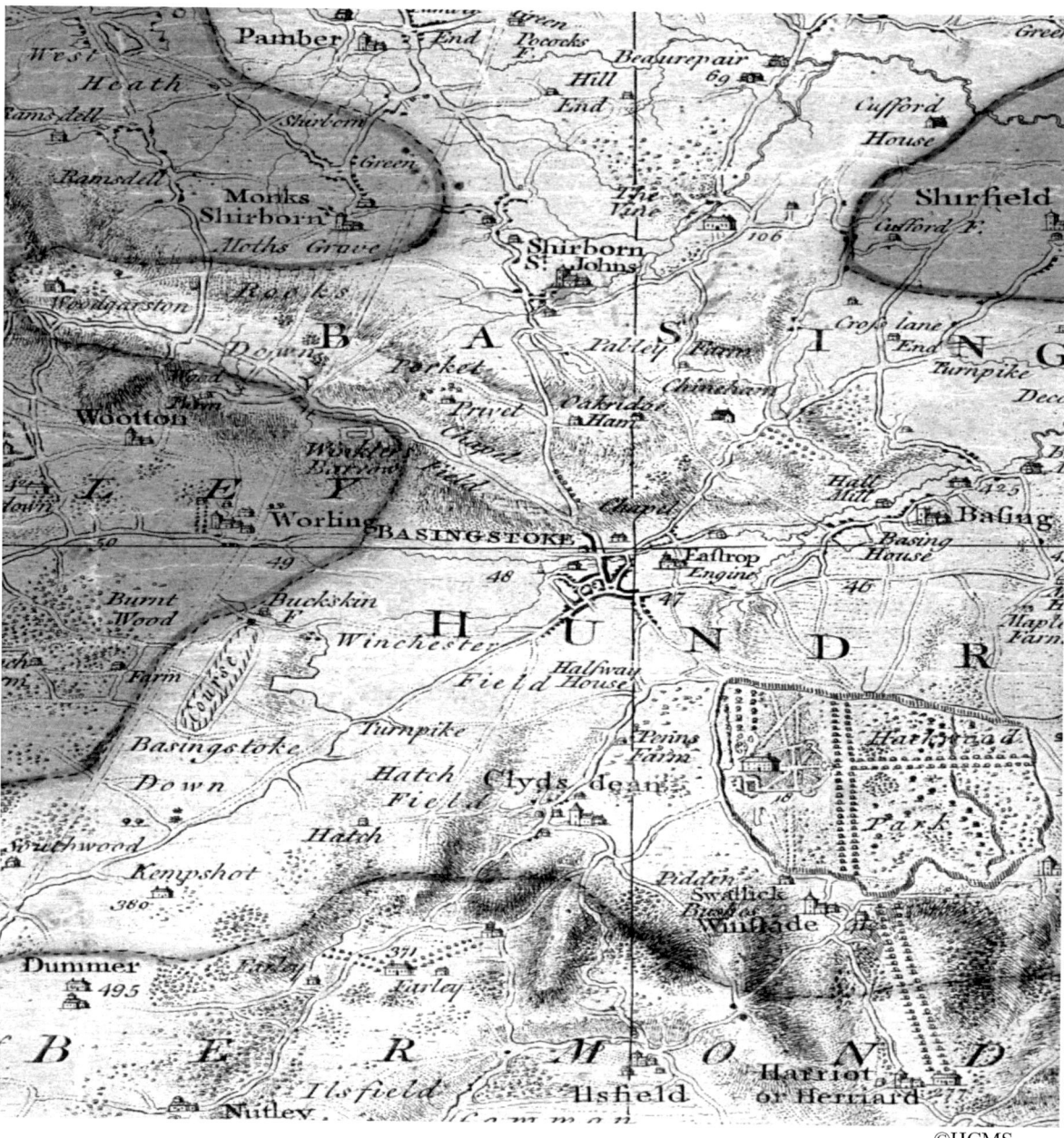

©HCMS

An extract from Isaac Taylor's 1759 1 inch map of Hampshire
This is one of the first maps to show a reasonably accurate plan of the layout of the streets

[If this map and the map on the next page are compared it can be seen that the growth of the town was slow, mainly by infilling.]

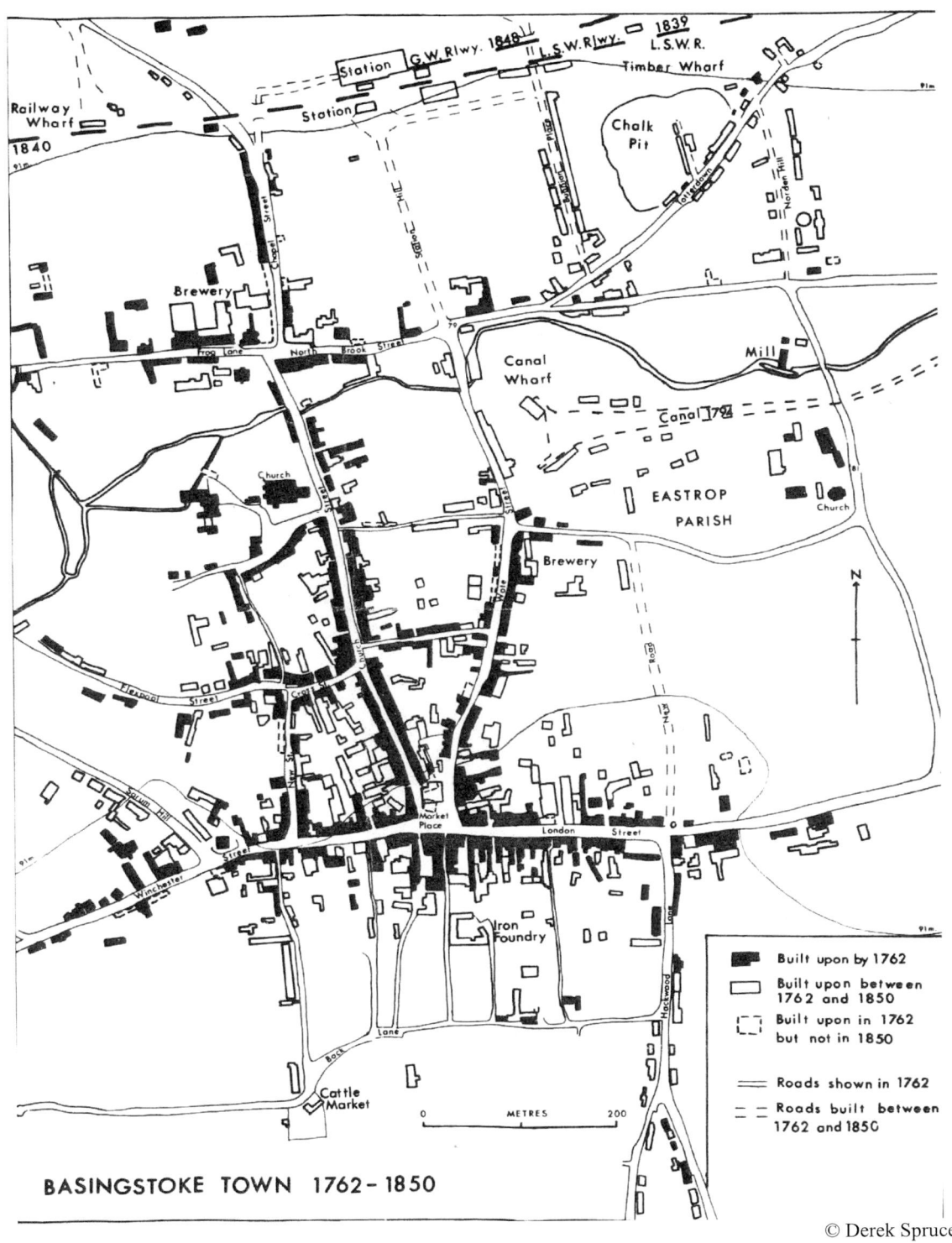

Map showing the development of Basingstoke between 1762 and 1850

The importance of agriculture

When the Commissioners came to look into the 'state' of Basingstoke in 1834, (in order to prepare their recommendations for the reform of local government), they found a small town serving as a market and shopping centre for the surrounding countryside and providing such services as would not be found in the villages round about. Although large 'manufactories', such as those characterising the industrial north of England, were absent, various forms of manufacturing were carried on. Assuming that the area which the town served was formed by the civil parishes making up the Basingstoke Registration District, it was in 1801 a central place for a population of nearly 10,000 people, of which the town contributed about 2,600. By 1841, the same area had a population of over 14,000, the town contributing 4,066 to the total. By 1901, the area's population had reached nearly 19,000; the town's population was then about 9,500.

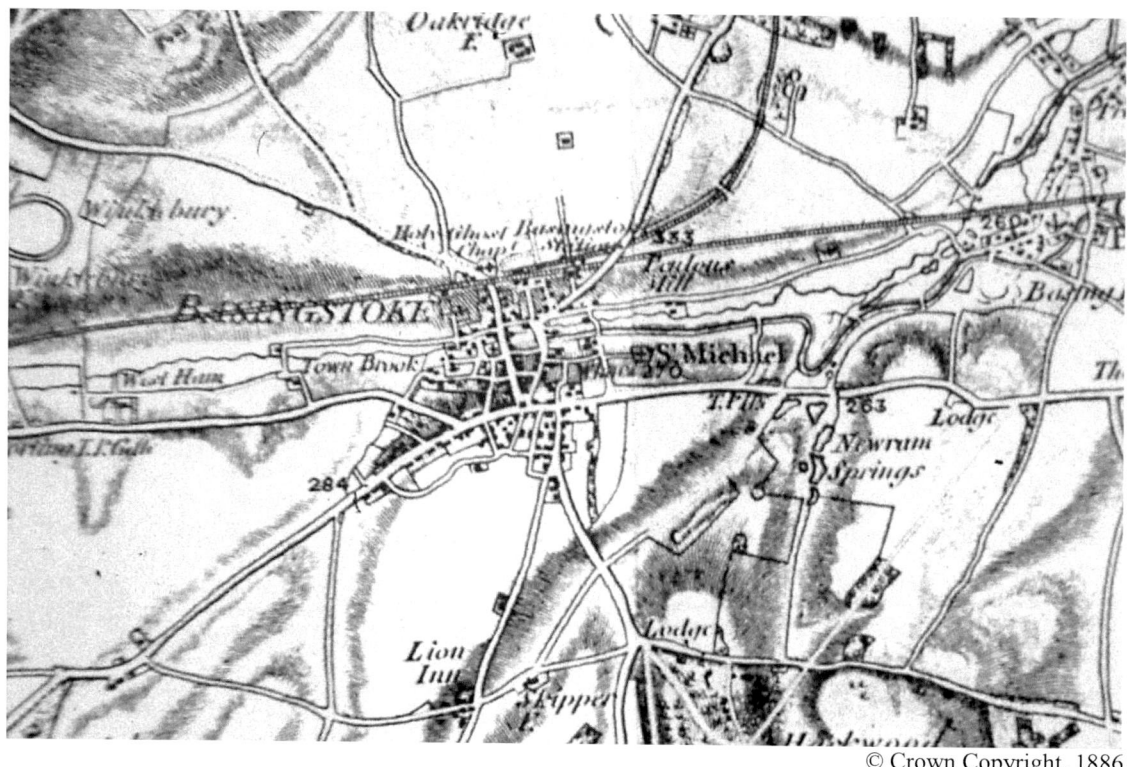

© Crown Copyright, 1886
Photo: Mary Oliver

An extract from the 1886 O.S. map

[This O.S. map is the 1817 map with later additions, particularly the railways. It does not necessarily give an accurate representation of the town in 1886 (May Street is not shown). The Municipal Corporations Boundaries Commission map of 1836 (See page 123) shows exactly the same town area.

Note the position of a church marked **St Michael** *in Eastrop parish. Can this be correct? St Michael's church is shown in the correct position in Church Street but is not named. However, St Mary's Eastrop is not shown. According to the records a chapel did exist roughly in the position marked, but it had been deconsecrated and demolished by the time of the commission; Eastrop farm is noted in this position on later maps. See the section on St Mary's in Chapter 17.]*

The only resource of the district was the land, and so the greater part of the town's economic activity was dependent on the basic land-use - agriculture. Around the town were the estates of large landowners; for example, the Chutes at The Vyne, the Jervoises at Herriard, the Portsmouths, with their farms large and small. There were also farms within the borough; three of these, now largely built over - Buckskin, South Ham and Viables - give their names to parts of the south-western sector of the town. Lord Bolton at Hackwood was another important landowner, as were also Winchester College and Merton College, Oxford. Deep Lane and Glebe farms formed part of the 600 acres farmed by members of the May family, who described themselves as 'brewsters, maltsters and farmers'. They became the leading brewers in the town. Other brewing concerns were those of Thomas and Henry Downs,

Edward and Robert Barrett (later Barrett and Hindes), the Pentons and Edward Adams. The extensive arable lands of the district, as described by Abraham and William Driver (1794) and by Caird (1850) provided the raw material for both brewing and milling. Henry Portsmouth was both farmer and miller; his mill was at Eastrop, near the site of the present Eastrop roundabout. Not far away, downstream towards Basing, was another mill at Vince's Farm.

The farmers of the district were able to represent their views through membership of the Basingstoke branch of the Winchester Farmers' Club or through *ad hoc* bodies formed for specific purposes, for example, to protest at the levying, in 1850, of market dues which they had hitherto not been called upon to pay (Chapter 6). They also came together in meetings of the North Hants Agricultural Society. At their annual general meetings, it was the custom for members to award prizes to their employees in various categories. One of these was for 'married men who have brought up respectably the largest family with the least parochial relief' (a reminder that the wages of farm workers often fell short of what was necessary for bringing up a family). Another category was 'length of well-conducted employment with one employer.' The notice of the 1841 meeting mentioned the availability of a satisfactory sum of money for distribution among 'shepherds and other meritorious labourers.' The notice continued rather condescendingly, saying that the prizes were 'a demonstration by those whom Providence had made affluent that they are not regardless of the comfort and necessities of the honest and industrious peasantry.'

Making use of timber transported in from the wooded areas round about, Edwin White, originally from the village of Greywell, carried on a sawmilling business at the Wharf, where he produced sawn timber for a variety of uses. There were occasional sales of timber here; in October 1850, 50 good, useful elms and seven oaks, were on offer.

Engineering

Machinery of various kinds was increasingly required by farmers. This need was met locally by the important firm of Wallis and Haslam, later Wallis and Steevens. The Wallis family came originally from Reading, where they had been in business as farmers and corn merchants. Before moving in 1856 to a site at the junction of Station Hill and Basing Road - the North Hants Ironworks, the firm had a foundry in Caston's Yard. This had previously been owned by George Caston, who in 1834 had taken a leading part in providing the town with a gasworks (Chapter 10). General engineering was carried on by John Hale and also by Mills and Watson, millwrights (of Totterdown, Reading Road). Another business in the engineering field was that of John Burgess Soper, 'engineer, gun-maker and ironmonger.' His business was to prosper, as the town became provided with a piped water-supply and as the sewerage system was slowly extended.

Coachbuilding

The town's function as a 'thoroughfare' provided the need and the opportunity for the provision of maintenance and repair facilities for horse-drawn vehicles. Joel Passmore had his workshop in London Street; Thomas Dyer and John Fencot also described themselves as coachbuilders. The former had his business in Winton Square; the latter employed 12 men and 2 boys in Old Crown Yard (Joice's Yard). As can be seen, they were all well placed along the busy route through the town. Good custom for new vehicles would have come from the gentry of the neighbourhood as well as from the tradesmen of the town.

[In the early 1880s, the exact date is uncertain, John Joice established his coachbuilding business in Old Crown Yard. This became the major coachbuilding business in the town. In 1888 he bought a much larger business in Staines. (Freeman, M D, 1972).]

Photo: © R Applin

An example of a Joice gig in Milestones Museum

Trades and businesses

We have seen in Chapter 6 the part played by the market and by fairs in the economic life of the town. A large number of shops, some of which had workshops attached, also existed to meet the requirements of town and country customers. Many shops were providers of food and drink. Distinct from the inns and taverns were the large number of beerhouses. Among the retailers of beer were Edward Adams, (the name Adams was to become better known in the 1880s at the time of the Salvation Army Riots, see Chapter 17); Thomas Goodall, Thomas Leavey and John Hacker, who also performed the duties of night watchman and town crier! There were numerous bakers/confectioners as well as grocers. Perhaps the best-known of the latter were George Franklin and George Gibbs, both of whom regularly received some of their goods from London via the Canal. The more important bakers/confectioners were Joseph Hunt, William and James Moody, William Penton and James Poulter.

Among the businesses concerned with the sale of clothing was one owned by Mr J Tubb. His shop was in London House, Church Street. In 1841 he told 'the nobility, gentry and the public generally' that he had been highly flattered by their custom and that because of 'the daily increase of his business' he had decided to turn over part of his house to the sale of various goods. He said that he received weekly supplies of 'novelties of the season, Parisian costumes of the newest design, every description of table linen, Leghorn, Tuscany and Dunstable bonnets, gentlemen's summer hats, waistcoats, etc.' He offered 5s. rebate on all parcels of £5 upwards.

Better known in the clothing trade and eventually serving a much wider market was Thomas Burberry, who started his business in the town some time before 1859. He was later to go into clothing manufacture. Eventually he would be known in particular for the waterproof raincoat known as a 'Burberry'. We are told that 'when this tradesman established himself in the town some years ago, without signs of pretentious demonstration, he providently secured premises eminently suitable and capable of expansion.' The newspaper account of 19th April, 1879 added that the business took 'astonishing strides', so much so that more space had to be found. Later he transferred 'the general manufacturing side of the trade' to two of his employees, Mr Gerrish and Mr Ames. In this way, a new factory, described as 'a steam factory for making workingmen's clothes' was opened on Station Hill in 1878, the new firm taking the name Gerrish, Ames and Simpkins. He retained the made-to-measure side of his business but later disposed of it to Mr Mares, so that he could concentrate on the manufacture of gabardine cloth. In 1892 a new Burberry factory was opened in London Street, where the firm's tailoring business had been carried on. The buildings in Winchester Street where the firm was founded were badly damaged by fire in April 1905. Mr Burberry, a true entrepreneur, was not deterred by this. The site was redeveloped into a shop selling a wide variety of goods, thoroughly deserving of the name 'emporium' by which it was known. Burberry, and its two offshoot firms were, of course, large employers of women workers.

White's Gazetteer for 1859 lists thirteen 'firms' under the heading 'Boot and shoe makers'. One of these - that of Alfred Milward - was to achieve a more than local importance and eventually grew into a business with many branches throughout Southern England and South Wales. The business was founded in 1857, with boots and shoes being made by hand in small premises situated in Church Street. Later Mr Milward decided to increase his business by selling to his customers in their homes. He acquired a hawker's licence and began making regular calls on 'the Clergy, Gentry and Inhabitants generally of Basingstoke and its vicinity', carrying with him, in his horse-drawn cart a selection from a stock of boots and shoes from 'some of the largest Wholesale Shoe Houses in England', as stated by the handbill advertising his business. (Hampshire Museums & Archives Service)

Another well-known businessman was Robert Cottle. A native of Taunton, he had come to the town early in the century and had set up in business as a stationer and bookseller. In 1841 we find him selling copies of the inaugural address of the Mechanics' Institute, printed and published by himself. His name also occurs frequently as printer of public notices put out by the Corporation. From 1814 until his death in 1859 he held the position of Post-Master. Outside his shop was the town's only post-box, a fact which cannot have been without some advantage to his business generally!

[His billheads show his shop and the post-box which is now in the Willis Museum. His shop is shown as property 8 in Winchester Street on the 1851 Archer Davis Map, also in the Willis Museum. The Liten Tree now occupies the site; however, the upper part of the building is still recognisably Cottle's.]

Canal transport enabled cargoes to be moved in greater bulk and at lower rates. Coal was one commodity which constantly became cheaper. The coming of the railway reduced the cost of transport even further. One business to benefit was that of Mr Richard Wallis, who traded in coal and corn. His premises were in Wote Street and at the railway station. An advertisement dated 13th December, 1841, giving details of the various grades of coal he had on offer, reads as follows:

> Best 32s. per ton; seconds 27s.; best Welsh culm 38s.; anthracite 40s.;
> coke 45s. per ton.
>
> All prices cash.

Frederick Bushell, George Etheridge and Henry Jesse also carried on business as corn, coal and/or timber merchants.

The professions

Of course, the town also had its professional men - its doctors and solicitors. They provided a service to town and country people, as did also those who set themselves up as bankers. In the early part of the 19th century banking was still essentially a local affair, where associations of local business and professional men, (frequently solicitors) were prepared to act as lenders of money. Messrs Raggett, Graham, Seymour and Co (giving their address as the Market Place) was one such company, in 1808. The partners changed over time. In 1840 it was known by the names Cole, Seymour, Lamb, Brook and Hillier. By about 1859 it had become the Basingstoke and Odiham Bank. In 1864 it was absorbed into the Hampshire Banking Company, which later became the Hampshire and North Wiltshire Banking Company. Further amalgamation in 1879 produced the Capital and Counties Bank, the name that was still in use in 1915. Banking services were also provided by the London and County Banking Company. Although its address in 1859 is given as Winchester Street, by about 1880 it is shown as being on the site which today is occupied by the NatWest Bank in London Street. Indeed, its name appears in 1915 as London, County and Westminster Bank Limited. It is interesting to record that the Basingstoke Corporation borrowed from Messrs Raggett and Co £300 in 1816 and £200 in the following year. The town also had a thriving savings bank, which in 1841 had just over 1,000 depositors, detailed as: 'Friendly and charitable societies 34; petty tradesmen 48; mechanics 103; minors 341; servants 355; labourers 124.' Deposits were shown as £140,761 and withdrawals as £97,741. The bank had rather restricted opening hours: in 1859 it was shown as being open on Wednesday, from 11 to 12. The secretary was Joseph Shebbeare, solicitor, who was also the Town Clerk.

A number of medical men (they were all described as surgeons) looked after the health of the town and its district. Among them the more important in the early part of the 19th century, were Thomas Workman, Charles Lyford and Charles Covey. Besides providing treatment and care for their own patients, they also shared responsibility for the 'public health' of the town, there being as yet no office of Medical Officer of Health. Between them they were supposed to care not only for poor people resident in the town, but also for travellers. One reason for this was that there was a real fear of the spread of epidemic diseases such as smallpox and cholera. In April 1817 a dispute arose between the above-named and the Vestry (still responsible for meeting the cost through the poor rate). The medical men wanted to limit their services to the poor of Basingstoke, for which they asked the sum of £105 per year. The Vestry's reply was directly to the point, the doctors would be expected to provide services to the poor, including the itinerant poor, for an annual remuneration of £90 per year.

No serious attempt was made to improve the public health of the town until much later on. The Ballard report of 1871 (Chapter 10) pointed out what was necessary, but it was a very long time before anything was done to set matters right, in respect of water-supply and sewerage.

Ancillary to the doctors were those who carried on the business of chemist/druggist: Frederick Blunden, Robert Hulbert and Robert Meatyard. There appears to have been no-one resident in the town who described himself as a dentist; it must be assumed that dental ailments were dealt with by the doctors. However, those who wished to do so could consult a visiting dentist, every Wednesday, at Mr Gibbs, Basingstoke. A notice, advertising the visits of Monsieur Mallam, surgeon-dentist, of London, appeared in the *Hampshire Chronicle* of 10th October, 1840. It was addressed 'To the nobility, gentry and public generally of Basingstoke and its vicinity.'

There was obviously a demand for legal services in the town; much business would come from local businessmen; much also from the landed gentry of the neighbourhood. About the middle of the 19th century the more important of the solicitors' partnerships were those of Messrs Lamb, Brooks, Son and Challis, of Winchester Street, Messrs Shebbeare and

Chandler and Messrs Prickett and King, with their offices in Church Street. It was quite usual for a local solicitor to be appointed (elected) to the office of town clerk. This happened in 1821, when Mr William Anthony Lewis, attorney-at-law, was elected 'town clerk and clerk of the peace in the room of James Warne for one whole year or during the time wherein the said James Warne shall be Mayor of the town.' Mr. Lewis later became the first town clerk to the new Corporation established in December 1835.

As would be expected in a town whose economy was closely related to farming, there were a number of auctioneers in business. *White's Directory for Hampshire* for 1859 names five firms of auctioneers/estate agents. Taking one of these, that of Mr Charles Paice, as representative of the type of business carried on, we find that gentleman in 1841 selling property belonging to Mr Charles Lyford, 'removing to a distant county'. In 1849, by auction at the Wharf, Mr Paice sold 'a large quantity of capital book-shelves made especially for a neighbouring mansion and well adapted for fitting-up of offices.' In April of the same year he sold paintings and wine at premises in Winchester Street. The farming side of his business is well shown in the sale in January 1850 of 350 tons of clover hay and meadow hay. The sale notice gives the location of each of 15 lots and adds that 'the hay is well situate for removal, being close to good roads and near the Basingstoke railway station and canal.' Later on in the year we find him selling five 'recently erected and well-built brick and slate dwelling houses with good gardens, remarkably well situated in Bunnian Place.'

The *Hampshire Chronicle* of 21st September, 1850 had a notice, addressed to 'Capitalists, Brewers and others', of a sale by auction of important properties forming the estate of Mr Richard Curtis, innkeeper and farmer. These properties were stated to offer 'most secure and advantageous investment'. The estate was a considerable one, consisting of the Lickpit [Lychpit] Estate and Manor (at Basing); land in Old Castle Field; *The Angel Inn*, 'an hotel of the best repute, doing an extensive trade, with ample accommodation; a capital brewery; stabling for near 100 horses; granaries, barn, farmyard etc.' Included also was *The Black Boy Tavern* (in Church Street), and *The Crown Inn* (in Winchester Street), together with several plots of building land in Basingstoke and also at Cliddesden and Bagshot. The sale notice stressed the suitability of the land at Old Castle Field for building - '15 acres of the best land in the parish.' It was also Mr Paice who advertised for sale 46 acres of building land (this will be described more fully in Chapter 14). The sale notice of March 1851 in the *Hampshire Chronicle* refers to it as deserving the attention of 'a builder who would be able to give a fit display of his ability in a profitable undertaking.' The most important building firm at this time was G B Mussellwhite and Son. Established in 1798, it continued in operation until the 1970s. Another local builder was Robert Nicholls who, in 1861, described himself as 'Auctioneer, Surveyor and Builder'. It was he who built the new Queen Mary's School in Worting Road in 1855. The quickening pace of growth from the 1870s onwards, and more particularly towards the turn of the century, provided plenty of opportunity for the town's building firms, first of all in that part of the town to which the name Newtown was given *[the May Street area]*, and later in the Fairfields area, to the south of the town centre. The initiative in providing houses was taken by local businessmen, including the builders themselves, who saw the provision of housing in a growing town as a profitable investment.

[A large number of original nineteenth century auctioneers' notices can be inspected in the Resources Room at the Willis Museum. Many refer to auctions conducted by Charles Paice, and most were printed by Robert Cottle or by his successor C J Jacob.]

Inns and taverns

Besides the large number of 'businesses' which were described as 'beerhouses', there were those classified in *White's Directory* as 'Inns and Taverns'. The role of some of these - *The Red Lion, The Feathers, The Angel* and *The Wheatsheaf* - has been mentioned in connection with the coaching trade (Chapter 8) *[See appendices 1 & 2 for the location and current name/use of the inns mentioned in this chapter.*] In addition to responding to the requirements of travellers, they were frequently used for meetings, because of the hospitality they could provide. We see them being the venue for gatherings of the parish officers when they met to 'examine intruders', travellers whose presence was not welcome in the town. Auction sales were also held on their premises; in March 1841, *The Angel* was used for the sale by auction of the tolls for the Baughurst and Worting Gate Turnpike. The same venue was also used in June 1849, when houses, a workshop and land belonging to Mr W Glover (plumber, glazier and painter) were put up for auction.

As 'termini' for the services operated by carriers between the town and the surrounding villages, inns formed an integral part of the local transport network. *The Anchor Inn,* at one time known as *The Chequers,* provided a base for services to Ellisfield on Wednesdays and Saturdays (market days). To Upton Grey there was a more frequent service, on four days a week; Mondays, Wednesdays, Fridays and Saturdays. *The Rose* was another inn to and from which carriers operated. A weekly service to Kingsclere, worked by Mr Rolfe, went from there. A similar service went to Odiham from *The Feathers,* which was also the pick-up point for services to Bramley and Whitchurch (on three days each week). From *The Self-Defence* went the service to Monk Sherborne provided by Mr Monger.

Public buildings

Photo of print © R Applin

Basingstoke Old Town Hall

Winchester Street is the road on the left, with Church Street behind the Town Hall. The buildings in the background were also demolished.

Change in the appearance of the town and neighbourhood accompanied the steady growth in population and the gradual increase in the volume of business activities, attributed to 'the improvement of railway facilities.' By 'town' we mean, of course, a relatively small built-up area of about 200 acres, in the north-eastern part of a large parish of about 4,000 acres. Change had begun towards the end of the 18th century, with the enclosure of the open fields (1788) and the completion of the canal (1796), with the Wharf, at 'the bottom of the town'. The enlargement of the Market Place, under an Act of 1829, the erection of the gasworks in 1834 and the coming of the railway in 1839, followed by the link with Reading in 1848, continued the process of growth. New single buildings had appeared, the first of these being two churches, one for the Congregationalists in London Street in 1800, the other in Wote Street for the Countess of Huntingdon's Connexion in 1802.

In 1832, on 20 May, the 'taking-down' of the old Town Hall began. It was replaced by a new building erected on the north side of the enlarged Market Place. In the diary of Samuel Attwood we have an account of the laying of the first stone, on 8th June: 'The first stone of the new Town Hall was laid with great ceremony by J Simmons, Esq. Mayor, attended by the Corporation, several gentry, the Band and a large concourse of spectators – a new sovereign, crown piece, penny, halfpenny and a farthing were deposited in the stone, all new coins of King William.' The new building, which cost in all nearly £10,000, stood on pillars, leaving an open space below, which served as the Corn Exchange. *[See the print on page 52 which shows the new Town Hall as built.]*

Basingstoke Town Hall in 1906.

The clock tower was the gift of Lt. Col. John May to commemorate Queen Victoria's Golden Jubilee. It was taken down as unsafe in 1969. The clock is in the Willis Museum

Photo of Print © R Applin

Besides being used for regulating the affairs of the town, including the administration of justice, the new building was the scene of various other activities - meetings of the North Hampshire Agricultural Society, lectures to the Mechanics' Institute, and the Easter County Balls, which were such a feature of the local social scene.

Until they gained a building of their own in New Street, in October 1869, the members of the Mechanics' Institute held their meetings in the Town Hall. It was here, on 28th March, 1841, that Mr C E Lefroy gave the inaugural address, for which he chose a Biblical text, 'The night cometh when no man can work.' As can be seen in Chapter 18, from the variety of topics dealt with by visiting lecturers, the Basingstoke Institute did its best to meet George Birkbeck's aim, which was that of 'instructing artisans in the scientific principles of arts and manufactures.'

The poor

Poverty was, of course, the lot of many inhabitants of the town. In the 1837 report we are told of the non-rating of one hundred houses, because of the poverty of their inhabitants. A practical demonstration of this can be seen from the fact that it was quite normal for the soup kitchen to be provided at the Town Hall, whenever severe winter weather made it necessary. The *Hampshire Chronicle* of 12th January, 1850 reported the opening of the soup kitchen, 'which, during the last three winters, has proved to be so beneficial to the poor, from which they will be supplied twice a week, with most excellent nutritious soup, at a penny a quart, which, as heretofore, will no doubt be received by a large number of our poor townspeople as an acceptable boon during the inclement season.' The soup was described as being 'prepared according to the formula of preceding years.'

The conditions under which the poorer inhabitants lived left much to be desired. Dr Ballard, in his report of 1871 (Chapter 10), said that, in many places, 'the residences of the poor were totally unfit for human habitation, damp, dilapidated, low and unventilated.' He quoted the example of ten low thatched cottages in Totterdown Dell, the twelve houses making up Ford's Buildings in Brook Street and, on the west side of Church Square, 'a group of cottages newly built - and very badly built, too.' These would have contrasted strikingly with the houses of the more affluent inhabitants such as the one belonging to Mr W A Lewis (solicitor and town clerk). This was advertised for sale in June 1841. It was described as 'a genteel family residence - 5 bedrooms; manservant's room; WC; drawing room 20ft x 16ft; brewhouse with pump of excellent water. A most gentlemanly residence. Convenient for station (London 2 hours).' The houses of Lady Anna Maria Colquhoun (Bramblys House), Richard Wallis (Eastlands) and William Apletree (Goldings) cannot have been any less genteel.

Given the appropriate opportunity, for example, the Michaelmas Fair, the townspeople could give themselves over to enjoying themselves to the full. A special reason for rejoicing presented itself in 1887 with the Golden Jubilee of Queen Victoria. Celebrations, processions, illuminations, feasting and sports took place over two days. On the first day, there was a procession of children from the Sunday Schools in the town. The music was provided by the band of 'K' Company of the 1st Hampshire Rifle Volunteers, and his Worship the Mayor, John May, was on horseback for the occasion. *[Lt Col May was commandant of 'K' Company; he established the Company and provided its Drill Hall at Sarum Hill. (Ray, F 1904)]*

After the procession there was tea for the children at tables outside the Town Hall. The day was rounded off with games and sports on the Common, at the end of which the Mayor called for three hearty cheers for the Queen.

The second day was somewhat similar, except that it was the turn of the grown-ups. The day began with the Mayor's breakfast for members of the Council and the Borough officials. The adults too had their procession: all branches of civic life were represented in a perambulation of the town, which lasted about three-quarters of an hour, ending just before noon. The festal dinner, at which there were no less than 2,500 diners, was eaten at tables set all along London Street and Winchester Street. The day ended, as had the previous one, with sports and games on the Common.

Riots

There were occasions when the word 'riot' was used to describe unruly happenings in the town. The first of these was the local disturbance associated with the agricultural unrest, known as the Swing Riots, which occurred in 1830. We are told that Down Grange Farm was the scene of a disturbance in that year. A mob armed with sticks came demanding money and saying that they were going 'to rise in a body to have their wages risen'. The owner, Cassandra Hankey, gave them money and they went away, but only after they had broken her winnowing machine. Samuel Attwood in his Diary recorded the events of 21st November, 1830 as follows: 'A great number of riotous persons assembled in a disorderly manner, breaking all machines, demanding money and committing robberies. Two hundred special constables sworn in. Military sent for. Nineteenth Lancers arrived. Shops shut in the evening; a number of prisoners brought in and all the town and neighbourhood in confusion.' A public notice gave the names of the 55 rioters who were 'apprehended on 23rd November' Twenty-one were committed to Winchester Gaol; the remaining 34 were discharged after being 'suitably admonished'.

More unrest, which became known as 'the Basingstoke Brawl' occurred 50 years later. This, also called the 'Salvation Army Riots' began with the arrival of the 'Army' in the town in September 1880. Trouble resulted when its strongly pro-temperance mission came into sharp conflict with local brewing (and drinking) interests. Baigent and Millard in their *History of Basingstoke* described the situation in these words: 'The rigid temperance principles of the Salvation Army rendered it obnoxious to those who frequented and to those who had a pecuniary interest in places licensed for the sale of strong liquor.' Those with 'pecuniary interests' such as the Adams brothers, of the Victoria Inn and Brewery, were able to organize 'the ruder class of opponents' with a hostile mob, which came to be known as 'the Massagainians', presumably because they could be persuaded to 'mass again' in protest, whenever called upon to do so.

Sunday, 20th March, 1881 was one day on which there was trouble; it is said that a crowd of about a thousand, two hundred of them armed with sticks and weapons, assembled in the Market Place to oppose the Salvationists. The following Sunday, a mob of about three thousand gathered in Brook Street to threaten members of the 'Army', at their headquarters, a former silk mill. The scale of the disturbances on this occasion was such that the Mayor thought it his duty to read the Riot Act. It so happened that a battery of Horse Artillery was billeted in the town and they were called upon to clear the streets, 'which was very effectually done'. Ten of the participants were charged, convicted and sent to Winchester Gaol. After a few days they were brought back, triumphant, to Basingstoke and were fêted as heroes at a banquet in the Corn Exchange.

[A more detailed account of the 'Basingstoke Brawl' can be found in Arthur Attwood's 'The Illustrated History of Basingstoke' and in the Resources Room of the Museum. The editions of the Hants & Berks Gazette of the time have very full accounts of these disturbances. An account from the Salvation Army viewpoint is given Ken Clement's Two Feeble Women, *(Clements K, undated)]*

Damage by the Massagainians to Hillside, 'Soper's castle', in Vyne Rd.
[Now demolished]

Evolution

If, at the beginning of the 19th century, Basingstoke was the typical small market-town, largely dependent for its prosperity on the health of local agriculture, by the time the century was coming to an end it had already taken on some of the features of a town where manufacturing was to assume the leading role. Its real change in character began when, with the coming of the railway, its hinterland was considerably increased. Further change resulted from the expansion of the firm of Wallis and Steevens, which diversified its business into the manufacture of traction engines for haulage purposes and road rollers, gaining a reputation not only nationally but also internationally, The enterprise of Thomas Burberry and subsequent developments in the clothing trade contributed further to the change in character. The decision of the motor vehicle manufacturer, Thornycroft, to set up its works in the town in 1898 reinforced the move towards more manufacturing.

This trend might have occurred in another way. In the late 1870s, the possibility of the London & South Western Railway establishing a carriage works in the town was being discussed. There were those members of the Council who thought that they should encourage the scheme, arguing that it would promote the well-being of the town; there were others who objected to it on the grounds that it would bring a class of people to the town that would lower its reputation. A letter to the local paper in May 1879 under the heading 'Look ahead, Basingstoke', criticised those in authority in the following terms: 'Had it not been for some of them, we should have the fields between here and Worting covered with houses and railway works, but they, as now, could not see an inch before their eyes and, for fear of the gross immorality that would be introduced into the quiet town of Basingstoke, they opposed in every way the now powerful SW Railway Company having any works here, and to this day the Company have never forgotten it.'

The town's population continued to grow, sometimes achieving a rate of growth nearly twice the national average. By 1901 it had reached 9,793. The provision of housing failed to keep pace with increasing numbers, and concern was expressed that this could have a harmful effect on the future prosperity of the town. This was one more difficulty for the Corporation already pre-occupied with the related problem of ensuring a pure, safe water supply and of providing a sewerage system adequate for the needs of a growing town.

[An article by Jonathan Brown, 'Market Towns and Downland in Hampshire 1780-1914' in Southern History Vol 2, 2006, includes Basingstoke in its area of study. In particular it advances reasons why Winchester, Andover and Basingstoke became the dominant towns of the Hampshire Downlands. These towns grew, at times at the expense of the smaller towns such as Whitchurch and Odiham, because of their geographical positions in relation to trade routes, and especially to the sheep trade. It is a well-researched paper that adds extra dimensions to the contents of this chapter. It has very full notes and list of sources; for serious students it should be on their reading list.]

14 NATURAL GROWTH

Population

In 1801 the population was recorded by the Census as being 2,589 (587 families occupying 501 inhabited houses). Fifty years later it was 4,263; in 1901 it had reached 9,510. By 1961, when its most rapid growth was about to begin, mainly by the reception of overspill population from London, the borough had 16,978 inhabitants; by coincidence, the population of the surrounding Basingstoke Rural District was exactly the same.

The decade 1831-1841 saw the town's population grow from 3,581 to 4,066, giving a rate of increase just under that for England and Wales. It was during this time that the railway line from London to Southampton was completed. A through journey was possible from June 1840 onwards. Although improved communications would eventually contribute considerably to the prosperity of the town and thus encourage further growth, the effect of these was yet to be seen.

The Town area

During the same time (1837) the Commissioners for Municipal Corporation Boundaries reported on the state of the town. Although several new houses had been built 'within the last two or three years on all sides of the town', buildings occupied only a small area (200 acres estimated) in the north-east corner of a large parish of about 4,000 acres.

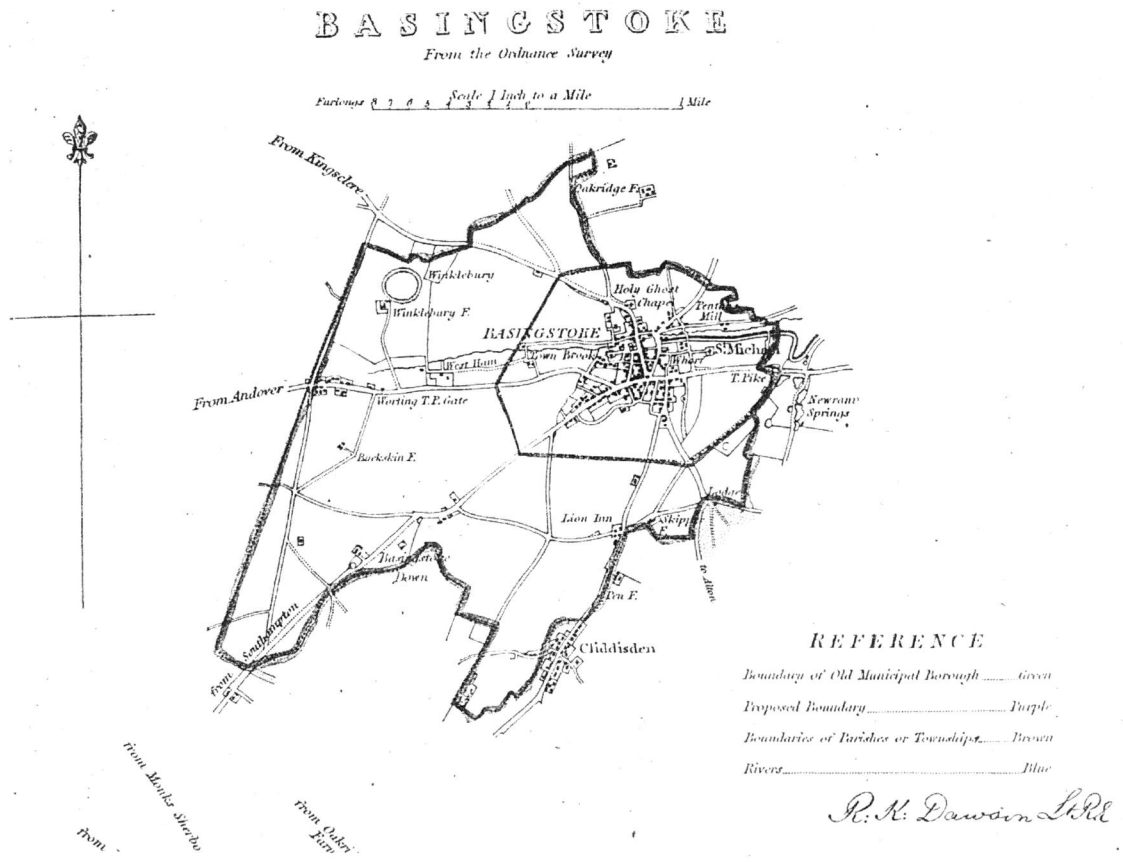

This map was included with the 1837 Boundary Commissioners' report for Basingstoke

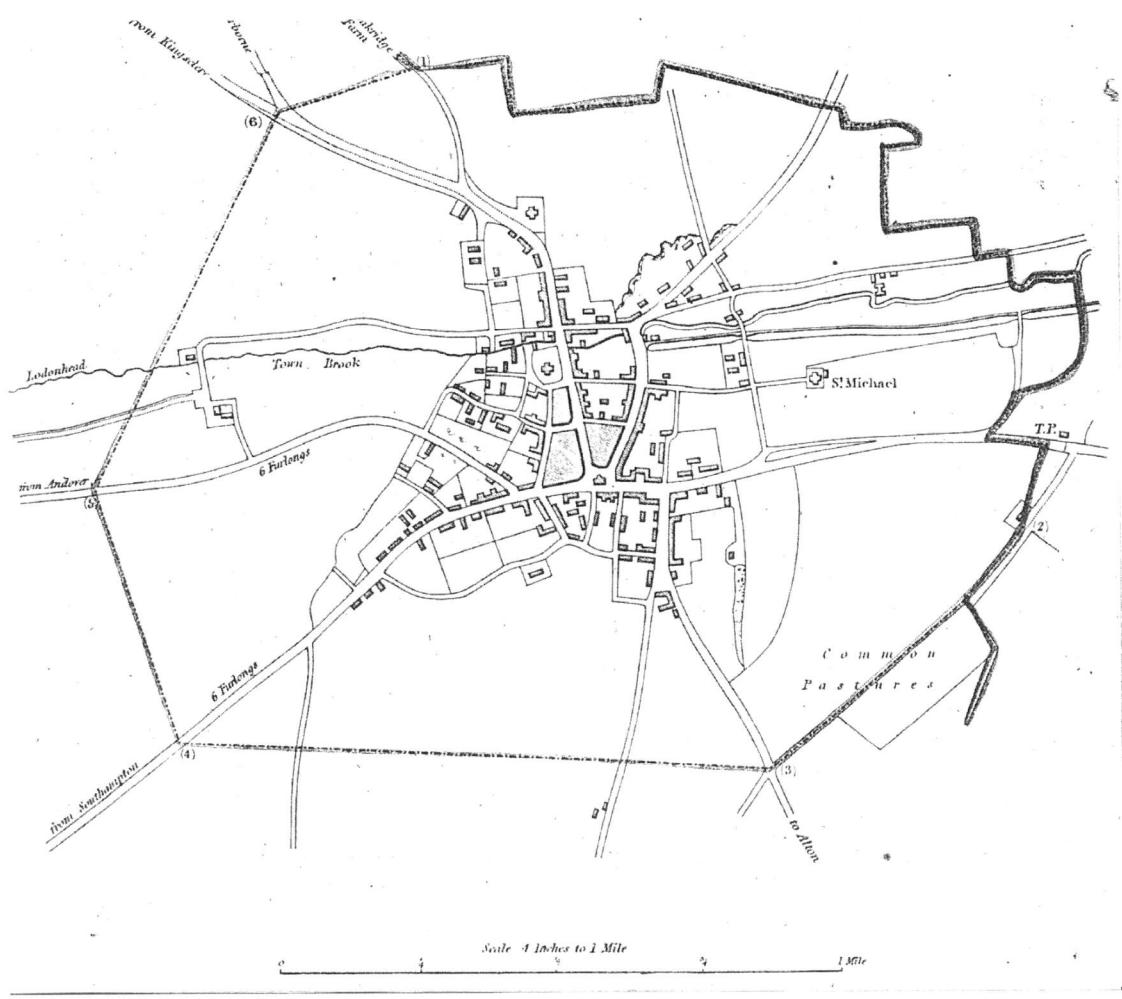

Detail from the map on the previous page
See the comments on the 1886 O.S. Map extract on page 110

It occurred to the Commissioners that a reduction in the area of the borough (which was co-extensive with the parish) was desirable: 'on all sides but the north-east the boundaries reach between one and two miles from the town. On the latter side, the parish boundary is at such a distance from the town that it can conveniently be retained for the future boundary of the borough. On the other sides, however, the present limits are much too extensive for municipal purposes.'

Their report included the maps above to show the proposed boundaries; these were thought 'to allow sufficient space for whatever extension of the town may take place along any of the high roads.' The boundaries appear not to have been altered, and the official area of the borough continued to be given as 4,036 acres. For most of the 20th century, the official figure has been 5,180 acres; this was increased to 5,580 acres in 1966-67.

As can be seen from the 1851 map of the town, overleaf, a traveller leaving the town to go via Chapel Street and Chapel Hill to Kingsclere and Newbury would see that beyond the railway bridge there was no continuous built-up area. On the east side of the road was the open space known as the Maiden Acre, part of which was called the Liten. Here were the ruined Holy Ghost and Holy Trinity chapels. On the west side were a few buildings, two of which were inns, *The Half-Moon* and *The Rising Sun*. Near the latter, at the top of the hill, stood one of the town's tollgates. The road to Sherborne St John led off from here.

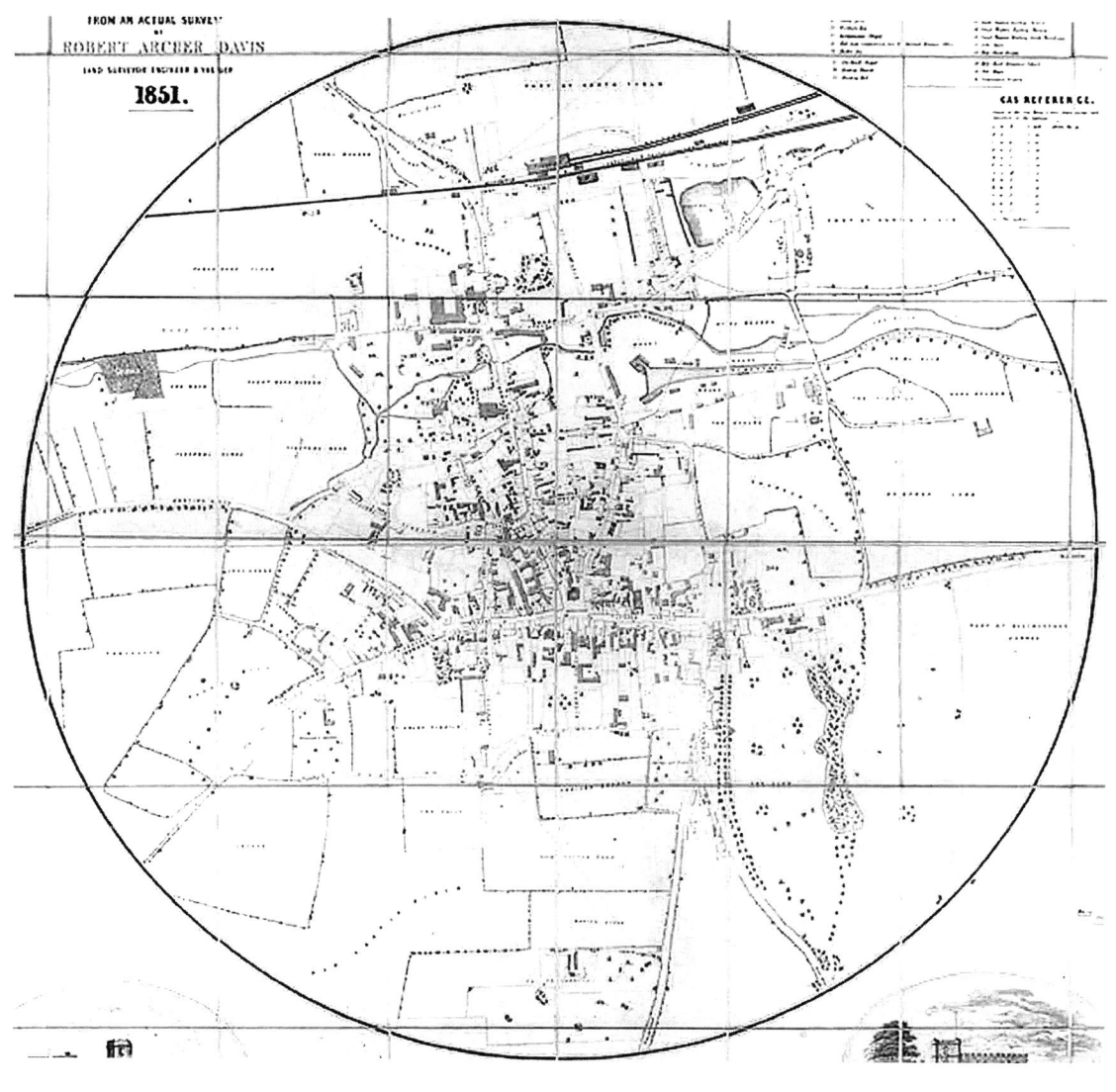

© HCMAS

The 1851 'Archer Davis' Map of Basingstoke
A copy is displayed in the Resource Room of the Willis Museum

If the traveller's destination was Reading, he would leave the town to proceed via Totterdown and Norn Hill. In so doing he would pass the end of a line of cottages in Bunnian Place and the large Chalk-pit, known as the Steam Dell, for long the source of the town's water-supply. He would find buildings more or less continuous as far as *The Castle Inn*. Beyond *The Castle Inn*, railway installations were a relatively new intrusion into an otherwise rural landscape. Especially prominent to the north was the terminus station of the Great Western Railway line from Reading. Between the eastern part of the town, where the Wharf occupied a large area of the flat valley floor, and the village of Basing was land liable to flooding. This discouraged the development of a continuously built-up area, but buildings were not completely absent. In addition to two mills, one at Eastrop, the other at Vince's Farm (where the footbridge over Churchill Way East is), there were the gas-works, dating from 1834, and, further east, the 'Union' workhouse, opened in 1855-56. *[Both of these establishments were on the northern slope of the Loddon valley above the flood plain.]*

On the opposite side of the valley ran the 'high road' to London. Two buildings were prominent: the house known as Goldings, standing in its park and farmland, and The White Hart Inn, beyond which, once again, was open country, including the Common (dating from 1788).

To the south of the town, the continuous built-up area more or less ceased along the line of what is today Southern Road, then known as Back Lane, which was linked in places to Winchester Street and London Street by 'twitchens or twitters' like Bishop's Alley. Near where the road to Cliddesden branched off from Duke's Lane (Hackwood Road) stood another of the town's tollgates (the Kiosk). Names such as Jubilee Meadow, and Viables Pightle remind us that the countryside was not far away.

In Winton Square the high road from London divided into two routes, one leading to Winchester and the other to Salisbury. Taking the road to Winchester past the yard of Brinkletts Farm (now a car park), the traveller would find the houses extended along the road only as far as Hardy Lane (formerly Foulflood Lane), beyond which he would find himself in the open country. A journey westward would take him via Sarum Hill (then known as Salisbury Hill) and Worting Road. Apart from a few buildings at the top of the hill, there was open country as far as the village of Worting, where another turnpike gate was situated. In 1851, there was as yet no *New Inn* at Flaxfield, and the move of Queen Mary's School to its new site had yet to be made (in 1855). *[There were, however, three large houses: Downsland House (next to Stowell's Funeral Directors), Highfield House (Devonshire Place) and West Ham House (West Ham Industrial Estate) on the way to Worting.]*

Along the Loddon valley, Northbrook Street (later simply Brook Street) led westward via Frog Lane and Water Lane. Prominent buildings were the brewery of May and Company and Ford's Buildings which formed the workhouse, until replaced by the new one in Basing Road. Not far away, nearer the railway, was the pesthouse. Within a very short distance the scene became rural, as may be judged from field-names such as Sheep Wash Meadow and Hog Mead.

Physical growth

Already in 1851 there were suggestions that the town had potential for growth. A notice appeared in the *Reading Mercury* on 2nd August giving the information that there was an opportunity for 'any Builder or Capitalist who may be inclined to erect PRIVATE RESIDENCES in the parish and near the town of BASINGSTOKE.' The location was described as being 'a most healthy and commanding site, overlooking the beautiful and luxuriant domain of Hackwood Park and the picturesque ruins of Basing House.' A similar notice had already appeared in the *Hampshire Chronicle* of 15th March, 1851. This referred to 46 acres of superior freehold land with a homestead being available on the Basingstoke to Preston Candover Road, within five minutes of the town. The neighbourhood was described as being 'of the first respectability' and one that would appeal to the builder of good taste. He would 'at first sight discover the groundwork for a fit display of his ability in a profitable undertaking.' The notice further pointed out that 'applications are daily made for houses of a respectable character.' Charles Paice, Auctioneer and Appraiser, made much of the advantages of the town in respect of 'the salubrity of the air and the pureness of the water.' There was also the almost obligatory reference to 'the proximity of the South-Western and Great Western Railways which furnish a ready and speedy communication with all parts of the kingdom', a selling-point of which more was to be made in the future.

In April 1867, the *St. Michael's Parish Magazine* stressed the need for more housing to rent. Referring to the founding of the Basingstoke Benefit Building Society, it reported: 'There is notoriously a great want of cottages in this town. Rents are consequently too high, and yet the labourer or mechanic has but little choice when seeking for a home, but has often to put up with one which does not suit him.' In the previous year (1866) it had pointed out the connection between overcrowding and crime: 'The inhabitants are overcrowded and over-crowding means dirt, foul air, necessary indecency, a consequent immorality, disorder, wrong-doing and the police court.' It is interesting that the writer thought in terms of the new dwellings being 'suited to strangers who might wish to find a house not far from London.' He concluded on an optimistic note: 'Meanwhile we may have good hope that the remedies will come, for our rulers are fellow-townsmen. What all want, they want too, and having done much, we may well believe that they will not stay their hand from doing more.'

Five years later, in 1871, the national census showed the population as 5,574, with the number of inhabited houses as 1,164. In the same year, Dr Ballard in his report on T*he Sanitary Condition of Basingstoke [see Chapter 10]* stated: 'The new houses have been principally erected in the suburbs and especially on the level land at the lower part of the town.' The town had begun to grow out from the nucleus of the old built-up area westward along the Loddon Valley, to form the area which we today know as Brookvale, but which was then known as Longcroft or Newtown. The 1873 6 inch OS Map shows that some of the open spaces within the borough boundary had been filled in with housing and new street names had appeared. For example, immediately to the south of London Street and Winchester Street, Castons Road and Cambridge Terrace had come into existence. Back Lane had received the name Southern Road as far as its junction with Victoria Street, beyond which it now continued as Bounty Road, to join up with Winchester Road. As yet no building had taken place to the south of that line. Jubilee Meadows and Old Castle Field were still rural land with advertised potential for development.

By 1878, mention is being made of housing in other parts of the town e.g. 'new cottages beyond the station and in roads leading from Essex Road; new villas in Worting Road, new cottages in Flaxfield.' By 1880, it was possible to report that of the 95 houses which had been built in Longcroft, 90 had been occupied. These new developments prompted the writer of a letter to the local paper in September 1878 to say 'It is impossible, judging from what is going on in the town, to come to any other conclusion than that Basingstoke is growing and prosperous.' Not everyone was satisfied with the progress being made. Another correspondent, on 15th February, 1879, pointed out the need for more housing in the following critical terms: 'If the authorities wish to discourage private enterprise in meeting what is admitted to be one of the town's sorest needs, viz. the creation of cottages for the largely increased number of its working population, they cannot do better than pursue the course they are doing.' The letter then referred to the apparent unwillingness to allow working men to settle down among the select population of Basingstoke. It concluded: 'such a course, it is clearly seen, must be fraught with evil consequences for the prosperity of the town.'

By 1881, it was becoming obvious that a proposal by the London & South-Western Railway to transfer its carriage works from Nine Elms to the town had come to nothing. Regret was expressed by some at the lost opportunity. 'But for the obtuseness of the men in authority some years ago, this would have been a flourishing commercial town of probably twice the size and importance, as the London & South-Western Company were prepared to commence and develop an industry which would have required hundreds of new houses and would have immediately increased the circulation of money in the town.' In the event, the railway company set up its works at Bishopstoke (Eastleigh). There, over the period 1891-1901, during which time the transfer took place, the population grew from 3,613 to 7,779, an increase of 115%.

Street names sometimes serve to show when development of an area for housing purposes took place. This would appear to be the case with Beaconsfield Road, named after the great Victorian Prime Minister, Disraeli, who was created Earl of Beaconsfield in 1876, and Jubilee Road, which appears to remind us that 1887 was the Golden Jubilee of Queen Victoria, though we should note that the 1851 map of the town shows Jubilee Meadow in the same area. Change was certainly occurring in this part of the town, which we know as Fairfields, after the area of land allocated under the Enclosure Award for the purpose of holding the annual Sheep Fairs. It was here that 'large and stately' Board Schools were opened on 16th February, 1888.

The year before (1887), a correspondent writing to the local paper about 'mixed schools or separate departments', with reference to Fairfields Schools, used the phrase 'miniature metropolis for north Hampshire' to describe the town. For the villages round about, the town was certainly a focus of activity, a central place which acted as a market for the produce of their farms and provided them with goods and services. The day would come when the town would seek to extend not just its influence but also its authority over a larger area.

In 1889, what was referred to as 'the rectification of the borough boundary' came up for discussion at a meeting of the Urban Sanitary Authority. It was reported that the Local Government Board did not approve of the Borough's proposal to incorporate parts of neighbouring parishes, since they took 'no heed of existing boundaries either natural or artificial and – in one instance, at least – bisect a house.' The inhabitants of the parishes most likely to be affected - Eastrop, Sherborne St John, Monk Sherborne, Basing and Cliddesden - had, not surprisingly, objected to the proposals. Boundary questions were to crop up again in the 1930s, in 1948, and most recently in 1974.

By the end of the 19th century, the town's population was growing at roughly twice the national rate. Between 1881 and 1891 the population increased from 6,681 to 7,960, an increase of 19.1%, the national rate being 11.7%. In the following decade, the increase was 23%, from 7,960 to 9,793. We can obtain some idea of the corresponding physical growth of the town from housing proposals submitted by developers to the Works Committee of the Corporation.

During the period 1878 to 1899, plans were approved for nearly 200 dwellings, most of which were described as 'terraced cottages'. Among the roads where building was proposed were Phoenix Park Terrace (1879), May Street (1882), Southern Road (1882), Soper Grove (1885), Lower Brook Street (1898), George Street (1899), Mortimer Lane (1899), Alexandra Road (1899) and Worting Road (1899). Most proposals were for the May Street, Brook Street, George Street and Alexandra Road area of the town.

More limited development was taking place north of the centre of the town, as shown in a Directory for 1891. Of Phoenix Park Terrace it said that 22 of the railway cottages were occupied; of Vyne Road the account was of 'only some half dozen houses including Hillside.' There were six occupied houses in Soper Grove. Between Vyne Road and Sherborne Road, the gradual transition from town to country is shown by the following:

Burgess Road	16 houses
Cromwell Road	7 houses
Richmond Road	4 houses
Darlington Road	2 houses (well and truly out in the country)

The year 1901 saw the beginning of the use of a less central part of the borough. This was Winklebury, where plots of land for housing were offered in Bury Road and West Ham Road, as well as in Worting Road. Larger plots of 2-10 acres or 12-20 acres were described as being suitable for poultry farming or market gardening. The area was later to become one where there was considerable concentration of the former activity.

[Similar development at Kempshott took place when Homestead Estates of Poole (hence Homesteads Rd) purchased what was once part of Basingstoke Down from the Town and resold plots for building and smallholding. The earliest bungalow, now much modified, in Kempshott Lane dates from 1910. (Personal communication to the Editors by a previous owner)]

In 1902, at a meeting of the Works Committee of the Council, on 10th May, plans were approved for new dwellings in various parts of the town – Alexandra Road, Kingsclere Road and Cliddesden Road. At the meeting, Alderman Powell announced the establishment in the town of the People's Investment Company Ltd of Reading, to encourage working men to borrow money to build their own homes. In this connection, he referred to a proposed new road, leading off the Reading Road, to be known as Coronation Road. The figure of 200 was suggested as the likely number of houses to be built here. By August 1902 the company had received approval for the building of five cottages in Reading Road and seven in Coronation Road.

Towards the end of 1902 we learn of another company – the Basingstoke and District Mutual Building Society. The notice advertising its establishment listed the names of the directors, all of whom were prominent in the business life of the town – Mr W Cannon, Mr J Mares, Mr W Wadmore, Mr W Higgs, Mr W Milsom and Mr W Powell. The stated aim of the Company, with its capital of £62,500 was 'to advance money to its members to enable them to purchase the houses they live in or any other property or to build houses for themselves.'

At about the same time, Lord Bolton, who owned considerable land in the borough, sought permission to develop part of the South View area into an estate, where plots could be made available for building houses to rent. The details of the scheme included the names proposed for the roads. Where we now have Queen Mary Avenue was to be Bolton Road. This would have led into Powlett Road (i.e. Reading Road). Family forenames were also to be used – e.g. Algar Road, Myra Road. Swing-Swang Lane was to become Lickpit Road. Oakridge Towers (the only residential tower block in the town) was later built in the area which was to have been served by Orde Road (Orde-Powlett was the family name of the Dukes of Bolton). The scheme put forward by Lord Bolton was not proceeded with; instead, the area was developed for local authority housing in the years following the 1939-45 war (Lefroy Avenue, Doswell Way, etc). Further building took place in the early stages of the 1960s overspill described in Chapter 16 – a series of closes (Martin Close, Westway Close, etc.) leading off from the Reading Road.

Despite all the building that had taken place, the town continued to have a housing problem. Accommodation was nowhere equal to the demand. By passing the Housing of the Working Classes Acts of 1885 and 1890, followed by the Housing and Town Planning Act of 1909, Parliament had provided the means whereby local authorities could build municipal (council) housing for rent, if they thought it an appropriate course to take. However, although the Corporation had had its Housing for the Working Classes committee since at least 1902, it had not put forward any proposal to take advantage of the legislation available. There was disagreement among councillors about the real extent of the problem and also as to the right solution.

Those who favoured 'council housing' put forward three reasons for doing so. There was the general one that, since 'such things as water, gas and electricity were coming more and more into the hands of the municipal authorities', there was no reason why housing should not be treated in the same way. The second reason had particular reference to the future of the town: 'If therefore the development and prospects of the town are being endangered by the want of housing, there seems a good case for the local authority to step in and meet the demand.' The third reason advanced was that families were entitled to 'a good house with suitable accommodation at a fair rent.' The local authority had a duty to meet the demand; the provisions of the various Acts gave it the powers to do so.

Those who were opposed to provision and ownership by the Council made the point that housing was not like other municipal undertakings such as electricity, public baths, recreation grounds, etc. It was open to 'the free play of competition'. There was obviously concern about the financing of a house-building programme. To the suggestion that 200 dwellings should be built, the objection was made that this would 'saddle the town with an enormous debt for the sake of comparatively few people, who might not be in the town five or six years hence. The Council would then have a large number of houses on their hands.' The view prevailed that private development would provide the best answer. The provision of housing should be left to the 'speculator' or 'capitalist', who would only undertake the risk if he could see a fair return for his money. The Corporation would need to intervene only if the private developer failed to meet the demand.

Although it appeared to be accepted that the town required 'more workmen's cottages at a rent workmen could afford', there was some doubt about how much they could be expected to pay. One councillor thought 8s. or 9s. a week a reasonable sum; another thought that it would be difficult for a man earning only £1 per week to afford that amount. Another thought that 5s.6d. or 6s. would be a more easily affordable sum.

The matter again came up for consideration when the Council had before it a proposal and estimates prepared by the Borough Surveyor for building 20 cottages on the King George V playing-field, subject to the approval of the Local Government Board. Another site considered was a plot of land adjoining Southernhay (in Brook Street), owned by Messrs May. Nothing came of these proposals. No council housing was built until 1914, when a crescent of 28 houses was completed in Cranbourne Lane, near its junction with Winchester Road. These were taken down in 1965 to allow for road alteration.

The views of a pressure group – the Ratepayers' Association – were made known at a public meeting held in December 1913. Examples were quoted to show the extent of the housing shortage. This included reference to the need to replace unfit properties. The main argument put forward was that the Council should expedite any housing scheme they were considering, in order to meet the needs of industrial development. Basingstoke was said to be 'one of those places which could hardly help being prosperous but there could be no more industries without more housing.' One firm, Messrs Thornycroft, had written to the Council in September 1913, saying they were having difficulty in employing married men 'owing to the want of houses.'

The meeting ended with the following motion being carried: 'That in view of the serious lack of housing provision in Basingstoke this public meeting urges upon the Town Council the necessity of putting into operation the powers in regard to housing which have been conferred upon them by Act of Parliament.'

In the 1930s two differing views were put forward about the future development of the town. In 1930, Mr G G Clark spoke to the Rotary Club of Basingstoke on 25th January. His talk was entitled 'The Architectural Development of Basingstoke'. His theme was that the town's future was bound up with the extension of employment. The town was well provided with transport facilities; it should adopt policies which would attract new industrial firms. Although he thought that the town ought to be able to become reasonably self-contained in the matter of employment, he suggested that, 'if a suitable early morning train service to London could be arranged, there would be a tendency for Basingstoke to become, on a small scale, a dormitory town.'

Increased residential population, with a consequential upward turn to prosperity, was the theme of a similar talk by Mr P M Crosse, given to the Rotary Club on 4th June, 1937. He referred to the building development already taking place in and around Basingstoke. As a traffic consultant, he had a professional interest in advocating the building of houses for those who would commute to employment outside the town: 'With a clean, fast and frequent train service can you imagine the number of people who would decide to make their homes at Basingstoke? The number of season-ticket holders would soon rival the number of Brighton season-ticket holders, land values would increase, [prophetic words!] building activities would be redoubled and careful control by the local authority would ensure that only suitable development would take place.'

The building referred to by Mr Crosse was of housing for sale. It was most in evidence along the roads radiating out from the town to the South and West, i.e. along Winchester and Worting Roads. It shows well what was meant by 'ribbon development'. The 'suburbs' of the town also experienced a considerable expansion, with new building taking place in Kempshott (Buckskin Lane, Kempshott Lane and Pack Lane) and Winklebury.

In the years immediately preceding the 1939-45 war, local estate agents regularly advertised houses for sale on estates in and about the town. In March 1938, there were houses for sale on the Highfield Estate (Deep Lane) at prices ranging from £595 to £650. In the same year plans were submitted to the Council for 84 houses in the Bramblys Grange area. At the same time houses were becoming available in Cumberland Avenue. Outside the borough, houses were being built in Hatch Lane and Linden Avenue, on what was known as the Byfleet Estate, at Old Basing.

As the following summary shows, houses were also being built for the Local Authority during the 1920s and 1930s.

Area of Town	No. of houses	Date of completion
Kingsclere and Sherborne Road	135	1920 - 22
Merton Road	74	1926
Hackwood Road	26	1927
Grove Road	40	1930
South Ham	272	1932 - 38
Grove Close (Hackwood Road)	6	1938
	553	
Cranbourne Lane	28	1914
Total Local Authority Housing	581	

The increase in the population of the town and the accompanying physical growth made it necessary for the men in authority to adopt policies to accommodate the changes inseparable from that growth. This meant taking decisions about the changed infrastructure required – a satisfactory sewerage system, a pure water supply, improved means of rubbish disposal, electricity supply, a hospital.

Public utilities

The coming of gas to the town in 1834 was described in Chapter 10. Eventually, with the advent of North Sea Gas, it became possible to dispense with the large gas-holders which were such a prominent feature of the eastern end of the town. Some time after 1966, the sites of the gasworks and the nearby Town Yard were cleared. They now form part of Basing View, the location of a number of large office buildings.

The establishment of a competitor to gas, of course, came much later. The possibility of the town being provided with electricity was first considered in 1894, when Mr R Hammond, a consulting electrical engineer, reported on the feasibility of providing a generating plant for the town. It was not until 1900 that the Borough Council decided to take the necessary action. They obtained the required provisional order from the Board of Trade and entered into negotiations with the National Electricity Construction Company for the construction of the works. They also applied to the Local Government Board for permission to obtain a loan.

In 1901, a second report was made to the Council by Mr R P Wilson. He reported on the environmental and financial aspects of the proposal. Much discussion followed, particularly in 1904 and 1905, not only about where the plant might be located but also about whether it was really needed. The town was said to be 'not ripe for an electric light scheme.' While some wanted to know who would be the consumers, others argued that a new source of power could lead to an increase in business activity, which would be for the good of the town as a whole. It had to be decided who should operate the undertaking. Some preferred ownership by the Corporation, while others favoured a private company to do the job – 'they all knew that private undertakings as a rule worked more economically than municipal ones.' In the meantime it was found that the Corporation's order could not legally be put into operation. The proposal lost its immediacy and the order was abandoned in 1907.

One interesting line of argument for this proposal was that it would be more economic, less damaging to the environment if all the Corporation's 'utilities' were located together in one place, rather than being scattered throughout the town. This led to the rather modern idea being put forward that electricity might be more cheaply generated if the town's rubbish could be burnt in a rubbish destructor (a 'dust destructor'), to provide heat for the generating station's boilers. It was also suggested that public baths on or near the site could make use of the hot water produced in the condensation of steam. It is interesting to see to what extent attention was paid to environmental considerations, at a time when there was as yet no town-planning legislation to regulate such matters; not until the Housing, Town Planning etc, Act of 1909. Among the points stressed were the noise and vibration which the plant would cause, the smoke and gases inseparable from such an operation, and the appearance of the site. In particular it was thought that care should be taken to avoid having tall chimneys in the centre of the town. Planning is concerned with anticipation of change. Those responsible for finding a site for the generating plant showed their understanding of this by taking into account the possibility that the Flaxfield area, where the Corporation had its town yard, might, in the future, be used for more housing.

When it obtained a new order in 1913, the Corporation proceeded more quickly with its electricity scheme. The generating plant was erected in Brook Street in 1913 and it started to supply the town in the following year. It continued to do so for a number of years, though latterly only as an emergency source of supply. It was demolished in 1969, as town development got under way. *[A major substation is still on part of the site.]*

Basingstoke Electricity Generating Station, 1964

Photo: © Sid Penney

Not everyone looked with favour on the various infra-structural changes taking place. The attitude of those who did not want change is well conveyed by the following quotation from the Borough Guide Book of 1906: 'As a country town, Basingstoke remains unique among its compeers of equal population and extent – it has so far resisted the introduction of such improvements as electric light, the electric tram and the motor omnibus.' The account goes on to say that, although these may be appropriate to larger towns, they are, in smaller towns, 'merely the ebullition of a too rapid civilization.'

Whereas the Borough Council of 1906 appears to have been unwilling to accept too rapid a process of civilization, their successors in 1935 were prepared to consider the change that the aeroplane might bring. In that year the Council negotiated with the Portsmouth Estates Improvement Co Ltd, to purchase about 100 acres of land for use as something all progressive towns should have – a municipal airport.

© Crown copyright 1947

Basingstoke in 1947 - a compact country town

EDITORIAL UPDATE

From the late 19th century, until the late 1930s when Kelvin, Bottomley and Baird and Eli Lilly established factories in Basingstoke as a result of promotion of the town by the Borough Council, and the earlier establishment of the Auto Tyre Services at Worting, employment in the town was dominated by the two engineering companies, Thornycroft and Wallis & Steevens, and the railway. For women the clothing factories of Burberry, John Mares and Gerrish, Ames and Simpkins were the major employers. The remainder of the larger businesses in the town employed several tens of staff rather than hundreds, although the Gas works, May's brewery, Mussellwhite the builders, Fisher's leather works and the two timber yards (White's at the Wharf and Taggart's in Kingsclere Road) cumulatively employed many hundred staff. Otherwise the numerous small firms in the building and allied trades, garages, shops and the service industries, along with all aspects of the catering trade, provided the bulk of the employment opportunities in the town. Shop work, that came with the arrival of the multiple grocers such as International Stores and Home & Colonial and later, chain stores like Marks & Spencer, Woolworth, Boots, and Smiths, provided additional jobs for women (and men) as an alternative to domestic service. The establishment of the Basingstoke Cooperative Society also provided jobs in a large range of retail and allied trades. Clerical work was provided by the banks, solicitors' offices and the factory offices. A major, and often overlooked, source of local employment was the Park Prewett Psychiatric Hospital on the outskirts of the town; also the Nurseries at Cranbourne employed a significant number of men and women. See page 190 for a brief discussion of the post war expansion of industrial employment before the LCC/GLC overspill scheme.

Photo DPAAOR19: © HCMAS

Basingstoke in the mid 1950s from the north-east and a vertical view

Photo DPAAOT99: © HCMAS

15   THE MOTOR-CAR AGE

Basingstoke: South's First Town of the Motor-car Age

Basingstoke Gazette 16th August 1962

Basingstoke's first acquaintance with a mechanically-propelled vehicle – a locomotive– occurred in 1830. This was the steam carriage built by Ogle and Summers (Nathaniel Ogle of Millbrook, Southampton and William Summers of Whitechapel, London), which made two unsuccessful attempts to travel from London to Southampton in March of that year. On its first attempt it broke down at Brentford; on the second it broke down within a few miles of Basingstoke. (It was shipped back to London via the Basingstoke Canal.) At the third attempt it reached Southampton, despite operating difficulties, having achieved in part of its route a speed of 20 mph.

Samuel Attwood very briefly recorded the event in his diary for 22nd August: 'The steam coach, passed through the town to Southampton.' This happening, although something to be wondered at by the local inhabitants, had no effect on the coaching trade passing through the town. The horse-drawn coach, carriage and wagon remained the chief means of transport, whether for long-distance travel or for journeys in the immediate locality. There were in the town businesses engaged in making and repairing these vehicles. In 1841, Joel Passmore was carrying on such a business at his premises in London Street; the 1861 Census recorded Thomas Dyer (employing five men and one boy) as being similarly engaged at his works in Winton Square. About twenty years later, another carriage manufactory was established by Mr John Joice, who came to the town from Essex. This firm supplied all types of horse-drawn vehicles to the local gentry and tradespeople. It finally ceased business in 1950, *(Freeman, MD 1972)*. Another local firm, Wallis and Steevens, although mainly concerned with making agricultural machinery and steam rollers, also produced 'road engines', which were applied to the task of hauling pantechnicons of goods about the country, *(Whitehead, R A 1983)*.

The town was to have much more to do with vehicles, following the opening of the Thornycroft works here in 1898. The technique of building road vehicles powered by petrol engines was still only in its early stages; the first vehicles produced in the Basingstoke works were in fact wagons driven by steam. In the same year Mr Watson, cycle agent and pioneer motorist, of Wote Street, advertised his 'Motette', built by the Coventry Motor Company, 'on the French Bollée System.' He claimed for it the ability to make the journey from London to Basingstoke in 3¾ hours, 'burning' a gallon and a half of petrol at a cost of 1s.5d. The notice proudly proclaimed that it would 'mount any hill at 5 mph.'

In the early part of the next century the town saw more activity by motor vehicles, activity that infringed the legal speed limit of 12 mph. Charged with breaking the law was the Hon John Scott Montagu, of Palace House, Beaulieu. The details are given in the history of the Automobile Association, *(Barty-King, H 1960)*. The charge against Lord Montagu read: 'that [he] being the driver or person in charge of a certain light locomotive on a certain highway ... called Winchester Road, unlawfully did drive the said light locomotive at a greater speed than 12 miles an hour on the said highway contrary to the Regulations contained in the Light Locomotive on Highways Order 1896 ...' The offence was committed on Good Friday, 1902; the speed of the car was 21¼ mph. The case, heard on 22nd April, resulted in a fine of £1 with 12s. costs.

In 1903 the County Council discussed the regulation of motor traffic against the background of the Motor Car Act of that year, which besides raising the speed limit to 20 mph, made registration and identification of cars compulsory and introduced licensing for drivers. Vehicles were no longer 'light locomotives'; they had become 'motor-cars'. Members were concerned to protect the public; setting a maximum speed was one way of doing this. Requests had been received from some parts of the county for the maximum to be set at 8 mph. On this occasion the Council was considering whether or not to make 10 mph the limit. The decision was taken not to do so. The need for careful enforcement of the legislation was illustrated in the case of the Prime Minister's driver who, it was stated, had been fined for 'driving through Hook village at a rate of 33 mph.' Members did, however, recommend the erection of 'caution posts' at dangerous cross-roads, corners and 'precipitious places'. They were not concerned only with safety; they were also having to take note of the fact that road surfaces which were adequate for the slower movement of horse-drawn vehicles were liable to be damaged by the greater speed and in most cases the very much greater weight of motor vehicles. They had already (in 1901) found it necessary to strengthen some of the County's bridges liable to damage by heavy traction engines.

In 1904, the police appeared to have made a determined effort to enforce the law. It is now that we first hear of the so-called 'speed-trap', the assessment of the speed of a vehicle by timing it over a measured furlong. One place where this was done was on the Winchester Road, near *The Wheatsheaf Inn* at Popham . Two cases came before the Borough Magistrates in June 1904. In the first, a Dr S Andrews, referred to as a medical practitioner, of Basingstoke, was charged with riding his motor-cycle at a speed of 30 mph. He disputed the accuracy of the timing and argued that the stop-watches should have been sealed before they were produced in court. He was fined two guineas, including costs. On the same day, the driver of a motor-car was stopped by the police and it was shown that he had covered the measured furlong in 13 seconds, giving a speed of 34 mph. There was some difficulty with the case, as the evidence of the defendant was difficult to follow, 'his English being somewhat indifferent.' Besides casting doubt on the reliability of the stop-watch and implying inaccuracies in the distance measured, the defendant, aided by his employer-passenger, argued that his speed was not dangerous, since there were no people, no horses and no turnings in the road. For good measure he argued that the car was too heavy to travel at 34 mph!

It is to be regretted that Dr Andrews appears to have been once again an offender; in September 1905, while returning from visiting a patient at Dummer, he travelled the measured furlong at a speed of 28 mph. Despite his plea that 'everyone knew that he did not go racing about,' he was fined £3, with 8s. costs. Appearing before the Magistrates on the same day was Mr F Watson, who pleaded guilty to exceeding the speed limit along the Winchester Road.

The Borough Council was, of course, concerned at the way in which motorists drove through the narrow streets of the town. They expressed the view that it was not unreasonable to set a maximum limit of 10-12 mph within the main built-up area. There were recognised danger-spots in the town. One of these was the London Road - Hackwood Road Junction; the entrance to Dark Lane (Eastrop Lane) was another. It was thought appropriate to indicate these by means of warning-boards. At the same meeting attention was drawn to the increased registration of vehicles nationally; there was a realisation that this would inevitably have an impact on traffic in the local area.

Regulation of traffic again came up for discussion in 1911. The Works Committee recommended the Council to ask the County Council for permission to enforce a 10 mph limit in parts of the town. The need to do so was emphasised by one member who said that he had seen a car 'come up Wote Street at certainly 20 mph'!

The 1914-1918 War saw a huge increase in the use of motor vehicles. The local lorry-builder, Thornycroft, made a significant contribution to the war effort by supplying vehicles for various military purposes. With the return of peace, there were surplus vehicles available for use in the civil field. Such vehicles were obtained by those who had gained experience in their operation and maintenance. It was in this way that local bus services originated. Commonly, of course, operators of these services were also 'Motor Engineers', providing maintenance and repair facilities for the private car-owner. A 1915 directory for Hampshire shows several local firms engaged in the motor trade to varying degrees: Watsons (motor engineers); Webbers (motor engineers and agents, garage, cars for hire); Julians (ironmongers and motor engineers); Scard (motor garage); other businesses having to do with vehicles were: Joice (coach and motor body builders); Rogers (coach builders), Wallis and Steevens (iron founders, engineers, agricultural implements and road engine makers). One firm, which concealed itself under the telegraphic address 'Groithwil', Sarum Hill, was in fact Grover, Smith and Willis (mechanical engineers) who advertised that they had cars for hire and that they undertook repairs of every description.

In 1921, an advertisement appeared of a 'bus service' being provided by Mobility Ltd of Ludgershall. The firm was proposing to run a service between Andover and Basingstoke. The single fare proposed was 2s.6d. The advertisement included the cautionary note: 'Intending passengers are advised to travel, where possible, on days other than Market days, to avoid disappointment.' Towards the end of the year, the service was extended to Alton, so that it was then possible to leave Andover at 9.00 am, arrive at Basingstoke at 10.35 and arrive at Alton at 11.35 am. The fare for the journey was 3s.6d single. The Company's schedule later provided for three services each way on Wednesdays and Saturdays, two each way on Mondays, Thursdays and Fridays, and one each way on Sundays. *The Wheatsheaf*, in Winton Square, was the staging-point for the service, as it was later for a service established by Transit Motor Coaches (of Southampton) who provided a through service from Southampton to London.

Enterprise in providing local services also came from within the town itself. Two Basingstoke firms, King's Motor Garage, of Brook Street and the Basingstoke Charabanc and Motor Company, had advertised their services on 12th March, 1921. The latter firm (part of Watsons of Wote Street) said that it would provide two services each way between Basingstoke and Basing on weekdays and Saturdays; in May the same firm advertised a service to Odiham 'every fine Sunday until further notice.'

© Roy Reynolds

Mr Reynolds of Basing with a charabanc party c 1930

Other local providers of services to and from the town were Huntly (of Wootton St. Lawrence), Kent (of Baughurst); Porter (of Dummer), Wood (of Empress Garage, Roman Road, Basingstoke) and Reynolds (of Old Basing).

In 1926 there was a major development in local public transport. A new company was established, mainly on the initiative of Thornycrofts. It was called Venture Ltd. It had its garage in Victoria Street and it operated its services from The Barge. By 1933 it had become the largest of the local operators connecting Basingstoke with its immediate hinterland as well as the more distant towns of Alton, Andover and Newbury. In 1945 the company was taken over by Red and White Motor Services, a South Wales Company. In 1951 it became part of the Wilts and Dorset Company.

The effect of all these developments was to provide more convenient links between the town and other parts. There was, of course, also a slow but steady increase in private motoring. Webbers and Watsons were the two main agents for a wide range of makes – Fords, Studebaker, Singer, Morris Oxford, Austin, Wolseley, etc. Webbers were confidently able to announce 'we supplied twenty new cars to customers during 1913 and we know we can say every buyer is pleased, both with the car we sold him and the way we treated him.' Another local firm, Burberry, took advantage of the arrival on the scene of the motor-car to advertise its products – the Automo slip-on and the Gabardine lap-robe. Gabardine was stated to be proof against rain, dust, sleet, snow and cold winds – 'No motor-car can be complete without them.'

The 1930s were years of continuing depression; there was, nevertheless, an increase in the number of vehicles using the roads. This was true of the road from London to the South and West, which, passing along London Street, divided in Winton Square, into the 'South Road', leading to Winchester and Southampton, and the 'Western Highway', the route which took the traveller to Salisbury, Exeter and the West Country. Although the volume of traffic was small compared with what it was later to become, it all had to pass through the bottleneck of the Market Place. It is not surprising that Mr Clark, in his talk to the Rotary Club of Basingstoke in January 1930, said of the Market Place: 'Traffic immediately confronts us – traffic of every description, from enormous stacks of milk churns on wheels (milk on its way from the West Country to London) to the normal small cars – obviously the road is too small for the traffic.' The narrow streets of the town were further congested by traffic passing between Reading and Southampton.

The idea of solving the problem by building a by-pass was first considered on 26th November, 1921. Eventually a decision was made to undertake the work. Construction was begun in November 1930, and the new road was opened to traffic in December 1932. Men from the depressed areas were employed in the work. In this way, the cost to the Hampshire ratepayer was reduced, because under the terms of the Unemployment (Relief Work) Act of 1920, 80% of the cost of the work was met from Government funds. What had been a quiet country lane – the Harrow Way – had become a busy arterial road, which was itself later to prove inadequate to handle the volume of traffic which wished to use it, particularly at weekends in the summer months.

Reducing the volume of traffic through the town did not mean the end of congestion and delay. The town was about to experience the problem of the parked car, left stationary by its owner as near as possible to his intended destination within the town. Difficulties were already occurring in 1931 in certain streets – New Street came in for special mention. The need for a suitably located car park was discussed in the Council on several occasions. On one of these, in February 1934, Councillor Mrs Weston proposed that land in the Barge area should be purchased. Her argument was that it would be convenient for the private motorist, as it was near 'the hub of road traffic in the town.' She reinforced the convenience argument with an environmental one. The provision of the car park could be a means of improving 'that corner of the town which is ugly, garish and untidy.'

Those responsible in the early 1960s for drawing up the plan for the future development of the town (see Chapter 16) had to produce solutions which would accommodate a greatly increased population and would allow for car ownership on a much larger scale than hitherto. There would obviously be much greater flows of traffic between home and workplace, as well as between home and shops. Any plan had to permit traffic to move freely about the town; equally important, in the interest of safety, was the separation, wherever possible, of pedestrians and vehicle movements.

The solution proposed was a large multi-storey car park located centrally, with space for 3,500 cars, integrated with the new, vehicle-free, platform shopping area. Accompanying this provision, which was massive by the standards of thirty years previously, when the council had been facing up to the problem of the motor-car, there was a radically new road pattern, consisting of a spine road running east-west along the Loddon Valley, together with a new loop road system, and an outer ring road, which would later link to the M3 Motorway, to the south-east of the town.

The routing of the ring road presented a problem. Particularly sensitive was the area to the south of the town, where the Common and Memorial Park formed the town's most extensive open space. To the west of the town, it had been possible to use the route of the former Basingstoke to Alton Railway and the line to Park Prewett for the alignment of the ring road. The 1962 Map showed that most of the Common was to become a residential area. From the map it was also apparent that it was intended to direct the A30 (the former by-pass) to a new alignment across the Common, to link in with another stretch of ring road leading to Winchester Road. The idea of using the A30 as the basis for the ring road had been examined by the planners, who rejected it in favour of the road across the Common. This was approved by the Public Inquiry held in 1963, but not everyone was satisfied. The views of those who objected to the Park and the Common being used in this way were made known at the Community Conference in July 1969. They were made more strongly known at the Public Inquiry in August 1971 into the proposal to acquire the Common by compulsory purchase. However, the use of the A30 alignment was rejected on the grounds that it would involve the costly demolition of far too many properties, together with other undesirable environmental damage.

Work on the construction of the Southern Ringway between Black Dam and Winchester Road began in May 1974. The Ringway was opened as a continuous route in August 1976. As a report of the opening has it: 'From then on drivers were able to appreciate the full advantages of the ringway system.' The road pattern was further modified by alterations at the Town Centre East Junction to improve the link between the spine road and the ring road. Later a new link was built to join Basing View to Daneshill. All these changes in the road pattern were made in the interests of easier movement about the town by motor vehicle. It was no longer possible to say, as Mr Clark had said in his talk to Rotary, 25th January, 1930, 'It is obvious that the road system in the town itself was not designed for motor traffic.' Although some road closures caused dissatisfaction, the motorist had good reason to accept that his needs had indeed been taken into account. This is not to say that all was well.

A newspaper report of October 1986, referring to the regular 'snarling-up' of traffic in the town, said 'The more successful the town becomes, the harder it is to get to work.' The town now faced the consequences of the high degree of prosperity it had achieved – a morning and evening rush hour resulting from the considerable increase in the volume of commuting to and from places of employment in the town. Increased commuting by train, mainly to London, had added to the problem. The 1962 plan had envisaged an extension of car-parking to the station area. The original provision – the Vyne Road car park – proved to be insufficient to meet the demand, so large parts of the former railway goods yards, both north and south of the railway, were converted to accommodate cars. In a further attempt to improve the situation, consideration is now being given to the possibility of building new 'commuter stations' in the locality. These, which could be located at places such as Oakley, Worting, Basing or Chineham, would go some way towards reducing the problem of the relatively constricted area around the station.

EDITORIAL UPDATE

Currently the proposal for local commuter stations appears to be very much 'on the back burner'. The commuter traffic into and out of the town has continued to increase, to the extent that there are now daily traffic queues at the M3 junction and most of the major roundabouts at rush hour. This is despite major traffic management schemes to ease the flow of traffic.

Within the residential areas of the town, many areas now have restricted parking for residents only and various forms of traffic calming.

16 PLANNED GROWTH

The ultimate aim of any overspill development must be well-planned, agreeable expansion for the benefit of the people who will live in the area.

Comment: *Hants & Berks Gazette*   November 1960

When drawing up the Greater London Plan of 1944, Sir Patrick Abercrombie took note of the recommendations made in the Barlow Commission Report of 1940, 'The Distribution of the Industrial Population'. He proposed the dispersal of over a million people from the Metropolitan area. It is here that the town is first officially mentioned as a potential contributor to the plan. It was included in the category 'Additions to existing towns outside the Greater London Plan boundaries, mostly between 40 and 50 miles from London.' It was proposed that Basingstoke should receive 20,000 people from the Greater London Plan area. Aylesbury and Bletchley were also named in the same category.

In March 1945 the Planning Officer for the Basingstoke area referred to changes that might take place. He said that these would be dependent on 'the ultimate size of the town and whether it might be required to take some overspill from London.' On 16th May, 1947, a report appeared in the local paper, under the heading 'Greater London Plan – 40,000 Population for Basingstoke.' After giving details of the plan, the article concluded, 'The proposal is not an unacceptable one; in fact, something of the kind was foreshadowed before it was actually mooted.'

The proposals for accommodating overspill were incorporated in the 1950 Development Plan for the County. Assuming that the 'decanted' population would be 20,000 and that there would be a natural increase of 3,230 over a period of 20 years, it estimated that the 1971 population would be 40,000. The 'target population' was reduced in 1955 to 32,000, to take account of the need to preserve agricultural land in the immediate neighbourhood of the town.

The provisions of a piece of legislation passed by Parliament in 1952 – the Town Development Act – were to be of importance for the future of the town. The Act enabled small towns to finance schemes of expansion more easily than otherwise would have been the case. In the same year the London County Council (LCC) made tentative approaches about accommodating overspill. It was interested in an initial programme of 1,500 houses. At the same time, proposals were being considered which would result in the construction of 200 houses, (later increased to 400), for people who would work at the Atomic Weapons Research Establishment at Aldermaston.

After 1945, over the country as a whole, there was a shortage of housing. The demand for new homes was met by both public and private development. For several years the number of local authority houses built was well in excess of the number built for sale. This was the case in Basingstoke. In the earlier years of the post-war period, the ratio of council to private houses was between 10:1 and 15:1. In 1950, 165 Council and 11 private houses were built. The ratio decreased, to average 2:1 between 1951 and 1954. By the end of that year, of the 5,569 dwellings assessed for borough purposes, 1,584 (28.4%) were owned by the Council. Two parts of the town received most of this early post-war development – South View and South Ham, the latter an extension of building that had occurred in the 1930s.

The town's population grew slowly, from an estimated 15,850 in 1946 to 16,978 in 1951. It was to grow more rapidly during the decade 1951-1961, reaching 25,940 by the latter date. This was still a period of natural growth, during which over 7,000 people moved to the town,

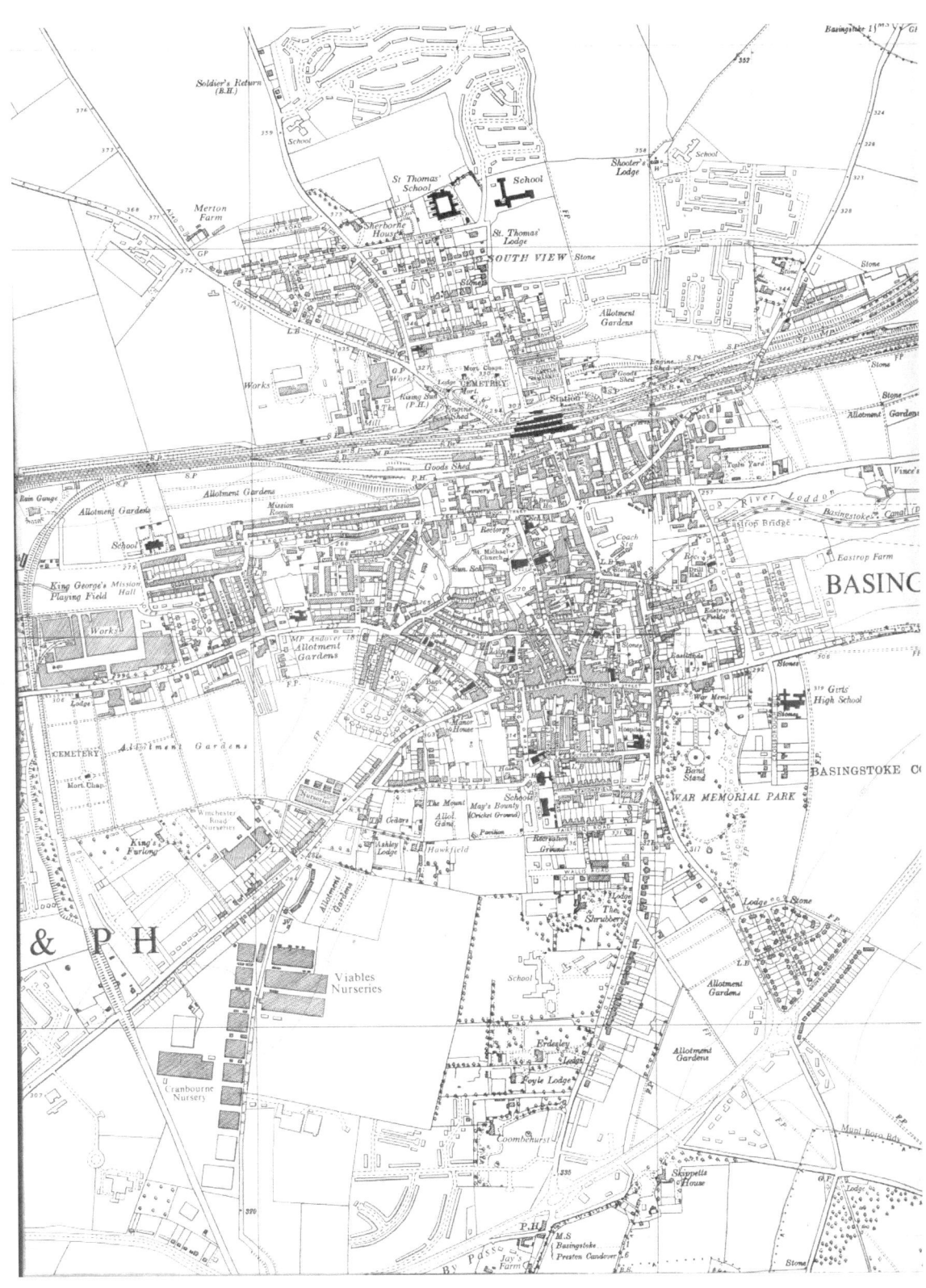

6 inch Ordnance Survey Map – 1961

The map extract shows the extent of the central built-up area before clearance and re-development of the centre of the town.

Reproduced by permission of Ordnance Survey on behalf of HMSO
© Crown copyright 2008. All rights reserved. Ordnance Survey Licence number 100048022.

in response to greater employment opportunity and also to increasing availability of houses for sale. This growth in the population represented a great increase in purchasing power, with a corresponding effect on the prosperity of shops and services in the town, a prosperity that was further increased by the fact that the town continued to be the shopping-centre for a hinterland where population was also growing, though not at the same rate.

As there had been differing views in the 1880s about proposals to establish railway carriage works in the town (Chapter 13), so there were now differences of opinion about the rightness or otherwise of the plan to move Londoners to the town. The year 1955 was one in which a great deal of public discussion took place. One view, strongly expressed, was that the LCC expansion scheme was not in the best interests of the borough, the argument being that the provision of a large number of council houses would result in too heavy a burden on the rates. This line of argument prompted a local firm of estate agents to put forward a scheme which would have used private money to build not only houses but also factories, offices and shops. The houses (500 was the figure mentioned) could be leased in block leases to the Council and the factories could be for sale or rental. Such a scheme, it was argued, would have the advantage that the town itself would be able to control its own development and there would be little or no burden on the rates.

It was, of course, realised that expansion would result in a loss of farm-land greater than had hitherto been experienced. Not unnaturally, the local farming community made known their opposition. It was suggested that, as an alternative, land of lower agricultural value elsewhere in the county could be used. The heath-lands in the east of the county, around Fleet and Farnborough, were mentioned as suitable areas.

There were those who argued that the town would be presented with problems, even if its growth was natural, i.e. without overspill, since even a slow increase in population would ultimately make increased demands on water, sewerage and other services. The cost of these could be less of a burden if the LCC scheme was adopted. Mr George Willis had warned his fellow-members of the Council in 1936, when a proposed rate increase of 3d. in the pound to 10s.3d. was under discussion: 'An increase in the rates is inevitable in a live town. Basingstoke is a growing town; it is also an old town and some of its services are getting a little shaky!'

Others saw a scheme such as the one proposed as a means of improving local employment opportunities. This was something the Council had attempted to achieve, in a small way, in pre-war years. Diversification of employment would be a means of increasing local prosperity.

Some said that it was not possible to give a considered opinion on the matter, because there were so many unknowns. They made the point that to discuss the implications of an overspill scheme with representatives of the LCC would not commit the Council in any way. More information, particularly about methods of financing, was required before a decision could be reached. Eventually, a delegation from the Borough Council met representatives of the County Council, and, with them, members of the LCC. As a result, a joint approach was made to the Minister of Housing and Local Government, in order to learn his reaction to the proposal and especially to find out what financial assistance would be available from Central Government. A letter of 26th April, 1955 from the Minister to the Borough Council explained how expansion schemes could be financed. With assurances of financial assistance from central government, the town could now go ahead with a deliberate, planned expansion over a definite period of time. The alternative to this would be private development over an unspecified period with no financial assistance for water and sewerage works, and perhaps without the provision of sufficient employment for the future labour force. Four years were to go by before an agreement was signed with the LCC (October 1959).

This envisaged the building of 3,500 homes, to accommodate an overspill population estimated at between 11,000 and 12,000. These local developments should be set against a background of what was happening elsewhere. The process of dispersing people and employment to the New Towns had been proceeding for several years, but this was not achieving all that was necessary to implement the LCC's own development plan. So overspill agreements were made with places such as Swindon and Bletchley, and these were soon in operation. Later, negotiations were entered into with a number of other towns situated south-east of a line from the Wash to the Solent. Aylesbury was one of these. County Councils had already been asked to suggest towns within their boundaries which might be suitable for expansion. As planning authorities, they would be closely involved in such schemes of expansion. As early as 1947, the Hampshire County Council had asked to be given an opportunity to join in any discussions that the Borough Council might have with the LCC.

The County Council was now to have the opportunity to join in. The LCC had been investigating the possibility of building a new town somewhere in the region permitted by the Ministry of Housing and Local Government – i.e. inside (south-east of) the Wash-Solent line. From the 70 sites looked at, Hook was eventually chosen as being the most suitable. In October 1958, the proposal to develop a town in the Hook area, to accommodate 'upwards of 100,000 people', was published. The proposal met with opposition from many quarters. Drawing attention to the 'formidable total' of population grouped in the nearby towns of Aldershot, Basingstoke, Camberley, Farnborough, Fleet, Reading and Wokingham, the Hartley Wintney Rural District Council expressed concern at a further extension of 'urban sprawl', which would destroy the rural character of the area. The Hampshire Branch of the Country Landowners' Association was also against the scheme and recommended that an area of Government-owned land, mainly heathland in the east of the county, should be used. They specifically mentioned the Whitehill (Bordon) area as being suitable. Important and influential local residents also saw to it that their objections to the proposal were made known in the right quarters.

The publication of the Hook plan seems to have raised some doubts about the intentions of the LCC in respect of the expansion of Basingstoke. The opinion was even expressed that the LCC did not now appear to be so keen to reach an agreement with the Basingstoke Borough Council.

The County Council discussed the Hook scheme on 25th November, 1958. There was some dissatisfaction with the way in which the LCC had gone about the selection of Hook and the preparation of its plan. No member of the Council spoke in favour of the plan; many, in fact, opposed it very strongly. The attitude of members can be attributed to the concern they felt about the problems the county was already facing; the rapid growth of the county's population by immigration taking place independently of any overspill scheme; the growth of the three County Boroughs, Portsmouth, Southampton and Bournemouth, creating their own overspill problems; and fear of too great a concentration of new urban development in one part of the county. Eventually, discussions took place between the HCC and the LCC, covering the whole field of overspill policy, so far as it might affect Hampshire. These discussions produced an alternative scheme. The LCC would agree to abandon its idea of creating a new town at Hook. In return, Hampshire would agree to the expansion of Basingstoke, Andover and Tadley. The LCC accepted this situation at its meeting on 8th November, 1960.

The end result, so far as Basingstoke was concerned, was that the overspill agreement of October 1959 was replaced by a new, tripartite one between Basingstoke Borough Council, Hampshire County Council and the London County Council, signed on 31st October, 1961. This provided for the construction of 11,500 dwellings. This would represent an estimated intake of overspill population of 36,800. It was envisaged that there would continue to be private migration into the town.

Table 5 below shows the population in Basingstoke Town Map Area 1959 and 1982 (as estimated in the Draft Town Map).

The higher values, marked *, which were obtained by assuming a higher rate of natural increase and a more rapid in-migration, are given by J H Dunning in *Economic Planning and Town Expansion*.

TABLE 5

	1959 Town Area	**Draft Town Map Area**
1. Population mid June 1959	23,130	30,130
2. Intake of overspill from London	36,800	36,800
Private Migration	6,300	6,300
Total Migration	43,100	43,100
3. Natural increase from 1	2,950	4,200
" " " 2	8,800	8,800
Total natural increase	11,750	13,000
4. Population 1982	77,980	86,230
* Dunning's estimate	85,180*	93,430*

It was essential to form some idea of the number of homes required by the increased population. One estimate made in August 1962, in *'Basingstoke – Town Development – description of the scheme'* by *Basingstoke Town Development Joint Committee*, was that a total of 19,270 would require to be provided over a period of 20 years. Of these, 11,500 would be for the purpose of accommodating overspill (i.e. people moving from London, having been nominated by the LCC). It was thought that 4,850 would be required for other new residents and for the natural increase of the incoming population and the need to replace existing houses, through redevelopment, would account for another 2,920. It was the intention of the Basingstoke Town Development Joint Committee to achieve and maintain a building rate of 1,300 homes a year. They hoped that, in addition, it would in the long run be possible for private development to provide 350 homes a year. There was always concern about preserving a suitable balance between public local authority housing and housing built for private ownership.

Gradually, as sites became available and when the necessary infrastructure had been provided, this large-scale programme began to be implemented. Initially, development took place in two areas of the town: South Ham, where council houses had been built between 1932 and 1938, and from 1950 onwards, and Winklebury, where much private house building had taken place during the natural growth period of the 1950s. Later, in 1964, building began in another area – Oakridge. Included in the housing here was the Oakridge Tower block, the only such residential accommodation provided in the town, although more had at one time been proposed. In 1965, work was begun on a smaller area, nearer the centre of the town – King's Furlong. Over the period 1965-69 about 300 houses were built here. In contrast it now

Photo: © HCMAS P1959.38 DPAAOR17

An 1959 aerial view showing the central re-development area from the north. Note the large areas of derelict land between Wote Street and Church Street and the Wharf (bottom left).

Photo: © HCMAS P1985.194/4

Aerial view of the same area showing the first stage of the Central Area re-development c 1985.

became the turn of an area far out from the centre, towards the north-east, separated from Oakridge by Ringway North. It was here, in the large area known as Popley, that construction began in 1966. This eventually added about 3,200 dwellings to the housing stock of the town. Its three major sub-divisions were identifiable by being named respectively after poets, abbeys and islands. Between 1967 and 1972, about 139 acres of land at Buckskin Farm, situated on the western edge of the borough, gradually became built over, to provide 1,100 new dwellings. One of the town's county councillors had farmed this land. He, like his fellow-farmers, had consistently argued against the loss of so much farmland. Their objections to loss of land and livelihood had prevailed in the 1950s, leading to a reduction in the proposed intake of population. On this occasion they were less fortunate, defeated, as they would say, by the extension of urban sprawl.

In December 1975, the Greater London Council published a consultative document 'Planned Growth outside London'. This expressed that council's concern about the economic and social effects of the decline in London's population, and also about the shortfall in the resources available for carrying out its policies of dispersal and urban renewal. It was a means of pointing out to the new and expanding towns that a new policy would need to be adopted, one of discouraging the movement of firms and people out of its area.

No town can separate itself off from what is happening to the national economy. The economic climate had worsened and firms which had been considering expansion and making a move from London were obliged by the increasing cost of construction and transfer to defer and cancel their plans. Basingstoke did not escape this slowing-down of economic activity and the consequent reduction in employment opportunity. Fewer people now wished to move to the town; there was a surplus of overspill houses; the authorities could economise by reducing the house-building programme to meet the changed circumstances.

A new unit of local government, the Basingstoke District Council (renamed Basingstoke & Deane Borough Council in 1978), had come into existence on 1st April, 1974.

The amalgamation of two predominantly rural areas – the Basingstoke Rural District Council and Kingsclere and Whitchurch Rural District Council – meant that, for the first time, rural members of the new body could directly influence decisions about the future growth of the town. They contributed to the formation of majority opinion against the continuation of the overspill scheme. Their views coincided with the GLC's wish to divert its reduced resources to schemes within its own area, and so the ground was prepared for the termination of the agreement which had done so much to alter the physical appearance of the town and its economic and social characteristics.

The final decision to bring the scheme to an end was taken in April 1976; it was to come into effect on 31st December, 1977. The *Borough Information Digest* of July 1976 reported, 'The District Council has decided ... that the time has come to slow down the forced expansion of Basingstoke by building council houses specifically for Londoners, and to concentrate on a more natural growth of the town and district by encouraging private development.'

It was expected that the employment opportunities to be offered by the growing town would attract people to Basingstoke independently of any overspill scheme, and so it was always intended that houses would be built for sale. In the 1963-64 *Annual Report of the Town Development Joint Committee* we read that it was the objective of the committee 'to keep private house-building in step with its own housing programme at a ratio of four council houses to one built for sale.' From 1979 onwards, when the last houses for overspill purposes were completed, building for private ownership would be the rule.

During the period 1965-1975, the triangle of land bounded by Hackwood Road, Cliddesden Road and the A30 was built on to form what came to be known as the Camrose estate. The

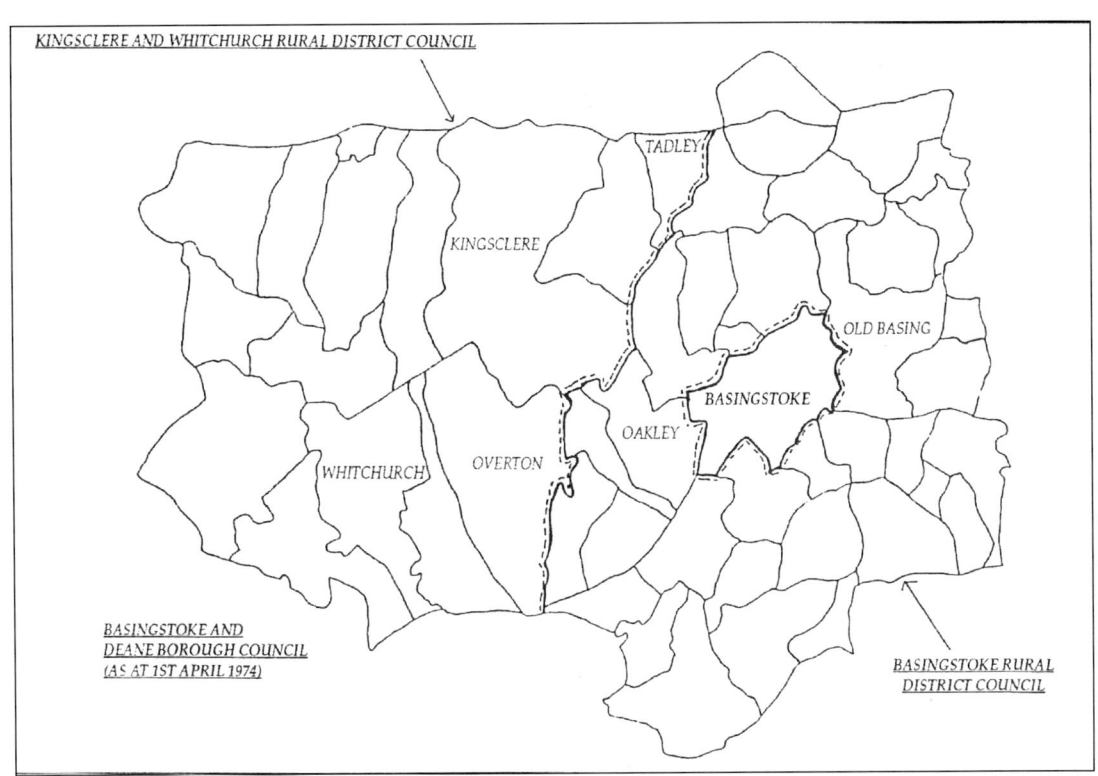

Map of the Borough of Basingstoke and Deane

Also shown are the areas administered by the pre-amalgamation Rural District Councils

development of the area had begun in 1955 with local authority housing. Side-by-side provision of private and council housing was in line with the stated policy of the County Council as planning authority. In 1968, building began on land at Eastrop, between the London Road and Eastrop Park, It continued until 1972. The pattern of closes, drives, walks and ways, including Loddon Drive and Thames Court, became known as Riverdene. The year 1968 was described as showing 'a noticeable and welcome increase in private housing'. Building was then in progress on ten different sites. From this time on, two of these, Kempshott and Brighton Hill, became the main areas of private housing in the town.

Brighton Hill was first mentioned as a possible area for housing in November 1967, when application was made for outline planning permission to use about 350 acres of land to build 3,200-3,500 dwellings. The location of this area of land, to the south-west of the town, between the A30 and the M3, was known only vaguely, if at all, to the majority of the townspeople. It became better known during the lengthy discussions which took place as the Town Map was being reviewed. An important contribution to the discussion came from the document *Basingstoke – Further Growth,* published by the Hampshire County Council in June 1970. This set out the arguments in support of future expansion. The available supply of land was being used up more quickly than had been anticipated. The main cause of this was that, in order to provide more open space and larger gardens, houses had been built to lower density than had been envisaged in the 1963 Town Map. The housing target set in the Town Development agreement would not be reached unless more land could be made available. Other arguments put forward were that it would not be possible to meet the demand, an increasing one, for private housing. There was also the need to anticipate the requirement of the town's second generation – the children who were growing up in the town and who would eventually be looking for employment and homes there. The further point was made that, because of the town's potential for growth, there would still be an impetus to expand after the completion of the overspill commitment.

The arguments in favour of further expansion were supported by estimates of the population of the Town Map Area. It was thought that this could be expected to rise from about 64,000 in 1971 to about 115,000 in 1986. Existing plans provided for a 1986 population of 89,000. The requirement, therefore, was for land to accommodate an estimated 26,000 people. After a study of areas considered suitable, it was thought that development could most appropriately occur in two places. These were: an area in extension of already existing housing at Brighton Hill requiring 623 acres and another one, to the north-east of the town, which consisted of Basing and the very much smaller community of Chineham, with the valley of the River Loddon in between, requiring 1,100 acres.

The proposals for these developments and the ideas underlying them were presented at public meetings held during the summer of 1970. From these meetings and other representations made, it became apparent that there was a strong body of opinion which favoured setting a limit to the growth of the town. The view of the Basingstoke RDC was clearly conveyed in a report in the *Basingstoke Gazette* of 14th August, 1970. 'The RDC accepts that Basingstoke should be allowed to grow, but more slowly. The upheaval of the last few years must be allowed to settle down, and growth should be limited to the minimum necessary to keep a live and balanced community.' A letter in the paper in March 1972 expressed the same opinion: 'Is there not an optimum size for a country town like Basingstoke? And is not Basingstoke already in danger of exceeding that optimum? Would it not be a good idea to call a halt, and instead of elaborating and expanding, take steps to consolidate, as a balanced, integrated, live community, the town as it is today?'

In May 1972, the County Council published *Draft proposals for Second Review Town Map*. This set out in greater detail what was likely to happen in the two areas most affected, and allowed discussion to continue. Bodies such as Country Watch, Cliddesden Action Group and the North Hampshire branch of the Council for the Protection of Rural England were active in opposition.

Country Watch was set up to reflect the views of the inhabitants of Basing/Chineham; it concerned itself also with the possible effects of future planning policy on rural communities in north-east Hampshire generally. Near neighbours, such as Sherborne St John and Sherfield-on-Loddon, made certain that their attitudes were made known, as did also the residents of the existing Brighton Hill development, of Cliddesden and of Kempshott. The authorities were left in no doubt about what was not wanted. The Basingstoke RDC was anxious to safeguard the area's rural character and so could not agree that it was necessary to provide for the population increase proposed. The outward growth of Basingstoke should be limited by means of a 'green belt'. More specifically, the proposed Loddon Valley Road should be abandoned. The interests of existing and new residential areas would be better served if the valley were to be developed as a 'linear park'. The proposals of the authorities were put before a public enquiry in November/December 1973. Following this, the area of land which it was proposing to develop at Chineham was reduced by 200 acres; the Loddon Valley Road was removed from the programme. In April 1977, the Council was able to announce the details of the plan for the Chineham area. Enough land would be made available to accommodate a population which would rise to about 12,000. This would involve the construction of about 3,800 houses, almost all of them for sale.

Chineham is now constituted a separate civil parish. In 1985 (October) it had a population of 3,194; at the 1991 Census it numbered 6,047. Brighton Hill South, also known as Hatch Warren (from the farm of that name) was able to be used for housing. Here land was to be made available for about 2,200 dwellings, all of them for sale. By the end of 1989 new housing covered almost the whole area.

Surprising though it may seem, the possibility of such a development had been mentioned as long ago as 1904, at the annual dinner of the Hants Imperial Yeomanry. The Rev G Jones,

Vicar of Dummer, in proposing the toast to the town and trade of Basingstoke, said that he hoped to see building taking place on Kempshott Hill. He said that he had read in the local paper that such an idea had been under discussion. The idea seemed to be that they were 'going to turn Basingstoke into a kind of west end of London.' He added that he was 'thankful however' that he lived on the other side of the little stone on the top of the hill. 'Nimbyism', it would seem, is not a new phenomenon.

[A much expanded account of the growth of the Town, and the effect of the overspill scheme, up to 1980, is given in Eric's Basingstoke – Expanding Town, WEA, 1980.

Doughnuts Galore – Basingstoke's London overspill days – the people's story, Mogg, C, 1997, *is a well-researched and well-written account of the London overspill era from the point of view of some of the people involved, which gives a human dimension to Eric's more formal account. Quoting from Roger Morris's Foreword (he was Mayor when the book was published): 'Utilising his journalistic talent and skills he portrays the human side of this period ... His graphic account of the effects this had on numbers of people born and bred in Basingstoke, together with the incoming Londoners, reminds us of the personal sacrifices many had to pay.*

The Basingstoke Talking History Project has recorded the memoirs of the upheaval of the overspill scheme of both incomers and original residents. These are available for access in the Resources Room of the Willis Museum.]

EDITORIAL UPDATE

The series of extracts from the 1:50000 Ordnance Survey maps for the period 1972 to 2005 on the following pages illustrates dramatically the growth of the town.

House building has continued at a steady pace. Since this draft was written, houses have been/are being built in the following town areas: 600 apartments at Victory Hill (the former Western Goods Yard); continued expansion at Chineham, Lychpit and Hatch Warren; and new development at Beggarwood Lane, Park Prewett; Merton Farm (Popley) and Old Kempshott Lane (Worting). Also at Chineham substantial office/warehouse/light industry building has continued in the various Business Parks.

Several of the Town Centre office blocks have been converted or are planned for conversion to apartments for sale or rent.

Considerable work has been carried out by the Housing Associations in redeveloping and infilling social housing areas, particularly parts of the original Oakridge overspill housing, to provide a mix of social, essential-user and rent-to-buy housing. The original monolithic maisonette blocks at Oakridge have been demolished to provide more people-friendly 'neighbourhood areas' with integral shops and facilities in an attempt to limit the scope for vandalism and other antisocial behaviour. Similar redevelopment is planned at Popley.

In October 2006 the Government named the borough as one of the country's 29 'New Growth Points' – areas where the population and economy are rapidly growing – and gave the Borough Council a £340,000 grant to fund studies into improving infrastructure, such as roads and sewerage, to support this expansion. Since then a further £5 million of government funding has been announced 'to help solve the borough's infrastructure issues and support major improvement projects over the next three years' (Basingstoke & Deane Today, Spring 2008). The South East England Regional Development Agency (SEEDA) has also labelled Basingstoke as one of the region's eight 'Diamonds for Growth' – economic power houses that will need Government investment to secure their future prosperity.

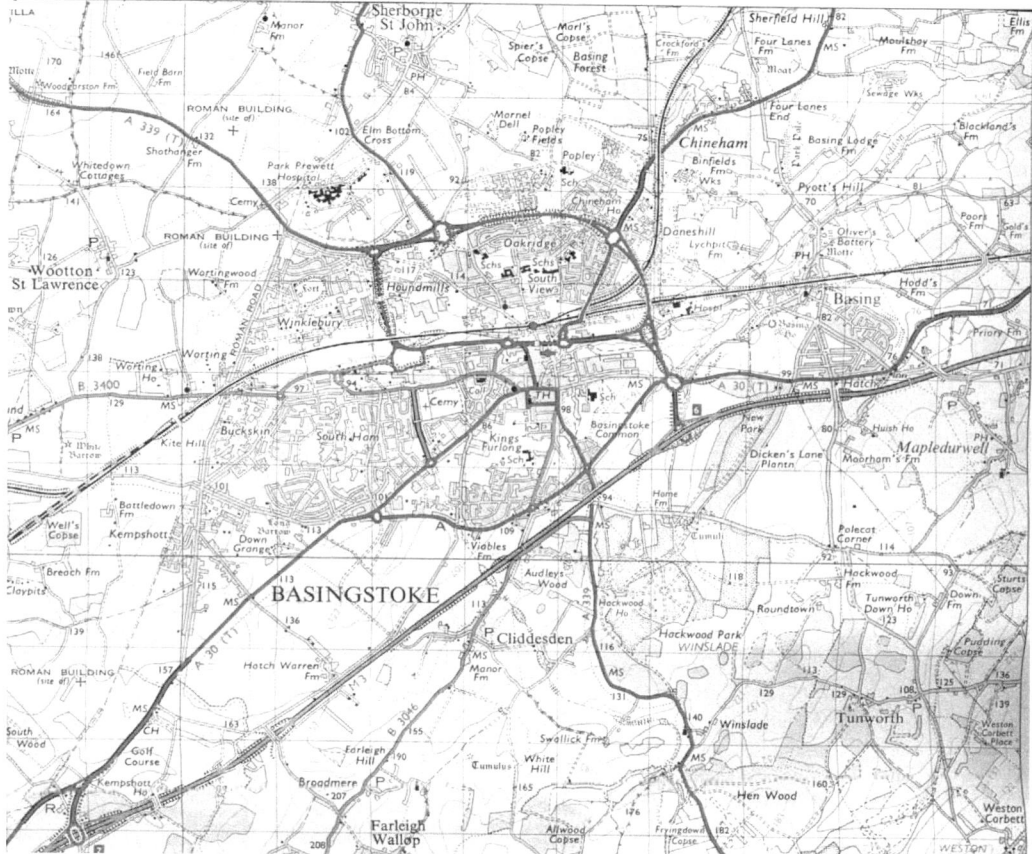

1972

Both maps: © Crown copyright. All rights reserved. Licence No100048022

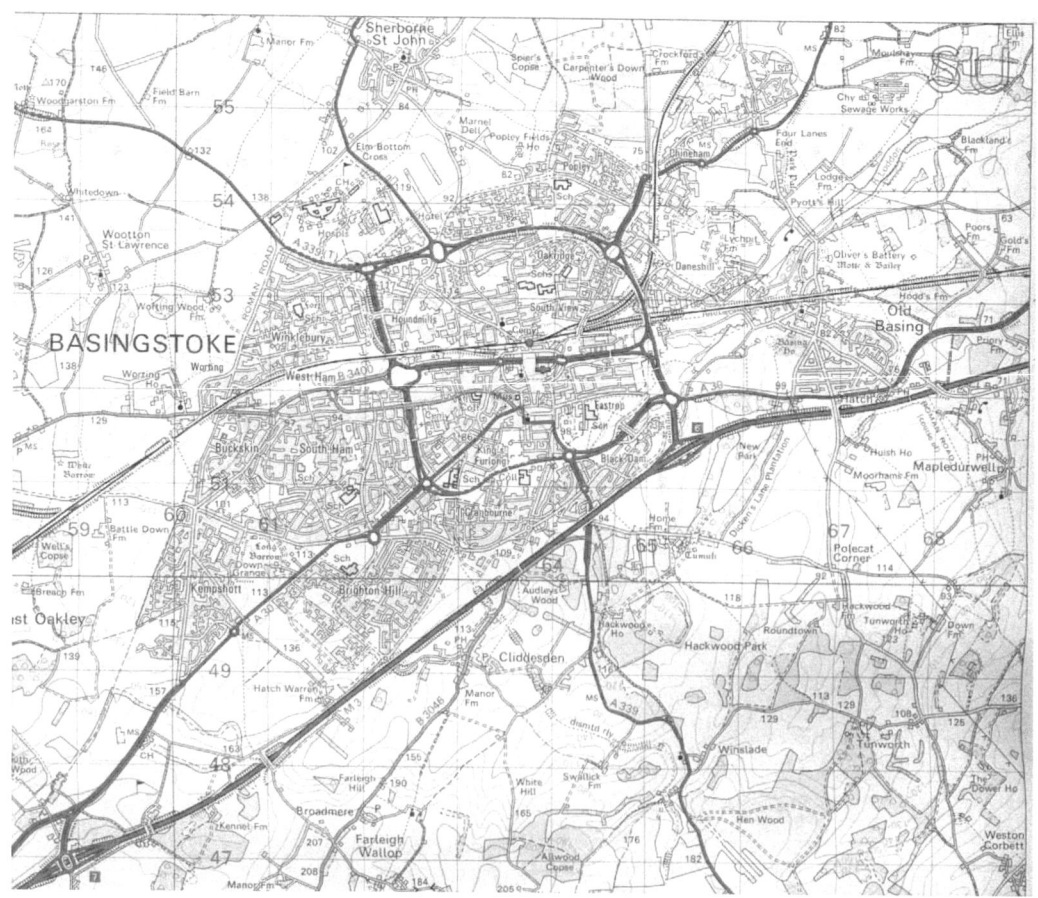

1982

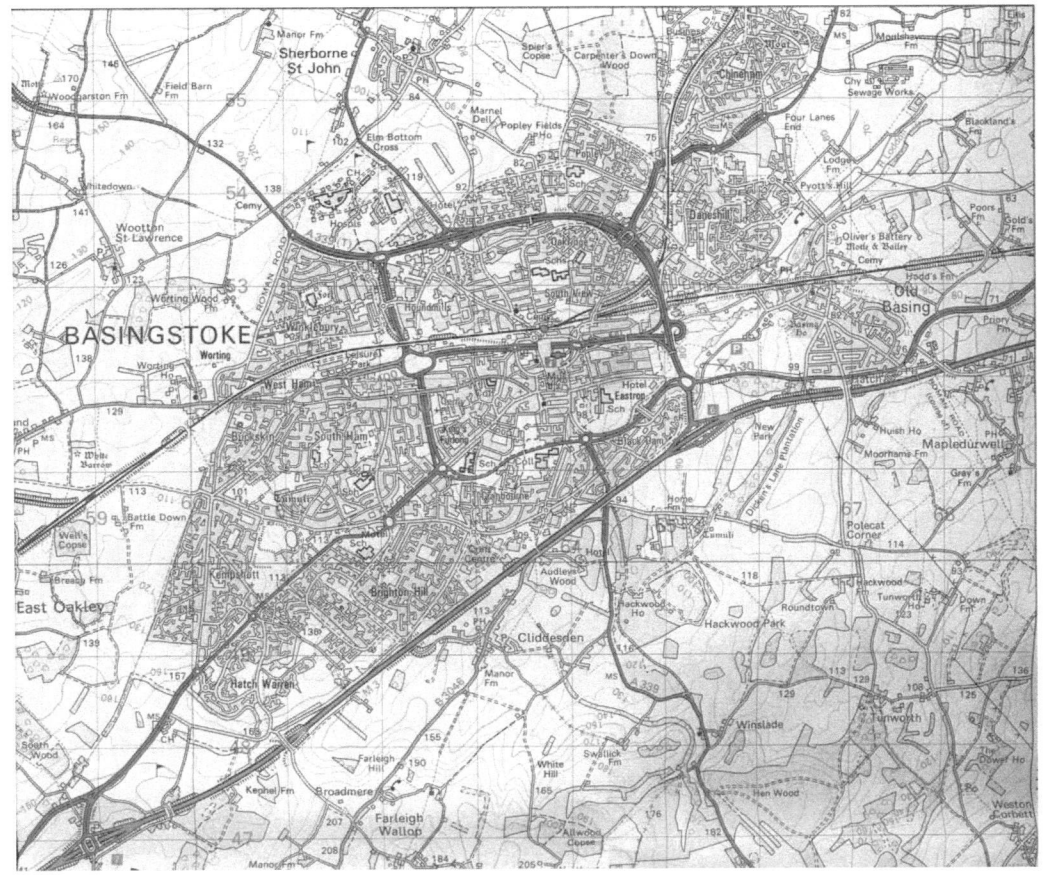

1994

Both maps: © Crown copyright. All rights reserved. Licence No100048022

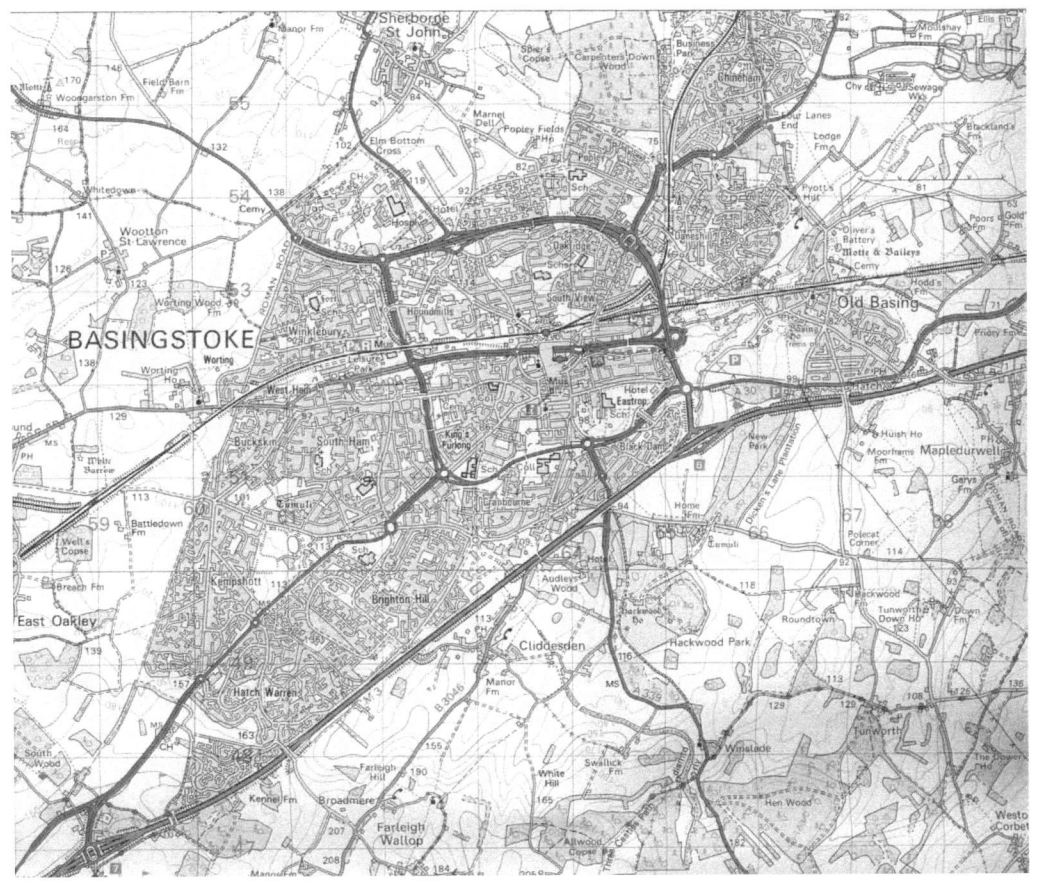

2005

17   RELIGION

Basingstoke – notoriously difficult to move in religious matters. But results encouraging!

Report on a Wesleyan Mission to the town

St Michael's Church

It is unfortunate that lack of records prevents us from giving as detailed an account as we should like of the early history of St Michael's Church. A church in the town is first mentioned in Domesday: 'The Church of St Michael on the Mount holds of the King [William 1] one church with one hide and the tithes of the Manor of Basingstoke. One priest is there, and two villeins [villagers] and four boors [smallholders] with one plough [land], a mill let at 20 shillings, and two acres of meadow. The whole worth 4 pounds and 5 shillings. Bishop Walter [of Hereford] held the land under King Edward [the Confessor], but it did not belong to his bishopric.' The monks of the Abbey of St Michael had been given the church and tithes in 1077. It is probable that, following this gift, an original small Saxon church was replaced by a larger one, dedicated to St Michael.

The next important event in the history of the church occurred in 1233, when Peter de Rupibus, Bishop of Winchester, purchased the advowson (the right of patronage or presentation to a living) of the church at Basing, Basingstoke and Selborne. This provided him with the means of establishing a priory at Selborne. In 1244, the Bishop of Winchester, William de Raleigh, decreed that the work of the church in Basingstoke, Basing and Nately should be carried out by a vicar and four chaplains. Basingstoke was to be served by the vicar himself, with the assistance of two chaplains, 'one for the living, the other for the dead.' The vicar, or his chaplain, was responsible, 'as in olden times' for the chapel at Nately; he was to find 'two fit chaplains' to minister to the people at Basing. The patronage of all three places was retained by the priory at Selborne until 1486. In that year, the priory was dissolved by Pope Innocent VIII, its possessions being transferred to Magdalen College, Oxford.

The fabric of the church underwent change in 1464, with the rebuilding of the chancel (at a cost of £120). St Michael's took on its present proportions and appearance during the early years of the 16th century, more particularly between 1510 and 1521. The work involved the taking down of the main body of the church and the complete rebuilding of the nave, aisle and tower. The south porch of the church and the parvise were both added in 1539. The inspirer of the work was Bishop Fox. The external appearance remained the same until the tower received 'the stately diadem of pinnacled turrets for which it [had] waited some 400 years.' *[Vicar's letter in* Parish Magazine, *January 1879]* Further change occurred with the addition of the memorial chapel to commemorate those who had lost their lives in the 1914-18 War.

Most people have throughout the centuries been more than satisfied with the appearance of the church. We should probably find it difficult to recognize it from the description it received in 1669: 'a small and very indifferent building.' This was how Cosmo III, Grand Duke of Tuscany, saw it when he came to the town, while engaged on the Grand Tour of Europe. Thomas Hardy appears not to have been impressed either. In 1896, in *Jude the Obscure* he referred to Stoke Barehills (his name for Basingstoke) with its 'gaunt, unattractive ancient church.'

The intertwining of religion and politics during the 16th century gave rise to unsettling events in the life of the nation. However, the changes which accompanied Henry VIII's break with Rome appear to have had little impact on the religious life of the people of Basingstoke. In August 1538, Thomas Cromwell, Lord Privy Seal, ordered William Sandys to have an 'idolatrous image' removed from St Michael's Church. It was to be transported to London, pending its destruction. Although the offending figure was one which appeared to have been 'greatly venerated by the people', there is no record of anything untoward having happened to disturb the way of life of the ordinary citizen. It might have been expected that the policy of dissolving religious bodies, whether monasteries or religious guilds, would have been applied to the town in the case of the Guild of the Holy Ghost, but this did not happen. The Guild was in fact suppressed under Edward VI, only to be re-founded by Mary in 1556. During the reigns of Edward, Mary and Elizabeth, local priest and parishioner seem to have been able to adapt to the changing circumstances of the times.

The interaction of politics and religion was again much in evidence in the 17th century – locally, very much so, particularly following the outbreak of the Civil War in 1642. The struggle between King and Parliament was to place Basingstoke at the centre of the nation's affairs, given that Basing House, the home of John Paulet, 5th Marquess of Winchester, was 'the greatest Royalist strong point in the county.' St Michael's Church was indirectly involved in events. During the siege of Basing House, which began in November 1643 and continued with varying intensity until October 1645, Parliamentary forces quartered in Basingstoke used the church as a store for gunpowder. This exploded, seriously damaging the church. The Churchwardens' Accounts for 1646 refer to donations given towards the repair of the church and to a petition 'to the Committee at Winchester for allowance towards the reparation of the church, very much torn by the blowing-up of gunpowder lying in the church.' Another reference is to materials being brought from the demolition of Basing House to be used in repairing the church. In the 1643-44 accounts there was some reference to the digging of graves for soldiers.

The Society of Friends

The Restoration of the monarchy, in the person of Charles II, in 1660, meant a return to the forms of organization and worship of the Established Church. There were those who were unwilling to accept the Anglican way and were prepared to show dissent or non-conformity. This began to manifest itself in the form of the Quaker movement, later to be better known as the Society of Friends. The Society appears to have come into being some time after 1647, the year in which George Fox made his first converts in Manchester. On his travels he visited Basingstoke in 1656. In his *'Journal of the Travels and Sufferings of George Fox'* he wrote, 'Then, leaving Farnham, we came to Basingstoke, a very rude town, where they had formerly much abused Friends. There I had a Meeting in the evening, which was quiet, for the Lord's power chained the unruly.'

In *A Collection of the Sufferings of the People called Quakers, for the Testimoney of a Good Conscience, from the time of their first being distinguished by that name, in the year 1650 to the Time of the Act, commonly called the Act of Toleration, etc*, we are told what happened in July 1655, when Thomas Robertson and Ambrose Ring came to Basingstoke, and held a meeting there. The 'glowing ardour' of their preaching was objected to, in particular by the Vicar of Basingstoke, Stephen Evered (alias Webb). He was reported to have 'uttered several invective speeches against them.' Accompanied by a Justice of the Peace and others, he tried to persuade them to cease their preaching, by insisting on their swearing the oath of Abjuration. As they were quite unwilling to do this, they were committed to prison, where they remained for fifteen weeks. In attempting to visit them Robert Hodgson was also imprisoned – for sixteen weeks.

In 1657, it is recorded that Mary Spicer suffered ten months imprisonment for 'reproving the priest at Basingstoke.' We do not know what occasioned the reproof but it seems an excessively heavy sentence.

In the same and following years we find that others were put in prison for the non-payment of rates for church purposes. References in the Churchwardens' accounts reveal the way in which the authorities 'distraine' the possessions of those who were in arrears. In 1731, there is an entry to the effect that 10 bushels of malt belonging to Robert Applegarth were sold for 31s.8d. to cover the sum of 30s.8d. John Mitchell owed 9s., so 18 lb of his pewter (dishes and plates etc) were sold at 6d. per lb. An entry for 1737 listed 'the arrears that we strained [sic] from the Quakers for what was due for the years 1734-35 and 1736.' Among the offenders were Mr Applegarth, Mr Portsmouth, Mr Mitchell and Mr Hack, who, between them, owed the sum of £2.13s.6d. The sale of items such as wheat, oats, beans, pewter, spades and nails brought in £2.16s.10d. The difference of 3s.4d. is recorded as being due to the Quakers.

A Basingstoke Meeting of the Society of Friends was established in 1668 and a meeting-house was erected in the Reading Road in the following year. From 1696 another building in the same road was used. A small area of ground on the north side of that road, near where Goddard's Lane joined Reading Road, came into use as a burial ground. Later another meeting-house came into use on the west side of Wote Street. It was rebuilt in 1849. It was demolished in 1966, when the clearance of the town centre took place.

The passage of the Act of Toleration of 1689 ensured for Friends the right to worship freely according to their own principles and beliefs. They no longer had to face the hostility of the clergy of the Established Church; they were no longer ill-used by the mob who either would not or could not understand the Quaker way. In course of time they came to be respected for their own good works, both nationally and in the local community. Among the well-known local Friends were members of the Sterry, Steevens and Wallis families.

The fortunes of the Basingstoke Meeting have fluctuated over the years. Today, although numbers continue small, there is still a Quaker presence in the town. For a period in the later 20th century they made use of a house in Cromwell Road as a Meeting House and for social welfare purposes.

Methodism

In the 18th century, the town experienced another form of dissent: that associated with what became known as the Methodist Revival. This originated as a result of the two Wesley brothers, John and Charles, joining with some of their contemporaries at Oxford to form a 'Holy Club', devoted to the strict methodical practice of their religious beliefs.

Both brothers were moved to take their religion to the people, particularly to the 'neglected poor'. They travelled countrywide, preaching wherever people would assemble to hear them. Where they were not prevented by the opposition of local clergy, they would hold services in the parish church (both had been ordained priests of the Church of England). Often their meetings would take place in the open air; on occasions they would make use of an inn to address an assembled congregation, as is shown by a letter written by the Vicar of Basingstoke, the Rev. T Warton, to the Town Clerk, Mr John Russell, Attorney at law. It is dated 13th February, 1738-9: 'They write from Basingstoke, that on Sunday last the Reverend Mr Charles Kinchin MA, Rector of the Church of Dummer in the Bishop of Winchester's diocese, and Fellow of Corpus Christi College [where his Lordship is Visitor] held a publick meeting consisting chiefly of Dissenters of both sexes, who were very numerous at the Crown Inn in that town, where he prayed much extempore and expounded or preached after the manner of the Methodists, taking a whole chapter for his text; the noted Mr Whitfield, an itinerant Preacher lately arrived from Georgia, having done the same at The King's Head on the Thursday, and at The Crown on the Friday and Saturday next preceding. NB. It is presumed that the aforesaid Inns have licence to sell Ale and other Liquors usually retailed at Publick Houses, but for no other purpose whatsoever.'

John Wesley first came to Basingstoke in the following year, on Saturday, 10th March, 1739. He wrote in his journal, 'In the afternoon I came to Dummer and on Sunday morning had a large and intelligent congregation. I was desired to expound in the evening at Basingstoke.' On a later visit on 10th February, 1759, he must have met with a certain amount of opposition. The entry in his journal reads, 'In the afternoon we rode to Basingstoke, where the people put me in mind of the wild beasts of Ephesus. Yet they were unusually attentive in the evening.' He came again the same year, on 24th September; then he found his congregation to be 'a people slow of heart and dull of understanding.'

He was more optimistic on the occasion of his visit, on 30th September, 1763, for he then wrote, 'From Whitchurch to Basingstoke. Even here there is at length some prospect of doing good. A large number of people attended, to whom God enabled me to speak strong words, and they seemed to sink into the hearts of the hearers.'

Wesley's preaching and that of others was effective for, despite the intolerance and discouragement they had to face, Methodism took hold in the town. In the early days meetings used to be held in an upper room in Potters Lane (part of a granary). In November 1875, a purpose-built chapel was opened in Church Street. This was replaced by a larger building in March 1905. Unfortunately, it was badly damaged by bombing in August 1940. It was no longer able to be used for worship; it became instead an emergency food store. After the war it was rebuilt and re-opened in 1950 (7th September) only to be demolished in 1967, when the Town Centre was cleared, preparatory to re-development. The site it occupied is marked by a stone set into the paved area of Clifton Walk, which leads from Church Street to Porchester Square.

The Countess of Huntingdon's Connexion (Immanuel Church)

Selina, Countess of Huntingdon (1707-1791) became a member of Wesley's first Methodist Society, founded in Fetter Lane, London in 1739. She gradually came more under the influence of George Whitfield, eventually making him her domestic chaplain. It was Whitfield who, through the force of his personality and preaching, attracted many well-known and well-placed people to her house in Park Lane. She hoped that her 'dissenting connexion' would have some appeal to members of the upper classes. Following-up this idea, she encouraged the setting-up of chapels at various places where people of quality used to foregather. The first three were fashionable watering-places – Brighton (1761), Bath (1765), Tunbridge Wells (1769).

Apart from the fact that both Wesley and Whitfield were occasional visitors to the town, we do not know why Basingstoke should have preceded those places with a place of worship established in Church Street in 1755; we do know that it was replaced in 1775 by a chapel in Wote Street, which later (1802) had to be enlarged because of the increasing size of the congregation.

The use of the term 'connexion' is interesting, reinforcing, as it does, the point that there was initially no break with the Church of England. This did not occur until 1783. So far as Basingstoke was concerned, the trust deed drawn up for the new Chapel stipulated that the liturgy of the Church of England was to be used in its services. We are told that the Rev. Thomas Thorne, 'one of Lady Huntingdon's ministers', was the minister from 1799. When the new chapel was opened, on 11th June, 1802, it was he who read the 'prayers of the Established Church.'

The building, together with its associated manse and small burial ground, formerly occupied the site next to that later occupied by Jukes, the Chemist, in Wote Street. *[Now the Bakehouse Pie Shop]*

The United Reformed Church

The church which we today know as the United Reformed Church was formerly known as the Congregational Church. The building - the Meeting House – first came into use in 1801, but Congregationalism has a longer history than that. It dates from 1663.

An Act of Uniformity was passed in 1662, which, like its predecessors of 1549 and 1559, was intended as a means of regularising the services of the Church of England. The Act provided for the expulsion of priests from the established Church, if they were unwilling to conform, particularly in the use of the liturgy of the new Prayer Book. It is estimated that some 2,000 priests found it impossible to do so and resigned their livings. One of these was John Hook, whose ministry to the Independent community lasted from 1663 to 1719. Meetings could not be held publicly, so members resorted to holding services in their own homes.

The passage of the Toleration Acts of 1689-1695 gave official recognition to Non-conformists; from then it was possible for them to meet openly. They did so in a meeting-place next to the former Blue Coat School in Cross Street. This was used until an increasing congregation made the provision of a new building necessary. The new building was opened on 25th August, 1801, and underwent enlargement in 1839 and 1870.

Among the ministers who served the Independent community in Basingstoke was one John Curwen, who achieved distinction, nationally and internationally, by devising and applying a new system of music notation – the Tonic Sol-fa.

The Baptists

In their chapter 'Non-conformists in Basingstoke 1650-1888', in their *History of Basingstoke*, Baigent and Millard made very brief mention of two small religious communities, then relatively newly established in the religious life of the town: 'The Baptists have a small chapel of recent date (1867) in Church Street, and the Roman Catholics a chapel in the Burgess Road.' The small chapel of the Baptists was the building which later became the Moose Hall. Better known is the building on Sarum Hill, later used by the King's School. This building, opened originally in 1841, to house the British School, was purchased in 1908 by a small group who decided to establish a meeting place there. They were helped in their endeavours by the Rev. Alfred Bird and other Baptists from Whitchurch. The official opening took place on the 9th July 1908.

*The Baptist church in Church Street
An earlier, smaller chapel was built in Flaxfield Road.*

Photo: © Sid Penney

The Roman Catholics

The Act of Toleration of 1689 did not apply to Roman Catholics and so they continued to live and worship under a number of disabilities. These were gradually removed by legislation passed between 1771 and 1791. An Act passed in the latter year granted Catholics, both clerical and lay, the right to worship in public. In Basingstoke this did not bring about any immediate changes. As elsewhere, the Catholic community remained small and without the services of a priest. A change occurred in 1866, when a priest first started coming from Fleet. He held services in an inn, probably *The Barge Inn*, at the bottom of Wote Street.

Further changes came in 1878, with the arrival of Father James Daly, to become the first resident Roman Catholic priest in the town. We are told that he bought No 4 Burgess Road and also a small plot of land at the corner of the cemetery. On the day on which the first sod was to be cut for the site of the new building, a party of about 120 men marched up Chapel Street, with the intention of preventing the work from going ahead. Father Daly was equally determined that it should proceed. Taking off his coat, he showed that they would have to deal with him first. His display of 'Muscular Christianity' (he was over six feet tall) gained him the day. Many of the men remained to help with the work. The *Hants & Berks Gazette* of 18th May, 1878 records, 'The Holy Ghost Chapel, recently erected in Burgess Road, was opened by the Bishop of Southwark.' It continued in use as a church until 1899, also serving as a school during the week. Its name, of course, was derived from the original early 13th century Holy Ghost Chapel, the ruins of which are situated not far away, in the Liten.

The present Church of the Holy Ghost was built through the vision and effort of Canon Scholes, at a time when there was a proposal by the Bishop of Portsmouth to withdraw the resident priest from Basingstoke, reverting to the practice of former times of having a priest visit from Fleet. Canon Scholes, who was a trained architect, had built a Holy Ghost Church at Yeovil. He had seen the Holy Ghost 'ruins' at Basingstoke, as he passed by in the train. Inspired by their related history, he offered to come to Basingstoke to serve as priest and to build another Holy Ghost Church. He came in 1899 and by December of that year had built a presbytery. The work was completed in 1903, the consecration of the church taking place on 9th September of that year.

'The Basingstoke Brawl'

The Salvation Army arrived in the town in September 1880. It met with opposition when its strongly pro-temperance mission came into sharp conflict with local brewery interests, 'The Basingstoke Brawl' described in Chapter 13, resulting in the reading of the Riot Act.

Members of local non-conformist congregations tended to side with the Salvationists, but the Established Church was less sure what its attitude should be. Although it was willing to acknowledge that the 'Army' succeeded in 'securing the adhesion of many who had stood entirely aloof from all religious influences', it was not sure how to treat such a 'novel and highly emotional form of religion.'

Confrontation, which continued from time to time for two or three more years, was eventually replaced by acceptance. Baigent and Millard were able to write in 1889, 'All this excitement has long since happily subsided. The people of Basingstoke, have acquiesced in the wisdom of leaving the 'Army' to its own devices, and the result has been that it has tempered its zeal with discretion, and has ceased to be in any way a serious cause of annoyance.'

Since then the Salvation Army has maintained without interference its regular Sunday morning parades round the town, besides engaging in its normal welfare work, necessary even in prosperous Basingstoke. *[In 2007, the Salvation Army opened their new Basingstoke Citadel in Wessex Close.*

The Hampshire Record Office has a collection of Dissenters' Meeting House certificates (licences), **HRO 21M65/F2***, that include several for Basingstoke properties. The earliest is for James Jackson, Baptist, in Wote Street, 16/6/1729.]*

EDITORIAL UPDATE

The Anglican Church

Contributed by Mary Oliver, former Churchwarden of St Michael's

The Anglican community continues to evolve to meet the changing circumstances in the town. With the growth in population in the later 19th century, St Michael's established mission churches in Reading Road and May Street.

May Street Mission church

Photo: © Sid Penney

With the further expansion south and west, the Vicar, in 1900, Dr Cooper Smith, and his sisters bought in a site at the corner of Southern Road for a new church. An iron church was erected and came into use in 1902. It was decided to make this a more permanent building, and serious fund-raising began in 1914, in spite of the outbreak of war. A retired clergyman who lived in the town, Rev. Alexander Hall, gave very generously to this project, enabling the splendid Gothic design of the architect, Temple Moore, to be fully realised. Chilmark stone was used, and the interior furniture and fittings were also either designed or overseen by Temple Moore. In recent times, more works of art have been given to All Saints Church, including Dame Elizabeth Frink's 'Head of Christ', and stained glass windows designed by Cecil Collins and made by Patrick Reyntiens. By tradition, the church has always belonged to the catholic wing of the Church of England, but also is in the forefront of developments in the church – it was one of the first in 1994 to have a woman priest on the staff.

Expansion to the west was catered for by the establishment of St Peter's Church in South Ham. To begin with, the church community met in a building in King's Road, now the Labour Hall, but in 1964/5 a new church in an exciting modern style designed by Ronald Sims was opened in Pinkerton Road.

Further expansion led to the setting up of a caravan church in Popley in 1967, which later became a permanent building - the Bethlehem Chapel - in 1973, and finally expanded into St Gabriel's Church in 1991.

Christ the King at Brighton Hill also began as a caravan church, later transformed into a permanent building. For many years until 2006, it was a shared building with the Roman Catholics. It has just (2007) celebrated its 30th anniversary.

The five churches – St Michael's, All Saints, St Peter's, St Gabriel's, and Christ the King work closely together as a Team Ministry, led by the Rector at St Michael's. This was set up in 1970. One of the two suffragan bishops of the diocese of Winchester bears the title of Bishop of Basingstoke, recognising Basingstoke's position as the largest centre of population in the north of the county.

Expansion to the west has also been catered for by the church of St Thomas of Canterbury at Worting. The medieval parish church here was rebuilt in 1848 to a design by Henry Woodyer. Also within the Worting parish now are the Church of the Good Shepherd at Winklebury, and St Mark's at Kempshott.

To the east, the parish of Old Basing, still served by its ancient church, St Mary's, supported the establishment of a new church at Chineham, Christchurch, which has recently become a separate parish.

Eastrop remains a separate parish.

MO

St Mary's Church, Eastrop   Contributed by Derek Wren

The parish of Eastrop is one of Basingstoke's anomalies – a small parish on the east side of Basingstoke, as the name describes it, which, after remaining unchanged for hundreds of years, is now at the very centre of the town. It remained a separate parish outside Basingstoke until 1892 when the civil parish was split into two parts, the urban area becoming a ward of the borough and the rural area going to Basing; the ecclesiastical parish remained independent.

The manor was first created by the Saxon king Edmund the Elder in 945. After the Conquest William gave it to Alfred of Marlborough who let it to Hugh (Baigent & Millard, p55). Hugh de Port also held Basing and other manors around Basingstoke. The entry in the Domesday Book describes the population as consisting of 23 villagers, 15 smallholders and 3 slaves. It is believed that a manor house and mill were built by the river Loddon, with a chapel attached to the house. The manor was held by different owners until 1805 when the last 4/5ths were sold to the local landowner, Lord Bolton. The lords of the manor seem not to have lived in Eastrop since the 16th century and the manor house ceased to exist sometime in the 16th century.

A church was built on the present site in about 1540 at the instigation of the Rector, Dr Lesse. The chapel was then disendowed. Nothing appears to remain of that original building.

The present building is an odd mixture – a late Georgian chancel of brick; a Victorian rebuild of the nave in 1886, brick on the inside and faced with stone with a flint dado on the outside; and the Edwardian nave, designed by Sir Thomas Jackson, built in 1912. This was the first phase of a larger scheme, which was never completed. The nave is rendered on the inside and faced with stone on the outside and consists of three bays with a tiled roof carried on timber trusses. Its proportions with its high roof suggest it was intended to be much longer.

Photo of print © R Applin

*A print of Worting Church before its fire and Victorian restoration.
St Mary's Eastrop probably looked very similar, although it was thatched.*

In a directory of 1865 St Mary's was claimed to be one of the smallest churches in Hampshire. Dimensions on a picture of the church, painted about 1800 and kept in the cathedral at Winchester, give the church a length of 38 feet and a width of 22 feet. Subsequent extensions show how the population of the parish was growing. In 1676 there were only 24 inhabitants; in 1859 there were 62 but by 1901 the number was 300. Now the whole parish, which is a small part of Basingstoke, is residential

In the eighteenth century two brothers who, in succession, held the living of Eastrop, went on to achieve fame in the world of literature. They were the sons of Thomas Warton, who had himself been Professor of Poetry at Oxford before becoming Vicar of St Michael's in 1723. When his eldest son Joseph came down from Oxford, he was inducted as Curate of Eastrop, being made Vicar a few years later. His brother Thomas took over from him. Both became well known afterwards for their poetry, biographies and literary criticism, but it is Thomas who was appointed Poet Laureate in 1785. He is best remembered for his 'History of English Poetry.'

During the rebuilding of the nave in 1886, the thatch was removed from the roof and replaced by tiles. It seems that a gallery at the west end had been erected before 1886, possibly even as early as 1746. This was taken down in the 1912 extension. Pews had first been put in the church in 1794.

During the years between 1965 and 1980, when the Rev. Denis Boumon was Rector, the congregation began to grow and the decisive move was made to the Evangelical wing of the Church of England. St Mary's drew worshippers in, not only from other parts of the town but from beyond the boundaries of Basingstoke. By the 1990s the church could not accommodate the numbers of people attending. Architects Plinke, Leaman and Browning, who had already designed St Mark's at Kempshott, were asked to prepare plans for a new extension which would seat 500. This church, known as the Auditorium was built to the south west of the existing church It is joined to the old church by an entrance hall and parish office The Auditorium is separated from the church hall, built in 1980, by a wide corridor with a glazed roof. This space is known as the coffee shop where coffee and cakes are available every weekday morning. The new church was consecrated in 1995.

The Auditorium is a large, roughly square structure, mostly of brick, with a massive pyramidal tiled roof crowned by a small glazed lantern. A submerged font for baptism by total immersion was formed in front of the altar. The money for this work, which cost a million pounds, was all raised by the congregation.

Both the old and the new churches are used for services. In 2002 the old church was restored, the pews removed, the floors carpeted and chairs installed. A moveable screen was installed which separates the 1912 nave from the rest of the church. This area is used for meetings unless the screen is folded back so that the whole church can be used for services. The whole complex provides spaces and facilities to meet every requirement. The parish of Eastrop is now a very small part of Basingstoke but its parish church, once noted for being so small, is now one of the largest, if not the largest church, in the town.

DW

The Methodists built St Andrews in Western Way in the mid 1950s and in the 1960s a new church/hall at Oakridge Centre but consolidated their resources by building a new church, Trinity, in Sarum Hill to replace the Church Street building demolished for Town development and their existing church in Sarum Hill; their George Street Mission chapel was later sold. The long-established church in Kempshott Lane continues to provide pastoral care for the Kempshott area. This building, despite having a modern entrance, is a good example of an early 20th century 'tin tabernacle'.

For the expanding Catholic community, the Portsmouth diocese has made a continuing increase in provision. From the mid 1950s St Joseph's parish on the western side of town was established, building its first church in Western Way (now Carpenter's Court) and later the modern building in the grounds of Bishop Challoner School in St Michael's Road. The Holy Ghost church in Burgess Road became too small and, to a certain extent, is in the wrong place for its modern congregation. A new 400-seat church, St Bede's, has been opened in Popley Way. The Holy Ghost church, a grade II listed building, continues in use for funerals and weddings but is no longer a parish church. One aspect has come almost full circle. For many years after World War 2, Masses were provided in Polish for a substantial Polish community in the displaced persons' camp, at Bramley. Now, with the accession of Poland to the EU and an influx of Poles to the town, translation into Polish of Bible readings at Masses are being offered. The fall in the number of priests has led to the loss of Masses at the

Anglican churches at Oakley and Old Basing and the shared church at Brighton Hill, and priests and deacons now have to work not just in their existing parishes but also in the wider 'Pastoral Area' of Andover, Basingstoke, Tadley and Hook.

Photo © Charlotte Wood kindly supplied by JBKS Architects Ltd

St Bede's Roman Catholic church, Popley. Consecrated in 2007, this is a fine addition to the modern architecture of the town.

The Baptist Church has moved from its Sarum Hill church, which has become The King's School, to Brighton Hill.

Other minor sects such Spiritualist, Jehovah's Witness have been established in the town for many years. As the town has expanded, other Christian and non-Christian denominations have established places of worship for their congregations, reflecting the wide diversity of the modern population.

18   EDUCATION

I believe it will be absolutely necessary that you should prevail on our future masters to learn their letters.

Robert Lowe - 15th July, 1867 House of Commons

Lowe was speaking on the 1867 Reform Bill. Sixty years before, another MP, Davies Giddy, had questioned the value of educating the poor, 'However specious in theory the project might be of giving education to the labouring classes of the poor, it would be prejudicial to their morals and their happiness; it would teach them to despise their lot in life, instead of making them good servants in agriculture and other laborious employments; instead of teaching them subordination, it would render them fractious and refractory.'

Towards the end of the 19th century it was becoming increasingly recognised that a lack of satisfactory basic (elementary) education was a major underlying cause of failure to develop new techniques and apply new processes to industry. At the time Lowe was speaking of 'educating our masters' the vast majority of children attended school only irregularly and for too short a time. The Newcastle Commission (the Duke of Newcastle was its chairman) had been set up in 1858 to 'inquire into the Present State of Popular Education in England and to consider and report what measures, if any, are required for the Extension of sound and cheap Elementary Instruction to all Classes of the People.' Although the first grant from public funds (the sum of £20,000) had been made in 1833, the State remained very much on the sidelines. It was not until 1870 that Parliament legislated to ensure improvement in the existing provision of elementary education.

It was characteristic of the *laissez-faire* attitudes of the times that the provision of education was left to the initiative of individuals or societies. We see this in the work of the Sunday Schools and the parochial charity schools; it can also be seen in the education provided by the two societies which benefited from the grant of public money in 1833. These were the Royal Lancastrian Association, founded in 1810 (renamed the British and Foreign Bible Society in 1814), and the National Society (for promoting the education of the poor in the Principles of the Established Church throughout England and Wales), which was founded in 1811 and took over the work of the charity schools.

Both these societies were established in the town and made a great contribution to the education of its children. The British Schools were started as an infants' school in 1838 in the Congregational Church, and in 1840 were situated on Sarum Hill. The building later became the Baptist Church; and later the King's School. No building was ever specially provided for the sole use of the National Schools. In the middle of the 19th century infants were being taught in the Vicarage; use was also being made of 'a large but homely building called the Malthouse' (Church Cottage) from 1871. The buildings of Richard Aldworth School, re-opened in Cross Street in 1862, were also used by the National Schools.

An interesting insight into the prevailing attitude towards educating children is given by the report of 25th December, 1852 on the end-of-term examination. We are told that the Vicar, the Rev. Blatch, conducted the examination and interrogated the children in the various branches of their education. The pupils acquitted themselves very satisfactorily and for those 'who were most deserving because of their regular attendance and diligent attention there were handsome presents of good and useful clothing.' The report concluded with a reference to the 'benevolence, liberality and Munificence' of those who provided the gifts, among whom were the Dowager Lady Bolton, Mrs R Apletree and the Rev. Blatch himself.

By the 1870s, both societies were facing difficulties in providing education for a rapidly increasing child population. It would seem that the Corporation had ceased to contribute to the maintenance of the Schools. Without the existence of a School Board, they had no legal powers to do this from the rates; they could, however, make sums available from other sources e.g. income from property. On 3rd August, 1878, Canon Millard, on behalf of the National Schools, wrote a letter to the Corporation, asking that it should make the grant previously given to the schools. On the 19th of the same month, in a letter published in the local paper, we have the following details: 500 children were being educated by the National Schools and there was a proposal to open an additional school for 70 children at Totterdown (Reading Road). His letter continues, 'The National Schools which a few years ago were deeply in debt are now solvent and have all the necessary plant in good condition.'

A similar letter was written by Mr Wallis on behalf of the British Schools. In this it was stated that the two departments of the School (upper and infants) were, in 1877, educating a total of 325 children, that the schools were well equipped and that they had been well reported on by HM Inspector, Mr T W Green, in February 1878. In his report, this gentleman had given the information that between 1st April, 1843 and 31st January, 1878, a total of 2,540 pupils (1,622 boys, 918 girls) had attended the British Schools in Basingstoke. Reference was also made to the Legislation of recent years (the 1870 Education Act) and the hope was expressed that the local authorities would use compulsory powers to implement this. The need seems to have been greater in respect of the National Schools, for the buildings being used were condemned by an inspector as failing to meet the requirements of the Education Department and for being too small to meet the growing demand for places. In February 1880, it was educating 114 boys, 107 girls, while there were 102 in the infants' department.

It is necessary to remind ourselves that, besides an annual grant from the government and any contribution that might be available from the Corporation, the schools depended on income from fees. As a note in the St Michael's *Parish Magazine* of June 1864 shows, parents were usually expected to pay 2 pence weekly for the first child attending the National School and one penny for each of the other children. The November 1865 issue explains that the fees paid are insufficient by themselves to defray the cost of education: 'What is wanting is made up of gifts by the richer neighbours and a grant from Government. The grant can only be received in respect of each child who passes an examination and puts in the required number of attendances.' So there is an appeal to parents to ensure that their children (the particular reference is to daughters) attend regularly. Besides reminding parents that 'in our day, education is money and that it was often difficult to gather the money that is needed', mention was made of the school feast which is open only to those who have been at school 'half the school time'.

In October 1878, Canon Millard and the Rev. Barron went as a delegation to the Town Council. Both stressed the need for increased provision of accommodation, using the argument that they had been compelled to turn some children away. The town was growing and so consideration should be given to future requirements. Canon Millard was of the opinion that the situation was one which might lead to a request for a School Board to be set up. By this means it would be legal to expend rate income for educational purposes.

School Board

The idea of a School Board, first hinted at in 1878, assumed greater significance in 1884. In October, Canon Millard gave a pointed reminder that the National Schools were having to make use of buildings which failed to meet the minimum standard defined by government regulations; that grants would be withheld, if deficiencies were not put right. They had no real 'home of their own'; they were dependent on the goodwill of others. Annual subscriptions were failing to meet current running expenses. They were having to reject children who should be receiving education. Looking to the future, he suggested that plans should be laid for the proper education of 1,500 pupils.

One solution, already mooted, would be to establish a School Board, which would be financed by a precept from the Corporation. Inevitably there would be an increase in the rate, equally inevitably described as 'already too burdensome'. The argument was continued in the following year. The writer of a letter, signed 'Order and Regularity', and printed in the *Hants & Berks Gazette* of 3rd January, 1885, was obviously opposed to the idea of a board school, describing it as 'an incubus' involving 'ever more widely opened purses'. An alternative could be for the Corporation to raise a loan on some of its property and build a school which would take the overflow from the other schools. It would be 'an undenominational, Godless school, but it would keep out the Board School.' The inspectorate had reported unfavourably on the Totterdown School; this should be bought by the Corporation, knocked down and replaced by a school which could meet the demand. The letter went on to suggest 'a head-count of the different denominations'. A public meeting was also proposed 'to see whether much is wanted for any other School except the Totterdown one.'

The matter was taken up again in a letter dated 25th March, 1885, 'The threatened School Board for Basingstoke'. The writer attacked the Managers of the National Schools for their failure 'to put their own schools in proper order.' The Corporation should not be expected to spend ratepayers' money on private property: 'if their activity and apathy have brought their schools to their present shameful condition, justice and fairness require that they and theirs only should suffer for it and not the whole town be burdened with additional rates in these days of dull trade and industry.'

Eventually, a School Board was set up, on 14th May, 1885. Its members were: Mr G F Dunn (Chairman) Mr R S Wallis (Vice-chairman), the Rev. Canon J E Millard, Mr E Adams, Mr E C White, the Rev. H Barron and Mr C Pinder. On 29th November, 1885 the foundation stone of a new School was laid on a site at Fairfields. In June 1887 the local paper could report that only slow progress was being made, the continuous frosts of winter being blamed for the delay. Questions were asked about the cost and the probable burden on the rates. There appeared to be a reluctance to meet the demand of educational progress. The opinion was even expressed that 'the old system' was better.

In October 1887, the following figures were given in the local paper, under the heading 'Local Schools and Parliamentary Grants'.

	Accommodation	Average Attendance	Annual grant
Basingstoke British	347	284	£243.15s.3d.
Basingstoke National	543	415	£363. 4s.4d.
Basingstoke Holy Ghost	59	32	£26. 3s.4d.

Fairfields, the town's first Board School, was officially opened on 16th February, 1888. It was designed to accommodate 1,300 children. Part of it is still serving the community today as an infants' and junior school.

Twenty-one years later, in February 1909, another Council School was officially opened in Lower Brook Street, to serve in particular the needs of that part of the town which had become known as Newtown. The dignitaries who attended 'a ceremony of simple but interesting character' included the Mayor (Mr Cannon) and the local clergy; the Director of Education for Hampshire was present, as well as 120 children.

Private Schools

None of this educational provision was entirely free. Fees, however small, continued to be payable at elementary schools (both Board and voluntary) until their final abolition in 1918. The fact that the middle and upper classes of society were able to afford to pay more for the education of their children encouraged the setting-up of private schools. As elsewhere, these played a part in Basingstoke.

In 1841, a notice in the *Hampshire Chronicle* referred to the education provided by a 'Young Ladies Seminary', owned and run by Mrs and Miss Lowman. In that year it was transferred to the ownership of Mrs Kirby and her daughters. The notice thanked 'numerous friends for patronage'. It also emphasized that the girls would be certain to have the comfort of home, together with the advantages of scholastic instruction: 'Improvement of the pupils and the approbation of the parents will be the object of their study.' Their health would 'benefit from attending a school in the country.' The service provided by the London and South-Western Railway was an added advantage! The Misses Dusautoy ran a similar establishment in Winton Square. The 1861 Census showed that 20 pupils were boarders at the Winton Boarding School for Girls. In 1887 we read of another private school, the Southfield Collegiate School for Girls. It was located in Soper Grove; the Misses Bloodworth owned and ran it.

Increased private educational provision for boys was being advertised in December 1887. The notice referred to the opening of North Hants College, by Mr Wearing, formerly headmaster of Tunstall Grammar School. It was described as a high-class boarding and day-school, specifically for middle-class boys. Its premises were in Cliddesden Road.

A similar, but larger, institution had existed for many years in Flaxfield Road. In June 1840, there is mention of Flaxfield House as 'an establishment for young gentlemen.' This later became known as Flaxfield College. From January 1878 it was run by Dr Greenwood successor to Robert Brown, Esq. The nature and aims of the college were made clear in a notice which appeared in the *Hants & Berks Gazette* of 25th December, 1880: 'In this old-established School boys are thoroughly trained for business pursuits. Backward boys rapidly advanced. The locality is exceedingly healthy and the premises spacious. Pupils are kindly treated and no pains are spared to give them a solid and refined education. Preparatory class for little boys between the ages of 5 and 7 years, under a separate master. Terms moderate. Prospectus on application to the Principal. School will reopen on January 19th, 1881.'

Before 'breaking-up' for the Christmas holidays, the boys had been examined by Mr A W Roberts, a graduate of Lincoln College, Oxford. He seems to have been satisfied with the results of the oral and written examination which he gave the boys: 'In the first place, I cannot speak too highly of the good order and discipline which prevails in the school. During the two days on which examination took place, I did not observe a single instance of inattention, far less of misbehaviour, among the 70 or 80 boys who came under my notice. All seemed anxious to acquit themselves creditably and I should think a very excellent spirit pervades the whole establishment.'

Entertainments were also a feature of the end of the Christmas term. The report of the one that occurred in December 1852 shows well a praiseworthy Victorian attitude to learning: 'The end-of-term entertainment included recitations and dramatic representations.' One of these was the trial scene in *The Merchant of Venice*. 'Altogether the whole exhibition seems calculated to excite and improve a taste for literature and the exercise of the mental faculties by familiarising youth with the beautiful productions of minds acknowledged to be endowed with the noble gift of genius.'

The re-establishment of the college stimulated a certain amount of rivalry with the Queen's School [*as Queen Mary's School was known at the time*]. The minutes of the governing body of that school in 1879 refer to the revival of 'an old and popular school under new and energetic management.' The headmaster, the Rev. Rutty, reported that three boys had left to join Flaxfield College; he thought the reason was that they preferred 'a school where Latin does not form part of the curriculum.'

St John's School

Another school had been opened on 3rd June, 1901, on a site at the bottom of Church Street. It was given the name of St John's because here, by the side of the Loddon, was the site of the Hospital of St John, founded in 1261 by Walter de Merton (Chapter 5). By the 1880s, all trace of that building had disappeared.

Anticipating the possibility of building new Sunday Schools, the Vicar (the Rev. Cooper Smith) acquired the site some time during the 1890s. Advantage was taken of the Voluntary Schools Act of 1897 to obtain a grant to meet the cost of building. Very soon, there were nearly 200 pupils attending in the two departments.

A short account of the history of the school, compiled by Mr C Holmes, who was acting headmaster from 1964 to the closure of the school, gives some interesting details of the early days. The first headmaster, Mr F J Brown, received a salary of £120 per year; the headmistress, in charge of the infants' department, was paid £90; the assistant teachers were each paid £45. Apart from salaries, the main items of expenditure were books and stationery - £14.13s.1d.; Apparatus £9.14s.4d.; fuel, light and cleaning £25.10s.0d. The record contains two interesting items for the latter part of 1901. On 7th November, the school received a gift of 40 neat, serviceable rifles from Colonel John May! In the same month the school was reported on officially as follows: 'The school has made a promising start. The tone of the school is good and the instruction capable, bright and well directed. The accommodation is insufficient for the numbers in attendance.' The inspector recommended that attendance should be reduced and accommodation increased. A new wing was opened in June 1906.

The school was beset by difficulties at various times during its existence. For a time, during the early years of the 1914-1918 War, the building was requisitioned and the children attended in three different places: Brook Street School, Church Cottage and the Grammar School (Queen Mary's). A greater difficulty was the shortage of teachers. In 1915-1916 there were four teachers for 243 children; later, in 1917, the situation was even worse – 218 children being taught by two teachers.

The school was closed in 1966 and was demolished to make way for new buildings in the Central Development Area. Its name is perpetuated in the replacement school built in Kingsmill Road.

Basingstoke High School

The Basingstoke High School for Girls was opened on 1st April, 1908, in Brook House, a converted private house, which stood on the north side of Brook Street, opposite St John's School and the Fire Station. There were 41 pupils. Besides Miss Hinton, the Headmistress, there were three full-time members of staff. Visiting instructors taught cooking and horticulture. For indoor recreation and lessons such as singing, drawing and drill, use was made of a corrugated iron hut, known as 'The Iron Room', specially added in 1908. By 1912, there were 60 pupils. Fifteen of these were pupil teachers; 18 others held County Scholarships, two were Aldworth Scholars. The age range was from 8 to 19 years.

Already in January 1909 the Hampshire Education Committee had unanimously accepted a recommendation from its finance sub-committee that a site should be purchased for a new school. Land was purchased at Crossborough Hill in April 1911 and so, in course of time, there appeared a new building - 'a handsome and commodious pile' - designed to accommodate 160 pupils. Eighty pupils and six members of staff moved in on 24th September, 1912. Within a very short time it was found necessary to extend the buildings. This resulted in the addition of hutted accommodation in 1920, by which time there were 205 pupils. Brook House had its 'Iron Room'; Crossborough Hill had its 'Black Huts'. There is a wealth of meaning in the sentence which appears in the brief account of the school's history, 'Various *so-called temporary* buildings were added over these years.'

As time went on, in common with the other schools in the town, the High School needed new buildings to accommodate growing numbers. By 1961 these had reached 550. The required new construction work was completed in 1964. Complicated arrangements for sharing facilities with other institutions were now no longer necessary.

Further changes came with secondary reorganisation. Under this the school became a co-educational 11-16 comprehensive, named after Harriet Costello, who was Headmistress from 1915 to 1935. *[It is now Costello Technology College.]*

A major change was the amalgamation of the school's Sixth Form with their counterparts from Queen Mary's School to form the nucleus of the new Queen Mary's College.

Richard Aldworth School *(The Blue Coat School)*

In 1966, when the centre of the town was being cleared for redevelopment, the buildings which were 'taken down' in Cross Street included one which had originally served as a school - the Richard Aldworth School. It had been re-opened, after rebuilding, on this site in 1862. It originated from the beneficence of Richard Aldworth, a merchant of Reading, who in his will dated 21st December, 1646 left a sum of money to the town to be used for charitable purposes. The terms of the bequest, so far as education was concerned, were that it should provide for the education and up-bringing of ten poor boys of Basingstoke, up to about the age of 15, after which they were to be apprenticed to trades in the town. It was the responsibility of the Corporation to nominate the boys to the school. The sum of £6.13s.4d. was to be expended annually on each boy; in addition to having free education, each would be provided with food and clothing. They were to be provided with a blue coat and a blue cap (as at Christ's Hospital) 'so that they might by their habit be known from other children.'

All were to be housed in the schoolmaster's home, which was to be provided with five bedsteads 'and all other furniture necessary for the lodging of such children.' The master, appointed by the Corporation, was to be 'an honest, godly and learned man.' He was to teach the boys to read, write and cypher. He was also to instruct them in the catechism and 'such learning as should make them fit for apprentices.' In 1834 guidance was given as to the behaviour expected of the master: 'As the credit and well-being of the school might depend in great measure on the conduct of the master, it is expected that he do not associate himself with persons of an inferior sort, frequent public-houses, attend revels, mayings, or any meeting of that kind, nor attach himself to any band of musicians for the purpose either of pleasure or profit, nor attend concerts, balls or public entertainment as a singer or musician.'

His salary for his educational duties – and for the example he was expected to set – was £10 per annum.

The 1837 report on the town gave the number of boys in the school as nine. Later, when the number had fallen to seven, the Vicar, the Rev. James Blatch, gave money in trust so that the number might again be raised to ten. The trustees, realising that some change in the application of the charity was necessary, approached the Charity Commissioners to see in what way this could be done. There was initially disagreement between the trustees and the Commission over the proposed amendments to the scheme, but eventually a new scheme was introduced. This provided for the establishment of the Aldworth Exhibition Foundation, administered by a governing body of 12. Funds arising from the endowment were now to be disbursed in the form of Exhibitions tenable at other schools. In practice that meant Queen Mary's School and later the Girl's High School. 'Every exhibition and other benefit of the scheme to be given as a reward of merit and to be freely and openly competed for. If the holder shall, in the judgement of the governors, be guilty of idleness or fail to maintain a reasonable standard of proficiency or willfully cease to pursue his education, the governors may at once determine [i.e. end] the exhibition or other benefit on the report of the proper authorities of the school or place of education at which the exhibition or other benefit is held, or on such evidence as the governors think sufficient.'

Richard Aldworth's Blue Coat School, Cross St, prior to demolition.

Photo: © HCMAS

We read that an examination was held in the Town Hall on 26th March, 1887 for two Aldworth Exhibitions worth £16 each. The 45 candidates who applied were examined by the Rev. G H Chadwick, Master of the Queen's School, Mr G Gage, Master of the British School and Mr H Weeks, Master of the National School. The applicants sat an examination in reading, writing, arithmetic, grammar and geography. The six top boys had a further examination in Holy Scripture, etc. Arthur Kent, of the British School, and Stephen F Powell, of the National School, were the successful candidates. They were therefore entitled to receive education at the Queen's School or any other place of higher class education approved of by the Trustees. The same competition was open to girls. In 1912 two of the girls at Basingstoke High School were Aldworth Scholars.

Towards the end of the century, we find the Aldworth School being run as a fee-paying school by Mr H Weeks. An advertisement in December 1888 states that it is a Higher Grade School for the sons of tradesmen and others. 'The course of education embraces those subjects more especially essential to those boys about to engage in commercial pursuits, including book-keeping and shorthand.' There was a preparatory department and boarding facilities were available.

[James Lancaster, a generation before Richard Aldworth, had endowed a 'Petty School' in Basingstoke. In 1810 the Corporation decided to pay the Blue Coat Master an additional remuneration for teaching the Petty School children with his existing pupils at the Cross Street premises. By 1820 the Petty School, which was by then under the auspices of the National School Society (the Established Church society founded in 1811 to provide elementary education), erected a new schoolroom at the rear of the Blue Coat School to accommodate the extra pupils. See the first part of this chapter for an explanation of National and British schools and their shortcomings. The Blue Coat charity school closed in 1879 after surviving against the odds for 220 years; however the premises continued in use as a private school run by the last headmaster. It finally closed in 1896 due to bankruptcy. Information from Peter Davis in the Newsletter of the Friends of The Willis Museum, March 2004.*]*

The Aldworth Science College – formerly Richard Aldworth School – in Western Way is a suitable reminder of the benefaction of Richard Aldworth. The trustees of the Aldworth Charities still continue to make small grants to individuals for educational-welfare purposes.

Queen Mary's School

Spiritum Nolite Extinguire

The origins of Queen Mary's School are to be found in a medieval religious Guild – 'The Guild of the Holy Ghost' also known as 'The Brotherhood of the Chapel of the Holy Ghost'. It is not known when this Guild was founded, but, as is explained in Chapter 5, it was certainly in existence in the early years of the 13th century. Although in the beginning the priest seems to have had no educational duties to perform, in course of time these seem to have been undertaken. In all probability, the teaching would have taken place in the chapel porch or perhaps within the chapel itself. It was in this way that the Holy Ghost School (as it was called until about the middle of the 19th century) originated. In 1524, Lord Sandys (of the Vyne) obtained from Henry VIII a licence giving the Guild the right to hold property and to derive income from it. It appears from a chantry certificate of 1548 that from its legal incorporation in 1524 some of the Guild's money was employed 'to fynde a scole master to teche children grammar.'

The Guild escaped suppression under Henry VIII but had its properties confiscated under Edward VI. However, there was no interruption of the educational work of the Guild, for it was supported by Crown revenues throughout Edward's reign.

The year 1556 was an important one, for it was in that year that Queen Mary Tudor, in response to a petition from the townspeople, re-founded the Guild by granting a new charter. This confirmed what had already been granted by the licence of Henry VIII, namely, the right to hold property. It also stated that the Guild's revenues were to be used to provide a priest, 'as well for the celebration of divine service in the said chapel as for the education and instruction of young men and boys of the said town'.

Although, with the accession of Elizabeth to the throne in 1558, some changes might have been expected, in fact the Guild continued with its educational provision. The year 1559 was the first in which there is mention of the appointment of a schoolmaster as distinct from a priest, at a salary of £12 a year. He was unnamed; he remained in the post for less than a year. The ensuing gap was filled by the Vicar, the Rev. Thomas Browne, who gave his services for twenty shillings a quarter. It is suggested that the smaller salary reflects the fact he was called upon to teach only two or three days each week. We read in the Wardens' accounts for 1566:

'Paid to Mr Browne, the Vicar, for the teaching of the free school for one whole year ended at Our Lady-day last past for the year of our Lord, 1566, £4.'

Eventually a separate building came into use. Old prints show a half-timbered building standing on the west side of the ruined chapel.

Repairs to the school are mentioned in the account-book of the Wardens of the Guild. The building seems to have been demolished in 1636, then rebuilt by one Edwards, who was paid £11 for the work. Repairs were again necessary in 1652, presumably because of neglect and damage during Cromwellian times. Both the school and the Guild seem to have been suppressed during at least part of this time. Samuel Loggon, writing in 1742, describes the school building as 'consisting of one large regular room about forty feet in length and twenty-four in breadth.' It was 'in but indifferent repair.'

Photo of print © R Applin

From time to time, the story of the Guild and school is one of argument and litigation, concerning disputes which arose between various masters of the school and the Corporation, which had increasingly assumed responsibility for the affairs of the Guild. The first of these disputes involved Edward Webbe, son of the then vicar, Ambrose Webbe, who was appointed master in 1639. He argued that, by failing over a number of years to provide a priest to carry on the educational work, the Corporation had not correctly fulfilled the terms of the 1556 Philip and Mary charter. He further accused the Corporation of using the Guild's revenues for their own purposes, thus depriving him of emoluments to which he was entitled. In December 1642, he obtained from Charles I[st] letters patent, which appointed him chaplain and master *for life*. The Corporation obtained a sequestration order against him for the return of their property. Eventually both he and the Corporation agreed to submit to arbitration by the Bishop of Winchester, George Morley. The bishop decided against Webbe, but out of the arbitration came a ruling that the bishop should appoint the master, who would be entitled to all rent and profits of the estate during his term of office. The town acknowledged the services of the bishop by means of an inscription in Latin on the wall of the old Chapel school: 'In the year of our Lord, 1670, George Edwards being Mayor of the Town, the Right Reverend George Morley, DD, Bishop of Winchester, a distinguished promoter of Learning, entitled himself to the everlasting praise of posterity by re-opening this School after it had been closed for many years, and by religiously restoring its revenues which had long been alienated.'

Among other disputes involving litigation was one associated with the Rev. Samuel Loggon, who, having been appointed usher (second master) of the school in 1740, became master in 1743. In 1744 he addressed a 'memorial' to the Lord Chancellor, stating, apparently with some justification, that 'there hath not been anyone regularly nominated to the Place or Office for many years last past, on account of a dispute about the right of patronage.' In his petition, Loggon draws attention to the ruinous state of the buildings, even going to the extent of providing estimates of the cost of repairs. Perhaps more importantly, he accuses the Corporation of diverting to its own use revenues which should rightly be devoted to the furthering of the aims of the charter of Philip and Mary. In support of his attack on the Corporation for its malpractices, Loggon wrote *The History of the Brotherhood or Guild of the Holy Ghost,* which was published in Reading in 1742.

Samuel Loggon was not without his faults. In October 1745, the Town Clerk was authorised by the Corporation to take proceedings against him for having 'in a great measure neglected the education of the youth of the said town; sometimes by totally absenting himself from the said town, and, at other times, when there, by attending the said school for only one or two hours of a day; to the total ruin of the said free school, and repugnant to the wills of the donors establishing the same.' In the following year, the Corporation petitioned the Lord Chancellor to ensure that Loggon should be obliged to attend to his duties as schoolmaster or be removed from that office.

In 1825, Commissioners appointed by Parliament reviewed the functioning of charitable bodies, including those concerned with education. The report on the school shows that there was a master appointed by the Crown and an usher (assistant master) appointed by the Corporation. The master at the time of the report was the Rev. William Workman; his annual salary was £150. The average number of pupils was stated to be 12 and they were all fee-paying. Boys from the town paid 15 shillings a quarter; for those from the surrounding countryside the fee was £1 a quarter. The subjects studied were classics, history, geography, writing and arithmetic. The master considered himself bound to teach only classics.

In 1849 a public meeting was held in the town to discuss measures for 'the extension and improvement of the instruction and discipline of the said school and for applying its revenues in a manner more suitable to the present time.' As a result of a petition to the Lord Chancellor, a new scheme for the administration of the school was approved in 1852. It was from this date that the school became known as the Queen's Free School. Within three years of the change in organisation and name, the School moved to a new location in the Worting Road, where the building today forms part of the Technical College *[now Basingstoke College of Technology].* The laying of the foundation stone of the new building, on 31st May, 1855, was described in a newspaper account as 'worthy of being recorded among the greater events in the history of the town.' It was certainly a day of great local rejoicing, with a procession, bands playing, bells ringing, and a public dinner.

Towards the end of 1869 some of the townspeople were again looking for changes in the education provided by the school. At a meeting called by the Mayor, the view was expressed that the town and its neighbourhood would benefit greatly if the course of instruction could be 'more specially directed than at present to such subjects as will prepare boys for commercial and agricultural pursuits.' The Trustees thought that no change was necessary in 'the very comprehensive scheme of education laid down for the school.' Latin (and Greek where required) would continue to be taught, but 'the lower but more essential subjects of reading, writing, arithmetic and spelling should be equally or more strictly adhered to.'

A few years later it is apparent that there was concern about the reduced number of boys on the school roll, since this directly affected the fee income and thus, indirectly, the education the school could provide. In 1879 the Headmaster thought it necessary to express his concern over the decline in the number of day-boys applying to the school. He returned to this theme at the prize-giving in the same year. Basingstoke in itself was not large enough to provide a sufficient number of day-boys. The school needed the boarders 'in order to keep its staff and reputation.' There was also concern about the increased income received in the form of rent on property (mainly farmland) owned by the Trustees. In order to meet increased expenditure such as that made necessary by the broadening of the curriculum, more money had to be found in the form of grants and public subscriptions.

In July 1879 a misunderstanding gave rise to a situation, to which the term 'riot' was applied. It concerned the assumed right of the boys of the town to make use of the school's grounds for recreational purposes. The argument was that they had been accustomed to use the grounds of the school in the Liten as a playground and this right had been transferred to the school's new location. In the last week of July 'an assembly of persons' trespassed on the school's ground on two occasions. On a third occasion the Headmaster complained of 'a mob of people congregating in the road opposite the school and shouting and using irritating language and threatening to take forcible possession of the premises.' The trouble began with the town boys assembling and marching to the school, 'apparently with the intention of annihilating their opponents.' They had to be content with 'using language the reverse of complimentary and threatening the impertinent ones with a severe dressing on the first available opportunity.' When it was seen that there was increased participation by adults, the Trustees thought it advisable to publish a notice about trespassing on the property and to call in the police. The newspaper account reads: 'To enforce this the more vigorously the aid of the police was sought. Superintendent Hibberd and three or four constables have in consequence been making a little overtime. On Monday night, an immense crowd infested the lower part of Worting Road and, considering the amount of animus imported into the situation, it is a matter of surprise that the proceedings were not of a more tumultuous nature.' A later development was the swearing-in of 14 special constables to guard the playground in order to prevent a breach of the peace. The report of the affair concludes: 'These public officers had in their possession a copy of that awe-inspiring piece of legislation known as the Riot Act.'

In 1886 a new scheme of management began to operate. Under it, tuition fees for each boy were fixed at £8 per annum; boarders were required to pay £45 in addition. The Headmaster received a capitation fee of £4 for each boy in the school, and he was allowed the sum of £220 to employ three assistant masters. In 1889 the Headmaster reported to the Trustees that 85 boys were attending the school, the largest number ever; of these 55 were day-boys. There were five members of staff.

The teaching of science and technical subjects was introduced into the curriculum from about 1890 onwards. In 1888, the Headmaster sought to provide a small laboratory by voluntary subscription. Ten years later, on 5th July, 1898, a letter to the local paper explained that a physics room had been built and equipped to the standard laid down in the Science and Art Department, South Kensington. It is significant that the letter pointed out the need for further subscriptions from the townspeople in order to ensure the continuance of annual grants from the Science and Art Department and from the Hampshire County Council.

The early part of the 20th century was a time of further change. It was anticipated that new legislation for secondary education would increase the demand for places in the school. The governors realised that, even with the assistance already being received from the Local

Education Authority (LEA), the school could not produce enough income to meet its costs. Thus began the idea that it might be advisable to transfer the administration of the school to the LEA.

Discussion along these lines took place from 1920 onwards. In 1930 a report to the Higher Education Committee, on the state of secondary education in the county, stated: 'The postponement of the erection of a new boys' school at Basingstoke to replace Queen Mary's School is now no longer possible. An increase in numbers may be expected with adequate accommodation, especially as Basingstoke is geographically well situated.' The Committee then recommended that a new school should be built for 250 boys, at an estimated cost of £20,000.

On 6th November, 1931 under the heading 'County Education Economies – Secondary School Building Programme', the following report appeared in the *Hants & Berks Gazette*: 'The present school buildings are in a bad condition and unsuitable for use as a secondary school. It has been the intention of the authorities to replace them in the near future. A new school will cost approximately £20,000 and, in the present crisis the Committee consider it should be possible to continue in the existing buildings for a year or two longer, provided that the necessary repairs are carried out.' The number of boys attending the school had been increasing over the years; in the report for 1931-1932, the Headmaster could say, 'The number of boys in the school is 153, the largest I believe, in its history.' He added that examinations were not the sole aim of the classroom work: 'I would remind all that the aim of the school is to provide as comprehensive an education as possible.' (The time would come when the word 'Comprehensive' would take on a new and special meaning.)

It was not until May 1940 that the new building was opened, in Vyne Road, not all that far from the school's original site in the Liten.

In the immediate post-war period there were *ad hoc* modifications not forming part of a plan. In 1945 Queen Mary's had surplus classroom space, whereas the Girls' High School was under-provided, so for the first time in its history, the school provided education for girls. The Headmaster, Mr J S Shields, wrote, 'The experiment was not a success; thirty girls do not create a co-educational school. By December 1948 there were only three girls left and for them there was now room at the High School.' For a short time, from 1950 to 1957, the school had the status of a 'bilateral'. About 40 boys, who had just missed passing the 11+ examination, were formed into a 'technical stream'. They spent about two-thirds of their time in the school, attending the Technical College for the remaining third. Some of these came daily by train from as far away as Winchester. These schemes, although temporary, were pointers to changes in educational provision which the town has since come to take for granted.

These more considerable changes were foreshadowed in Circular 10/65 from the Department of Education and Science which laid it down that local education authorities should reorganise secondary education on comprehensive lines. As elsewhere, there were in Basingstoke differing opinions about what the pattern of provision should be. There was much consultation and public debate on the matter and various schemes were suggested. Of these, two proved to be more acceptable than the others. One view was that the town and its catchment area should be served by a number of neighbourhood comprehensive schools for the age-range 11-18. The alternative scheme was for pupils to attend neighbourhood comprehensives from 11 (or 12) to the age of 16, after which those wishing to continue their education could do so either in a Technical or Further Education college, or proceed instead to a new and as yet not fully tried institution, variously described as a 'junior' college, a 'sixth form' college, or more accurately, a 'comprehensive' college. Both schemes were discussed at a special meeting of the Hampshire County Council early in January 1968.

Voting was overwhelmingly in favour of adopting two forms of comprehensive education for the county. At the same time the idea of retaining grammar schools was rejected.

The opening, in September 1967, of Cranbourne Bi-lateral School, designated to serve the whole age-range 11-18, had appeared to indicate that the Local Education Authority was intending to adopt a scheme of all-through comprehensives for the Basingstoke area. Cranbourne saw itself as setting the ideal pattern for the future development of secondary education in the town and campaigned vigorously for the 11-18 idea. In the event, it was the other concept that prevailed. The scheme of reorganisation was approved by the Department of Education in January 1970, and plans were laid for the stage-by-stage implementation of the proposals. It was to be completed by September 1972.

The first change occurred in September 1970, when Queen Mary's School was amalgamated with Charles Chute School, its neighbour 'over the fence'. *[Charles Chute School was built in the late 1950s on land adjacent to Queen Mary's. The site is now a housing estate.]* Change continued with the announcement in March 1972 that this rather awkwardly named amalgam of Queen Mary's/Charles Chute School would, with very good historical justification, assume the name The Vyne School.

The announcement dated 29th March, 1972 and signed by the then Headmaster, Mr W H Rhodes, read: 'The Governors of Queen Mary's/Charles Chute School have unanimously agreed that the School should be called the Vyne School, Basingstoke from this September.' The announcement concluded, 'At which time some two hundred and twenty sixth-formers will be transferred to the new Sixth Form College, taking the title of Queen Mary's with them.' Since co-education was now going to be the rule, they were to be joined by about 180 girls from the sixth form of Basingstoke High School.

The first College bulletin, of May 1972, stated: 'There are likely to be about 540 students and 50 staff when the College opens in September.' It would be found that these students came, not only from the Basingstoke schools, but from the Hurst (in Baughurst) and Amery Hill (Alton) and a wide range of other educational backgrounds. Gradually the new system settled down and was found to work well. *[Eric Macfarlane was the first Principal of Queen Mary's College. His autobiography,* The Making of a Maverick, Macfarlane, E, 2007, *contains chapters on the establishment and development of the ethos of the College (pp 203 -252).]*

Technical education

It was a long time before technical education obtained a proper home of its own – a purpose-built college in Worting Road. The 'Technical Day Classes' that were provided for apprentices at the Thornycroft works, in the firm's West Ham House, formed the nucleus from which the College grew. Responsibility for these was later taken over by the County Council. It was in this way that the first technical college in Hampshire (apart from those in the county boroughs of Portsmouth and Southampton) came into existence, from 1948 onwards.

The move in 1940 of Queen Mary's School to its new site in Vyne Road had left the old school buildings, in Worting Road, vacant. The 'Institute' began using these premises in September 1950. Modifications were made to the building, but it soon became apparent that it would not be able to meet the requirements of a growing local economy.

The Institute was designated a college in 1954. A decision was eventually taken to provide new buildings and these were opened in 1960, subsequently enlarged in the 1970s to accommodate (in its five departments) a greatly increased number of students, drawn from a wide area of north Hampshire.

Adult education

In the mid 19th century, some evening lectures on matters of science and technology were being organised by the Mechanics' Institute (see Chapter 19). At that time, when new technology was being applied to manufacturing processes, it was realised that the work force needed to be better educated in order to become more highly skilled. The requirement for what we today call Adult Basic Education had been recognised in the provision of Adult Education Evening Classes by St Michael's Church. The *Parish Magazine* of December 1865 contained the announcement that 'these classes which are open to all men over 17 years of age who wish to learn how to read, write and sum are held at the National Schools on Monday, Wednesday and Thursday from 7.30 pm to 9.00 pm.' The cost to class members (there were 55 at the time of the notice) was one penny weekly, payable every Monday.

In October of the following year, an announcement of the classes contains a special invitation to 'married men whose education has been neglected.' Mention was also made of a room being set aside for 'classes for lads under 17 years of age.' It will be noticed that no mention is made of any requirement for the improvement of women's education.

The need to increase local educational facilities for adults was recognised in 1890. In January a number of influential people met in the Town Hall to look into the desirability of forming an association to provide evening classes, the lead being taken by the Vicar, Canon Millard. He wanted to know if enough people would come forward to undertake the teaching. It appears that they did. Among them were the Rev. Chadwick (Head Master of Queen Mary's School), who undertook to teach English Grammar and Arithmetic; Mr W Higgs (Secretary of the Gas Company) who offered Elementary Science; Mr H Wills Chandler (Solicitor) who was willing to teach Reading, Elocution and English Literature. Geography was offered by Mr Myland; Miss Blatch was prepared to teach Musical Drill and Mr Lunn undertook the teaching of Writing. Other subjects on offer were French, Drawing, Carpentry and Chemistry. The meeting decided to form the Basingstoke Evening Schools Association, with a paid Superintendent of Classes.

Two years before, on 29th September, 1888, there had been a special meeting of the School Board. Besides discussing how they might use the proceeds of the sale of redundant buildings, (no longer required now that the new Board School was functioning), the Board considered the matter of technical education. One member, Mr G F Dunn, spoke of what he understood the Swiss to have done in respect of technical education. He said that they had been 'greatly impressed with the necessity of making every child become a source of profit instead of a source of disgrace to the country.' They had established technical schools and as a result 'there had been a great increase in the wealth of Switzerland as a manufacturing and producing country.' The Board was not thinking of establishing a technical school; all that was envisaged was the improvement of facilities in existing institutions.

Following the report of the Royal Commission on Technical Instruction (1884), the Government passed the Technical Instruction Act (1889). This empowered local authorities to levy a penny rate to 'supply or aid in supplying technical or manual instruction.' The County and County Borough Councils, created by the Local Government Act of 1888, became the 'responsible bodies' for this purpose.

In December 1890, the Trustees of the British Schools and the School Board jointly put forward the proposal that the British Schools Committee should cease to function and any funds which it might have should go to the School Board, to be used for educational purposes. One suggestion was that a workshop should be established in which technical instruction could be given. In the following January, the committee of the Basingstoke Evening Schools Association, under its chairman, Mr E C White, decided to apply to the Hampshire County Council for 'a substantial grant towards the establishment of technical evening classes.' Basingstoke was considered to have a strong claim upon funds for this purpose; the sum of £9,000-10,000 was considered appropriate. This was the early beginning of what came to be commonly known as Night School. On 12th October, 1892, Mr George Gage, Headmaster of Fairfields School, who was the organising secretary of the Association, wrote to the local paper, pointing out that there were vacancies on courses in such subjects as Machine Drawing, Woodwork, Carving etc. The report of Her Majesty's inspectors, which had appeared in June of that year, reads: 'This school is doing very good work. The elementary subjects in the 5th Standard are very well done, and in algebra, elementary science and cooking the instruction is creditable. Regret is expressed that geography is hardly good enough for a special grant.' 24 pupils took examinations, earning a grant of £17. 4s. 0d.

This was the general pattern of provision until 1926, when the term 'Evening Institute' came to be officially applied to the various local arrangements under which such evening classes were organised. Basingstoke had its Institute, which, in addition to the more formal classes put on in different centres – mainly schools – in the town, also provided rehearsal facilities for the Basingstoke Choral Society, the Basingstoke Orchestral Society and for drama groups. It was the characteristic combination of vocational and non-vocational education.

A more recent development, since 1982, when Hampshire divided up its area into 13 Adult Education Institutes, was the establishment, as a co-ordinating body, of the Deane Institute of Adult Education, later known as the Deane Institute of Community Education. Courses covering a wide range of subjects, activities and interests, were organized, not only in the town's community schools but also in other venues. Later, a countywide reorganisation of adult education services removed the institutes' co-ordinating role. This passed instead to the county's technical or further education colleges. In Basingstoke, the provision of a comprehensive programme of courses is now the responsibility of the Basingstoke College of Technology. The provision includes courses organised in some nearby villages. The scene is very different from that of the last century, recreational activities of all kinds having assumed a much greater importance.

The extent of facilities for physical recreation provided, for example, in the form of sports halls would perhaps surprise the early advocates of *mens sana in corpore sano. [A healthy mind in a healthy body.]*

Such provision had not been entirely lacking before that date, however, as we can read in the St Michael's *Parish Magazine* of July 1867:

> 'The Gymnasium Basingstoke has now, within a few weeks, added to its somewhat scanty opportunities for recreation spacious and excellent Public Baths and a covered Gymnasium sufficiently furnished with apparatus. A visitor to the latter will find an old barn-like building, open to the ridge of the roof, with white-washed walls and the floor thickly covered with sawdust, to prevent injury in case of a fall. The machines are varied in character so as to promote agility as well as strength and develop the muscular power of different parts of the body. Among these are parallel, horizontal and vaulting bars, a vaulting horse, double and single climbing poles, a climbing rope, bridge ladder, ladder-plank, with iron bars and dumb-bells of different weights and sizes. One end of the building is screened off to serve as a dressing room.
>
> In a town where many persons are engaged in sedentary employment for the greater part of the day, any provision for harmless amusement is a gain. But it is a further advantage if such amusement can be found in exercises calculated to improve bodily health and strength, expand the chest, and distribute out muscular action equally throughout the frame. The amusement can be enjoyed by middle-aged as well as young men, and in wet weather as well as fine. Each exercise is set by a competent leader and practised in succession by a class.

A society of about 30 members, elected by a ballot, has become responsible for the management and expenditure of the Gymnasium. They will probably admit others to the practices on payment of a very moderate subscription. All information will be supplied by Mr Wade, New Street.'

EDITORIAL UPDATE

Queen Mary College (QMC) now (2008) has 2,000+ students and is one of the country's top Sixth Form Colleges. It is surprising that QMC is only very briefly mentioned. As noted above, an account of its establishment and first years is given in The Making of a Maverick, *Eric Macfarlane, 2007 (Chapters 16 onwards). Mr Macfarlane was the first Principal.*

In line with current Government policy, the town's secondary schools have become self-governing entities; several having achieved specialist status. The 1960s John Hunt of Everest School at Popley closed in 2007 with the site being redeveloped for housing; it has been replaced by the 'state-of-the-art' Everest Community College in the new Merton development.

Fairfields School is now a Primary and Junior School occupying the original main building. The former Primary School houses the Fairfields Arts Centre. Brook Street School (later Brookvale School) has been converted to apartments. Basingstoke College of Technology (BCOT) continues to expand, providing a huge range of vocational and non-vocational courses, both full- and part-time, for those aged 16 and over. As this up-date is written (February – May 2008) there is considerable discussion about whether a new Higher Education Facility incorporating BCOT should be established at the Eli Lilly factory site.

The University of Winchester has established an outpost in Chute House offering Business and Social Studies degree courses.

The Open University has a Study Centre at QMC.

For those wishing to study in a less formal environment the WEA and the University of the Third Age offer a range of courses.

19   CULTURE AND ENTERTAINMENT

'Basingstoke is not the cultural and social desert it is often said to be and although no-one would describe it as the entertainment Mecca of the South-east, a glance at the notice boards in the Central Library shows that there is plenty going on.' So wrote a correspondent of *The Times* in May 1972. Ten years earlier, *Basingstoke – A Social Survey*, produced by the local branch of the Workers' Educational Association, had expressed a similar view, referring to a range of cultural organisations that many large towns would be proud of – among them, the Concert Club, the Choral Society, the Art Club and the Haymarket Theatre.

Corn Exchange/Haymarket

The Haymarket Theatre was originally the Corn Exchange. It was opened for its main function on 1st March, 1865. A few years later, the building was being used for a variety of purposes. In September 1878 audiences would have been able to see the skill of Tanaker's troupe of Japanese acrobats, billed as a novel, clever entertainment surpassing previous displays. In April 1892 they could have enjoyed another kind of entertainment. It was advertised as being given by 'The Great Duprez, the Magician of the World'. To make sure that his potential audience knew his real worth, he allowed himself to be described as being 'unequalled, unrivalled and unparalleled by any conjurer of the world.' The notice went on to say that his performances had been 'recently witnessed by thousands at the Crystal Palace.' Mention is made of 'wonders in mesmerism, marvels in spiritualism, startling miracles and beautiful transformations.' For good measure, learned dogs, vanishing birds and sparkling music formed part of the act.

In 1879 concerts of music were being given there. A letter sent to the local paper, but addressed to the Mayor and Corporation, had the heading 'Promenade Concerts'. The letter read: 'Gentlemen, I do not like to make a complaint without a cause. The last two nights the band in the Corn Exchange has been playing for about three hours, and with a large drum, which shakes my rooms and wakes up the children, no easy task to get them to sleep again. If they could dispense with the drum, it would be a great favour. I am, gentlemen, Yours truly A Portsmouth.' A reply came from the conductor, Mr Neville, explaining that the drum made a necessary contribution to the music. On 17th September, 1908, music was being provided in another way. Mr H E Powell, another of the town's leading musicians, invited the townspeople to a gramophone concert in the Corn Exchange. The programme, which included selections played by the band of the Coldstream Guards, the Black Diamonds Band and the White Viennese Band, was described as a grand concert produced by the Auxeto-gramophone, a contemporary amplifying instrument.

The Corn Exchange was sometimes the venue for public lectures. One was advertised, for 3rd March 1888, as being 'of interest to all who have to do with horses'. The lecturer was Professor N F Hieronymus 'the celebrated scientific horse trainer and tamer from Australia.' In the same year, Mr John Grant, of the Inner Temple, gave a 'dissolving views' lecture on quite a different theme, 'Ireland, the question of the present'. Ten years previously, in January 1878, an audience of six or seven hundred had been present at a lecture 'describing by word and experiment the wonderful little instrument – the telephone.'

The building has experienced many changes. On 28th November, 1908 a change of name was announced. It became the Palace Vaudeville; from now on seats were regularly provided for the audience. In April 1913 it was let as a Cinematograph Theatre, the lessee being a Mr Casey of Eastleigh. On 12th June, still not sure of its true identity, it became the Grand Exchange Cinema and Vaudeville Theatre. For two or three years before this date, it had provided facilities for roller-skating, as the following advertisement of 12th August, 1911 shows: 'Corn Hall [sic]. Skating 6 - 10.30 p.m. Admission 6d. for each session. Hire - ball bearing skates 6d. Free tuition to beginners. Music at each session.'

In March 1925 the building was badly damaged by fire. Complete reconstruction of the interior was necessary, so the opportunity was taken to fit it out properly as a theatre. From this time on, until the outbreak of war in 1939, it was used for showing films; but from time to time plays were performed by both professional and amateur companies. (This was the period when the town could boast of four cinemas - the *Grand*, the *Waldorf*, the *Savoy* and the *Plaza*, all forming part of Casey's Theatres Ltd. It is interesting to read in notices advertising the film programmes such names as Godfrey Tearle, Herbert Marshall, Jack Hulbert and J Robertson Hare.) In 1940, the Borough Council carried out further alterations to both the stage and the seating. For a time, a repertory company was in residence. At the same time it was possible to see Variety acts, presented by such well-known performers as Tommy Handley, Elsie and Doris Walters and later Ernie Wise, Anona Winn, Norman Wisdom, Frankie Howerd, Stainless Stephen *et. al*. It was leased to Hammer Theatres Ltd, who continued its use as a variety theatre until 1950. Then its fortunes again changed, and there was doubt about what its future might be; or whether, in fact, it had a future at all.

The building had also been used in these early days for dramatic performances by visiting theatrical companies, for example, the Pickwick Histrionic Club of London (under the auspices of the Mechanics' Institute). Such presentations pointed the way to the 1950s visits by the Salisbury Arts Theatre Company, which were a regular feature of the local theatrical scene. A number of local dramatic societies – the Grange Players, the Kelvin Players, the Phoenix and the Basingstoke Amateur Theatrical Society – were all helped by the foundation of the Basingstoke Theatre Association. This was set up in 1950 as a non-profit-making organisation, whose members agreed to guarantee a regular annual payment, to offset any losses incurred. The Borough Council made its contribution by letting the building at a nominal rent. At the same time the building received its new name, The Haymarket, a reminder of what had been its original function.

Over a number of years, a regular annual event in the Haymarket Calendar has been the presentation of a Gilbert and Sullivan opera by the Basingstoke Amateur Operatic Society. The original society – the Thornycroft Operatic Society – started life (to quote the account printed in the Society's 1955 programme) 'on a wet Saturday afternoon, in September 1921, in the pavilion of May's Bounty, when the members of the local hockey team, awaiting the arrival of their opponents, got into discussion about amateur operatics. In March 1987 the society thought it appropriate to present *Ruddigore* on the centenary of the first performance in London. It is not known if the members of the cast or the audience achieved any clearer understanding of the "hidden meaning" attributed by Gilbert to the name "Basingstoke".'

During 1992/93, the Haymarket underwent a large-scale refurbishment, to improve facilities for both performers and audience.

[In 2007 a further refurbishment was carried out when management of the Haymarket was transferred to the Anvil Trust, following withdrawal of its Arts Council grant and some County Council and Borough Council funding. A more in-depth history of theatre and cinema in Basingstoke is in Mervyn Gould's Basingstoke Entertained, *(2007).]*

Drill Hall

On 28th June, 1883, a new building was opened at the top of Sarum Hill. This was the Drill Hall, presented to the town by Colonel John May, for the use of 'K' Company Volunteers, of which he was the Company Commander. During the period of the Michaelmas Fair 1888, it was the venue for an exhibition by the Art Club. It is to be regretted that the event was not as well attended as the organizers had hoped it would be. Of the poor attendance, a writer to the local paper said: 'Apparently we will have to wait some time before the people of Basingstoke are brought to the required standard of the appreciation of efforts of this kind.'

Thoroughly in line with Victorian earnestness in matters of intellectual improvement, the account concluded: 'We trust the working classes will not miss it.' The suggestion was made that the occasion could be livened up by music from a string band! There had been such enlivening music there, on 11th November, 1883, when Mr D'Oyley Carte's Opera Company presented, for one night only, Gilbert and Sullivan's *The Pirates of Penzance*.

Mechanics' Institute

Meetings of various bodies also took place in the Town Hall. One of these, which used this venue regularly, was the Mechanics' Institute, which was founded on 26th February, 1841. Its purpose was 'the instruction of its members in science and useful knowledge, by means of lectures, conversations and readings, at stated periods.' The inaugural address was given on 28th March, 1841, by Mr C E Lefroy, who, wishing to point out the value of leisure time, chose the following Biblical text as his theme, 'The night cometh, when no man can work'. Mr Robert Cottle printed and published the text of the address, with the intention of devoting all the proceeds to the purchase of some useful philosophical apparatus to be presented to the institution.

In the following month, the Institute held its first lecture. Mr Carter, of Flaxfield House, was the lecturer; his subject was Arithmetic. It was 'numerously and respectably attended by an audience which, far from finding the talk dry and uninteresting, listened attentively to an account of the history of numbers and frequently applauded the lecturer for his mastery of the subject.' Among the topics which were the subject of lectures during the first year of the Institute's existence were:

'The Philosophy of Memory', Mr Pearsall (of Andover)
'Mental culture as a means of combating social backwardness and political despotism', Mr White (of Reading)
'The Technical Properties of Steam', Mr Burt (of Southampton)
'The sensible motion of bodies', Mr Lefroy (of Basingstoke)
'The conflict between religion and science', Rev. Bigg Wither (of Manydown Park)
'Ornithology', Mr Mudie (of Portsmouth)
'The principle and practice of cooking by gas', Mr Sharp (of Winchester)

Other themes were not neglected; literature and geography were included in the programme. In September, 1851, members were introduced, however briefly, to 'Eras in literature and their effects in promoting moral and social advancement.' The lecturer, Mrs Balfour, had an audience of over 200. Geographical topics included, for example, a lecture, in March 1885, on mountains and their features; Canon Millard called his talk 'The Upper Realms of Frost'.

The Annual Report for 1857 spoke of 'steady but sure progress'. The lecture programme for that year included such titles as 'Sugar, its history and preparation', 'The Great French Revolution' and one with the type of wordy title that appeared to appeal to some lecturers at that time, 'The Normans in England, and their influence in moulding our national character'. The report also refers to elementary classes in reading, writing and arithmetic, given to the 'adult working classes' of the town. According to the report, these, together with the normal lectures, would improve the 'mental, moral and social advantages' of the students, and thereby provide 'one of the best and most effectual antidotes to the spread of ignorance, infidelity, vice and crime.'

From 1869, the Institute (and Club) was able to make use of a new building in New Street, opened officially by Canon Charles Kingsley, the Rector of Eversley *[author of* The Water

Babies] on 13th October of that year. It was possibly soon after this that it became known as the Mechanics' Institute and Club. By 1904-5, when the annual report says that the lectures were poorly attended, the recreational facilities provided were 'an increasing source of entertainment'. These were the library, the reading room, the billiard table and the brass band. The band was an institution in its own right; it made its existence known at various events of importance in the life of the town. In July 1898, for example, it provided music on the occasion of the start of the work on the Basingstoke and Alton Railway. It performed on the last night of the 19th century. We are told that 'in the Market Place, from 9 to 10.30 pm, the band of the Mechanics' Institute, under the direction of Mr Bedford, discoursed an excellent programme of music, their brilliant playing being listened to with pleasure by a large assembly.' It goes almost without saying that it would be in attendance at the Institute's annual rural fêtes, which took place on August Bank Holidays at Malshanger Park, kindly lent for the occasion by Wyndham B Portal, Esq, one of a number of local gentlemen who helped to foster the work of the Institute.

Library

In 1928 the building and the assets of the Mechanics' Institute were transferred to the Borough Council, to form the nucleus of a Library and Museum. It remained in use for these two purposes until 1969, when the Library (by now a Hampshire County Council responsibility) moved to new premises in the town centre, in Westminster House. The opening ceremony was performed by the Rt. Hon. Harold Macmillan.

There have always been some people who have questioned the provision of such amenities as libraries and museums on the rates. When, in 1900, the question was being asked: 'Should Basingstoke have a free public library?' a letter signed *Pro bono publico* supplied an appropriate answer: 'If it is necessary for the health of the inhabitants that they have pure water, perfect drains and good scavenging, surely it is the more necessary that they have healthy provision for the mind, and no institution which has yet been provided in any part of the country so thoroughly does this as public libraries.' The people of Basingstoke, as well as many visitors to the town, find the library a ready source of information on a wide variety of questions. The author is pleased to acknowledge the assistance he has received from the library staff. *[As are the Editors.]*

Museum

An interest in the town and district as it used to be is safeguarded by the Willis Museum, with its associated Friends of the Willis Museum. Its home is now the building which many will continue to think of as the Town Hall. The idea for a museum came from a talk given to the town's Rotary Club in December 1927. The speaker was Mr George Willis, who said that he saw the purpose of the museum as 'explaining Basingstoke'. By assembling archaeological and historical materials as well as those relating to the geology and the natural history of the area, it would serve as a source for the study of the town and its neighbourhood. Most of the archaeological collection resulted from the efforts of Mr Willis himself, helped by friends who accompanied him on his frequent explorations of the surrounding countryside. Among those was Mr J R Ellaway. The two of them became joint honorary curators of the Museum and Art Gallery that was established on the upper floor of the old Mechanics' Institute. It was the enthusiasm of Mr Willis, combined with the generosity of Mr T B Allnutt (who made a gift of £500) that persuaded the Borough Council to turn the idea into a reality, at a time of financial stringency, when it might have been argued that funds should not be made available for such an undertaking.

[The Borough Council passed responsibility for both the Museum and Library to the County Council in 1945. The museum was then renamed the Willis Museum. The establishment of the

museum and Mr Willis' honorary curatorship are discussed in Derek Wren's Dear Mr Willis.*]*

Understanding of the past is also fostered by the work of the Basingstoke Archaeological and Historical Society, as the published papers of the Society show. The Society has a regular programme of lectures. Since its foundation in 1971, its members have contributed in a very practical way to the investigation of the archaeological features of the district. It has published several books and recorded some of its discoveries in a video entitled *Beneath Basingstoke.*

Queen Mary's Centre

Located on the campus of Queen Mary's College and forming part of Queen Mary's Centre is 'Basingstoke's other theatre', visited by professional companies presenting plays by new as well as established writers. The Central Studio is used for concerts by small musical groups and for other presentations. 'The Street', a covered way in the main part of the College, is used for exhibitions, while the College Hall is the venue for concerts, including those arranged by the Basingstoke Concert Club. *[2008 – The Concert Club now meets at Trinity Methodist Church.]*

Music

In the 1880s there were two societies devoted to the performance of choral works: the Harmonic Society, whose conductor was Mr Liddle, and the Choral Society under Mr Powell. The latter gave a concert in the Town Hall on 15th December, 1887. The main work was an oratorio, *The Prodigal Son*, by Sir Arthur Sullivan. At its Spring concert in 1898 the society sang Haydn's *Creation*. At a later date, in 1904, Coleridge-Taylor's *Hiawatha* was one of the works performed.

Choral singing and orchestral playing have long been a feature of the life of the town. Today, the Basingstoke Symphony Orchestra and Basingstoke Choral Society provide enjoyment to performers and audiences alike.

The need for an orchestra in a growing town was firmly put forward in 1904, when on 9th April, an account was given of an Amateur Orchestra Concert. We are told that the concert was given 'under the patronage of an audience which completely filled the room in the Town Hall.' The writer suggested that this seemed to indicate a desire on the part of the Musical section of the community to help forward the establishment of a permanent orchestra – an institution which a town of 10,000 inhabitants surely ought to possess. A welcome was given to 'the first emergence of the Basingstoke Amateur Orchestra from the practice room into the concert hall.' The hope was expressed that it would go on 'to improve its talents and please the public ear.' The report concluded with praise for the skill and enthusiasm shown by the conductor, Mr Knight.

There was further mention of an Orchestral Society in 1921. On 8th January a letter from a Mr Duncan Hume to the *Hants & Berks Gazette* mentioned a meeting to be held to discuss the advisability of forming or re-forming such a society. The writer concluded: 'Music, choral and instrumental is nowadays reckoned as a most valuable asset in any town, and I can see no reason why our town should not succeed in this direction as well as in so many other methods of progress.'

Ten years later, on 13th March, there was a report of a concert given in the hall of St John's School. The players, 40 of them, under the direction of Mr A G Wood, received most cordial encouragement from a house that would have been quite full, if all who had taken seats had occupied them. Dr Housden a member of the orchestra, used the occasion to speak of the re-animation of the Basingstoke Amateur Orchestra. He said that there were those who said it was impossible to assemble an orchestra in Basingstoke. His remarks included the interesting observation, not without its relevance to the present day, 'If only we had a large concert hall in this town, it would be very well used. There are many things we could do if we had an ample hall.'

The Basingstoke Symphony Orchestra, formerly the Basingstoke Orchestral Society, has seen its membership increase considerably as the town has grown. Its efforts in the period following the 1939-45 war were much helped by forming itself into an evening class which met for practices under the aegis of the Basingstoke Evening Institute.

In the 1930s, there is reference to the Ladies' Choral Society: '25 voices responsive to the will of the conductor, Mr J Edward Garrett.' The concert they gave on 2nd February 1931, included works by Palestrina, Purcell and Vaughan Williams. The writer of a report on the concert, saying that the hall was 'but a quarter full', wondered for what reason 'this and other similar functions [were] passed over by the inhabitants of Basingstoke.'

The Basingstoke Choral Society in its present form, originated in 1947 as an evening class put on by the Basingstoke Evening Institute. Its membership has increased considerably with the growth of the town and today numbers about 140. Newcomers to the town and district have brought their experience and enthusiasm to the Society, which is now able to undertake with confidence the performance of more demanding works such as Bach's *Mass in B Minor*, Verdi's *Requiem* and Carl Orff's *Carmina Burana*.

Today, a similar society, the Basingstoke Ladies' Choir, (with a membership of 50) contributes in a variety of ways to the musical life of the town, and, together with other local musical societies, ensures that Basingstoke is not 'a town without music'.

The Anvil

In the recent past, two local organisations put forward the idea that the town should have a cultural centre. One of these, the Federation of Basingstoke Societies, proposed in 1969-70 that such a centre would be created around the nucleus provided by the Town Hall and the Haymarket Theatre, both of which would be retained.

The Basingstoke Consumer Group had previously, in 1969, suggested that the Town Hall and the Haymarket should be demolished, leaving the site available for the erection of a purpose-built complex of buildings, to serve a variety of needs.

Although the suggestions of both organisations were put before the Council, nothing came of them. Obviously the idea of having what was sometimes also referred to as an Arts Centre was in advance of its time.

There was a temporary revival of the idea of a Civic Hall in 1973. One suggestion considered was that there should be a joint venture between the County Council and the Borough Council to provide a hall and a small theatre (to seat 300), as an extension of the Technical College. One objection to this was that it was thought that the town would prefer to have a building which it could call its own. The matter was discussed again in 1976, when arguments about the difficulties of financing such a scheme carried the day.

At long last, the town is well on the way to getting its 'ample hall'. On 23rd April, 1992 it was announced that 'a Concert, Conference and Entertainment Centre' would be built on a site between Churchill Way and Alençon Link. It will provide a large auditorium to seat up to 1,400 people, a second 'space' to accommodate up to 150; and several smaller rooms. It is planned to include other facilities, including a restaurant. The Centre, which will be known as

The Anvil will be officially opened on 3rd May, 1994.' It is good to be able to report that the long-awaited building has been provided without the Haymarket Theatre and the Town Hall (now the Willis Museum) having to be 'taken down', as was at one time suggested.

EDITORIAL UPDATE

The town also has a thriving Art Club that celebrated its 60th anniversary in 2008 and a huge range of special interest and sports clubs, some equally long established, that provide for the leisure activities of the local population.

The Anvil has gone from strength to strength, putting on a wide range of shows, often to capacity audiences, with people coming from considerable distances to hear and see world-class orchestras, bands, dancers, entertainers etc. It has recently been given the responsibility for running the Haymarket Theatre, which had been forced to close after supporting grants were withdrawn, when it re-opened in late 2007 after refurbishment.

Hampshire County Council, supported by the Basingstoke & Deane Borough Council and a Lottery grant, built a major county museum in the town, which opened in November 2000. Milestones Museum tells the story of the industrial, transport and social history of the County from roughly 1840 to 1940/50 (the social history element has been extended to the 1970s). It is a County museum that is in Basingstoke, rather than a Basingstoke museum, but it does have major displays of Thornycroft and Wallis & Steevens vehicles and replica buildings, as well as a replica front of George Willis's Wote St jeweller's shop.

The Willis Museum continues to be the museum of the local area. Much local information can be found in its Resources Room, as well as at the Basingstoke Library. It is scheduled to undergo a major refurbishment in 2008. The planned security enhancements will enable national touring exhibitions to be staged in Basingstoke. The redisplay and upgrading of the galleries to allow more frequent updating will be a major improvement. More controversial are the County Council's plans to change the Library and Museum to an integrated 'Discovery Centre'. There are no final dates for the integration, but assurances have been given that there are no plans to close the Willis Museum.

Basing House, also a Hampshire County Council property, presents the story of the Civil War sieges and its destruction. It has recently obtained substantial Lottery grant funding to enable enhanced facilities, particularly for presentation of the Civil War to school parties, to be provided. It is planned that these will be in place by 2010.

20 BASINGSTOKE TODAY

[See the Editorial Update for information beyond the dates given in this chapter]

Population

In Chapter 3 we took our account of the town's population as far as 1976. Since that date there has been a considerable slowing-down of the rate of growth of the population of the area. An idea of the change can be gained by comparing the estimated population of the Borough in 1971 (104,600) with the corresponding value for 1981 (130,400). This shows an annual increase of about 2.5 %. For the following decade the increase was from 130,400 to 143,800 (13,400 or about 1.0 % per annum). Given that the forecast population for 2001 is 149,600, the average rate of increase for the current decade is estimated at 0.4% annually. The Basingstoke Urban Area, defined as the unparished area of Basingstoke plus the Park Prewett area and the parishes of Chineham and Old Basing, had an estimated population of 87,900 in 1992 (January). This is forecast to rise to 91,600 by April 2001, an increase of about 0.5% per annum. This shows well what is meant when there is reference to the Borough requiring a 'breathing space' in its development.

Approximately 60% of the population of the Borough is within the Basingstoke Urban Area. Other centres of population are the second largest settlement in the Borough, Tadley, which, with neighbouring parts of Baughurst, Heath End and Pamber Heath, had a population of about 16,700 (1991), Tadley parish having 11,407; and Oakley with a 1991 population of about 5,900. *[See the Editorial update to Chapter 3.]*

Housing

The local authority has made plans appropriate to the forecast limited increase in population of the Borough. These involve the building of 7,200 houses over the decade 1991-2001. The eleven westernmost parishes of the Borough were covered by the *Draft Whitchurch Area Local Plan*. The corresponding document for the remainder of the borough is the *Draft Basingstoke Area Local Plan*. Both plans were published together in July 1992 as the *Basingstoke and Deane Borough Local Plan*.

About 4,500 of the allocated 7,200 houses will be built on sites on the fringes of the town, e.g. at Beggarwood Lane (extension of Hatch Warren) and Park Prewett; some also at Kempshott and Basingfield (Old Basing). Closer in to the centre of the town, Riverdene will be extended eastwards out towards the Ringway. The plan provides for more building to take place outside the Basingstoke Town Area, in the western part of the borough. Here it is Whitchurch for which most development is proposed, with smaller provision for Kingsclere, Highclere and Burghclere.

Protecting the environment

The plans produced show the attention that is increasingly given to matters of conservation. Covering most of the north-western part of the Borough is the extensive Area of Outstanding Natural Beauty (AONB) of the North Wessex Downs. The chalk downland has several prominent hills – Cottington's Hill, White Hill, Ladle Hill and Beacon Hill - from which it is possible to view the contrasting landscape of the London basin to the north.

At the edge of the chalk is the small but interesting feature known as the Vale of Kingsclere, which runs more or less east-west for about six miles, taking in parts of Kingsclere itself,

Sydmonton, Ecchinswell and Burghclere. This small area was first studied in 1819 by Dr Buckland, pioneer geologist, of Oxford. He noted similar features to those of the Weald of Kent and Sussex. It has been appropriately called 'a miniature Weald'.

Many will know of Richard Adams and his rabbits of Watership Down. Less well-known, but only a short distance away, is Nuthanger Farm, where, for a time in 1934, the environment experienced an exploratory drilling for oil, in what proved to be a vain search. Many will have seen racehorses exercising on the downs; they will know of the racing stables to the south of Kingsclere. As the traveller makes his way along the Hampshire Trackway, he will be able to see away to the north the Atomic Weapons Establishment at Aldermaston and the former Greenham Common airfield and consider their particular contribution to the environment. He might also think of what might have been – a river valley in the middle distance, drowned to provide a reservoir for the Metropolitan Water Board. Such is the demand for water.

Other parts of the borough are indicated as being Areas of Particular Landscape Importance (APLI). The area to the south of the M3 motorway, extending towards Odiham, Alton, Alresford and Winchester, is one such area. It displays a varied chalkland scenery; through part of it flows the Candover Stream, a tributary of the River Itchen. Elsewhere, a similar description applies to the area around Whitchurch. Included is part of the valley of the River Test, which, with its tributary, the Bourne Rivulet, is designated a Countryside Heritage Area.

Some localities are shown as being sites of Special Scientific Interest (SSI). These include Beacon Hill and Ladle Hill for their archaeological features; Greywell Tunnel, on the Basingstoke Canal, on account of its unique bat population; and the Kingsclere Stream, which flows northward to join the River Enborne.

Conservation Areas

In its policy of preserving and enhancing features of particular historic, architectural and archaeological interest, the Borough has designated a total of 40 conservation areas. Besides the more obvious localities – Old Basing, the Basingstoke Canal and Silchester – this number includes smaller places like Deane and Hannington as well as the larger Kingsclere and Whitchurch. There are also conservation areas within Basingstoke town. Three, in addition to Basingstoke Old Town Centre, are the 'older housing neighbourhoods' of Brookvale, part of South View and the Fairfields area. Enhancement is also proposed for the area situated between South View and the Railway Station.

Strategic Gaps

Throughout the expansion of the town, the built-up area has been gradually reaching out towards the surrounding villages of Sherborne St John, Sherfield-on-Loddon, Basing and Oakley. They were always concerned, as was the Basingstoke Rural District Council, about the way in which urban sprawl might engulf them. Hence the calls for a limit to be set to the growth of the town. In order to preserve the separate identity of these places, together with Bramley, strategic gaps will be maintained between them and the built-up area of Basingstoke.

Employment

J H Dunning, author of *Economic Planning and Town Expansion,* speaking to the local productivity committee in 1963, described Basingstoke as 'a very attractively located town'. He was referring not to its setting in attractive countryside but to its potential attractiveness to industry and commerce 'because of where it is'. Although some had doubts, he was firmly of the opinion that the town would have no difficulty in attracting firms and in maintaining prosperity. This has certainly proved to be the case.

Assessments of the town's economic success have been made in recent years. In 1985, a study by the Centre for Urban and Regional Development Studies of the University of Newcastle examined 'five measures of economic well-being' for 280 Local Labour Market Areas throughout the country. These were combined to produce an index for each place. The study showed Winchester to be the most prosperous place in the whole country. Basingstoke was ranked 6th. A similar survey was carried out in 1988. This placed Basingstoke 9th out of these same 280 places.

One of the five measures entering into the index was the unemployment rate. For the two years 1985 and 1992 the percentages of the workforce unemployed were:

	1985	1992 (January)
Basingstoke and Alton Employment Area	6.5	5.7
Hampshire	10.0	8.1
Nationally	13.3	9.4

Relatively low values have been a common feature for a number of years; the rate during the later 1980s was consistently less than half the national rate.

Under the 1960s overspill agreement, planning was directed towards accommodating firms re-locating from the London area. The firms which moved occupied sites on five main industrial estates – Daneshill, Houndmills (the largest), Viables, West Ham and Winchester Road. To these was later added the Basing View Business Area. This had originally been intended for service industry. The change was made to meet the increased demand by firms for office accommodation. An early occupant of a site here was the Automobile Association, which established its headquarters there in 1973. Another early arrival was Wiggins Teape (now Antalis). More recently land was allocated for warehouse and industrial use to the north-east of the town, at Crockford's Lane, in the Chineham area. Here there has been a new development, the establishment of the Chineham Business Park and the Hampshire International Business Park.

It is obvious that the large employers, most of them nationally or internationally important, contribute greatly to the economic health of the town. They provide a varied pattern of employment, as can be seen from the following list of names: De La Rue, IBM, Linde, Macmillan, Provident Life *[now Winterthur Life]*, Sainsbury. No less important is the part played by the large number of smaller companies which it is the policy of the local authority to encourage.

BCSS

The letters stand for the Basingstoke Council for Social Service. In 1969 the local authorities involved with the Town Development Scheme, with the support of the BCSS, organised a Community Conference. It was at this conference that concern was expressed that Basingstoke might become 'a monochrome society', a town with a sameness of outlook, thought to be particularly associated with lack of variety in housing. A few years later, a similar view was expressed: 'it would be tragic if it became essentially a one-class society. We want all sorts here, to make it a balanced community.' To judge from the membership of the variety of organisations affiliated to the Council of Community Service (to give it its present name), 'all sorts' have arrived and are contributing their varied expertise in fostering many different interests and in performing voluntary service of all kinds. The BCSS sees it as its rôle to promote, develop, support and co-ordinate that voluntary activity.

Over the years, it has widened the scope of its activities, until today there are 300 organisations affiliated to it. Some of these are local branches of national or international organisations, but most are local ones which have originated through local initiative. All along it has seen the necessity for close co-operation between statutory authorities and voluntary bodies and between voluntary bodies themselves. It receives financial support from both the Basingstoke and Deane Borough Council and the Hampshire County Council. Local firms and organisations contribute financially and in kind to the work of the Council.

The BCSS continues to be an important contributor to the social development of the town and district.

The present system of local government for Hampshire, consisting of a County Council with 13 District Councils (to give them their original description) came into operation on 1st April, 1974. Currently, *[early 1990s.]* a Local Government Commission is carrying out a review of the county, assembling facts and opinions about proposals for reorganisation. This is to enable decisions to be taken about whether the existing authorities shall be replaced by a system of unitary (all-purpose) bodies. As with the previous reorganisation of twenty years ago, difficult questions arise about how to put detailed changes into operation.

There is no need for a standard solution to be applied everywhere, but any scheme proposed by the Commission must:

- reflect the historic and natural communities of Hampshire – your loyalties and where you feel you belong.
- be accountable locally to the electorate.
- be effective and offer value for money.
- make sure people get good local services.
- respond quickly to changing needs.

A Hampshire County Council leaflet, in the Summer of 1993, stated that for the northern part of the county, three options were currently being considered:

1 Amalgamation of Basingstoke and Deane with Hart and Rushmoor.
2 Amalgamation of Basingstoke and Deane with the northern part of Test Valley.
3 Basingstoke and Deane within present boundaries.

The leaflet continued, 'The decision of the Government is due to be announced in October 1994. No change will come into operation before April 1996.'

[2008, There has been no change to the local government district; the Borough of Basingstoke and Deane remains a separate entity, however, the Borough Council now provides some specialist functions to Hart on a repayment basis.]

Conclusion - Perceptions of the town

Travellers have from time to time voiced their criticisms of the town. In 1669 Cosmo III, Grand Duke of Tuscany, made a rather casual visit to the town, while engaged in the grand tour of Europe, regarded as essential to the education of persons of distinction. We have seen already that he was disparaging of St Michael's Church. He also criticised the town itself, as he walked through it. He found it 'wretched, both in regard to the buildings, the greater part of which are of wood, and the total absence of trade.' About three hundred years later, Elsie Sandell, writing in the *Southern Evening Echo* in May 1961, had this to say, 'Basingstoke? Oh, yes. Isn't it really rather a dull place? Of course, it is a good road centre and it has the by-pass. And, of course it's got a railway station where you seem to be able to change for anywhere ...' Obviously an opinion based on experience. In March 1980 we have the view of a motorist passing the town at speed on the motorway. He has the good grace to admit, 'I do not claim to be fully familiar with this singularly unlovely North Hampshire town.' He goes on to say, 'But I am sufficiently versed in the soulless symmetry of its overspill geography to feel an acute ecological depression - even from a safe distance on the fast lane of the M3.'

Others have commented more severely, as the following quotations show:

1 'Singularly lacking in evidences of the past' (1908)
2 'A most unlovable town' (1960s)
3 'Singularly devoid of architectural pleasures' (1967)
4 'Work-a-day' (1967)
5 'A colourless place with few or no attractions' (1976)
6 'A characterless mixture of large housing estates and wealth created by the computer revolution' (1983)

It is fortunate that it is possible to find views which go some way towards counteracting these criticisms:

1 'A prosperous modern town set in a charming countryside' (1935)
2 'A thriving market and shopping centre' (1944)
3 'A very attractively located town' (in the economic sense) (1963)
4 'A very buoyant town despite its ups and downs' (1972)
5 'An up-and-coming industrial town of quite considerable importance' (1976)
6 '"Booming" Basingstoke set to grow still more' (1981)
7 'An active and exciting place to live' (1982)

EDITORIAL UPDATE

It is this chapter that shows most clearly that this text was still in draft form when Eric Stokes fell ill and that, had he lived, he would have updated the statistics and other information that it contains. No attempt has being made to deal with the statistics, since they can be researched at the Basingstoke Library. However, the editors wish to provide a more up-beat ending, to try to show that 'Basingstoke: a Place to be Proud of' is not simply an empty 21st-century slogan. Additional contributions by Debbie Reavell, Derek Wren and Malcolm Parker help to make this point.

Basingstoke, as Eric Stokes has demonstrated, has become the town it has because of its location and it has grown and progressed, at times despite the efforts of those who wished to maintain the status quo, usually to keep the Rates down. The continued population growth of the town has been dealt with in the notes to Chapter 16. Since the 1980s Basingstoke has changed in character from a manufacturing town to one with a thoroughly mixed economy. The manufacturing companies that moved to the town in the post-war period and during the initial phase of town development, have, in most cases, moved on, usually for economic reasons: for example, Haskins and Hubbards (both sheet metal fabricators), Van Moppes (diamond drilling tools) and McCorquodales (bank note printers). The notable exception is Lansing Bagnall (now Linde). Similarly firms that were established in the 1930s have closed their manufacturing operations in the town: Smiths Industries (aeronautical instruments – previously Kelvin Hughes, and initially Kelvin Bottomley and Baird) and Eli Lilly (pharmaceuticals). This loss of manufacturing employment, as well as that which occurred with the closure of the Thornycroft and Wallis & Steevens works, has happened over a period of time and is part of the trend for manufacturing industry generally to move away from south-east England. It is indicative of Basingstoke's strength and success that these losses were absorbed without major unemployment problems. However, there are many companies such as the AA, Sainsbury, Wella, Blatchfords, Macmillan etc that came with the overspill development that are still active in the town.

Basingstoke in 2008 is a thriving major town in North Hampshire, with a population for the 'town area' of about 90,000. (This figure excludes those living in Basing and Sherborne wards, some of whom live in the town area. The way in which the census statistics are analysed by local government ward makes obtaining a closer estimate difficult.) It has a huge range of employment opportunities, from light manufacturing industry and Information Technology to the service industries; several international companies have their UK headquarters in the town. It is also a major commuter centre. It has the area's major hospital (and biggest employer), which employs internationally-recognised specialist surgeons. (The changes in health provision over the years have been explored in Barbara Applin's Taking the Pulse of Basingstoke, *which draws on interviews with a broad range of health professionals and patients recorded by the Basingstoke Talking History project. It discusses the changes that have taken place from the pre-war cottage hospital and small, often single doctor, medical practices to the modern multi-doctor health centres and the North Hampshire Hospital.) It is claimed that the revamped shopping centre, Festival Place, is eighth in the shopping mall league. The Anvil is a major attraction of regional importance, and the 'Top of Town' and Festival Place bars and restaurants cater for aspects of night life. The Leisure Park caters for the more active: bowling, swimming, bowls, ice-skating, ice hockey, etc. On the non-commercial front, there are hundreds of clubs and societies covering a huge range of activities. The Borough Council sponsors or supports a wide range of activities, from Balloons over Basingstoke and Jamming in the Park to performances and displays in the Walled Garden at Down Grange. The Sports Centre, built as part of the original new town centre, has undergone a major refurbishment. The Down Grange Sports Centre is a major asset, having all-weather athletics facilities; it is also home to the Basingstoke Rugby Club.*

There is, however, a downside; the popularity of the 'Top of Town' bars can cause late-night problems, and certain areas of the town suffer from vandalism and anti-social behaviour, but probably no more than in any other town of equivalent size. Despite the success of Festival Place, there is a perceived lack of specialist shops, such as are found in Winchester, Salisbury or Farnham. This is in part because, during the 1960s town development, the majority of the small, owner-occupied shops were swept away in the central area clearance and insufficient thought was given to providing affordable permanent replacements. The Council is working currently on plans to redevelop the car parks in New Road and has proposed some smaller shops in the scheme.

Quotes 1 and 7 in the final paragraph of this chapter neatly sum up the current Basingstoke. It is a prosperous modern town, set in charming countryside; it is an active and exciting place to live.

Debbie Reavell, Chairman of Basingstoke Heritage Society, has contributed the following:

Basingstoke has lived long in the shadow of the smarter towns around it. Its 19th century expansion was manufacturing and engineering; the entrance to the town from the station, down Station Hill, with Wallis and Steevens and Gerrish, Ames and Simpkins, expressed exactly what the town did. The town was visibly hard-working, run, like many, on the clash between brewer and non-conformist!

Basingstoke was an ordinary town, workaday. As soon as the motor car arrived, it is evident from census information that the businessmen, by and large, moved their homes into the villages around. In the late 19th century, the lawyers, doctors and company owners lived in *the town, but this had changed dramatically by the early 20th century. Basingstoke possesses only Sherborne House which was (built for W H Bayley and later home to Charles Steevens) and Erdesley, where John Wallis lived. Demolition consent is already in place for the latter. Even under town development, insufficient homes were available for the managers and executives whose companies moved to Basingstoke and they too bought outside. Living in a town is not a natural aspiration of the English middle class and towns suffer from this. The beginning of the Basingstoke Heritage Society (sometimes thought of as about as likely as the Swiss Navy!) came about as yet again, but piecemeal this time, older properties were being demolished without any thought given to their possible retention and adaptation for modern use. The society campaigns for a better Basingstoke and for an intelligent connection with the past, challenging the often-believed idea that Basingstoke was built in the 1960s!*

Basingstoke has lived too long in the shadow of Winchester; rather looked down on as a poor relation. But this has changed. Now it is Basingstoke which has The Ark at the North Hants Hospital with its formidable reputation for internationally-renowned health care. It is Basingstoke which has The Anvil, already mentioned for its excellent acoustics and prime location, which attracts first-class music events and an audience from far around. It is Basingstoke, too, which has opened Festival Place, one of the most attractive of the many malls in the south.

DR September 2007

Derek Wren has contributed the following:

I am sorry I have to say this but the 'old' Basingstoke was an unloved town as far as its buildings were concerned. Possibly Brook House was someone's home and the vicarage to St. Michael's was a Georgian house. All the others had been turned into offices, with the exception of Queen Anne House, which had been a solicitor's office but was empty, apparently abandoned, when I first saw it in 1962. Church Cottage, which, fortunately, I was able to restore, was considered to be only worth renting if you couldn't find anywhere else. The central area between Potter's Lane and Brook Street was filled with derelict greenhouses. No doubt any improvements had been held back because everyone knew that complete redevelopment was a distinct possibility.

Traffic congestion was also a serious problem. Basingstoke was ripe for development, although this is no excuse for not making any attempt to preserve any of the Georgian houses.

If there is one theme which runs right through this book, it is that Basingstoke was driven by its location to develop in the way it has done.

It could also never have avoided moving with the times, changing like other towns as our pattern of life changed. For example, the introduction of supermarkets from the late 1950s onward; shopping becoming a major source of pleasure with, in the last decade, shops open seven days a week; cars becoming available for most people; more of the population looking for leisure interests after retirement; more eating out and the growth of commuting – this started in the 1930s with two men going up to London each day.

So, in my view, any evaluation of Basingstoke, as it is today, must be done not as compared with the town it was in 1960 but in comparison with other towns of the same size, preferably those in the vicinity, such as Aldershot, Farnborough, Camberley and Reading.

Basingstoke has benefited from the layout of new roads that was the basis of all the planning. The ring road is still not used as much as I imagine Allan McCulloch [the Director of the Town Development Corporation] envisaged, but the growth of the town has gone beyond the limits set by the original plan and traffic has increased far beyond anything that could have been expected forty years ago. At peak periods traffic jams are mainly caused by the fact that so many people who live in the town work somewhere else, while much of the work in the town is done by people who come in each day. Basingstoke is still much easier to move about in and get in and out of than, say, Reading or Wokingham.

First impressions of Basingstoke, coming out of the railway station, with the steps going down to the town centre, are far better than the first impressions of Oxford, Winchester or Salisbury! The same could be said about the approach to the town along Churchill Way. Eastrop Park is particularly well landscaped with good displays of flowers and the view across to Basing View with its office blocks, designed by some of Britain's best-known architects. Many of these buildings, sadly, now stand empty.

There has been a shift right across the south of England from manufacturing to service industries so that firms which grew up in the town, such as Wallis & Steevens, and firms which moved here a hundred years ago, such as Thornycrofts, have all disappeared. The first international firm to arrive here was Eli Lilly, which came in 1938. This has now closed as a manufacturing facility, although the company still has offices in the town.

Shops have undergone the same change. The enclosed shopping centre, built in three phases, is as good as, but not better than, similar centres such as the Oracle in Reading. The same shops can be found in all of them. The shops which were kept by well-known local people, often active in the life of the town in other ways, have almost entirely disappeared. Most of these shopkeepers retired when they lost their premises in the 1960s.

Since development started there has been an enormous growth in provision for leisure activities – schools providing classes for a wide range of interests, new libraries, the formation of hundreds of societies, the building of cinemas, swimming pools, an ice rink, bowling alleys and so on. It is true to say that The Anvil sets Basingstoke apart from all the other towns in the area. The Hexagon in Reading is certainly not comparable. A multi-purpose-use building is notoriously difficult to make a success of and here the architects were designing for a small awkward site. Sir Simon Rattle considers, as other musicians do, the acoustics to be amongst the best of any concert hall in this country.

DW

Malcolm Parker in the Introduction to his recent compilation of archive photographs, Images of England: Basingstoke, *has a relevant summary which makes a cogent conclusion to this update. Many of the 'publications' on Basingstoke's recent development view the pre-1960s town through 'rose-coloured spectacles'; this quotation from the summary (by kind permission of Tempus Publishing Ltd) and Derek Wren's and Debbie Reavell's contributions above provide an alternative view with which the editors concur.*

Basingstoke's original street patterns were becoming well established by the fifteenth century and while the overall area of the town changed very little for the next 500 years, what were large gardens or agricultural plots, between the shops and houses that lined the street fronts were gradually encroached upon through the nineteenth century. Storerooms, outbuildings and workshops gradually filled the gaps. ……….. The only remaining viewpoint in the town centre, to give a hint of what it looked like then, is the view from the Library balcony towards Cross Street and Church Street.

The town has produced or played host to some important figures during its history, although not all are as widely acclaimed as they might be. Thomas Warton is celebrated as Poet Laureate, but perhaps deserves higher praise for his talents as an academic and researcher; indeed his brother and father might be said to have been equally noteworthy figures. John Arlott became famous as a charismatic cricket commentator, but his essays for the Hampshire Magazine and his other writings should not be overlooked. Harriot Stanton Blatch, one of the most important figures in the American Women's Rights movement, and as celebrated as Emmeline Pankhurst there, lived in Basingstoke for about twenty years. Finally Gilbert White, perhaps the greatest naturalist in British history, received much of his early education here, even if he did admit to assisting other boys in the 'wanton destruction of the Holy Ghost Chapel'.

Pick up almost any Hampshire guide book from the 1950s or 1960s and it's clear that few outsiders could see anything notable about Basingstoke beyond the concentrated urbanity of the town; Pevsner's famous guide The Buildings of England is particularly damning. In truth, Victoriana was then heavily out of fashion and generally ignored, the streets of Basingstoke, though much widened, were woefully inadequate to cope with the ever-increasing traffic and much of the town centre was looking pretty shabby.

Basingstoke's redevelopment in the 1960s will always remain controversial, but many of the changes that came with it, particularly the loss of small independent shops and long-established businesses and the immeasurable change in society from one of generally respectful servitude to what some now regard as arrogant self-interest and self-obsession were symptomatic of changes to English society as a whole. Basingstoke changed monumentally, but so did the rest of the country. In the unlikely event that Basingstoke had remained untouched by developers, it is inconceivable that the small happy community that existed just after the war would have continued unchanged. Like a much-loved old coat, the town was worn at the seams, no longer fitted properly and had simply gone out of fashion, but when we look back we only tend to remember what it was like on the first day that we wore it and wish longingly that somehow we had managed to keep it………… Crime, violence, depression, drunkenness, litter and ignorance certainly did not begin in 1967 and then, like now, happiness was really all about your own state of mind.

MP

Eric Stokes, whilst appreciating our shared heritage and promoting its study and preservation, did not live for the past; he was forward-looking and with his geographer's eye could appreciate why Basingstoke has become the town that it has. This is why he spent considerable time and effort in producing this story of 'The Making of Basingstoke'. He would have been more than pleased that his ideas are appreciated and shared by our contributors.

APPENDIX 1

Location of places mentioned in the text that have changed names or no longer exist

Anchor Inn	Anchor Court. Just to the east of the *Red Lion*, London Street, earlier *The Chequers*.
Angel Inn	Barclay's Bank, Market Square.
Barge (The)	This was the local name, taken from *The Barge* public house at the junction of Wote Street and Brook Street, for an area (roughly) from the Waldorf cinema in Wote Street to Station Hill, and Basing Road from Station Hill to the Reading Road junction. Both roads were very wide at these points and the area was used as the main bus interchange. Very roughly, it is the area occupied by part of Churchill Way, Eastrop roundabout and Churchill Plaza.
Basingstoke Wharf	Under (approximately) Debenhams to BHS in Festival Place.
Black Boy Tavern later The Hopleaf	CENSO Restaurant, Church Street.
Burberry's Emporium later Lanham's, then Thomas Wallis	Café Rouge and Chicago Rock Café, Winchester Street.
Cattle Market Inn	*The Bounty Inn*
Chequers	See Anchor.
Countess of Huntington's Connexion (Immanuel Church)	Wote Street. Site is now part of Sinclair Young.
Crown Inn	Joice's Yard, Winchester Street.
Feathers Inn	*Laarsen's*, Wote Street.
Ford's Buildings	In Brook Street, approximately where Alençon Link joins Victory Roundabout.
Frog/Water Lane	Became Lower Brook Street, now partly under Churchill Way West.
Gashouse Road	Approximately on the line of the present Norn Hill from The Castle public house to Eastrop Roundabout and on to Eastrop Lane.
Goddard's Lane	A short road linking Reading Road and Basing Road- roughly opposite Bunnian Place which extended to the Reading Road.
Half Moon	Near *The Way Inn* (*Rising Sun*) in Chapel Street.

Longcroft	See Newtown.
May's Brewery	North side of Brook Street westwards from Chapel St. Now Churchill Way and Anvil westwards.
National Westminster Bank	Nat West, London Street.
Newtown	The May Street/Lower Brook Street area of late Victorian housing that was cleared for the building of Churchill Way West.
Nine Saxons	Oakridge Centre –demolished 2005.
Old Castle Field	South and west of Fairfields Road. There is no known evidence of there ever being a castle or similar structure here. It is thought that 'Castle' or a variant was a previous owner's name.
Old Town Hall	On west side of Market Square –site partly occupied by LloydsTSB
Rising Sun	Now *The Way Inn*.
Rose	At the junction, east side, of Chapel Street and Brook Street. Now Churchill Way at the footbridge to the Anvil.
Self Defence	In (Lower) Church Street opposite the existing small row of shops.
Three Tuns	The coaching inn referred to in Chapter 8 was roughly at the junction of New Road (Victoria Street) and Winchester Street. It was demolished when Victoria Street was made in the 19th century. A replacement *Three Tuns* was built between the old and new Victoria Streets. Currently (Spring 2008) unoccupied.
Totterdown	Old name of Reading Road from its junction with Basing Road to the railway bridges.
Union Workhouse	Site now of the Hampshire Clinic, Basing Road.
Victoria Street	This street ran from Southern Road to Winchester St. Its northern section has been incorporated into New Road. The name is now applied to the narrow lane on the east side of Lamb Brooks, solicitors (previously *The Victoria* public house). The southern section of Victoria Street exists on its original route.
Wheatsheaf Inn	*The Winton*, Winton Square

APPENDIX 2

Basingstoke Public Houses Closed/Demolished since 1965

* Rebuilt/change of use. All others demolished

Anchor *	Anchor Court, London Street.
Angel Hotel	Wote Street/Potter's Lane-north side. The name was previously used for the town's major coaching inn, later a hotel, in the Market Square, closed in late 1800s.
Bass House *	Part of the original New Town Centre, now incorporated into Tesco Metro
Barge	Wote Street/Brook Street- Southwest side.
Black Boy/ Hopleaf/ McCarthy's *	Church Street. Now CENSO Restaurant
Cricketer's	Brook Terrace (Off Brook Street at Victory Square).
Engineer's Arms	Basing Road/Reading Road Junction.
Forester's Arms	Southern Road/Cambridge Terrace-east side.
George/ Hole-in-the-wall*	Zizzi's, Market Square.
Grapes	Wote Street.
Horse & Jockey	Hackwood Road.
Goat	Goat Lane.
Goat & Barge	New Market Square. In the original New Town Centre at the west side of New Market Square - demolished when Festival Place built.
Nine Saxons	Oakridge Centre, demolished 2005.
Old House at Home	Reading Road/Bunnian Place - northeast side.
Pear Tree	Flaxfield Road/New Street/Cross St junction - north side.
Pen & Parchment Popley	Popley. Demolished 2007.
Railway Arms	Brook Street/Station Hill- opposite *The Barge*.
Red Lion Tap	Sydenham Place.
Rose	Chapel Street/Brook Street - east side.

Rose and Crown	Church Street/Potters Lane-north side.
Royal Exchange	Wote Street, east side, north of Feathers Lane.
Self Defence	Church Street opposite the existing small row of shops near St Michael's church.
Station Hotel	Station Hill/Junction Road-north side.
Traveller's Rest	Wote Street, west side just south of Bedford Place.
Victoria*	Winchester Street/Victoria Street - south Side. Lamb Brooks Solicitors.
Victory	Victory Square (Essex Road/ Brook Street junction).

APPENDIX 3

Equivalent Contemporary Values of the Pound – October 2007

Comparative money values – the amount of money in 2007 that would be needed to purchase goods purchased for £1 at the date given.

The figures are derived from the Retail Prices Index, based at January 1987 = 100. The data for 1270 to 1914 has been taken from **Phelps Brown, E H and Hopkins, S V** *Seven Centuries of the Price of Consumables, compared with Builders' Wage-rates, Economica, 1981.* Care is needed when using this table for comparisons. The changing relative cost of items to each other because of availability, changing methods of production and distribution and land values etc, altered the costs relative to wages at various times. An example of how the relative prices of some goods have changed over the last 50 years is illustrated by comparing the prices of household white goods and electronic equipment in, for example 1960 and 2007. A trivial example is the price of a Mars bar; in the late 1940s/early 1950s it cost 2½p (6d.) without tax. Using the 1950 factor of 25 this equates to 62.5p; the current price in a local shop is 48p which includes VAT at 17½%.

Goods purchased for £1 in:	would cost in 2007
1270	£584
1300	£567
1350	£470
1400	£490
1450	£548
1500	£533
1550	£219
1600	£110
1650	£83
1700	£86
1750	£93
1800	£35
1820	£46
1840	£48
1860	£47
1880	£53
1900	£63
1910	£63
1920	£23
1930	£37
1940	£32
1950	£25
1960	£17
1970	£11
1980	£3
1990	£1.70
2000	£1.20
2006	£1.05

Note: The pre-decimal coinage was a pound of 20 shillings (20/- or 20s.) and a shilling of 12 pence (12d.).

BIBLIOGRAPHY AND FURTHER READING

Abbreviations

BAHS Basingstoke Archaeological & Historical Society
HBG Hants & Berks Gazette, later The Basingstoke Gazette and now The Gazette
HCC Hampshire County Council
HCMAS Hampshire County Museums and Archives Service
HFC Hampshire Field Club
HRO Hampshire Archives and Local Studies at the Hampshire Record Office

Introduction

Eric Stokes's text did not have a separate bibliography; his references were collected together as footnotes at the end of each chapter. The editors decided that the narrative would flow better if these references were in the body of the text with a cumulative bibliography as a separate entity at the end.

This bibliography has been expanded to an extensive, but probably not fully comprehensive, list of books and reports on local topics of historical and related relevance. This has been done to extend the usefulness of the text to the student of Basingstoke's history. Deliberately, no references have been included to the literature, of varying quality, (other than **Godwin**) on the Civil War at Basing House. An earlier compendium of references by **Margaret Willoughby,** *Bibliography of Basingstoke*, 1973, contains 162 references including 25 to Basing House. A copy is in the Local Studies section of Basingstoke Library. All documents referred to in the text are listed; these are marked * within the alphabetical list.

The Local Studies Section of Basingstoke Library has an extensive collection of local documents, books and booklets, including most of those referenced below. The Library's Local Studies catalogue is available on-line at **www.hants.gov.uk/library** - click on the on-line catalogue entry and search using '**Basingstoke**'. The *Hants & Berks Gazette* (fore-runner of *The Gazette)* and *The Gazette* are available on microfilm in the Library. For many years, until his death in 2002, the local amateur historian Arthur Attwood contributed a weekly article to *The Gazette.* Since then Robert Brown has done the same. The Monday edition of the paper has a regular feature, *Memories on Monday.* Prior to the establishment of *The Hants & Berks Gazette* in 1878, the main newspapers covering local news were *The Hampshire Chronicle*, Winchester, and *The Reading Mercury,* Reading; microfilm copies of these are available for consultation in the respective town libraries. The Basingstoke Library also holds copies of the *Basingstoke Review* published between 1958 and 1966 and *Expanding Basingstoke* bulletins 1967 – 1974 (also available in the Resources Room at the Willis Museum). A short-lived *Basingstoke Mail* was published between 1973 & 1976. The *Hampshire Magazine, Hampshire Life* and *The Hampshire Chronicle* have occasional articles on Basingstoke and its surrounding area; the Basingstoke Library displays the current issues of these journals. The *Basingstoke Observer* and the *Basingstoke Independent* are published (2007) as free-sheets and are noted here for completeness.

The Resources Room at The Willis Museum also has an extensive collection of Basingstoke documents, including an unpublished manuscript copy of a history of Eastrop parish (which contains errors) and transcripts of the Samuel Attwood, George Woodman and other diaries, as well as maps and a large collection of photographs. It also has a several notes on the derivation of Basingstoke street names and Arthur Attwood's collection of photographs;

these are currently being catalogued. A more extensive collection of photographs and a collection of 19th century Basingstoke traders' billheads are held at the Hampshire County Museum & Archives Service (HCMAS) headquarters at Chilcomb House, Winchester.

Hampshire Archives and Local Studies (HA&LS) at the Hampshire Record Office in Winchester hold the originals of many of the Borough and Church records from the earlier centuries, as well as documents relevant to Basingstoke from private sources. Many of these were transcribed (and in some cases translated from the Latin) by Baigent & Millard in the late 19th century for their *History of Basingstoke*. Serious students are recommended to consult this book which was one of the major sources used by Eric Stokes, particularly for some of his early chapters, and also to consult the HRO's catalogue, which can be accessed on-line at **www.hants.gov.uk/record-office/index.html.** A search using '**Basingstoke**' will produce over 13,500 references, whilst '**Basingstoke Corporation**' will refine this to 250 references. The documents referenced under **Finding 8M62, 10M57, 23M72, 46M74** and **148M71,** in particular the last reference, contain a wealth of information. HA&LS have produced an on-line resource, Access Hampshire Heritage, to provide access to typical archive sources for the history of a neighbourhood at **www3.hants.gov.uk/archives/ahh.htm**

Each of these collections (Library, Museum and HRO) should be searched thoroughly as they are the major sources of information and are updated continually. For example, the HRO recently were given the collection of documents that Arthur Attwood had gathered over many years and which he used as the basis of his weekly *Basingstoke Gazette* articles mentioned above: **HRO 50A07**.

The *Newsletters* of BAHS and the Friends of the Willis Museum regularly contain articles on Basingstoke topics.

Hampshire Studies (*The Proceedings of The Hampshire Field Club and Archaeological Society* until 1994: *Proc HFC*) and *The HFC Newsletter* carry articles on the archaeology and history of the Basingstoke area. A complete run of *Proc HFC* and *Hampshire Studies* is held by Southampton University's Hartley Library. See **King, Anthony** in the alphabetical listing for cumulative indices of volumes 21 to 60 (1958 - 2005). HCMAS headquarters at Chilcomb House, Winchester also hold a set (some of the earlier volumes appear incomplete) with an index to volumes 1-20.

All building developments have to have a PPG16 Archaeological Assessment prepared and the County Archaeologist can require investigations to be made prior to work starting and/or a watching brief kept during any ground disturbance. Reports of these operations are deposited with the County Archaeologist. The major excavations are published in *Hampshire Studies* or other archaeological journals. The County Archaeologist should be consulted for the references to the reports on the more recent archaeological work at Beggarwood Lane, Merton Farm, Rooksdown, Park Prewett and Old Kempshott Lane.

The Museum of English Rural Life at the University of Reading has the Wallis & Steevens archive and some information on other Basingstoke companies associated with agriculture.

The Thornycroft Basingstoke factory technical archive is held by HCMAS at their Chilcomb House headquarters at Winchester; there are no staff records in this archive but Wessex Film & Sound Archive at HRO have taped interviews with former Thornycroft workers. The Thornycroft Society also holds records of the Basingstoke factory's activities. The Lansing Bagnall photographic archive is held by HCMAS at Milestones Museum, Basingstoke.

The Basingstoke entry in *Hampshire Treasures*, noted below, published in 1979, contains, amongst other data, a comprehensive listing of the then-known archaeological sites and reported finds and a list of 'Buildings, Monuments and Engineering Works' that were considered worthy of recording. Each entry gives an Ordnance Survey Grid Reference, where known, and a brief description of the subject.

The *Victoria County History*, Hampshire, vol IV, 1911, has a major section on Basingstoke in the chapter for the Basingstoke Hundred; it draws heavily on the information in Baigent & Millard's *A History of the Ancient Town and Manor of Basingstoke* and provides an authoritative summary of the history of Basingstoke as understood in the first decade of the 20th century. It is currently being revised. During the revision, the input documents and data will be placed on the VCH web site, **www.victoriacountyhistory.ac.uk**, as they become available.

A website at **www.hantsphere.org.uk** gives sources of Hampshire information and photographs. A search using '**Basingstoke**' will produce over 200 images and over 900 text entries – many not on Basingstoke itself, but of the surrounding area and many not of relevance to a student of the history or the making of Basingstoke. It is nevertheless a worthwhile source to interrogate.

An additional website, **www.visionofbritain.org.uk**, has information on Basingstoke between 1801 and 2001 including maps, historical description and statistical trends from the censuses, however it is a commercial site and some information has to be paid for.

The Basingstoke Talking History project (a joint BAHS and Willis Museum project) is recording recollections of residents covering the inter-war period to the recent past and of medical professionals discussing the evolution of medical practice before and since the introduction of the NHS, information has been gathered over the past 15 years. This ongoing collection, with synopses and transcriptions of the interviews, is available for consultation in the Willis Museum's Resources Room. The master recordings have been deposited with the Wessex Film and Sound Archive at the HRO.

The editors are pleased to acknowledge the assistance of Derek and Wendy Spruce; Barry Meehan and Joy Needham (both Hants Library Service) and Malcolm Parker (Willis Museum) in the preparation of this bibliography.

BIBLIOGRAPHY

Where a publication is undated but the year of publication is known from other sources, this is noted in brackets (----). A * preceding an entry indicates a document referred to in the main text. **(Ed)** indicates that the entry is an edited collection of work. As stated above, we have attempted to make this bibliography as comprehensive as possible, but acknowledge that we may have missed some material. Also we make no claims for the quality or accuracy of the material cited.

* **Allen, M J** *et al* Food for the Living: A Reassessment of a Bronze Age Barrow at Buckskin, Basingstoke, *Proceedings of the Prehistoric Society,* 61, 1995, pp 157 - 189.

Applebaum, Shimon Distribution of the Romano-British Population in the Basingstoke Area, *Proc HFC 18,* 1953, pp 119 – 138.

Applin, Barbara, (Ed) *Past Pieces, extracts from the Newsletter,* BAHS, 1992.

Applin, Barbara *Roundabout Basingstoke,* BAHS, 1999.

* **Applin, Barbara** *Taking The Pulse of Basingstoke,* BAHS, 2005.

Attwood, Arthur *The Illustrated History of Basingstoke,* The Breedon Books Publishing Co Ltd, 2004.

Attwood, Arthur *Around Basingstoke,* Basingstoke Gazette, (1981).

Attwood, Arthur *Basingstoke- Arthur Attwood's Look into the Past,* Basingstoke Gazette.

Attwood, Arthur *St Michael's Church, Basingstoke – A short history,* (1984 & 1995).

Attwood, Arthur Collected papers, HRO, 50A07.

Attwood, Arthur & Boshier, Ron *Picture Basingstoke,* Basingstoke Gazette, (mid 1980s).

* **Attwood, Samuel** *Diary,* Transcript held at Willis Museum, original in HRO, 8M62/27.

* **Backhouse, Robert (ed),** *John Wesley's Journal,* Hodder & Stoughton, 1993. Abridged P L Parker, introduction H P Hughes, appreciation of the Journal A.Birrell.

* **Baigent, FW & Millard, JE** *A History of the Ancient Town and Manor of Basingstoke,* C J Jacob, 1889.

Baldwin, Nick *The Illustrated History of Thornycroft Trucks and Buses,* Haynes Publishing Group, 1989.

* **Barty-King, Hugh** *The AA – A History of the first 75 years of the Automobile Association,* AA, 1960.

Bigg-Wither, R F *History of the Foundation and of the chief incidents in the gradual establishment of St. Thomas' Home, Basingstoke: The Winchester Diocesan Penitentiary for Friendless and Fallen Women, with a chapter concerning the penitents.* CJ Jacob, no date.

Birmingham, Peter & Pearce, John *Venture Limited – The Story of Basingstoke's Own Bus Company.* No publisher noted, 1995.

Bloomfield, Ena *The School on Crossborough Hill 1908-1968.* No publisher /date.

Boshier, R *Boshier's Basingstoke – 40 years on,* Basingstoke Gazette, undated. Photos.

Brown, Jonathan Market Towns and Downland in Hampshire 1780-1914, *Southern History,* 28, 2006, pp 74-93.

Brown, R *Basingstoke A Walk through Time,* Basingstoke & Deane Borough Council, 1985.

Brown, R *A Chronicle of Basingstoke.* No publisher and date noted, last entry 1988. Library ref RH942.271

Brown, R *Basingstoke's Pictorial Past,* Milestone Publications, 1987.

Brown, R *Basingstoke A Pictorial History, 1935-65,* Phillimore, 1994.

Brown, R *Basingstoke in old picture postcards,* European Library, 1991.

Brown, R *Basingstoke in old picture postcards, volume 2,* European Library, 1997.

Brown, R *Basingstoke in the 1960s,* Sutton Publishing Ltd, 1999.

* **Burrows** *Basingstoke, Hants, an Ancient Town with Modern Amenities: an Official Guide,* Basingstoke Borough Council, 1932.

* **Butler, Brendan (Ed)** *The Dream Fulfilled, Basingstoke Town Development 1961- 1978,* Basingstoke Development Group, undated.

* **Brayley, Edward Wedlake & Britton, John** *Beauties of England and Wales,* Vol VI, Venor, Hood and Sharpe, 1805, pp 255 - 262.

* **Caird, James,** *English Agriculture in 1850-51,* Longman, 1852.

* **Camden, William** *Britannia* 1586, translated by Philemon Holland, 1637.

* **Carpenter Turner, Barbara** *A History of Hampshire,* Phillimore, 1976.

* **Cary** *New Itinerary,* 1810.

* **Celoria, Francis** *Teach Yourself Local History,* EUP, 1958.

Charlick, Reginald *Basingstoke Symphony Orchestra.* No publisher and date noted.

Clark, G G *The Architectural Development of Basingstoke.* Report of a talk to Basingstoke Rotary Club, HBG, 1930.

Clements, K *Two Feeble Women – The Early History of the Salvation Army in Basingstoke.* No publisher noted (early 1980s).

Coe, D & Newman, R Excavation of an early Iron Age Building & Romano-British enclosure on Brighton Hill South, Hampshire, *Proc HFC* 48, 1993, pp5 – 26.

* **Coghlan, H H** The Old Way from Basingstoke to Salisbury Plain, *Transactions of Newbury Field Club*, Vol VII, 1936, No 3.

Cottle, Robert (Publisher), *The report of the public charities belonging to the Town of Basingstoke, "Ordered by the House of Commons, 18th May, 1826",* Basingstoke, 1844.

Crocker, Glenys *The History of the Basingstoke Canal,* The Surrey and Hampshire Canal Society, 1973. Very brief, **Vine** – see below, is a comprehensive history.

* **Crosse, P M** Report of talk to Basingstoke Rotary Club, HBG, 4th June 1938.

* **Defoe, Daniel** *Tours Through England and Wales*, quoted in *The Agricultural Revolution 1760-1880*, Chambers & Mingay, Batsford, 1966.

Dean, Martin, Robertson, Kevin & Simmonds, Roger *The Basingstoke and Alton Light Railway,* Crusader Press, 1998.

* **Driver, Abraham & William,** *General View of the Agriculture of the County of Hants,* London, 1794.

* **Dunning, J H** *Economic Planning and Town Expansion,* Workers' Educational Association, Southampton, 1963.

* **Dunning, J H** Report of talk to the Basingstoke and North Hants Productivity Committee, HBG, 1963.

Dutton, Gerry (Ed), *Tithe Award for the Parish of Basingstoke*, 2003. A copy is held in the Local Studies Section of Basingstoke Library.

* **Dyer, Alan & Palliser D M (Ed)** *The Diocesan Population Returns for 1563 and 1603,* OUP for The British Academy, 2005.

* **East, Gordon** *The Geography Behind History,* Thomas Nelson, 1938.

Edwards, Bob *Historic rural settlement in Basingstoke & Deane and Test Valley: an Archaeological & Historical survey,* Bournemouth University, no date.

* **Ellaway, J R, Willis, G W & Rainbow, H** Field Notes of Archaeological Discoveries in the Basingstoke District, *Proc HFC,* 9, 1927.

* **Ellaway, J R & Willis G W,** Field Notes, *Proc HFC,* 12, 1934.

Evans, T *Basingstoke Past & Present,* Sutton Publishing Ltd, 1997 (photos).

Fasham, P J & Coe, D *Brighton Hill South (Hatch Warren):An Iron Age farmstead and deserted medieval village in Hampshire,* Wessex Archaeology, 1995.

Felgate, M & Applin, B *Going Down Church Street to the Felgate Bookshop,* BAHS, 1998.

* **Fox, Wilson** Agricultural wages in England and Wales during the last 50 years, *Journal of the Royal Statistical Society*, Vol 66, 1903.

Franks, Michael *The Clerk of Basingstoke - A life of Walter de Merton,* Alden Press, 2003.

Franks, Michael *The Basingstoke Admiral- A life of Sir James Lancaster,* The Hobnob Press, 2006.

* **Freeman, M D** *John Joice & Son, Coachbuilder, Basingstoke* – Note in *Transport History,* Nov 1972, pp 284-292.

Gibson, Catronia The Iron Age and Roman site of Viables Two (Jays Close), Basingstoke. *Hampshire Studies,* 59, 2004, pp 1- 30.

* **Giddy, Davies** *House of Commons*, 1807.

Godwin, G N *The Civil War in Hampshire,* 1904; Facsimile edition, Lawrence Oxley, 1973.

Gould, Mervyn *Basingstoke Entertained,* Mercia Cinema Society, 2007. A history of cinema in Basingstoke.

Grant, Moira The Small Towns of North Hampshire 1660 – c 1800. Part 1: Economy. *Hampshire Studies,* 62, 2007, pp 193-201. Part 2 : Population growth
Part 3: The case for 'urban renaissance' (both forthcoming).

Griffith, Edward C *Basingstoke & Alton Light Railway 1901-1936*, Basingstoke, 1947.

Grufferty, Fr Tom *Holy Ghost Church Basingstoke.* No publisher noted, 1992. A history of the Roman Catholic church in Sherborne Road.

* **Hadfield, Charles** *The Canal Age,* David & Charles, 1968.

Hall-Torrance, M & Weaver, S D G The Excavation of a Saxon Settlement at Riverdene, Basingstoke, *Hampshire Studies,* 58, 2003, pp 63-105.

* **Hardy, Thomas** *Jude the Obscure,* Macmillan, 1896.

Hare, John Church-building and Urban Prosperity on the Eve of the Reformation, *Hampshire Studies,* 62, 2007, pp 181-192.

Hawker, Anne *Voices of Basingstoke 1400 - 1600,* BAHS, 1983.

Hawker, Anne *The Story of Basingstoke,* HCMAS & BAHS, 1999.

Hawkes, C F Old Roads in Central Hampshire, *Proceedings of the Hampshire Field Club,* 9, part 3, 1925.

* **Hibbert, Christopher** *The English - a Social History - 1066-1945,* Grafton Books, 1987.

* **Hinde L,** *A Collection of the Sufferings of the People called Quakers, for the Testimoney of a Good Conscience, from the time of their first being distinguished by that name, in the year 1650 to the Time of the Act, commonly called the Act of Toleration, etc.,* London, 1753.

* **Hinton, David,** The Place of Basing in Mid-Saxon History, Proc HFC, 42, 1986, pp 162 – 164.

* **Holmes, Charles** *History of St John's School.* No publisher noted, 1967.

* **Hoskins, W G** *Local History in England*, Longman, 1972 or 1984.

* **Hounsell, Dan & Murray, John** *Viables 3, Jay's Close, Basingstoke, Hampshire, An Archaeological Excavation - 2001,* Hertfordshire Archaeological Trust, Report 859, 2002.

Howell, Lucy & Durden, Theresa Further Excavation of an Iron Age Enclosure at Danebury Road, Hatch Warren, Basingstoke, Hampshire, 1995. *Hampshire Studies,* 60, 2005, pp 39 - 63.

Houston, Sheila *Basingstoke Silver Band 1898 – 1998.* No publisher or date noted.

* **Hughes, Elizabeth & White Philippa (Ed),** *The Hampshire Hearth Tax Assessments, 1665,* Hampshire Records Series No 11, HRO, 1991.

* **Hughes, Michael** *The Small Towns of Hampshire,* Hants County Council, 1972.

Hutchins, Eric *The Basingstoke Terriers,* (Territorial Army), published by the Author, 1990.

* **Idle, Christopher** (abridged by*), The Journal of John Wesley,* Lion, 1986. See also **Backhouse**.

* **Jackson, W Eric** *Local Government in England and Wales,* Pelican, 1945.

* **Jebens, H Dieter** *Basingstoke Canal - the case for restoration,* Surrey & Hampshire Canal Society, 1968.

Jebens, H Dieter & Cansdale, Roger *Basingstoke Canal,* Tempus Publishing Ltd, 2007. A collection of photographs.

Jefferson, Joseph *Sketch of the History of the Holy Ghost Chapel at Basingstoke in Hampshire,* Basingstoke, 1808.

John, J R *Fairfields Schools Basingstoke 1888-1979,* published by the Author, 1980.

Kelly, Arthur *Chapel of the Holy Ghost and St Michael's Church,* Basingstoke, 1911.

King, Anthony A classified Author and Title Index to *Proceedings* 21- 40 (1958 - 1984) and to other Field Club publications issued during the period. *Proc HFC,* 44, 1988, pp 137 – 151.

King, Anthony A classified Author and Title Index to Proceedings 41 - 50 (1985 - 1995) and to other Field Club publications issued during the period. *Hampshire Studies,* 52, 1997, pp 179 – 192.

King, Anthony A classified Author and Title Index to Proceedings 51 - 60 (1986 - 2005) and to other Field Club publications issued during the period. *Hampshire Studies,* 60, 2005, pp 242 – 253.

Lefaye, D G Selbourne Priory and the Vicarage of Basingstoke, *Hampshire Studies,* Vol 46, 1990, pp 91-99.

* **Livingstone, Margaret** *A Case study of four Hampshire Villages,* Hampshire Council of Community Service, 1975.

* **Loggon, Samuel** *The History of the Brotherhood or Guild of the Holy Ghost in the Chapel of the Holy Ghost,* Basingstoke, 1742.

* **Lowe, Robert** *House of Commons,* 15th July 1867.

Luffrum, J & Williams, H *The House in Mary Ann's Garden known as the Shrubbery,* No publisher noted, 1995.

Macfarlane, Eric *The Making of a Maverick,* Pen Press Publications, 2007. Eric Macfarlane was the first Principal of Queen Mary's College, this autobiography contains chapters on the establishment of the college.

McKenzie, Barbara (Ed), *Historical Miscellany of Basingstoke,* The Crosby Press, 1972. A collection of articles on historical topics by a WEA Study Group.

* **Millard, James Elwin** *The book of the accounts of the Wardens of the Fraternity of the Holy Ghost in Basingstoke AD1557 – AD1654,* C J Jacob, 1882.

* **Millard, James Elwin** *A Short Account of Basingstoke, Basing and the Neighbourhood,* C J Jacob, (1880s).

* **Millett, M & James, Simon** Excavations at Cowdery's Down, Basingstoke 1978-81, *Archaeological Journal,* 140, 1983, pp 151-279.

* **Millett, M & Russell, D** An Iron Age Burial from Viables Farm, Basingstoke, *Archaeological Journal,* 139, 1982, pp 69 - 90.

* **Millett, M & Russell, D** Excavations at Viables Farm, Basingstoke, 1974-6, *Proc HFC,* 40, 1984, pp 151 - 279.

* **Millett, M & Schadla-Hall, T** Rescue excavations on a Bronze Age and Romano-British site at Daneshill, Basingstoke, 1980-1, *Proc HFC,* 47, 1992, pp 83-105.

* **Mogg, Cliff** *Doughnuts Galore, Britain's London Overspill Years – the people's story,* published by the Author, 1997.

* **Moutray Read, D H** *Highways & Byways in Hampshire,* Macmillan,1908.

* **Mudie, Robert**, *Hampshire, its past and present,* Laurence Oxley, 1974. Facsimile of the 1838 edition.

* **Munby, Julian** *Domesday, Hampshire,* Phillimore, 1982.

* **Oliver, M** Excavation of an Iron Age and Romano-British Settlement at Oakridge, Basingstoke 1965-6, *Proc HFC,* 48, 1993, pp 55-94.

Oliver, M *Church Cottage, Basingstoke: Historical Notes,* St Michael's Church Cottage Management Committee, 2007.

* **Oliver, M & Applin, B** Excavation of an Iron Age and Romano-British Settlement at Ructstall's Hill, Basingstoke, Hants 1972-5, *Proc HFC,* 35, 1978, pp 41-92.

Osbourne, Keith *Hampshire Hogsheads. The Lost Breweries of the County, Vol 1, North Hampshire,* Hampshire Hogsheads, 1996.

Parker, Malcolm *Images of England, Basingstoke,* Tempus Publishing Ltd, 2007.

Parker, Malcolm *Mrs Blunden,* Willis Museum, 2007. A collection of contemporary accounts.

Parker, Malcolm *The Pedestrian Feats and Humorous Adventures of the late Mr Charles Spiers,* Willis Museum, 2007. Accounts originally published in 1871, now with a modern preface.

Pitcher, Anne *A Pictorial Record of Basingstoke 1689 – 1966,* published by the Author, 1966. The author has also written numerous booklets on local topics.

* **Plumb, J R** *England in the 18th Century,* Pelican, 1950.

Pugh, Steven *Fairs & Markets of Basingstoke,* published by the Author, no date but after 2002.

* **Rance, Adrian** *Southampton – An Illustrated History,* Milestone Publications, 1986.

Ray, F *The Mays of Basingstoke,* Simpkin and Co, 1904.

Roberts, Len *Historical Guide to Basingstoke.* No publisher and date noted.

* **Robertson-Mackay, R** The Defences of the Iron Age Hillfort at Winklebury, Basingstoke, Hants, *Proceedings of the Prehistoric Society,* 43, 1977, pp 131 et seq.

* **Roe, D** *Gazetteer of British Lower and Middle Palaeolithic Sites,* Council for British Archaeology Research Report No 8, page 75, CBA, 1968.

Rolt, L T C *Lansing Bagnall, The first twenty-one years at Basingstoke,* Lansing Bagnall Ltd, 1970.

Saunders, Arthur W *Basingstoke in the 19th century,* (a series of four articles) Hants & Berks Gazette, 1940.

Shennan S J & Schadla-Hall R T (Eds) *The Archaeology of Hampshire,* HFC monograph No 1, 1981.

* **Shore, T W** *A History of Hampshire*, London, 1892.

Smith, Dilys *Park Prewett Hospital, The History 1898-1984,* D W Smith, 1986.

* **Smith, K** The Excavation of Winklebury Camp, Basingstoke, Hants, *Proceedings of the Prehistoric Society,* 43, 1977, pp 31-138.

Smith, R A *1907/08 Notes,* Proc Soc Antiquaries, London, 22, 1908, pp 63 – 86.

Spruce, Derek J *Basingstoke 1780 – 1860 Aspects of the Development of a North Hampshire Market Town.* MSc Dissertation, 1977. A copy is in the Reference Section of Basingstoke Library.

Stanley, Diana *Within Living Memory,* Charles Skipper & East Ltd, 1968.

* **Stevens, Joseph** *The Farm Labourer at home and in the field. A short account of the North Hampshire labourer in his cottage, wages, and in his schooling; with a review of the emigration question, strikes, etc.* Wyman, 1874.

Stoodley, Nick (ed) *A Review of Archaeology in Hampshire 1980-2000,* HFC, HCC & Hampshire Archaeological Committee, 2002.

* **Stokes, E G** *Basingstoke - Expanding Town,* WEA, 1980.

Stokes, E G Introductory article *Why Queen Mary's?* Eric Stokes in *Various views at Ten. Some recollections of the first 10 years,* QMC, 1982.

Stokes, E G *The Things They Say About Basingstoke.* Published by the Author, 1990 & revised edition 1997.

Stokes, E G & Crossman, R C *Queen Mary's School 1556 – 1972.* (Published by the Authors, 1973)

Timmins, Gordon *Basingstoke, a town history,* published by the Author, 2006.

Townsin, Alan *Thornycroft,* Ian Allan Publishing, 2001.

Twelvetrees, Richard *Thornycroft Road Transport Golden Jubilee,* John I Thornycroft & Co, Ltd, 1946.

* **Vancouver, Charles,** *General View of the Agriculture of Hampshire and the Isle of Wight*, Sherwood, Nealy & Jones, 1813.

* **Vaughn, Tom** *Viables Two (V2), Jay's Close, Basingstoke, Hampshire. An archaeological excavation -1999,* Hertfordshire Archaeological Trust Report No 582, 2000.

* **Vine, P A L** *London's Lost Route to Basingstoke,* David & Charles, 1968 & Alan Sutton Publishing, revised 2nd Ed, 1994.

Whitehead, R A, *Wallis and Steevens – A History,* The Road Locomotive Society, 1983

Willis, G W Bronze Age Burials found at Basingstoke & Two Roman sites near Basingstoke, *Proc HFC,* 18, 1953.

* **Willis, G W** *Basingstoke town guide,* No publisher and date noted (1950s).

Willoughby, Margaret *Bibliography of Basingstoke*, 1973. 162 references including 25 to Basing House. In the Local Studies section of Basingstoke Library.

* **Winbolt, S E** *Hampshire and the Isle of Wight,* Pelican, 1949.

Winbolt, S E Roman Sites on the Harroway in the Basingstoke area, *Proc HFC,* 15, 1943.

* **Whiteman, Anne (Ed)** *The Compton Census of 1676: A Critical Edition,* OUP for The British Academy, 1986.

Woodman, George Reminiscences of Basingstoke, *Hants & Berks Gazette,* 6th March, 1926.

Wren, Derek *Dear Mr Willis,* Fisher Miller Publishing, 1997.

OTHER SOURCES

Other Documentary Sources

* *Account book of the Guild of the Holy Ghost* HRO 46M74/PZ89

* *Angliae Metropolis,* 1690. The British Library on-line catalogue has no record of this. However, it does record as published in 1690, **Delaune, Thomas,** *The Present State of London, or Memorials Comprehending a Full and Succinct Account of the Ancient and Modern State Thereof.*

* *Basingstoke High School for Girls- A Brief History 1908 – 1968.* No Author or publisher noted, 1968.

Basingstoke 1968. A look forwards and a look back, Basingstoke Lion's Club, Basingstoke, 1968.

Basingstoke Town Trail, Basingstoke Heritage Society, Basingstoke, 2006.

Basingstoke Directory Entries 1784 – 1935. A compendium of photocopies in the Reference Section of Basingstoke Library.

Bear, William E *The Agricultural Labourer in the Poor Law Union of Basingstoke,* Report to the Royal Commission on Labour, 1892. HRO 72A07/2

* *Churchwardens' Accounts* 1646; 1731, 1737. HRO, No catalogue reference has been found .

Church Street Methodist Church, Basingstoke: Valedictory Service, closing 17th October 1965, and History of the Church, Basingstoke, 1965. In the Reference Section of Basingstoke Library.

* *Corporation Accounts,* 1832-3, HRO, No catalogue reference has been found .

* *Directory of Hampshire,* 1915.

Ellaway, J R*, HBG, 24/9/1937*

* *Guide to the L&SWR, L&SWR,* 1845.

* *Journal of the House of Commons,* 1737.

* *Journal of the Travels and Sufferings of George Fox.*

London Street [Basingstoke] United Reformed Church Souvenir Booklet, 2000, Basingstoke, 2000 (celebrating 200 years). In the Reference Section of Basingstoke Library.

* *Notice of share issue Southampton and London Railway,* 23st January 1832.

* *Overseers' Accounts* HRO 46M74A/PO1 (1668-1701), PO2 (1701-1735).

* *Paterson's Roads,* 18th ed, London, 1826.

* *Pigot's Hampshire Directory,* London, 1824.

* *Pigot's Hampshire Directory of Wagon and Coach Services,* London, 1824.

  Queen Mary's School 1556-1956, Queen Mary's School, Basingstoke, 1956.

  Railway Directory, 1839

* *Reprint of the 1st Edition Ordnance Survey (1886 Revision), Sheet No 78, Basingstoke,* David & Charles, Newton Abbot, 1980

* *Rules, Orders and Bye-laws for the Markets,* HRO 23M72/BO17.

* *Salisbury and Winchester Journal,* 29th October 1770.

* *Southen Evening Echo,* May 1961.

* *Survey of Basingstoke for the Duke of Bolton, 1762,* HRO 23M72P1.

* *The St Michael's Parish Magazine,* 1865; 1867, HRO 46M74/PZ1-87 (Bound copies 1865-1939).

* *The Times,* May 1972.

* *Transcript of parish registers* 1807-1812, HRO. No reference. In a box file containing Baptisms – photocopy of 1798-1812; Marriages, indexed – photocopy of 1807- 1812, and typescript compiled by the Society of Genealogists.

* *Vestry Minutes* HRO 46M74A/PV1 (1797-1841).

* *Victoria County History* – Hampshire, Vol 1, Vol 2, Vol 4, Constable, 1911.

* *White's Directory & Gazetteer,* 1859, 1878.

Video, DVD and photographic

* *The story of Basingstoke from earliest times to 1964,* The Regional Centre, Queen Mary's College. A video copy of a slide/tape show produced by Derek Wren and narrated by John Arlott. This is currently being revised and updated for publication in October 2008 in DVD format.

* *Beneath Basingstoke,* BAHS, 1994 A chronological history of the archaeology of Basingstoke and its immediate surrounding area from prehistory to the Saxon period, particularly highlighting the discoveries unearthed during the 1960s to 1980s housing developments. This was transferred to DVD in 2008.

  A Day in Tudor Basingstoke, BAHS, 2002 A video of the live performance of a historical entertainment in Church Cottage based on Basingstoke's 16th century archives.

  The Wessex Film and Sound Archive at the HRO have compiled a video collection of films dealing with Basingstoke topics; this is available on loan at Basingstoke Library.

  The HRO's Hampshire Photographic Project has digitised over 10,000 Hampshire photographs, including many from the Basingstoke area; these are available for viewing on the internet.

  On-line catalogues to both of the above are at **www.hants.gov.uk/record-office**

For the remainder of this bibliography all the references listed
are for information used in the text.

Acts of Parliament

An Act for making a navigable canal from the town of Basingstoke to communicate with the River Wey in the parish of Chertsey, County of Surrey, and to the south-west side of the turnpike road in the parish of Turgiss, County of Southampton. 18 Geo.III, 15.5.1778. HRO 8M72/134.

An Act for Dividing, Allotting and Inclosing, the Open and Common Fields, Common Downs, Common Pastures, Common Meadows, Wastelands and other Commonable Places within the Parish of Basingstoke in the County of Southampton, 26 Geo.III, 1786. HRO 148M71/1/4/6

An Act for paving the footpaths and crosspaths, and lighting, watching, cleansing, widening and otherwise improving the streets, lanes and other public passages and places in the Town of Basingstoke in the County of Southampton, 55 Geo.III, 23.3.1815.
(Basingstoke Improvements HRO 76M86/20; *Pavement Commission Minute Books* HRO 148M71/1/5/7/1&2).

An Act for enlarging the Market Place in the Town of Basingstoke, 10 Geo. IV, 14.5.1829. HRO 148M71/1/5/3

CHARTERS

Charter, Henry III, 1256. (Documents arising from, HRO 148M71/1/1/1)

Charter, King John.

Charter, Richard II.

Charter re-founding the Holy Ghost Guild, February 1557.   HRO 148M71/5/3/2

Charter of James I, 1622.   HRO   148M71/1/1/2

Charter of Charles I, 1641.   HRO 148M71/1/1/3

Charter of Charles II,   HRO 148M71/1/1/4

REPORTS

Ballard, Dr   *The Sanitary Condition of Basingstoke,* 1871. Medical Department of the Local Government Board, December, 1871. Copy in the Resources Room of the Willis Museum.

Basingstoke – Town Development – description of the scheme. Basingstoke Town Development Committee, Aug, 1962.

Farrar, Dr *Report* 1905. Report to the Borough Council on the typhoid outbreak. HRO 148M71/1/5/32/2 & 15

Planned Growth outside London, Greater London Council, 1975.

Draft proposals for Second Review Town Map, Hampshire County Council, May, 1972.

Basingstoke - Further Growth, Hampshire County Council. Undated.

Webb, Dr *Reports* 1891, 1894, 1895, 1896, 1903, 1905. Medical Officer's annual reports to the Borough Council. HRO 148M71/1/5/32/15.

Basingstoke - A Social Study, Workers' Educational Association, 1962.

Annual Report of the Mechanics' Institute, 1857, 1904-5. Minute Book HRO 148M71/13/1; Records 1854-1929 HRO 180M88.

Annual Report of the Town Development Joint Committee, Basingstoke, 1963-4. HRO H/CX1/8

Barlow Commission Report, The Distribution of the Industrial Population, HMSO, 1940.

Basingstoke and Deane Borough Local Plan, July, 1992.

Borough Information Digest – A yearly compendium of information compiled by Basingstoke & Deane Borough Council. Copies held by Basingstoke Library.

Hampshire Treasures, Vol 2, Basingstoke and Deane, Hampshire County Council, 1979.

Proceedings of the Society of Antiquaries, 22, 1907.

Report of Court Leet, 1880. HRO 148M71/2/2/9.

Report of the Commissioners for Municipal Corporation Boundaries, 1837. HRO H/CX1/8.

Report on a Wesleyan Mission to Basingstoke,

Royal Commission on Municipal Corporations, 1835.

The Salvation Army in Basingstoke – Reports on the proceedings before the magistrates on May 3rd and 9th 1881, HBG.

The Social Implications of a Town Development Scheme, Basingstoke WEA Study Group on Town Development, 1963.

INDEX

Numbers in bold print refer to illustrations or maps

A

Accurate survey of the town and manor of Basingstoke...(1762) **41-43**, 56
Acts of Toleration 153, 154, 156, 157
Acts of Uniformity 156
agriculture, 40-46, 109-111
- hayward, duties of 43
- impact of population growth 142
- medieval 40-43
- mower, duties of 44
- open field system 40-44, 45, **42, 43**
- preservation of agricultural land 142
- swineherd, duties of 43
- wages (1875-1890) 55
airing house 84
airport, proposed (1930s) 132
All Saints Church 158
Anglican churches 152-153, 158-161
Anvil, The 180, 184, 185, 190, 191, 193
archaeology 30-35
Arlott, John 193
Assize, The 48-53
Atomic Weapons (Research) Establishment (AWRE/AWE) 25
Attwood, Arthur 82, 119
Attwood, Samuel 51, 82, 88, 119, 134
auctions and auctioneers 115, 116
- auction market 51

B

Baigent & Millard's *History of Basingstoke* 37, 38, 44, 45, 75, 93, 119, 156
bailiffs 36, 38, 40, 50, 91, 92
bakers 48, 49
Ballard, Dr, *see Sanitary Conditions of Basingstoke (1871)*
banks and bankers 114
Baptists **155**, 156, 162
Barlow Commission Report (1940) 138
Basing/ Old Basing 14, 17, 22, 28, 65, 86, 107, 127, 130, 136, 148, 152, 186, 187
- archaeology 34
- population 22
- toll free market 51
Basing House 20, 125, 153, 185
Basing View 128, 138, 188
Basingstoke and Alton Light Railway, *see* railways
Basingstoke and Deane Borough Council, (1978) 28, 146, 189, map **147**
Basingstoke and Deane Local Plan, (1992) 186
Building and Benefit Societies
- Basingstoke and District Mutual Building Society 128
- Basingstoke Benefit Building Society 123
Basingstoke and Eastrop Waterworks Company 83, 98
- acquisition by Corporation (1883) 98
Basingstoke Borough Council 26, 27, 104, 143, 184
Basingstoke Canal, *see* canals
Basingstoke College of Technology (BCOT) 172, 175, 178, 184
Basingstoke Common 53, 58, 119,138

- grazing rights 58
- 'firebote' 58
Basingstoke Corporation 37, 57, 58, 63, 70, 74, 82, 87-108, 111-113, 115, 119, 125, 127, 129, 163-165, 168, 170 -172, 179
- impact of Municipal Reform Act (1835) 93-95
Basingstoke Council for Social Service 188-189
Basingstoke District Council 26-27, 146
Basingstoke District Hospital, *see* North Hampshire Hospital
Basingstoke Down **43**, 53
Basingstoke Evening Institute 177, 184
Basingstoke Evening Schools Association 176-177
Basingstoke Gas and Coke Company 88
Basingstoke "green belt" 148
Basingstoke High School for Girls 167-168, 174
Basingstoke Technical College, *see* Basingstoke College of Technology (BCOT)
Basingstoke Union Workhouse 80, 124, *see also* workhouse
Basingstoke Urban Area 186
beerhouses 112
Beggarwood Lane 149, 186
- archaeology 34
bellman, *see* law and order
Blue Coat School 156, 163, 168 - 170, **169,**
Bolton (titled) family 37, 44, 55, 56, 57, 93, 104, 108, 126, 157, 161
boot and shoe makers 113
Borough of Basingstoke and Deane, *see* Basingstoke and Deane Borough Council
Basingstoke Borough rate 95
Boundaries, town 122, 123, see also *Report of the Commissioners for Municipal Corporation Boundaries* (1837)
- proposed alterations, (1889) 127
brewers and brewing 68, 111, *see also* May & Co
bridewell, The, *see* law and order, cage & bridewell
Brighton Hill 19, 27, 28, 147, 148,159, 162
- archaeology 19, 34
British Schools 163, 164, 170, 176
Brook Street 11-13, 33, 80, 105, 118, 119, 125, 127, 129, 131, 136, 165, 167, 192, 195- 197
- school 167, 178
Brookvale 28, 126, 178, 187
Buckskin 11, 17, 28, 110, 130, 146
- archaeology 31
builders 115, 132
building societies 123, 125, 128
Burberrys 55, 112-113, 120, 132, 137, 195
burgesses 91, 92, 93-94
bus services 136-137
Bye laws 30

C

cage, The, *see* law and order
canals
- Basingstoke Canal 60, 63-66, 112, 113, 117, 134, 187; Enabling Act (1778) 64; opening (1794) 64; and Napoleonic Wars 64; impact of Kennet and Avon Canal 65; impact of L& SW Railway 65;

213

types of traffic 65; liquidation (1866) 66; winding up of company (1869) 66
- Berks and Hants Junction Canal (proposed) 64
- London and South Western Canal Company 66
- Maidenhead and Reading canal scheme (1769) 63
- New Basingstoke Canal Company 66
- Surrey and Hampshire Canal Corporation (1874) 66
- Woking, Aldershot and Basingstoke Canal and Navigation Company 65

carriage builders 136
carriers, *see* waggoners
Caston's Iron Works 23
cattle market, *see* Market
Central Development Area (1959) **145** (1985) **145**
Charles Chute School 175
Charters 36-38
- 1256 charter 37, 91
- 1392 charter 38, 89
- 1449 charter 53
- 1556 charter (Holy Ghost Guild) 170, 171, 172
- 1622 charter 22, 50, 53, 91-2
- 1641 charter 50, 53, 92-3
- 1671 charter 53
chemists/druggists 94, 114
Chineham 11, 19, 27, 28, 139, 149, 159, 186, 188
Christ the King, Church, Brighton Hill 159
Christchurch, Chineham 159
Church Cottage 192
- used as school 163, 167
Church Street 13, 45, 54, 87, 89, 104, 110, 112, 113, 115, 116, 145, 155, 156, 161, 167, 193, 196, 197, 198
churches 152-162, *see also under names of individual churches*
Church of the Holy Ghost, *see* Holy Ghost Church
Chute House, 14, 178
cinemas 179-180
Civic Hall, proposed (1973) 184
clothiers 112-113
coach builders 111-112
coaching, *see* stage coach services
Common, The, *see* Basingstoke Common
common grazing land 43
Common Seal, grant of 38
commuting 129, 138, 192
Congregational Church, *see* United Reformed Church
conservation areas 187
Corn Exchange (1865) 51-53, **52**, 117,119
- as entertainment centre 179
Corn Market 94-5
corn merchants
- medieval 39, 43, 50
- 19th century 51, 68, 98, 111, 113
Cosimo III, Grand Duke of Tuscany
- opinion of Basingstoke, (1669) 152, 189
Countess of Huntingdon's Connexion 117, 153, 155, 195
Court Rolls 36, 38, 39, 48
Courts 38-40
- of the Hundred 36, 38-40
- of Pie Powder 50
- Court Leet *or* View of Frank-pledge 38-40, 56
- of Record 91, 93
Cow Down Copse
- archaeology 31

Cowdery's Down
- archaeology 33-34
Cranbourne Bi-Lateral School 174
crime, *see also* Courts, law and order
- and overcrowding 125-126
- dishonest market practices 48-9

D
Daneshill 138, 188
- archaeology 32
Deane Institute of Adult (later 'Community') Education 177
dentistry 114
diseases, infectious, *see* infectious diseases
Domesday Book, Hampshire 36, 152, 159
- reference to market 47
Down, The (Kempshott) 19, 43, **43**, 44, 45, 53, 56, 57, 61
drainage 89, 90, 96, 98, 102, 104-107
- 1878 scheme 104
- New Street barrel drain 89
Drill Hall 118, 180-181

E
Eastrop 22, 28, 71, 85, 86, 98, 110, 111, 124, 127, 147, 159, 160, 161
- Manor 12, 14, 106, 147, 159, 192
- Park 104, 145, 190
education 97, 163-177, s*ee also names of individual school and colleges*
- adult education 176-177
- comprehensive schools 174
- Education Act (1870) 97, 164
- evening classes 176-177
- elementary education 163; Newcastle Commission (1858) 163
- funding 164-165
- private schools 166-167
- School Board 164-165, 176
- technical education 175, 176; Technical Instruction Act (1889) 176
- young ladies' seminaries 166
electricity supply 130-132; generating station **131**
Eli Lilly 25, 132, 178, 192
employment 187-188, 190
Enclosures 40, 41, 45, 53, 56-58, 63
- Basingstoke (1780-1790) 56
- *Petition to Parliament* (1786) 56
- 1788 Enclosures Award 40, 46, 50, 58, 85, 117
engineering 111, 132, 191
English Civil War 20, 33, 153, 185
engrossing, *see* market, unscrupulous practices
entertainment 179
environment, protection of 87, 131, 138, 186-187

F
Fairfields 50, 115, 126, 187
- cattle market 50, 51
Fairfields School 50, 51, 54, 97, 127, 165, 178
fairs 19, 53-54, 58, 68, 91, 92, 112
- hiring and pleasure fair (Michaelmas) 54-55, 91, 118, 180
- sheep fair 53-54, 127
- wool fair (1851) 94
farms 32, 45, 50, 110, 127, *see also agriculture*
Farrar Report, (1905) 101-102, 103

fee farm rent 36-38
Festival Place 190, 191
fields and pasture, *see* agriculture
fire (1392) 38
'firebote' 58
Flaxfield 13, 88, 99, 100, 125, 126, 131, 166
Flaxfield College/House 166, 167, 181
Ford's Building 80, 118, 125, 195
forestalling, *see* market
Frank-pledge, *see* Court Leet

G
gas works 88, 132
geographical location, 34, 120; and communications 16-21; and market 46; and employment 185-186; and stage coach services 59
Gerrish, Ames and Simpkins 23, 113, 132, 191
Great Western Railway, *see* railways
Greater London Plan (1944), 21, 22, 140
green belt, Basingstoke 148
Guild of the Holy Ghost 44, 48, 153, 170-172
Gymnasium, The 175

H
Hackwood Park 110, 125
Hampshire County Council 173, 174, 176, 189
- *Basingstoke: further growth* (1970 report) 147
Harriet Costello School 58, 175
Harrow Way, *see* tracks, ancient
Hatch Warren 148, 149, 186
- archaeology 19, 28, 34
Haymarket Theatre 179, 184, 185
hayward, *see* agriculture
health care 190
High Stewards of Basingstoke 91, 92
Highways Act (1555), *see* roads
History of Basingstoke, by Baigent & Millard, *see* Baigent and Millard
Holy Ghost Chapel 42, 53, **171**
- 1878 chapel 157
Holy Ghost Church 157, 161
Holy Ghost School 45, 93, 95, 170
Holy Trinity Chapel 42, 123
Hospital of St John (or St Mary and St John) 45, 167
housing 25, 140, 147, 184; council 128 -130; private 127, 147; workers 126, 129
Housing of the Working Classes Acts, (1885 and 1890) 128
Hundred of Basingstoke 36, 37-38
- Court 38-40

I
Infectious diseases 84, 101-103,
Immanuel Church, *see* Countess of Huntingdon's Connexion
immigration (inward movement of population into Basingstoke) 22-28
inns and taverns 115-6, 197-198
intruders 80

J
John Hunt of Everest School 178
Justices of the Peace, *see* law and order

K
Kempshott 19, 43, 127, 130, 147

- archaeology 18-19, 31, 34, 201

L
Lancaster, Sir James 170
Lansing Bagnall, 25, 201, 208
Lansing Linde, *see* Lansing Bagnall
law and order 80-82
- bellman, duties of 81
- Bye laws 30
- cage and bridewell 81
- Justices of the Peace 58, 75, 91-92
- Sessions of the Peace 93
- The Watch/watchmen 80-82, 88
Linde, *see* Lansing Bagnall
Library 180
Lesser Market, *see* Market
lighting 87-88
Liten, The (corpse land) 44, 123
Local Government Acts, (1858) 89, 96; (1888) 176
Local Government Board 90, 96, 99, 100, 101, 106, 127,
Loddon, River 11-15, 34, 31, 32, 100, 106, 107
- associated place names 12-13
- proposed sewage disposal scheme 106
London and South Western Railway, *see* railways
London overspill 25-27, 122, 140-149, 188
Longcroft 126, 196
Lychpit 34, 115, 149

M
Manor of Basingstoke 36-38
- *Accurate Survey of the Town and Manor of Basingstoke* **41-43**
- *Regulation and constitution of the Manor of Basingstoke* (1389) 43-44
Market 39, 47-54, 91-95, 112, 127
- 1622 and 1641 charters 50
- cattle market 50, 51
- Clerk of the Market, 49, 50
- Inquiry (1888) 51
- Lesser Market 51, **52,** 93
- market day 50
- unscrupulous practices: engrossing 49; forestalling 49; re-grating 49
Market Place 51, 89, 137
Massagainians 119, 120
- riot damage **119**
May & Co 99, 125
May family 50, 63, 87, 93-94, 100, 110, 117, 118, 167, 180, 207
May Street 33, 115, 127, 196
May's Bounty 180
mayor and aldermen 92-94
Mechanics' Institute 113, 118, 176, 181-182
medical practitioners 94, 114
Merton, Walter de 45, 167, 205
Methodists. 154-155, 161
Milestones Museum, *see* museums
motor engineers 136-137
motoring, early 134-136
mower (medieval court official) 44
Municipal Reform Act, (1835) 93-95
Museums 182, 185

N
National Schools 163-165, 176
New Street 89, 137, 175

Newtown 115, 126, 165
- archaeology 33
Noah's Island 12, 105
North Hampshire Hospital 190
North Hants Agricultural Society 111

O
Oakridge 25, 144, 146, 149
- archaeology 33
Oat Street (Wote Street) 50
Old Basing, see Basing
open field system 40-44, **41-43**
overseers of the poor 75, 76-79

P
Park Prewett 184, 208
- archaeology 34
- Hospital 133
- railway 138
paving and lighting 87
- Enabling Act (1815) 87
Paving and Lighting Commissioners 81, 82, 88, 94-96, 104
pesthouse 58, 76-78, 81, 84, 125
Pie Powder, Court of 50
Pipe Rolls 36
place names 12-13
- Saxon 34
policing 80-83
poor relief 75-81
- Act (1601) 74
- 'farming the poor' 76-78
Popley 34, 146, 149, 159, 161, 178
population 22-28, 69, 74, 90, 99, 101, 108, 110
- growth 22-28, 62, 107, 121, 122-133, 140
- planned growth 140-149
- impact of railways 74, 117
- size of town area in 1851 123
poultry farming 127
poverty 75-79, 118-119
- comments in Ballard report 118
- non-rating of houses 118
- soup kitchen 118
public buildings 116-118, see also Corn Exchange, Town Hall
public health 95-96
Public Library, see Library

Q
Quakers, see Society of Friends
Queen Mary's Centre 183
Queen Mary's College 168, 175, 183
Queen Mary's School 170-175
- 'riot' 173
Queen's Free School 170

R
railways 66-74, 137
- Basingstoke and Alton Light Railway 70
- GWR station **69**
- impact on Turnpike Trusts 71-73
- proposed carriage works 120, 126
- proposed commuter stations 137
rating of property 95
- non-rating of houses of the poor 118
refuse disposal 107, 131
re-grating, see markets, unscrupulous practices

Regulation and constitution of the Manor of Basingstoke (1389) 38
Report of the Commissioners for Municipal Corporation Boundaries, (1837) 53, 89, 108, 122
Richard Aldworth (Blue Coat) School 163, 168-170, **169**
- Aldworth Exhibition Foundation 170
riots 82, 119
- Queen Mary's School 173
- 'Salvation Army Riots' 119, 158
- Swing Riots (1830) 82, 119
Riverdene 147, 186
- archaeology 34
roads see also paving and lighting, tracks ancient, turnpike trusts,
- Highways Act (1555) 75, 85
- maintenance 17, 61, 75
- Roman roads 16-17
Roman Catholics 157, 161
Royal Navy- recruitment 85
Ructstall's Hill- archaeology 32

S
Salvation Army 157
- riots 119, 157
Sanitary condition of Basingstoke, The, 1871 (Dr Ballard's report) 84, 90, 96, 98, 114, 118, 126, 211
School Board, see education
schools, see education, see also names of individual schools
settlement, early 31-35
sewerage 98-107
- sewage farm 106, see also drainage
shops 112, 132, 191
smallpox 79, 84, 114
- innoculation 84
Society of Friends 153-154
- prosecution of Quakers 151
solicitors 114-115
South Ham 130, 140, 144
South View 128, 140
St Andrew's Methodist Church, Western Way 161
St Bede's Roman Catholic Church, Popley Way 161, **162**
St Gabriel's Church, Popley 159
St John's School 167
St Mary's Church, Eastrop 159-161
St Michael's Church, 152-153, 158, 187, 189
'St Michael's Church', Eastrop 110
St Michael's Parish Magazine 53, 125, 152, 164, 210
St Peter's Church, South Ham 158
St Thomas of Canterbury Church, Worting 1579, **160**
stage coach services 20, 58-62
- effects of railways 20, 71-73, schematic representation **73**
- inns 59
- impact on population growth (1801-1851) 73-74
Steam Dell water source 98, 100
streets
- cleaning 88
- names 126
- widening 88
swineherd, see agriculture
Swing Riots, (1830) see riots

216

T

Thornycroft, Messrs 23, 103, 120, 129, 132, 135, 137, 175, 201, 203, 208
Totterdown 118, 196
- School 164, 165
Town Development Scheme 5, 144, 211
Town Hall 51, **52,** 82, 91, **116,** 117
- as place for meetings 38, 75, 77, 82, 91, 92, 99, 118, 176, 181, 182, 183
- Easter County Balls 118
- Old Town Hall **116,** 196; replacement (1832) 51, 89, 117
- soup kitchen 118
trackways, ancient 16
- Harrow Way 16, 17, 21, 40, 137
trade regulations 48-49, 91-92
trades and traders 48-49, 112-113
- 15th and 16th centuries 47-48
travellers, payments to 79
Trinity Methodist Church, Sarum Hill 161
turnpike trusts, 19, 71-73, 116
typhoid outbreak, (1905) 101-103
- Farrar Report (1905) 101-103

U

unemployment 186
United Reformed Church (*formerly* Congregational Church) 103, 117, 156, 163
Urban Sanitary Authority 90, 104, 127
utilities 130-132, *see also* electricity, gas, sewerage, water
- siting of 131

V

vagrants 80
Venture Ltd 137
Vestry, The 14, 50, 76-86, 94, 114
Viables 186
- archaeology 32
View of Frank-pledge, *see* Courts, Court Leet
Voluntary Schools Act, (1897) 167
Vyne School, The 175

W

wages, agricultural, *see* agriculture
waggoners 59-60, 62, 116
waifs and strays 38-39
Wallis and Steevens 111, 120, 132, 134, 185, 189
Watch, The, *see* law and order
Watch Committee (1836) 94
watchmen, *see* law and order, The Watch
water supply 98-107
- contamination 101-103
- sources 98-100
Water Supply Committee 100, 102, 103
Webb, Dr Frere, Medical Officer of Health 98
- reports, 100, 101, 102-103, 104
Wesley, John 154, 155
West Ham
- archaeology 33
- water works site 100, 101, 102, 104
White Barrow
- archaeology 33
Wildmoor Sewage Treatment Plant 107
Willis Museum, *see* museums
Willis, George 31, 33, 142, 182, 183

Winchester Street 54, 61, 62, 87, 89, 119, 125, 126
Winklebury 16, 34, 39, 127, 130, 144
- hill fort 16, 33
- poultry farming 127
Winton Square 20, 111, 125, 134, 136
workhouse 58, 76-78, 80, 106, 124, 125, *see also* Basingstoke Union Workhouse
Worting 34, 85, 118, 120, 125, 132, 139, 159, 160
- archaeology 31, 34
Worting Road 33, 126, 127, 130
Wote Street 13, 44, 145

BASINGSTOKE ARCHAEOLOGICAL & HISTORICAL SOCIETY

(Registered Charity No. 1000263)   www.bahsoc.org.uk

The Society aims to investigate the history and prehistory of the Borough of Basingstoke & Deane, and to stimulate interest in archaeological and historical studies generally. There are lectures on the second Thursday of the month, from September to May, at 7.30 pm in Church Cottage, Basingstoke. As well as the Basingstoke Talking History project, the Society organises visits to places of archaeological & historical interest as well as training excavations, fieldwork and finds processing.

PUBLICATIONS

Taking the Pulse of Basingstoke   Ed Barbara Applin
ISBN 978-0-9508095-3-3
£13.00
Memories of health matters in the town before the coming of the National Health Service and right up to the present day from doctors, surgeons, nurses, midwives, dentists, chemists, opticians, community and district and hospital nurses and many patients

Voices of Basingstoke 1400-1600   Anne Hawker
ISBN 978-0-9508095-0-2
£3.00
Taken from Basingstoke records, identifying where and how people lived, describing the contents of property and the misdemeanours that led to fines.

Going Down Church Street to the Felgate Bookshop   Mary Felgate & Barbara Applin
ISBN 1-899077-06-5
£ 7.50
Mary Felgate's memories of her Grandmother's bible bookshop in the 1920s, with research into the history of properties in Church Street.

Roundabout Basingstoke   Barbara Applin
ISBN 978-0-9508095-1-9
£1.50
Stories of Basingstoke's many roundabouts: the highwayman, the Daneshill stones, the 'Chineham Wave' etc.

Beneath Basingstoke   **DVD**
£12.00
Archaeological discoveries made beneath and around Basingstoke from the Stone Age to the Saxons

A Day in Tudor Basingstoke   **VIDEO**
£10.00
A historical entertainment performed in Church Cottage, based on Basingstoke's archives, showing goings-on in the Market Place, people 'had up' at court and the cost of the townspeople's petition to Mary Tudor.